# THE
# BUCCANEER'S
# REALM

Also by Benerson Little

*The Sea Rover's Practice:*
*Pirate Tactics and Techniques, 1630–1730*

# THE BUCCANEER'S REALM

*Pirate Life on
the Spanish Main,
1674–1688*

BENERSON LITTLE

Potomac Books, Inc.
Washington, D.C.

Illustrations by David J. Meagher, except "Examples of Merchants' Marks"
by Bree Little.

Maps by Benerson Little and Courtney Little.

**Library of Congress Cataloging-in-Publication Data**
Library of Congress Cataloging-in-Publication Data

Little, Benerson, 1959-
The buccaneers realm : pirate life on the Spanish Main, 1674-1688 /
    Benerson Little.
p. cm.
ISBN 978-1-59797-101-0 (alk. paper)
1.  Pirates—Spanish Main—History—17th century. 2.  Buccaneers—
    History—17th century.  I. Title.
F2161.L58 2007
623.19729—dc22

                                        2007010230


ISBN-13:  978-1-59797-101-0

(alk. paper)

Printed in the United States of America on acid-free paper that meets the
American National Standards Institute Z39-48 Standard.

Potomac Books, Inc.
22841 Quicksilver Drive
Dulles, Virginia 20166

First Edition

10 9 8 7 6 5 4 3 2 1

For Bree and Courtney

# Contents

Maps     xi

Preface     xiii

1   Yo Ho, Yo Ho:     1
    A Life on the Margins for Me

2   Water, Water Everywhere:     13
    The Means of Freedom on the Main

3   Biscayers, Indians, Africans, and Greeks:     21
    Spain in the New World

4   Boucaniers, Flibustiers, and Buccaneers:     39
    Hunters Along the Main

5   Petit Goave and Port Royal:     57
    Pirate Asylums and Sanctuaries

6   Muscovado, Indigo, and Urcas,     73
    Not to Mention Sweet Virginia

7   Slaves, Monopolies, and Maroons:     83
    Africa on the Main

8   Contraband Cargaroon:     93
    The Sloop Trade

9   Pirates and Puritans:     99
    The New England Connection

**10** Gods, Devils, and Castaways:      107
Faith, Religion, and Superstition on the Main

**11** Lost Ships and Souls:      115
Wrecks, Wrecking, and Wreckers

**12** To the Slaughter, Gentle Beasts:      129
The Sea Turtle, Manatee, and Seal

**13** The Beginning of the End:      135
Native America Enslaved and Enraged

**14** Tarpaulin Cant and Spanish Lingua:      145
The Language of the Buccaneer

**15** Armadillas, Galleons, and Canoes:      151
Sea Battles in the Great South Sea

**16** Battle Wounds and Belly Timber:      159
Chirurgery, Physic, Diet, and Health

**17** The Torrid Zone:      165
Sex and Romance on the Main

**18** *Ladrones! Ladrones!*      171
Towns Plundered, Lives Violated

**19** Honor With An Edge:      189
Dueling and Swordplay on the Main

**20** Clean Bottoms and Lost Souls:      201
Keys, Cays, Isles, and Inlets

**21** Cannon, Sword, and Garrote:      207
Spain Strikes Back

**22** Yo Ho, Yo Ho:      215
A Pirate's Life for Me

Appendix A                                      223
   The Chasse-Partie

Appendix B                                      231
   Buccaneer Organization

Appendix C                                      235
   Captains and Their Vessels

Appendix D                                      243
   Roving Books and Authors, 1674–1699

Appendix E                                      247
   A Boucanier Barbecue

Appendix F                                      249
   "Pieces-of-Eight! Pieces-of-Eight!"

Appendix G                                      253
   Places Plundered, 1674–1688

Appendix H                                      255
   New World Exports and Plunder

Appendix I                                      259
   Weights, Measures, and Containers

Appendix J                                      263
   A Brief Glossary of Sea Terms

Notes                                           269

Bibliography                                    307

Index                                           325

About the Author                                343

# Maps

Campeche and Honduras ..... 5

The Treasure Fleets of 1674–1688 ..... 26

Jamaica, Hispaniola, and Porto Rico ..... 47

The Windward and Leeward Islands ..... 51

Petit Goave and Environs ..... 60

Port Royal Circa 1685 ..... 65

Cuba and the Bahamas ..... 122

The Isthmus of Darien ..... 153

# Preface

*I* was born on an island known in the seventeenth century as *Cayo de Huesos*—the Key of Bones—and anglicized today as Key West. My father, serving in the U.S. Navy, was stationed there, and without a doubt those three tropical years imprinted themselves on my psyche. The island then was not the tourist mecca it is today, but retained a sense of distant, exotic, tropical isolation and adventure. Some years later I read Rafael Sabatini's *Captain Blood*, the two collections of short stories that serve as its sequels, and *The Black Swan*. All of these tales are set during the period of 1674–88, when the buccaneer discovered his depredations against Spain were no longer as popular with his government as once they were—a time when the buccaneer and filibuster began to turn pirate.

When I wrote *The Sea Rover's Practice* to describe the tactics of pirates, privateers, and cruisers, I was acutely aware that while tactics may be observed, studied, dissected, and described, they are inseparable from their environment. In the case of the buccaneer and filibuster, the environment was the Spanish Main of the seventeenth century, a place and time that evokes romantic, adventurous images. Although these images are based much in fact, they are equally based on literary and cinematic interpretations designed to support a good story, not historical realities. Thankfully, the truth is far more interesting, even if it takes more effort to tell, and it is my purpose to present the world of the buccaneer and filibuster—the true pirates of the Caribbean— from 1674 to 1688, an era that led to the early eighteenth century and the time of the sea rovers who knew no nation and sailed under the black flag.

In writing this book, I was fortunate to have many friends who gave their assistance freely. I had far more kind offers than I could accept, and I am thankful for them all. To Brock Gordon, my thanks for reading the manuscript, and to Dave Young as well for his kind offer. Likewise, my thanks to Gareth Thomas of the Historical Maritime Combat Association for our e-mail conversations on the subject of arms and swordplay, as well as his review of the chapter on swordplay. To Christine Lampe, my thanks for putting me in touch with Gareth and his organization, and also for her support of my works on piracy. I owe thanks also to Mike Greene and Tim Ricks for their pragmatic suggestions on fencing and period arms. Tim worked with me on practical period swordplay, and Mike reviewed my first draft on the subject. My thanks to Mary E. Crouch for reviewing my Spanish translations, to Sara Leibold for shooting my jacket photograph, and to both for putting up with an occasionally difficult subject.

To Maj. Gary Leopold, USA (Ret.), teacher and historian, my many thanks for his comments on the historical method and for our discussions of arms and tactics. My thanks to Cherise Maddox in particular for her insight and for her review of several chapters on which I had questions of balance and presentation. To Ann Marie Martin—a fan of *Captain Blood* and *The Black Swan*—my gratitude for her articles on pirate literature (including mine) in the *Huntsville Times*. To David Meagher, my thanks as ever for his conversation and excellent illustrations.

My many thanks to Peter Vemming Hansen and Jens Christiansen of the Middelaldercentret (Medieval Center) in Nykøbing Falster, Denmark. Peter, a noted archaeologist as well as founder and director of the center, and Jens, an expert in many period subjects, including black-powder arms and pyrotechnics (not to mention a former Danish hussar), welcomed me warmly and significantly increased my "hands-on" knowledge of swivel guns and firepots, among several other subjects associated with *The Buccaneer's Realm*. The Middelaldercentret is not only a center of research, but also a historically accurate recreation of a fourteenth-century market town, complete with merchant vessels, trebuchets, and knights tilting in tournament, and should not be missed by any visitor to Denmark.

I must give special thanks to Chris Sondreal and producer Neil Laird of JWM Productions for the opportunity to work with the Medieval Center during the filming of the "Pirates of the Mediterranean" episode of the television documentary series *Digging for the Truth*. Neil and his team—associate producer Nicole Vinnola, director of photography Chris Cocuzzi Cox, sound recordist Malcolm Hirst, and host (not to mention stuntman, actor, and ex-Marine) Charles Ingram—were not only extraordinarily dedicated, professional, talented, and hospitable, but are some of the best people I've ever worked with. My thanks also to Jessica Harrington and to the staffs in general of both JWM Productions and the History Channel.

My thanks also to Professor Ted Cotton of Loyola University, New Orleans, an old friend and the only truly ambidextrous fencer I have ever known, for his insight into questions I had on Restoration comedies. Dr. Eugene Hamori, my old friend and fencing master, as always has my sincere appreciation for his insight and suggestions. My special thanks to Jamie Case for her enthusiasm for *The Sea Rover's Practice* and *The Buccaneer's Realm*, and as well for her conversation, sense of humor, and welcome advice.

To Don McKeon, my many thanks for his support both for *The Sea Rover's Practice* and *The Buccaneer's Realm*. I owe much thanks and praise to the outstanding staff at Potomac Books, in particular to my excellent production editor Laura Hymes, as well as to Claire Noble, Wendy Garner, Julie Kimmel, and Don Jacobs. Books are not created by their authors alone, and the staff at Potomac Books has always been a pleasure to work with.

My daughters, as usual, provided patience, humor, and, not least of all, assistance: Courtney with maps and Bree with manuscript preparation and research into merchant marks. I am forever grateful for all of this, and for their wonderful company as well. My thanks also to my brother, Keith, for his assistance during the testing of various arms. Last, my parents as ever are ready to assist as necessary. Special thanks to my mother for reading the manuscript, especially at the last minute, and to my father for conversation and sea stories over rum and brandy.

# 1 *Yo Ho, Yo Ho:*

## *A Life on the Margins for Me*

hey sail boldly and obviously, these men of Jamaica in 1674, into the shallow harbor of Salinas, Mexico. There is no need to do otherwise, no need to employ tactics of subtlety and deception. At anchor are a handful of Spanish barks, all loading salt gathered by the tribes of the coast. Each week forty or fifty families of local Native Americans come, replacing those who worked the previous week. They haul salt aboard the barks or rake it into large, conical piles, cover the piles with grass, and burn them to create a hard, protective coat against the rain.[1]

Perhaps these attackers from Jamaica claim, as often they do, to hold a letter of reprisal permitting them to attack and seize Spanish vessels and goods as compensation for Spanish attacks against them. Perhaps they even claim to hold a legitimate privateering commission from the French, a legal document permitting them to attack and plunder the enemy. In reality, many of these letters of reprisal are licenses that grant "Liberty to Fish, Fowl, and Hunt" on Hispaniola. Issued by the French governor at Petit Goave, they permit reprisals if attacked while hunting or fishing. Invariably, the licenses are expired or have been altered to exceed their original grant. They are mere pretenses. Salinas is nowhere near Hispaniola.[2]

There is no fight. The small crews of the barks flee, as they have done before and will do again when these *ladrones*, or thieves, come. What purpose is there in dying over a small cargo of salt? And what arms have they anyway, with which to defend themselves? At Campeche, on the Main, the crews will report the attack by pirates.

On the Main . . . the Spanish Main! What images this romantic term conjures! Pirate ships and Spanish galleons, and buccaneers and filibusters. Palm trees and rum, and sunken ships and buried treasure. Dark women and bawdy taverns, and haughty hidalgos and rapacious rapiers. Battles and duels at sea and ashore. And above all, adventure enough for several lifetimes. Along with the blood, dirt, disease, sweat, fear, and tragedy, many of these images are factual. Buccaneers—pirates or privateers who originated in the Caribbean in the late seventeenth century and who take their name from the pig and cattle hunters of Hispaniola, called *boucaniers*—were derived from a broad, diverse, and rich New World, of which they were but a small, albeit often central, part.

Strictly speaking, the Spanish Main was the Spanish-controlled mainland of America, both North and South. To a Spaniard, however, the Spanish Main included all land that Spain claimed, although those of other nations would not concede any such point unless proved by force of arms. "I explain that by Florida I mean only such portions as are actually settled, or can justly be claimed. For the Spaniards can hardly claim the whole country in virtue of two small castles," wrote the Earl of Doncaster, expressing a common attitude.[3]

The Spanish Main was usually referred to simply as the Main. This was practical shorthand and often poetic elegance. In the words of Sir Thomas Lynch, for example:

> The pirate was gone before she reached the coast of St. Domingo, so
> the captain got flesh, as I conclude at Porto Rico,* and thence made
> for the Virgins or the coast of the Main in search of La Trompeuse.[4]

The Main in 1674, as Spain saw it, ranged from Florida southward along the Central and South American coast until it was interrupted by the small Dutch and French colonies of Surinam, and Cayenne and the immense Portuguese colony of Brazil, then proceeded around Cape Horn and north to largely unexplored California. In a broader and modern sense, owing to travel writers, novelists, and Hollywood, the Main refers to the Caribbean, both sea and islands, particularly during the sea rover's Golden Age, from Queen Elizabeth's late-sixteenth-century sea dogs to the often bloody or rope-stretched end of the notorious Anglo-American pirates in the early eighteenth century. The British colonies of North America, bordering the Spanish Main and influencing all that happened there, must also be included in any discussion of the

---

*All quotations have been reprinted with their original spelling and punctuation.

romantic, epic, and often tragic history of this enormous land of two continents, America.

In 1674 it was three years since buccaneers, filibusters, and volunteer soldiers under Henry Morgan sacked the great city of Panama. Morgan, knighted by a grateful King Charles II, now served as lieutenant governor of Jamaica and was retired from piracy and privateering. If he plundered now, it was by pen and status in Port Royal, and not by musket and cutlass along the Main. In this year the two men who were destined to become both buccaneers and the greatest of buccaneer authors figuratively crossed paths: twenty-eight-year-old surgeon Alexander Exquemelin departed Saint Domingue (now Haiti) for France or the Netherlands, and twenty-two-year-old William Dampier departed England for Jamaica.[5] England was at peace with Spain, although Spain authorized the commissioning of local *corsarios* (privateers) to pursue and capture pirates, many of them not pirates at all, but innocent or interloping merchantmen. France still made war on Holland and Spain, permitting French filibusters to sail under legitimate privateering commissions. Between England and Spain the trade of slaves and smuggled goods strongly influenced policies in the region. England still needed her Caribbean "privateers" for defense in time of war, but in peace they were a two-edged sword: necessary for defense should war return, but liable to create trouble if their roving energies were not diverted from attacks on Spain.

Those men at Salinas, who captured several barks and "made bold . . . to sell both the Ships and the Indian Sailors that belonged to them," were not buccaneers or privateers at the time but worked as logwood cutters (also called *Bay men* and *Wood-Cutters*), and Salinas was merely a minor, profitable excursion.[6] Yet most people on the Main saw no distinction between logwood cutters and buccaneers, and rightly so. William Dampier was both a noted, amateur naturalist and variously a buccaneer, pirate, privateer, naval captain, explorer, and pilot to the South Sea, who early in his career made trading voyages to the logwood cutters in the Bay of Campeche. He noted the logwood cutters' origin:

> This Trade had its Rise from the decay of Privateering; for after Jamaica was well settled by the English, and a Peace established with Spain, the Privateers who had hitherto lived upon plundering the Spaniards, were put to their shifts; for they had prodigally spent whatever they got, and now wanting Subsistence, were forced either to go to Petit Guavas, where the Privateering Trade still continued, or into the Bay for Logwood.[7]

Operating from Petit Goave were filibusters, or French freebooters, counterparts of the English buccaneers, although in general the English called all sea rovers in the Caribbean *buccaneers*, while the French called them *flibustiers*. Unfortunately for English buccaneers, the Crown made it illegal to sail under a foreign commission, meaning English buccaneers could not work as privateers for the French or Dutch without fear of consequence.[8]

*T*hose logwood-cutting former buccaneers, who called themselves *privateers* to lend legitimacy to their acts of piracy (for privateering was legal but piracy was not), learned their roving trade from Henry Morgan and his ilk, and hardly considered the theft of a few salt barks to be worth anyone's notice. They were simply scratching an old itch. In addition, the barks were at anchor on the route from Jamaica to Trist, where the logwood lay stacked and waiting. The logwood cutters had not planned an act of piracy; an opportunity merely presented itself. Call it good business.

Logwood trade, which temporarily diverted a few hundred sea rovers from their natural instincts, exported several valuable woods, including "fustick, braziletto, *lignum vitae* . . . and ebony."[9] Logwood was used to make a valuable reddish-purple dye, and from it fortunes could be made. The early English raiders did not realize the value of the first piles of logs they came across in the bays of Campeche and Honduras. Quickly, though, they discovered a virtual gold mine of timber, and if they found no purchase—plunder, that is—in the Bay of Campeche they would sail to the "Champeton River [in Campeche], where they were certain to find large Piles cut to their Hand, and brought to the Sea-side ready to be shipped off."[10]

In theory, logwood cutting was an opportune trade at an opportune time for buccaneers who could no longer make a semi-legitimate living working as semi-legitimate privateers. Buccaneers were hardy enough to both cut and ferry logwood, and defend themselves against wild cattle, alligators, and Spaniards. They were strong enough to toil barefoot in water up to their knees, chopping down logwood trees, cutting them to length, and stacking what they cut. "When they have cut down the Tree, they Log it, and Chip it, which is cutting the Bark and Sap, and then lay it in Heaps, cutting away the Underwood, and making Paths to each Heap."[11] There the logwood remained "till the Land-Flood favours their bringing it into the River, and then Canoos are laden away with it, to lay in store at *Barcaderas* [embarcaderos]."[12]

To take advantage of the cool sea breezes, logwood cutters built palmetto-thatched huts near the shore. They made frames or grills, called *barbacoas*, or *barbecues*; covered them with leaves or earth; and used them for tables and beds. To protect themselves against the infernal multitude of "Sand-Flies and Muskitos," they erected "pavillions" or tents of "Ozenbrigs" (a coarse cloth of linen or hemp) above their beds inside their huts. Their clothing came from the same cloth much used by sailors for their clothing. They dined on beef, sea turtle, manatee, and jewfish (Goliath grouper). They swore; there

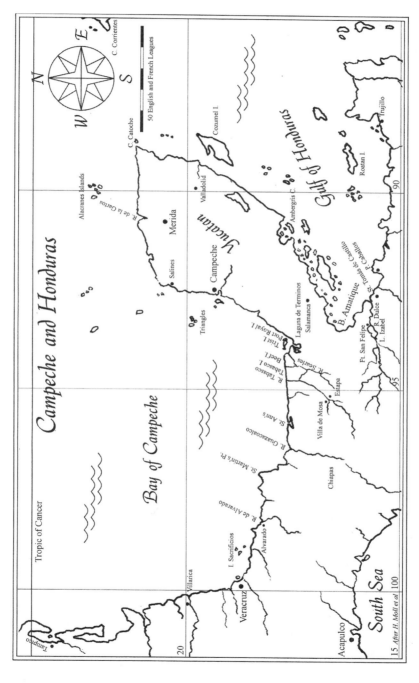

**BENERSON LITTLE AND COURTNEY LITTLE.**

was "little else to be heard but Blashphemy, Cursing and Swearing." They delighted in hunting cattle. When they shot one they cut it into four quarters, carved out the bones, and each of the four-man hunting party

> [m]akes a hole in the middle of his Quarter, just big enough for his Head to go thro', then puts it on like a Frock, and trudgeth home; and if he chances to tire, he cuts off some of it, and flings it away.

They stood their ground (so to speak) in a canoe when charged in the water by an angry wild cow or bull. They kept the bow toward the animal, so that it could only push them astern a hundred or more feet, rather than capsizing them, wetting their arms, and leaving them unable to use their weapons to defend against attack by alligators. They were "generally sturdy strong Fellows, and will carry Burthens of three or four hundred weight."[13]

Notoriously, the

> Wood-Cutters are generally a rude drunken Crew, some of which have been Pirates and most them Sailors; their chief Delight is in drinking; and when they broach a Quarter Cask or a Hogshead of Wine, they seldom stir from it while there is a Drop left,

wrote Captain Uring of those at Honduras.[14] Dampier described the logwood cutters of the Bay of Campeche similarly, noting that rum punch was their favorite drink, although they also drank cider and bottle ale. "[B]esides they had not forgot their old Drinking bouts, and would still spend 30 or 40 *l*. [pounds] at a sitting aboard the Ship that came hither from Jamaica; carousing and firing Guns three or four Days together."[15]

In the ranks of these tough men were John Coxon, Bartholomew Sharp, Joseph Banister, Jan Willems (called Yanky), Richard Sawkins, William Dampier, Helles de Lecat (called Yellows), and many others, of which much more will be told.[16]

Logwood cutters encountered problems because the bays of Campeche and Honduras were, in Spain's eyes at least, part of the Spanish Main. Spain did not appreciate foreign intruders taking Spanish property, and England eventually came to agree because Spain's complaints and reprisals were convincing, and because logwood was "almost all carried to Hamburgh, New England, Holland, &c., which injures us and customs and trade of the nation."[17] The trade grew dangerous to those who engaged in it, and the ships that laded logwood invariably kept "a strict Watch to prevent our being surpris'd by the *Spaniards*, having our Small Arms and Granado Shells always ready upon the Quarter Deck," while simultaneously entertaining staggering, drunk logwood cutters.[18]

$\mathcal{S}$o where would they go, those men who tentatively accepted peace between Spain, England, and, in four years, France? What was left for buccaneers and filibusters in place of their native trade, stealing by force of arms from the Spanish while under legitimate commission or reasonable pretense thereof? To stay in the good graces of the English government, they shifted to other trades. Logwood cutting remained hard but mundane work, and became more dangerous as the Spanish and English attempted to suppress it. There was *wrecking*, or the salvage of sunken treasure. There was turtling, the sloop trade, and hunting.

There was also, of course, the sailor's trade aboard merchant ships, but buccaneers and filibusters refused to follow it. The "seamen in Jamaica . . . are unwilling to sail in Ships, because there is more Work, and loath to go for Europe, for fear of being imprest," writes Captain Uring in the early eighteenth century, expressing a simple truth that had been in existence since the English captured Jamaica from the Spanish in 1655. Similarly, Father Labat, a French priest with much experience among filibusters, noted of "vessels of three masts . . . our corsairs [filibusters] serve in them little, or to speak more correctly, not at all." In peacetime ships were too much work, and as privateer or pirate vessels, they were expensive to outfit, required larger crews, and resulted in diminished shares of plunder.[19]

Employment aboard a merchant vessel hardly suited those who principally valued courage under fire. For those who had lived a largely egalitarian, largely democratic lifestyle of desperate adventure, where each man's vote was equal to another's (excepting only to the captain, who usually had two votes and two shares), where each man shared equally in the profits of plunder by force of arms, where each man was judged by his deeds, and where shooting, drinking, and whoring were the favorite pastimes, forays into mundane trades must have been a shock.[20]

Although their attitudes were more extreme than many of their contemporaries'—most men and women of the New World did not seek their fortunes as sea rovers or in such difficult, hazardous ventures as logwood cutting—their origins were the same. While members of the nobility, the middle class, and yeomanry made their home in the New World, most people who immigrated to the two continents were of the lower class and often described patronizingly. "These Indies are the refuge of people who are unable to make a living in England," wrote a French Huguenot in Virginia in 1686. He continued: "The country constitutes also the galleys of England, for those who have committed any crime short of hanging may be banished and condemned to service in America. It is also the refuge of bankrupts." He had nothing better to say of the women who hazarded their lives to better themselves in the brave New World.[21] Ironically, Governor Pouançay of Saint Domingue stated that the same Huguenots were those who "ill-governed their affairs [were bankrupts] and claim religious persecution in order to settle among the English in the New World."[22]

Ned Ward, a late seventeenth- and early eighteenth-century satirist, wrote of Jamaica in a similar vein: "Receptacle of Vagabonds, the Sanctuary of Bankrupts, and a Close-stool for the Purges of our Prisons."[23] Not only were they vagabonds, thieves, and bankrupts, they bred and mixed with other races, and took on airs. America was home to the *"Lacker-Face'd Creolean,"* also called a "Tawny Fac'd *Moletto* Strumpet," and men who "look as if they had just knock'd off their Fetters." Worse, they assumed social rank in a time not known for upward mobility: "A *Broken Apothecary* will make there a *Tipping Physician*; a *Barbers Prentice*, a good *Surgeon*; a *Bailiffs Follower*, a passable *Lawyer*; and an *English Knave*, a very *Honest Fellow*." Common men considered themselves officers and gentlemen, and common women put on impudent airs.[24]

Other observers were more positive. Giovanni Francesco Gemelli Careri, who traveled around the world in the late seventeenth century, noted that "many . . . Spaniards, from mean beginnings have arriv'd to vast wealth, and then finish'd prodigious works," and that that was typical. *"Dominick Laurencana* coming poor into the *Indies*, acquir'd so much wealth that he built the famous monastery of the *Incarnation*," and *"James del Castillo*, born at *Granada*, coming poor out of *Spain*, laid the foundation of his fortune by following the trade of a brazier."[25] Early in the seventeenth century, Catalina de Erauso—a novice turned swashbuckling picara (female rogue) disguised as a man—noted both cynically and optimistically about justice that "persistence and hard work can perform miracles, and it happens regularly—especially in the Indies!"[26]

Edward Barlow, a mariner for forty-four years whose fascinating journal is one of the principal sources on the maritime world of the period, noted that

> several that have gone over, servants, and some convicted by law for their roguery and transported out of Newgate or Bridwell and other prisons, live so well now in Jamaica that they keep their coach and horses, being worth a thousand a year, which they get by good plantations, which they have got by their care and industry.

For former buccaneers, however, it remained to be seen exactly how honest and upstanding they could be or pretend to be.[27]

In the seventeenth century a common punishment in the Netherlands was serving in a "rasp house," scraping dyewoods, including logwood. Many petty thieves, having served time rasping logwood, may have indentured themselves to barbarous *boucanier* masters in the Caribbean. Eventually, if he survived, an ex-thief from Amsterdam could cut logwood on the Main, make a fortune, and retire to a Caribbean estate with his "coach and four" (horses). Not a bad end for a man born poor across the Atlantic.[28]

*C*hanges in opportunity, character, and culture also occurred in America. Francis Rogers described the inhabitants of Jamaica as "of a fiery hot temper, haughty and apt to command and domineer," yet also "of an open, free, and generous spirit, very hospitable and civil to strangers."[29] Captain Uring praised a poor husband and wife in Virginia who housed him and helped him recover from smallpox. "I lived with these poor people very agreeably . . . and assisted the poor old Man in all his Plantation business."[30]

Excepting Native Americans, much of the New World population was not born there, but traveled from across the Atlantic. Some came as free men and women, escaping religious persecution or simply seeking new opportunities. Because the Spanish were required to petition for a license to cross the sea, and licenses were refused to foreigners, single women, Jews, Moors, mulatto slaves, and non-Catholics, among many others, many Spaniards claimed their population in America was superior to those of other nations, who sent their "rubbish."[31] But this was arrant nonsense. People of many nations, ethnicities, and faiths found their way to New Spain. Those who sneered at "rubbish" were merely engaging in social posturing.

Not all who came to the New World came as free men or women. Many were voluntarily indentured servants, transported criminals, or slaves. Native Americans, too, were displaced, sold as slaves, and transported to other regions of America to discourage them from fleeing their owners. In Spanish lands they were enslaved or forced to work under various labor systems as if they were slaves.[32] Africans were brought as slaves.

Many immigrated to the New World from across the Atlantic, but others were born along the Main. They, and other Europeans who made permanent homes in the Main, were called *Creoles* or *Creolians*. Native Americans were called *Indians*, *Natives*, "Americanes," or by the names of their tribes.[33] Africans were called *Blacks* or *Negroes*. Mixed races had many names. Mulattos were the offspring of a European and an African; mestizos were the offspring of European and a Native American (in Spanish the term *Criollo* was also used).[34] The Spanish had categories in depth: a *mustee* was "begot by *Spaniards* on *Indian* Women," and a *quarteroon de Negroes* was the offspring of a mulatto and a Spaniard.[35] A *zambo* or *alcatrace* was half Native American and half African. Those of mixed races or darker complexions were sometimes called *mongrels* by Europeans.[36] Africans and Native Americans were often considered, by Europeans, entirely inferior. Racism and bigotry were the inevitable products of such social stratification.

$\mathcal{T}$he New World was populated by a variety and blend of cultures: Europeans, West Africans, Native Americans, and small numbers of Asians. Spaniards were ubiquitous, including Castilians, Basques, Asturians, Navarrese, Aragonese, Valencians, and Galicians. The Portuguese inhabited Brazil and other places along the Main. Britons were represented by English, Welsh, Cornish, Scottish Highlanders and Lowlanders, and Anglo-Irish. The native Irish had also immigrated. There were large numbers of French from Gascons to Parisians. There were also men and women from the Low Countries, including Hollanders, Frisians, Flemings, and Walloons. West Africans were enslaved and shipped in large numbers. Tribes included the Ashanti, Igbo, Kalabari, Bini, and Songye, among others, although Europeans often referred to Africans by their region of origin: Gold Coast, Coromantines, Whidaw, Angola, and Alampo.[37] Small numbers of natives of the Coromandel coast of India were carried to the English colonies of North America.[38] Native American tribes were too many to enumerate, but included the Iroquois, Huron, Abenaki, Wampanoag, Narragansett, Apalache, Timucuan, Yamassee, Moskito, Darien (Cuna), Carib, and the descendants of the Aztec, Maya, and Inca. There were mulattos, mestizos, and zambos. In smaller numbers were Poles, Italians, Brandenburgers, Danes, Swiss, Germans, Swedes, Norwegians, Corsicans, Ragusians, Majorcans, Canary Islanders, Levanters (called Greeks), true Greeks, Slavs, North African Moors, and Jews of several nations. In Peru there were a few natives of India and China, carried first to Acapulco aboard the Manila galleons, and then taken to Peru by local merchantmen. Malays, Filipinos (sometimes known as Malays), and Chinese were found in Acapulco and beyond.[39]

For many people new to America, born there or carried there, opportunity was the key, and opportunities, legitimate and otherwise, abounded along the Spanish Main. They had little to lose and much to gain. Independent, they formed alliances with other like-minded individuals, both on the small scale of a buccaneer crew and on the larger scale of proto-nations. Regional identifications formed among New World inhabitants, and the Europeans began to see themselves as part of, yet separate from, their nations of origin. The many and diverse Native American tribes had always been independent. Africans, as slaves, lost their ties to their native tribes but retained much of their diverse cultures. All those cultures began to blend and change as they influenced each other in the New World.

All the people along the Spanish Main had one thing in common: they lived either at the edge of mainstream European society or beyond its pale. It was a world of marginal peoples, by European standards, and of varied cultures at the far edge of a world claimed and fought over by Europeans.

And in that pot of many cultures, new and old, grew the roots of significant, even profound, change. Native American insurrections were on the rise against the Spanish and English. African slaves rose against their masters and formed independent communities of Maroons. English planters lived in fear not only of African-slave uprisings, but also of indentured-servant uprisings.[40] Spaniards in New Spain feared that the "rabble of *Blacks* and *Tawnies* is so encreas'd ... [that] they may one day rebel, and make themselves masters of the country."[41] Spanish colonists subtly engaged in a form self-determination, in spite of contrary orders from Spain. The English colonies of North America were a hotbed of political uprisings. A century before the American Revolution, social and political upheaval—rebellion, that is—was already a habit, indeed a trait, of the New World. New social orders unconsciously grew. Immigrants needed only another century to develop a stronger identity of nationality, confederation, or mutual self-interest and to recognize the injustice of a government across the sea to ignite large-scale, world-class rebellions. Indeed, the American revolutions of the eighteenth and nineteenth centuries had their origins in the seventeenth.

Logwood cutters, nearly all of them former privateers—buccaneers and filibusters—represented the traits necessary to seize the opportunity of material gain presented by a far-flung, failing empire: independent, egalitarian, tough, brave, cunning, violent, hard playing, hard drinking, and, when they chose to be, hardworking. They were men of opportunistic calculation and courage who lived in a time and place that was wilder, larger, richer—a third of the world—than the wild American West or any other frontier in modern history ever was. In European eyes, not since the origin and dispersal of man, or in seventeenth-century terms, the expulsion of Adam and Eve from Eden, had such a frontier been known.

In such a wide new world, men who had grown accustomed to willful, independent adventure would scarcely give it up without a fight, if its fruits remained plentiful. "[N]either of these Employments affected them so much as Privateering," writes William Dampier.[42] Many quickly returned to their preferred trade. It was "a dry Business to toil at Cutting Wood," after all, notwithstanding that it was an "honest living" compared to "privateering."[43] It may not have mattered to buccaneers that both Spain and England discouraged logwood cutting. It was not long before the logwood-cutting buccaneers sallied from Trist to plunder Indian villages, keeping the women and selling the men, or seized salt barks at Salinas, selling the barks, cargo, and crews.[44]

Petty piracy to piracy on a grand scale was a small step for those men, although they did not consider their acts piracy if the prizes they sought were Spanish.[45] When governments prohibited attacks on the Spanish, "the Transition [was] easy from a Buccanier to a Pyrate; from plundering for others, to do it for themselves," and some did not resign themselves to piracy only against Spain.[46] Unflinchingly, unhesitatingly, unabashedly they began to take to the seas again for riches by force of arms, and their successes caused "all people of uncertain fortunes [to be] strangely tempted to join them."[47]

Dangerous free spirits turned to piracy, not on the scale of stealing a few salt barks at anchor in a tiny port such as Salinas but on a grand scale. In doing so, their deeds resounded far beyond their numbers of a few thousand. These men became the real pirates of the Caribbean, whose captains and deeds surpassed anything in fiction or film. Unlike most of their bastard progeny of the early eighteenth century—Blackbeard, Calico Jack Rackam, Bartholomew Roberts, and others—these pirates engaged heavily armed Spanish men-of-war and captured them. The formed armies and sacked cities, explored places largely unknown to Europeans, crossed the dangerous Darien afoot, sailed around Cape Horn, and even around the world. And they did so with little, if any, significant support of any state. Few nationalities, ethnicities, or cultures of the New World, of this Spanish Main, were left out of their crews, but the English, French, and Dutch dominated at sea among the enemies of Spain. Spain, too, produced its own notorious pirates along the Main, whose depredations against the English and French also became legend.

"[These buccaneers] are for the most part those who have long haunted these seas, and, finding themselves discouraged at their old trade, have joined together," writes Lieutenant Governor Hender Molesworth of Jamaica.[48] The buccaneers or privateers were already, in many instances, pirates; however, their acts were ignored or condoned locally. Spain was a rival and an enemy, in fact if not always by declaration. The buccaneers protected the vulnerable English colonies, and the filibusters protected the French. They brought goods and hard currency into struggling economies. Buccaneers were a necessary, and often praised, part of English aspirations along the Spanish Main.

But not after 1674. After peace was declared between Spain and England, buccaneers became a double-edged sword because they would not forget that "damned privateering business"; nor would the filibusters when peace came to the French. So for the fifteen years from 1674 to 1688 reigned the boldest, truest, and perhaps greatest pirates of the Caribbean, central to the history of a rich, rebellious, violent New World.[49]

# Water, Water Everywhere:
## The Means of Freedom on the Main

*N*ot long after soon-to-be-buccaneer William Dampier departs, in 1675, from Trist in the Bay of Campeche, aboard a ketch laden with log wood purchased with rum and sugar, the lookout espies two sails astern. Captain Hudsel does not wait to discover who they might be. Instead, wisely, he "edge[s] off more to Sea," and as soon as he does the two as yet unknown vessels "also alter'd their Course steering away still directly with us; so that we were now assured they were *Spaniards*."[1] The chase is on.

Water is unique among all things as the binding element of life. And it has its price: too much and too little will kill, in many forms. Along the Spanish Main in the late seventeenth century, water in the form of rivers and seas was the binding element not only of life in general, but of life as it expressed itself in peoples and cultures. It was the only conduit for travel, trade, and communication with the Old World and was the most significant conduit in the New World. The North and South Seas, better known today as the Atlantic and Pacific oceans, lapped against and broke upon hundreds of thousands of miles of shore, and thousands upon thousands of miles of rivers emptied into the seas. The surrounding seas and penetrating rivers led to and within a world of deserts, jungles, and temperate forests along a Spanish Main often viewed by Europeans as a dark, foreboding landscape of endless opportunity, peopled on its sparsely colonized shores and interior depths by voracious savages and beasts, and encroached on by avaricious enemies.

The waters were also the sea rover's highway. The seas led to merchant vessels and treasure ships, and the rivers led where "the Earth opens in this Country her most interiour* Bowels, to furnish with Gold and Precious Stones."[2] Making one's way about these waters, whether to trade honestly or live by the pirate and privateer's rule of "no prey, no pay," required seamanship and, obviously, ships, vessels, or craft. The New World seas were, in practical terms, largely uncontrolled, and anyone with a swift, armed, seaworthy vessel and a stout, armed crew was, if perhaps only briefly, master of his own destiny. Opportunities were many and often easy to seize if one had the means to travel the seas and their adjacent rivers. However, the successful outcome of such a seizure was another matter entirely.

*U*nderstanding the vessels and craft of the region is essential to understanding life and piracy on the Main. Smaller vessels were by far the most numerous, and the smallest, as well as the simplest, least expensive, and ubiquitous were the canoe and its larger cousin, the periager (in French a *pirogue*, in Spanish a *piragua*, from Carib *piraua*).[3] Carved from logs, the principal difference between the two was size. Canoes were used for coastal and river traffic, as ship's boats (and often carried aboard), and as light, general-purpose craft. Periagers, often rigged with sails, served in a similar fashion to longboats and launches, the largest of a ship's boats. They also served as cargo barges on rivers, and some were large enough to carry fifty or sixty barrels. Both craft were commonly used by Native Americans and Europeans, at sea and on inland waters, although Europeans usually rowed them, while Native Americans paddled them. They were also used by buccaneers, filibusters, and Spanish pirates.[4]

Boats were ubiquitous as well: yawls, pinnaces, longboats, launches (Spanish longboats, from *lancha*), and shallops.[5] Of single-mast vessels, the most significant was the sloop (from Dutch *sloep*, in French a *barque*, in Spanish a *balandra*). In her common form her mast had little rake (was mostly vertical), and she had a large gaff sail and one or two headsails. However, as a swift merchant, privateer, or pirate vessel she had a rakish mast, was made of Jamaica or Bermuda cedar and therefore was lightweight, and carried not only the common sloop sails, but also a square course (mainsail) and perhaps even a topsail to assist in maneuvering in a fight. Bermuda sloops were by far considered the best in quality, for the timber used in their construction, and their speed.[6]

*Bark* was the common term for a variety of vessels of one to three masts ferrying cargo along the coast and among the islands. The *barcalonga*

---

*All quotations have been reprinted with their original spelling and punctuation.

(sometimes written as *barco luengo*; in French a *barque-longue*) was usually described as a small vessel with a sharp bow and stern, with two masts and two or three square sails, often undecked, and swift under sail or oar.[7] The *corvette* was often described by the French as a type of barque-longue. The *brigantin* was a two-mast vessel, with square sails on the foremast and a single large gaff sail on the mainmast, while the *brigantine* (often equated with the corvette) was square-rigged on both masts. Both rowed well. The Bermuda boat had two masts and a triangular sail laced to each. The ketch was short (her beam was wide relative to her length), had a round stern and "great round bows," and carried a course and main topsail on her mainmast, and a triangular sail called a *lateen* (from *Latin*) on her mizzenmast. She was built for cargo, not for speed.[8]

The tartan, or *tarteen* (Spanish *tartana*), was an exotic Mediterranean vessel with a long sharp prow, two or three masts and conventional lateen sails; had a burthen of forty to seventy tons; and was much used on the Main as a fishing boat and advice boat. The *saëtia*, or settee, was another Mediterranean vessel much used in the Spanish New World, with a long sharp prow, two or three masts, and settee sails (a quadrilateral form of lateen).[9]

Three-mast, square-rigged vessels were, by definition, ships. The common merchant ship was built for cargo while the frigate, with her sleeker lines, was built for speed. The frigate was both a form of ship's hull as well as a type of light naval warship used for scouting and cruising. Among navies and rovers, light frigates were preferred for their speed and suitability for rowing in calms and light airs, while the man-of-war was usually frigate built. A common form of merchant ship was the *flute* (or *fluyt*), also known as a *flyboat* and in Spanish as an *urca*. She had a shallow draft, flat bottom, broad beam, and round or "pinked" stern; was lightly constructed; was long by the keel as compared to her beam, and was roughly of three hundred tons burthen, although the size varied. Her upper deck was often quite narrow compared to her beam, said to be a Dutch response designed to minimize Danish customs dues. The flute was the bulk carrier of her day and also often used as a *patache*, or tender. The pink was a ship with a pinked stern, much like a small flute (and defined as one in some French texts), and was an excellent sailor. The galleon, long recognized as a symbol of Spanish might, was, with perhaps a few rare exceptions, extinct. The term remained in use to describe Spanish men-of-war with high sterns, usually *fragatas* of more than four hundred tons, used to ferry treasure or other valuable goods. In general, all but the smallest ships of the Spanish treasure fleets were referred to as *galleons*.[10]

*T*he typical buccaneer or filibuster vessel might have been originally English, French, Spanish, Dutch, Portuguese, or even Danish. She might have been a French ship captured by the Spanish and recaptured by filibusters, or a Spanish ship built by the Dutch and captured by buccaneers, or a Danish ship taken in an act of piracy, or any other vessel that could be had by hook or by crook. Except for some Spanish vessels, Bermuda sloops, and a galley each at Jamaica and Saint Domingue, no vessels on the Spanish Main were designed and built intentionally as rovers. Most roving vessels were not ships, but sloops and small "topsail" vessels. A "fine barque with ten guns, sixteen patararoes and about fifty men" was a typical, if very well armed for its size, pirate vessel of the period.[11] Pirates did not usually fly their own colors, but those of their various nations.[12] Not until the early eighteenth century, when state-sponsored and state-abetted piracy ceased entirely, did pirates begin to fly the black flag with skull and bones. To intimidate the enemy, or to show themselves "undaunted," pirates did often fly the "bloody" red flag of no quarter, but this flag was often flown by men-of-war as well.

However, pirates were not only predators; they were often prey as well. To hunt them local governments used swift light frigates, hired sloops, large piraguas, and galleys that were "called half-galleys in the straits." A piragua could carry as many as "fifty-four men and two guns" (swivel cannon), while a half-galley had two masts (with a pair of gallows so they could be un-stepped and stowed when rowing) and fifty oars, was ninety to ninety-five feet long and sixteen or more feet abeam, had a hull depth of four or five feet and a draft of only a foot and a half, and carried sixty-five to one hundred and twenty men, one "Cushee piece" (a cannon rigged to fire forward in the chase) in the bow, and four to six patereroes (swivel cannon) astern. Periagers and galleys, often made of cedar, were particularly useful for their shallow draft and rowing speed. They could be pulled ashore and hidden during the day and then used to strike by night. They were ideal for quick coastal raids on shipping and small towns. Cuba in 1684 had seven pirate-hunting periagers and two half-galleys.[13]

*A* vessel was more than cannon, timbers, and sails, more than a "pretty thing" on the water. She had a crew and often passengers, and was not only a means of travel but also a home where people ate, slept, and lived. (Never mind the contradiction between merchant*man* or *man*-of-war and the otherwise feminine reference to a ship—one wit claimed a ship was feminine "because her Rigging, and Fitting forth, is always worth double her Carcase.")[14] It was cramped aboard all vessels, even aboard those with a small crew. There was nowhere to be alone except the great cabin, and that was the captain's berth unless he rented it for the voyage to one or more of his passengers. Common sailors slept in "hammacoes" in the forecastle and in the space beneath, or on deck when in the tropics:

In Privateers [buccaneers], especially when we are at an Anchor, the

Deck is spread with Mats to lie on each Night. Every Man has one, some two; and this with a Pillow for the Head and a Rug for a Covering, is all the Bedding that is necessary for Men of that Employ.[15]

Officers and petty officers of most vessels slept in beds called cradles or in hammocks in tiny, three-feet-by-five-and-a-half-feet cabins in the steerage. Even the "great cabin" was small, although more comfortable and appealing with its green paint, a landscape painted on the forward bulkhead, several stern "lights" (windows), and the nautical instruments, muskets, pistols, and swords hanging on the bulkheads.[16] Only aloft in the fore or maintop, or in one of the crannies in the depths of the hold, might anyone other than the captain find quiet solace. It was crowded everywhere, and not surprisingly some spoke of a "Sea-kennel, call'd a Ship."[17]

The decks themselves were crowded—or more correctly, "lumbered" or "pestered"—with goods and livestock. If she provisioned in the tropics, a ship might look like "a floating garden with such abundance of fruit and greens."[18] Two tiers of water casks filled most of the free space on the gun deck or between decks, to the point that the ship's cannon could not be used without first jettisoning goods or staving water barrels.[19] Indeed, it took an hour or two to make the ship clear for engaging a pirate—and by then it might be too late. Aboard some ships, many or even all of the "great guns" may have been "struck below" to make the ship more seaworthy in heavy seas, and were mounted only when nearing land.[20] There may have been clothing drying in the rigging after being washed or after a storm.[21] Lashed to one of the channels (platforms that support the shrouds) was the steep tub in which salt beef, salt pork, or *boucan* was soaked to make it more palatable. In the tropics a "boarded awning" was often rigged over the quarterdeck to provide shade.[22]

Amidship, the main hatch to the hold was "caulked up . . . close" and covered tightly with a tarpaulin to keep sea and sailor from the cargo, while the barrels and bale goods within were "heaved in so close with hand-screws that we could not stow one more."[23] If the ship was Spanish, much of the cargo, water, gunpowder, and provisions were stored in earthenware jars, although water casks were preferred for men-of-war.[24] Aboard common merchantmen, treasure was stowed in the great cabin in "a large chest, so heavy, that five or six men could but just draw it along the deck, full of pigs of silver, bags of pieces-of-eight, and some gold."[25]

Aboard most vessels, animals were everywhere: "sheep, hogs, turkeys, hens, ducks, monkeys, goats, dogs, parrots, and geese" were listed by one mariner.[26] Another was more detailed: at the taffrail at the stern were two chicken coops filled with hens, and somewhere a rooster or two, or even more for eating, and if a Spanish ship, cockfights for certain (although gambling was forbidden aboard Spanish galleons, as curiously were chicken coops on their quarterdecks). Four more hen coops were stowed about the ship, each hold-ing two dozen hens. Thirteen turkeys made their home in the forecastle, sit-ting upon the cannon. In the pinnace beneath the yawl were half a dozen each of hogs, sheep, and goats.[27] There may have been other animals stowed in the manger, a small partition set just abaft the hawseholes in the forecastle, which contained seawater entering at the hawse. Sea turtles, alive and recently cap-tured, often lay on their backs on deck or in the hold, unaware of their im-pending slaughter.[28]

There was often an "abundance of parrots aboard" purchased for five dollars (pieces-of-eight) each in the Caribbean. Any one parrot was "harder to maintain . . . aboard than I have since done a wife and two children."[29] If the ship came from Africa, "Parakets," purchased at forty for a half dollar, including a cane cage, were also aboard.[30] There were monkeys (often called *jackanapes*; three or four could be bought "for an old hat" on the African coast), pet dogs, a cat or two, and several piglets.[31] The piglets "run and tumble about the Ship during a Calm," and even hogs ran free at times.[32] The odors of the entire menagerie mixed with those of pine tar, wet wood, linseed oil, cordage, tal-low, pitch, wood and tobacco smoke, sea air, and unwashed bodies, and the noises of the animals—cackling, crowing, bleating, lowing, snorting, meow-ing, and barking—not to mention the cries of sea birds, all added to the creak-ing and groaning of hull and rigging. Further, the ships were infested with rats and cockroaches.[33] One mariner wrote about entering the gunroom of severely storm-damaged ship,

> Whilst I was thus goveling in the dark, I felt my body all over cover'd
> with rats, as thick as they could stand upon me, on my coat, arms,
> neck, and my very head, so that I was forc'd to make my escape into
> the light to get rid of those vermin.[34]

Sharks, called *requins* by the French (from *requiem*, or mass for the dead), followed in the wake of vessels, sniffing the rich, odiferous trail and hoping in their primitive brains for a meal of fish, beast, or man, dead or alive, fresh or foul.[35]

There were few differences between a merchant or trading vessel and a pirate vessel. Roving vessels were typically better armed, although often they carried only muskets and other small arms. In the pirate's hold, the only goods brought on, rather than captured, were food, wood, water, rum, and arms. Livestock was aboard in small numbers, except after the sacking of a town. Pets—parrots, monkeys, dogs, and cats, for the rats—were found in as great a number as aboard a merchantman. "So that with Provision, Chests, Hen-Coops and Parrot-Cages, our Ships were full of Lumber," writes Dampier of bucca-neer vessels after the sack of Alvarado.[36] After a long South Sea voyage, one pirate vessel's sails were patched with clothing, and her leaks stopped with coconut fiber.[37]

*I*n such conditions aboard various vessels, crew and passengers tempted fate on the seas. They battled "flaws" (brief stormy weather), tempests, "tornadoes" (thunderstorms), hurricanes, and "whirlwinds" (waterspouts), not to mention calms that forced the rationing of food and water. They battled navigational uncertainties that led to shoals, coral heads, and other "breaches" that could sink a ship and drown her crew, or leave the survivors marooned, starving, and dehydrated. Beyond the dangers of the sea were those of man: avarice, ineptitude, and mutiny, not to mention enemy men-of-war in times of war and pirates in times of peace.

Knowing now what these vessels on the Spanish Main were like, we return to the ketch chased by two vessels astern, certainly Spanish. If she could not outrun the "chasers," her captain would have to choose to bluff, fight, or surrender. If he bluffed, it would have to be believable:

> our commander threatening them hard, they fell astern of us again; and at last, seeing us resolute in keeping them off, they durst not attempt us, but made away, firing two guns with shot at us, which we returned in the like manner with interest.[38]

But the ketch ran first, and in a slow and dull-sailing vessel at that, so it would be difficult to bluff successfully.

If he decided to stand and fight, a merchant captain would have to choose the best tactics. If his vessel was lightly manned, he could not fight well with broadsides or repulse boarders by fighting from open decks. Thus he had to retreat to "closed quarters," let his enemy board him, and try to batter and chop his way through deck and bulkhead into the barricaded spaces, while braving a gauntlet of powder chests, small arms, grenades, and even a barrage of scrap metal fired from a cannon aimed into the ship's waist. The merchant captain, commanding from the steerage, also fired his cannon into the hull of the enemy alongside.[39] In a stern chase the gunner was in the great cabin; otherwise, his place was in the steerage. The carpenter would plug holes at or below the waterline and ensure that the enemy did not pry open the gun ports, while the mate commanded in the forecastle.[40]

This tactic often worked, if backed by a stout captain and crew. "Win her, and have her[!]" shouted a courageous commander in 1686 when threatened by a pirate. The rover

> thereupon boarded us for four or five hours, cutting our poop and ensign-staff; and his shot cut many of our shrouds. Our ship being

very much pester'd, we play'd but three or four of our guns; yet we beat his gunnel [gunwale or "gun'l"] in, and made him put off, and lie upon the careen. As soon as she was gone we came out of our close quarters, and found one of his men almost dead upon our poop, with a fuzee [a flintlock musket], an axe, a cartouch-box, a stinkpot, a pistol, and a cutlass.[41]

But Captain Hudsel would not bluff, fight, or surrender unless he had no recourse. He was a seaman and used seamanship to escape and save his cargo. A calm came, betwixt the land and sea breezes, and in the interval his crew "unbend the Foresail, and make a studding Sail of it." By rigging the foresail as a stuns'l (studding sail), probably alongside the fore topsail, and putting the ketch directly before the sea breeze when it sprang up, "all the Sail we had did us Service" for no sail could becalm another. But three-masted ships did not sail well with the wind directly astern, for the "After-sails becalm ... their Head-sails." The wind freshened, and the ketch escaped without having to heave the cargo overboard to increase speed. The case concluded with the best outcome: no harm done, only sweaty palms and a knot in the stomach for a while.[42]

William Dampier escaped, and with him his share of logwood profits. But logwood was hard work, and Dampier eventually turned to piracy, as many of his contemporaries had done, with his sights set on the riches of a declining Spain at peace with England. After all, why not chase instead of be chased? But much of the Spanish wealth was well protected, and stealing even a small part of it required much more than a sword waved and a yell of "Amain, dogs, strike your colors and your topsails!" and accompanied by a few cannon shots and musket balls fired at a frightened and poorly armed merchant crew. It required leadership, skill, and desperate courage, for Spain in the New World was often defended not by frightened merchants and their brave servants and slaves, but by battle-tested, courageous men-at-arms of many different New World peoples.

# 3 Biscayers, Indians, Africans, and Greeks:
## Spain in the New World

*I*t was more than well that Dampier's ketch escaped. Many of the Spaniards who chased pirates and interlopers had a deserved reputation of brutality and murder, and often gave no quarter.

> They lurk in the bushes by the shore, so that they see every passing vessel without being seen. When our sloops are at anchor they set them by their compasses in the daytime, and steal on them by night with little noise that they are aboard before they are discovered.

They "are of all nations, rogues culled out for the villanies* that they commit. They never hail a ship; and, so they can but master her, she is certain prize," wrote Hender Molesworth of Jamaica.[1] Doubtless there are *zaramullos* (criminal outcasts), *pícaros* (rogues), and *bandidos* (bandits) among them. Molesworth neglected to mention that the Spanish tactics and villainies were often those of English pirates. The only difference, if indeed it was a difference, was that Spanish governors condoned acts of Spanish piracy, while English governors claimed to decry (and some actually did decry) those of English buccaneers. That being said, the English and French much preferred to be captured by English or French pirates, for they were considered to be

---

*All quotations have been reprinted with their original spelling and punctuation.

21

more "humane and reasonable," and if a person survived their initial fury, he was likely to be given quarter and could then negotiate. But Spaniards, some said, never gave quarter.[2]

Dampier described Spaniards as

> ready to launch out, and seize any small Vessel, and seldom spare the Lives as well as the Goods of those that fall into their Hands for fear of telling Tales....The Merchants and Gentry indeed are no way guilty of such Actions, only the Soldiers and Rascality of the People; and these do commonly consist of Mulatoes or some other sort of Copper-colour'd Indians, who are accounted very barbarous and cruel.[3]

Others claimed likewise of race and villainy.

> They have committed barbarous cruelties and injustices, and better cannot be expected, for they are Corsicans, Slavonians, Greeks, mulattoes, a mongrel parcel of thieves and rogues that rob and murder all that come into their power without the least respect to humanity or common justice.[4]

They racked their captives mercilessly. They murdered a prisoner because he was sick. They hanged English seamen from yardarms and then shot them. Yet notwithstanding these instances of brutality, Spanish pirates did not commonly murder all or even part of the crews they captured, nor always torture them, unless they made a stout resistance.[5]

Caribbean pirates and privateers of all nations—Spanish, English, French, and Dutch—were often equally brutal; invariably composed of multiple races, nationalities, and ethnicities; and occasionally equally noble. Each had its butchers, each its merciful, although some argued that the Spanish could better afford to be brutal toward pirates and, unfortunately, toward interloping merchants who infested the waters of the Main. The Spaniard intended to relieve himself of vermin, preferably by extermination or incarceration, while the buccaneer intended to plunder and so often took a more pragmatic approach to his thieving. Gross brutality against the Spanish over time only served to harden Spanish resolve and thus diminished plunder, for defenders, particularly at sea where there was often no retreat, fought more vigorously if they believed no quarter would be given. Profit—wealth by force of arms—was the buccaneer's primary goal, not service to a national cause, vengeance, reprisal, or pretenses of preemptive self-defense, except when they were potentially profitable. If buccaneers and filibusters sought a utopia, it consisted of piracy without penalty.[6]

*H*owever, most important to understanding Spain in the New World is not her reputation for brutality, deserved or not, but the composition of the crews of Spanish vessels sent out to take the pirates of Britain, France, and the Netherlands. In nationalities, races, and ethnicities, Spanish crews reflected the reality of New Spain. The popular image of white Spanish hidalgos and their white, sloe-eyed Spanish wives (although they did exist in fair number), with a few African slaves and mission Indians tossed in to complete the background was inaccurate. Rather, the Spanish Main was colorful, and Native Americans, blacks, mestizos, and mulattoes in their many varieties made up the majority of the population.

For example, Acapulco in the late seventeenth century, except when the Manila Galleon arrived, "is inhabited by none but Blacks and Mulattoes [those born of blacks and whites, and probably meaning here mestizos as well]." There were white Spaniards in Acapulco, but most who could afford to moved inland during the hot rainy season, which gave the city the nickname "Mouth of Hell."[7] Likewise in Veracruz, Mexico, where most residents were blacks and mulattoes, the Spaniards (white and mestizo) remained in the city only while the flota was there. In Mexico in general the "*Mestizo, Mulatto,* and *Black* women . . . are the greatest number."[8] In 1671 in the great fortified city of Cartagena de Indias, the "People . . . for the most part are *Creolians* who are half *Spaniard* and half *Indian*; There are also many *Mulatto's* and *Negroes* amongst them."[9] In 1679 in Vaiaguana (Bayaguana) on Hispaniola, the "faithful number one hundred forty; thirty of them are Spanish men; twenty-one Spanish women, eleven slaves and the rest coloured freedmen." There were ten others, "wretched coloured folk," apparently nonbelievers.[10] Only a third of the population of this typical town was white, and many small villages were occupied only by mestizos, mulattoes, Indians, and blacks.

Santo Domingo, Hispaniola, had a population of 2,977 (including those who worked within fourteen leagues of the city) in 1679, and according to Father Navarette little more than half were white, and half of those were children. The rest were African slaves, mestizos, and mulattoes. Santiago de los Caballeros to the north was roughly a quarter each white Spaniard and African slave, and the remainder of the population was free mestizos and mulattoes.[11] In Veracruz, "most of the inhabitants are Mulattoes, that is of a tawny dark Colour."[12] Many mestizos and mulattoes "call themselves white . . . to honour themselves and by Way of Distinction from their Slaves, who are all Blacks and having got much Mony by their Labour, ransome themselves and sometimes become considerable Merchants."[13] Privateer Woodes Rogers, who listed eleven different racial castes in the early eighteenth century, stated categorically that in Peru the "Spaniards are the fewest by far of all the Inhabitants."[14] Even in the greatest city in New Spain, Mexico City, there were only seventy-two thousand whites in a population of four hundred thousand.[15] Spanish cities, towns, and villages in the New World were overwhelmingly multiracial and included former slaves, both men and women, many of whom were wealthy. In 1697, "there went aboard the galeons twenty doctors of *Peru*, being the sons of Spaniards and Indian women, going to court for preferment; and the least that every one of 'em carried was thirty thousand pieces-of-eight."[16]

*S*pain's New World subjects ranged from those in the great cities (*ciudades*) guarded by great castles, such as Havana, Veracruz, San Juan, Cartagena de Indias, and Panama, to those in the far more numerous towns and villages. Spread throughout the Spanish territories were agricultural works, including small farms called *estancias*, ranches or farms with various live-stock called *hattos*, ranches with cattle only called *vacadas*, and sugar and other factories called *ingenios*. Mines were common, and a great part of the world's silver and gold was dug from American earth, yet much of Spain in the New World was poor.

Spanish architecture along the Main was a combination of Spanish de-sign with its Moorish influences, local materials, and native influences. "Mud" (adobe) houses with one floor and a roof thatched with straw or palm leaves were common throughout Mexico. In Chile adobe houses had flat roofs, for rains were largely unknown. The walls were made of bricks "three Foot long, two Foot broad, and a Foot and a half thick." In the Caribbean simple houses with tile roofs were common, along with *boxios*, small, rude buildings often little more than huts, made of palm wood, reeds, and other materials and typically without windows. *Ajoupas* were also common and consisted of four poles, or "crutches," and a roof of palm leaves. Even a rural castellan (gover-nor) might have lived in a house thatched with palm. In the larger cities there were often fine houses, buildings, and churches, along with middling ones of mud and stone. In Veracruz, for example, the "Houses are handsome and regu-lar"; in Havana, "the Houses very handsome, but ill furnish'd"; and in Campeche, the houses are made of "good Stone [and] are not high, but the Walls very strong; the Roofs flattish, after the *Spanish* Fashion, and covered with Pan-tile." Houses with balconies and red tile roofs were typical of Spanish archi-tecture on the Main.[17]

In Cartagena houses were "well built with Stone, and covered with Tile ... and for the most part contiguous, and most of them four or five stories high, with Balconies of Wood and great Wooden Lattices as they have in *Spain*."[18] Towns and cities were laid out in a neat grid, with a government center, a market place, parade grounds, and at least one church at their center. In the great cities, churches were typically "magnificent, and enrich'd with Gold and Silver, Lamps, Candlesticks, and Ornaments for the Altars."[19] While the great cities were heavily fortified, most towns and villages had only stockades, palisades, or often hastily constructed barricades. An embarcadero, or landing, was in every city, town, or village near sea or river.

Spanish government in the New World was divided into the viceroyalties of New Spain and Peru, and each viceroyalty was subdivided into *audencias*, or districts. Regional differences in character already existed within districts, which would become the basis of national, if stereotyped, characteristics. A "babbling" merchant of Peru "according to the custom of that nation, endeavoring to talk me into a bargain, gave me a violent head-ach," wrote Gemelli Careri, yet the "Spaniards of New Spain [Mexico] are of another temper, for they deal generously and gentilely, as becomes them."[20]

$S$pain's crumbling empire was barely sustained by the treasures found in the New World. Every two to three years, and sometimes annually, Spain sent two fleets, sometimes called *treasure fleets* or *plate fleets* (from *plata*, or silver), to the Caribbean. They were called the Armada de Tierra Firma (or *Galeones*), which sailed first to Cartagena, and the Flota de Nueva España, which sailed to Veracruz. The two fleets traveled separately and departed in different months, and sometimes even in different years. When the Galeones arrived in the Caribbean (usually near Dominica), a single ship called the *patache* separated from the fleet and traveled to Margarita, La Guayra, Maracaibo, Río de la Hacha, and Santa Marta. If the great Honduras urca and its patache were traveling with the Galeones, they were dispatched to Trujillo and Puerto Cavallos as well. When the remainder of the Galeones arrived at Cartagena, word was sent "over Land to *Lima*, thro' the Southern Continent, and another by Sea to *Portobel*, with two Pacquets of Letters." From Portobello, the packet of letters traveled to Veracruz, then to Mexico City, while the Lima letters traveled via Panama. Receiving word of the Galeones, the Lima plate fleet in the South Sea, filled with silver from Potosí (Chile) via Arica (Chile), after stopping at Callao (the port serving Lima) for goods originating from other South Sea ports, sailed to Perico Island two leagues from Panama, where its goods and treasure were off-loaded and transported into Panama. Tidal range prevented these ships from unlading at the city itself.[21]

After about two months in Cartagena, the ships of the Galeones fleet sailed to Portobello, where they remained for a month. When the governor of Panama received word of their arrival, South Sea riches were transported from Panama to Portobello via long mule trains (*recuas*), filling storehouses with goods, silver, and gold. To avoid customs, merchants often smuggled goods via the Chagres River, passing through Venta Cruz (now underwater), then by sea to Portobello. Buccaneers knew this route as well and had captured "a whole Fleet of Periago's and Canoas." The smuggling and other extensive disregard

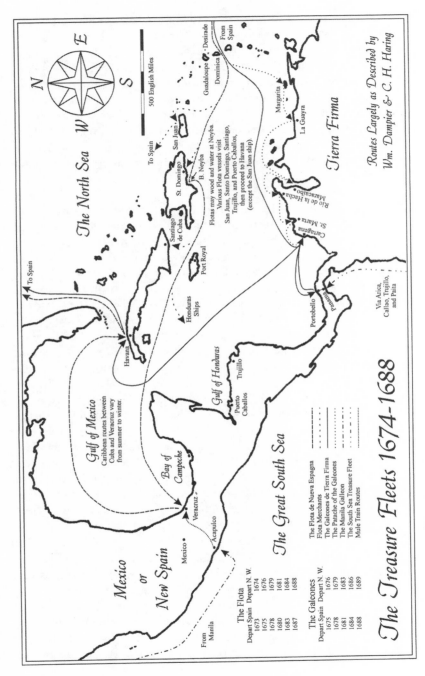

The Treasure Fleets 1674–1688

The Flota

| Depart Spain | Depart N. W. |
|---|---|
| 1673 | 1674 |
| 1675 | 1676 |
| 1678 | 1679 |
| 1680 | 1681 |
| 1683 | 1684 |
| 1687 | 1688 |

The Galcones

| Depart Spain | Depart N. W. |
|---|---|
| 1675 | 1676 |
| 1678 | 1679 |
| 1681 | 1683 |
| 1684 | 1686 |
| 1688 | 1689 |

The Flota de Nueva Espagna
Flota Merchants
The Galeones de Tierra Firma
The Patache of the Galeones
The Manila Galleon
The South Sea Treasure Fleet
Mule Train Routes

Routes Largely as Described by
*Wm. Dampier & C. H. Haring*

Flotas may wood and water at Neyba.
Various Flota vessels visit
San Juan, Santo Domingo, Santiago,
Trujillo, and Puerto Caballos,
then proceed to Havana
(except the San Juan ship).

Caribbean routes between
Cuba and Veracruz vary
from summer to winter.

Via Arica,
Callao, Trujillo,
and Paita

500 English Miles

BENERSON LITTLE AND COURTNEY LITTLE.

of laws and *cedulas* (edicts or mandates) of the Crown, was recognized in a phrase frequently used in the New World: *Obedesco pero non cumplo*; that is, "I obey but I do not comply."[22]

Prices rose in both Panama and Portobello when the treasure fleets arrived, as the treasures filled the cities, and "there is no hiring of an ordinary Slave under a Piece of Eight a Day; Houses, also Chambers, Beds and Victuals are extraordinarily dear." Portobello was a "Sickly place," so merchants remained there only as long as they must, but Panama was healthier, and the fair lasted longer.[23]

From Portobello, the Galeones returned to briefly to Cartagena to meet the patache. Then the fleet sailed to Havana. After 1670 or so, the Galeones and the flota no longer rendezvoused. The course of the flota was simpler: from Spain to Veracruz to Havana and back to Spain. The flota carried the riches and products of both Mexico and the Far East, because every year or so the Manila Galleon would arrive at Acapulco. Asian and East Indian goods were transported from Manila to Acapulco to Mexico City, and then to Veracruz to the flota. Both fleets departed for Spain from Havana. According to Elias al-Mûsili, an Arab traveler, the journey across the Atlantic was neither cheap nor comfortable: one thousand pieces-of-eight bought a passenger a space two yards long, one and one-third yards wide, and one and one-half yards high. However, Gemelli Careri received the same passage gratis: al-Mûsili may have been overcharged.[24]

Both treasure fleets were awe inspiring, not merely for the spectacle of the galleons themselves, but also because of what they held, or would soon hold, inside. The French priest Labat described his awe at watching a treasure fleet, probably the Galeones, sail through the Leeward Islands. There were seventeen galleons, several of them armed with fifty to sixty cannon, accompanied by two small frigates or pataches. The galleons were high sterned, higher than frigate-built men-of-war of comparable cargo capacity, and had to be heavily laden or they were dangerously top-heavy (although this may have been an excuse to ensure that the galleons were well laden with merchandise, both legitimate and illicit). Spain also sent "registry ships" independently of the treasure fleets to the Venezuelan ports of Caracas and Maracaibo; to the Cuban ports of Trinidad, Matanzas, and Havana; and to Puerto Rico, Santo Domingo, Honduras, Campeche, and Buenos Aires.[25]

*T*o support the plantations, ranches, mines, and other "machinery" of empire that rendered such treasure and trade possible, Spain used slave labor. While some Native Americans were enslaved, most Native American labor fell under a system called the *repartimiento* (distribution) in New Spain and the *mita* (the Incan word for "season") in Peru. The system was a periodic labor obligation much like a form of taxation in which Native Americans often worked as slaves. With some exceptions, Native American labor was insufficient to support the needs of empire, so Spain engaged in a significant African slave trade. The controlling monopoly was called the *asiento* (contractor agreement), through which licenses were granted to subcontractors of other nationalities.[26]

Unable to adequately defend her entire empire, Spain defended her great cities and her treasure fleets—the principal repositories of her New World wealth—and for the rest relied on often poorly armed local militia, *guardas costas* (local guard ships), *armadillas* (small armadas or vessels armed locally and sent out against pirates), the Armada de Barlovento and the Armada del Mar del Sur (small armadas in the North and South Seas, respectively), and reprisals by corsarios (privateers), who were often little more than pirates and no better than the foreign pirates against whom they sought reprisals. At one point privateers from Spain were granted permission to cruise for pirates and interlopers in the Caribbean. In the past such permission had been refused:

> Several Proposals have been made for permitting Biscay and Ostend Privateers to Scowre those Seas of Pirates, they promising to do it upon certain conditions, but were never admitted, the consequences of such a Toleration appearing to be no less mischievous than the evil they were to obviate.[27]

These privateers were typically commanded and crewed by "Biscayers" (Vizcayans)—Basques, that is—who ignored local authority and attacked other nations as they pleased, claiming to bear commissions from Spain, which meant they need not obey local authority. Even Spanish governors complained of them, although some Biscayers were commissioned locally.[28]

Biscayers, also called *Biscayners* and *Biscaneers*, were a significant part of the Spanish population along the Main, and all invariably considered themselves gentlemen: "As *Biscay* and *Navarre* were secur'd against the Attempts of the *Moors*, by the unaccessibleness of their Mountains, so there is scare a *Waterbearer* there but what boasts himself a Gentleman."[29] Buccaneers regarded Biscayers as the best of Spanish sailors and soldiers, and called them "Old Spain Men" to distinguish them from Criollos.[30] Their native language was Basque, and many Biscayers had to attend school to learn Spanish, which they referred to as "Romance."[31] The Biscayers of both Old and New Spain were a powerful element of the Spanish defense against piracy, a threat from which Spain itself was not free until after the first quarter of the eighteenth century.

*A*nd what else contributed to the spectacle of Spain in the New World, among peoples of many colors and customs? What else of the might and grandeur of Spain and her culture was found in the Main? How did Spaniards present themselves in the New World? Much was the same as in Spain, and much was not. Among the *Gachupines* (Spaniards born in Spain) and Criollos, dress was conservative and recognizably Spanish. The typical Spanish gentlemen wore

> Shoes without Heels; their Hair being strait cut, they part it on both sides, and put it behind their Ears, with a broad Hat, black habit, Taffaty or black Tabby Sleeves, a very long Sword, very strait Breeches, hanging Sleeves, and a Ponyard, and a black Frize Coat over all this.[32]

Often the Spanish gentleman carried a silver-headed cane, and spectacles were common. Wealthy men were often "richly habited, and adorned with Gold and Jewels, and many of them of the Orders of Saint *Jago*, *Calatrava*, and *Alcantara*," and were attended by retinues of richly dressed black servants and slaves.[33] The admiral of the Armada de Barlovento might dress in the French fashion, with a Spanish cloak on his shoulders and a large reliquary encased in crystal hanging from a large gold chain. Many of the residents of Havana dressed in the French fashion, and Biscayers might dress "half *French* and half *Spanish*." Morion and corselet (armor of helmet and breastplate), so popular with Hollywood costume designers, seemed to appear only in parades on holy days. This armor was largely relegated to pikemen (*piqueros*), although some soldiers in the field, both mounted and afoot, did wear steel or leather morions as well as leather or mail coats to defend against arrows.[34] Otherwise, the dress of the professional Spanish soldier was much like that of other nations.

For gentlewomen, the great farthingale that required they turn sideways to pass through doors was gone, replaced by a more discreet skirt. Breasts were hidden ("want of breasts is so far from being a Defect"), shoulders and back were bare, feet were covered in shoes of thin leather without heels, and the flesh beneath the dress was protected by a "plain Under-garment" under which were several other petticoats. Indeed, it was "almost impossible to conceive how such little lean *Creatures* as the *Spanish* Women are should be able to carry such a burthen without a great deal of trouble," wrote the baronne d'Aulnoy in 1691, although the baronne was known for occasional hyperbole. Around the waists of Spanish ladies, instead "of Girdles, they have a row of [religious] Medals and Relicks, and perhaps a Cord of some Order." They wore much jewelry and many were said to have long earlobes owing to the weight of their earrings. At the waist they typically wore a rosary: "these they use in the Streets, at Cards, whilst talking, making Love, backbiting, &c." They wore red makeup on their cheeks and shoulders, and "white Paint" on the face as well. As a "remedy against Poyson and some other Distempers," they daily ate pieces of a red clay pottery called *Portuguese earth* in English, *barros* in Spanish. They used egg whites "beat up with Sugar-candy" to clean the "Face and make it shine." When they "go abroad, they are cover'd with a Veil of black, having only a hole left for one Eye." Mulattoes and mestizas of the upper classes dressed similarly. [35]

In most Spanish cities of the New World, women of the upper classes seldom went "abroad, and then in Coaches or Chairs." In Havana, however, "the Women have more Liberty," yet they did not forgo their veils when they went out. At home women "keep retired above Stairs, not to be seen by Strangers," for their husbands were of a "jealous Temper." In private, women dressed only in "a Smock and silk Petticoat, with gold or silver Laces, without any Thing on their Heads, and their Hair platted with Ribbons, a gold Chain about their Neck, Bracelets of the same and Pendants of Emeralds in their Ears."[36]

In Mexico, the common

> *Mestizo, Mulatto*, and *Black* women . . . not being allow'd to wear veils, or be cloath'd after the *Spanish* fashion, and scorning on the other side the *Indian* habit, go in an extravagant garb, wearing a thing like a petticoat across their shoulders, or on their head, like a cloak.[37]

Black women were also forbidden, often unsuccessfully, to wear gold, silk, or pearls.[38] Native Americans generally wore native dress, which varied by locale. In Mexico Native American men wore wide breeches and a short doublet. "On their shoulders they wear a cloak of several colours," and on their feet they wore sandals instead of shoes.

> The women all wear the Guaipil (which is like a sack) under the Cobixa, which is a fine cotton cloth; to which they add another upon their back, when they are abroad, which when in the church they place upon their head.[39]

In Veracruz, residents of all ethnicities "live most upon Chocolate and Sweetmeats, extraordinarily sober, and eating little Flesh."[40] Spaniards of all classes in both the Old and New Worlds drank chocolate in great quantities. It was typically prepared from rolls or loaves of roasted cacao berries pounded to a powder, with sugar and vanilla, "Pimentone or Guiny-pepper [allspice], and a little *Acchiote* to give a colour."[41] Some Creole and Native American women ate "cacao-nuts" raw.[42] Compared to their neighbors, Spaniards were said to be "temperate in Wine [and] the worst Affront you can put upon a *Spaniard* is, to call him a *Drunkard*," although alcohol was actually as popular among Spaniards of all classes and ethnicities as it was among other nationalities.[43] In Mexico, for example, *pulquerías* (taverns serving *pulque*, an alcoholic drink made from the maguey plant) were ubiquitous.[44] Similarly, the inhabitants of Potosí imbibed great quantities of wine and *chicha* (an alcoholic beverage made from corn).[45] Spanish subjects of all classes attended bullfights (the *fiesta de toros*, where *lanceros* on horseback fought and killed bulls) and cockfights.[46] They gambled. Among officers and passengers of a man-of-war in the Armada de Barlovento, the game of choice was *para y pinto*, played with two dice. When gambling, at least among gentry, they engaged in *barato*, "a small Present of Money to the Standers-by, which they must not refuse," which could also be demanded by bystanders from winners. Also seen among Italians, the practice was unknown among the English and French.[47] Spaniards were as fond of the theater as the English were, and Spain's literature transcended national boundaries. Mexico City had an enormous trade in books, plus poetry contests complete with magnificent fiestas and fireworks. One of the world's great poets, Sister Juana Inés de la Cruz, composed her verses in Mexico City.[48]

*T*he Spanish were extraordinarily religious, even when blasphemous. Spanish sailors brought on deck a statue of San Antonio, patron saint of seafarers, to quell a violent sea and bit off his head if the storm continued.[49] Gachupines and Creoles were "the most orthodox and rigid Romanists [Catholics] in the World," while many Native Americans under the Spanish yoke modified the Catholic faith to incorporate their own beliefs.[50] The religion of Spain was an emphatically proselytizing one: priests and their orders were everywhere, seeking to convert the heretics and nonbelievers. The Spanish Inquisition, an ecclesiastical court with authority over much of daily life in Spain and her realm, remained a powerful force devoted primarily to the persecution of Jews and other "heretics." Its nature was, after a third-party denunciation followed by an investigation, to commit "a man to Prison without knowing his Crime or the Witnesses that depose against him," a process that promoted false confession and perhaps the true confession of acts for which one was not arrested.[51] The Spanish language was well suited to inquisition, and also to literature and love, for it was "grave, noble, and expressive. . . . *French* is the only language that may challenge the precedency before the *Spanish*."[52] It was, with its many sacred references, also a great language for swearing.

Distance affected culture in the New World. Spain was far away, physically and psychologically.

> So I say in all this that Spain was but a stepmother to me, for she bani-
> shed me to seek my fortune in strange lands, passing through varied
> climes. Here, I do what I could not do there, despite my inclination,

wrote don Diego de Vargas, soon to govern New Mexico, to his wife in
Spain in 1686.[53] His words epitomized the New World circumstances many
"Old Spain Men" found themselves in: the New World, the New Spain, was
both a land of opportunity and home, forever. Just as the Spanish Catholic
image of the Virgin Mary, mother of God, was being transformed in New Spain
by native peoples so was the image of Spain changing—no more Spain the
mother but Spain the stepmother, as de Vargas, a man of Old World nobility in
a rude New World, put it. Many New World Spaniards, sensing a distinction
between the two Spains, in particular between the privileged Gachupines
and the native Creoles, grew hostile to Old Spain.[54] Gachupines had hopes
and illusions about returning, although most knew they would live and probably die somewhere upon the Spanish Main. The culture of this new land,
developed from dozens if not hundreds of Spanish, Native American, and
African cultures, exerted as great an influence on residents as Spain. Most
Spaniards, whether Gachupines or Criollos, and most mestizos and mulattoes,
considered themselves neither occupiers nor colonists, but native citizens of
a new Spain. For most there was no motherland to return to, and so when
threatened they fought to defend the only homes and livelihoods they ever
knew. Spain was too far away—geographically, politically, psychologically—
to help in a crisis. Even the Spanish nobleman don Diego de Vargas, who
never broke with his Spanish heritage and sense of duty, died, as many of his
sort did, in the New World after decades of service there "to God and the king
our lord."[55] But he died a Spaniard of New Spain.

*N*ational prejudices and stereotypes abounded on the Main. The English called the Spanish lazy, and one xenophobic writer of the period referred to the "wretched laziness of the People, very like the *Welsh* and the
*Irish*, walking slowly and always cumbred with a great Cloak and long Sword."
The English were not immune to stereotypes themselves. "I must say, that the
English in these Colonies are too careless and lazy," wrote the French baron de
la Hontan.[56] Broadly speaking, none who built an empire or attempted to do
so, even with the labor of slaves and forced work programs, were lazy. Just as
common were insults about sex and women. The Spanish, some of the English
said, had a "multitude of Whores," and for "Fornication and Impurity they are
the worst of all Nations." In the lexicon of propaganda, the enemy's women
were always wanton whores and their men always ignorant cuckolds.[57]

*S*panish culture on the Main was one of fascinating contradictions, and its social stratification was typical of this paradoxical nature, in appearance more stratified than that of other European nations, yet in substance perhaps less so. Nearly every Spaniard claimed purity of blood (*limpieza de sangre*), thus granting him or her the right of honor normally due only the gentry. All wished to be, or pretended to be, descended from *Cristianos Viejos* (Old Christians) of gentle birth, "without any mixture of *Jewish* or *Moorish Families*," yet the blood of both Jews and Moors was pervasive in Spain, and unfounded claims of social stature abounded. Purity of blood was a fantasy similar to purity of culture, a myth that denied the Moorish influence on Spain. Even so, the false sense of a high social standing led to many haughty and arrogant Spaniards.[58] However, in a society that boasted strict social demarcations and was characterized by a high degree of racism, in practice it had a degree of social equality among free whites, rich or poor, that other nationalities in America were only beginning to find and between whites and other ethnicities that other nations were doing their utmost to prevent.

Public behavior was the most noticeable indicator of social stature. Men of the lower and middle classes from Old Spain were reputed by the English as "most horribly rude, insolent and imperious; uncivil to strangers," but the gentry, as a gentleman traveler of the period noted, were "very civil and well-bred."[59] Perhaps the gentry were more civil than lower- or middle-class men, but English gentlemen were probably offended more by a declaration of equality from the lower and middle classes than by any "insolent" behavior. A visiting Englishman did not consider the "gentry" to include the many haughty Spaniards of middling-to-poor social stature who wore a cape and sword and considered themselves equal to caballeros (knights) or hidalgos (gentlemen). Thomas Gage described the "gentleman Creoles or natives of Chiapa . . . as presumptuous and arrogant as if the noblest blood in the Court of Madrid ran through their veins."[60] Even common sailors and soldiers considered themselves *Signores Marineros, y los Signores Soldados*—deserving of the title *Señor*—and even ate separately, not in messes as the English, French, Dutch, and Germans did.[61] Indeed, not even poverty reduced a Spaniard to submissiveness: "Notwithstanding this general Indigency, the *Spaniards* abate nothing of their national haughtiness." Nor did Spaniards beg "unless it be in an imperious tone."[62]

In his description of Mexico in 1698, Gemelli Careri, an Italian, noted that "all the *Blacks* and *Mulattos* are insolent to the highest degree, and take upon 'em as much as *Spaniards*, whose habit they wear; so, among themselves, they take the title of captain, tho' they be not so." Henri Joutel, writing of a visit to Veracruz, noted that the men—most of them of a "tawny" color—were haughty as well.[63] Blacks, mulattoes, and mestizos were not insolent, as some described them. Rather, they merely put themselves on equal footing with, or at least considered themselves equal to, the white, Old Christian, Gachupines and Criollos. They too were Spaniards, although they did not have all of the rights or respect granted to a white Spaniard. In fact, the rights of free blacks were often restricted: they were not allowed out at night, or to have "any *Indians* to serve them," and they were forced to "live with Masters that are well known."[64]

Accompanied by the perceived haughtiness was a fierce sense of honor. Spaniards, including many mestizo and mulatto freemen, were punctilious about honor, and "so tenacious of Revenge, that they will not lay aside an Injury for twenty years after." For any insult, whether a slap in the face, the appellation of drunkard, or a word of disrespect regarding a wife's virtue, the offense "must be wip'd off with no less than the Blood of the Aggressors." Assassination of offenders was not unknown, even common according to some observers.[65] "Come, let's be gone whilst we're safe," said Belville in *The Rover*, "and remember these are Spaniards, a sort of people that know how to revenge an affront."[66] Assassination, murder, and armed gangs were prevalent in the larger Spanish cities of the New World, among all ethnicities and classes. Potosí was known to have one of the highest death rates in the New World, both in open "confrontations and in deeds of treachery."[67]

Even in issues of official protocol, Spaniards would resort to swords or daggers, or if duty precluded weapons, they engaged in ridiculous battles of will while seeking redress from the viceroy or king. Sir Thomas Lynch reported in 1683 that because the governor and the bishop in Cartagena could not agree whether Dominicans or Franciscans would confess a convent of nuns, no mass had been said for months.[68] In 1698 the captain of the Manila Galleon, believing his merchant vessel supreme by virtue of its independence in the Pacific, and the vice admiral of the Peru fleet, a man-of-war, argued in Acapulco over who should lower his flag to the other. Both kept them flying while waiting for the viceroy to "decide the controversy."[69] Even women were not immune to this sense of honor and pride. In 1679 a third of the women in Santo Domingo did not attend mass "because they have no suitable clothes." Likewise, the poor often attended mass at dawn or at night.[70]

New Spain also inherited a tradition of guerrilla warfare, although the word *guerrilla* was not used until the early nineteenth century. Spain carried on a partisan war against the Moors for generations until their expulsion in 1492 and brought that tradition of warfare to the New World. Spanish soldiers—many of them blacks and mulattoes—engaged in guerrilla warfare against General Venable's army in Hispaniola and Jamaica in the mid-1600s.[71]

Spanish privateers were manned by mestizos, mulattoes, blacks, Native Americans, and "Greeks," and their commanders were often mestizos, mulattoes, and even foreigners. They composed a majority of the population yet had no direct ties to Spain, but the men of these races and ethnicities were like the Europeans of the New World: they sought opportunity in the avenues open to them, and sea roving was both an open and suitable avenue. Without her population of black slaves, "tawny" workers, and "Greek" mercenaries, New Spain could have been overrun by pirates and privateers used by Spain's enemies. For the Spaniard in the New World, regardless of ethnicity, privateering and piracy were means of exploiting an opportunity of profitably and of honorable vengeance through guerrilla warfare against the unwelcome English, French, and Dutch nations. Spaniards believed other Europeans should be expelled from New Spain as the Moors were from Old Spain. To murder a pirate crew, or even that of a English merchant crew, was a practical exercise of Spanish honor against men who had none, or so it was rationalized by a Spanish pirate. And besides, murder left no witnesses.

*W*ho were those "strong desperate rogues," those pirates and privateers who seized the ships of Spanish enemies? They were, among many, *capitáns*: Don Francisco, Manuel Rodriguez, Pedro de Castro, Philip Fitzgerald, Juan Balosa, Pasqual Onan, Blas Miguel, Juan de Larco, Alonzo Martin, and the most notorious of them all, Juan Corso, also known as Corsario John.[72] Their craft were primarily large piraguas, barcalongas, and half galleys. But Spanish subjects were not the only ones employed in the defense of Spain. *Renegados* of other nations deserted their own countries to sail in defense of Spain, such as the English captains Bond and Beare, and the Dutchman Reyning. Others served ashore, like the Irishman John Murphy who killed one of his compatriot boucaniers on Tortuga in the 1630s, was accused of murder, deserted to the Spanish, and became don Juan Morfa Geraldino y Burco, who admirably defended New Spain against pirates for fifty years.[73]

Men also deserted from service to Spain, to the greater opportunity of service against Spain. One of them was Laurens de Graff, a Dutchman from Dordrecht. He was generally known by the Spanish as Lorenzo or Lorencillo, by the English as Laurens or Laurence, and by the French as Laurent. "Lorencillo" is the diminutive of Lorenzo, used perhaps because he was tall, much as "Little John" was the name used for Robin Hood's giant companion. Diminutives were also used as a sign of affection, and "Lorencillo" might have derived from Laurens's service with Spain:

> He had for a long time served the Spanish at sea against the filibusters themselves . . . and had been in combat many times against the filibusters of the islands of San Domingue, Tortuga, and Jamaica, and after many combats where he had taken many prisoners, he was himself captured,

wrote the venerable buccaneer-surgeon-author Alexander Exquemelin. He noted that Laurens witnessed many Spanish cruelties, and as a result volunteered to serve with his captors to punish Spain, or so Exquemelin claimed was Laurens's motivation. Governors Pouançay and Du Casse of Saint Domingue wrote simply that Laurens was a Dutchman who served Spain, then France, while the historian-priests Lepers and Charlevoix, writing in the early eighteenth century, stated that Laurens sailed first as a seaman, then as a gunner with the Spanish Navy in European waters, and later was promoted to captain and sent to the Caribbean. What was certain was that Laurens spent his entire adult life as a sea rover.[74]

According to Spanish folklore, Laurens's first major act of piracy was a largely unsuccessful attack on Campeche in 1672, followed immediately by the sacking and burning of the nearby village of Champotón. However, according to French records, he probably did not join the filibusters until 1676. Undoubtedly he was a gunner once, for he often demonstrated in battle that "one has never seen a better *cannonier*." Combining his skill at arms great and small with his seamanship and knowledge of Spanish tactics, he indeed punished the New World Spanish dearly, so much that they called him the *Scourge of the Indies*. Centuries later, mothers in Veracruz still frighten their children with his name. No other pirate, not even Morgan or L'Ollonois, ever achieved as much notoriety among the Spanish in the New World.[75]

*B*ut pirate attacks in 1675 were relatively insignificant compared to the years that led up to the sack of Panama in 1671 and that followed. John Coxon possessed a French commission to make reprisals against the Spanish, and there were roughly two hundred and fifty logwood cutters, mostly English, at Laguna de Términos in the Bay of Campeche. John Bennet captured the *Buen Jesus de las Almas* and almost fifty thousand pieces-of-eight. Filibusters under Lessone (La Sound) and the sieur de Bournano marched into the Isthmus of Darien but were driven back by the Spanish at Chepó. Darien Indians, whose assistance was made possible by the buccaneer captain Wright's adopted Darien son, accompanied them on the brief incursion. Spanish privateers sought pirates and interlopers, and English subjects were forbidden to sail under French commissions against the Spanish, under penalty of being charged with piracy and rebellion. In Jamaica, thirty-five members of an abortive slave rebellion were hanged by the English. Sir Henry Morgan arrived in Jamaica to serve as lieutenant governor, after a shipwreck en route and subsequent rescue by the buccaneer Thomas Rogers. A week later his superior, Governor Vaughan, arrived; Sir Henry had violated his orders by arriving first. Governor d'Ogeron of "Tortuga and the Coast of San Domingue" returned to France and died; the seigneur de Cussy governed briefly in his absence. Denmark colonized St. Thomas. The English colony of Suriname became Dutch, and many English colonists moved from Suriname to Jamaica. The Dutch colony of Nieuw Amsterdam became the English colony of New York. Warfare occupied the minds of local governments: France was at war with the Netherlands and Spain, among others, and her filibusters sailed honestly against the Spaniards. King Philip's War raged between New England colonists and Native Americans. And Laurens was still serving Spain. In such a hectic era Spain had reason to worry, for several thousand buccaneers and filibusters grew restless and needed only great commanders to unite them in great expeditions along the Spanish Main.

# Boucaniers, Flibustiers, and Buccaneers:
## Hunters Along the Main

Some argued unreasonably that the Spanish had only themselves to blame for men who itched to steal the tenuous riches of New Spain and Peru:

> Had it not been for the great care of the *Spaniards* in stocking the West-Indies with Hogs and Bullocks, the Privateers must have starved. But now the Main, as well as the Island, is plentifully provided; particularly the Bay of *Campeachy*, the Islands of *Cuba*, *Pines*, *Hispaniola*, *Portarica*, &c. Where, besides wild Hogs, there are Abundance of Crawls [corrals] or Hog farms; in some which, I have heard, there are no less than 1500. This was the main Subsistence of the Privateers,*

William Dampier wrote.[1]

Spaniards first set animals free on the large island of Hispaniola, whose name meant Little Spain. Its west coast remained largely unsettled until a variety of refugees and vagabonds began to populate a small island just off its north coast in the early seventeenth century. Called *Tortuga* by the English and Spanish and *la Tortue* by the French, the island was named for its resemblance to a swimming sea turtle. It was distinguished from Saltatudos, or Salt Tortuga, off the coast of Venezuela near Margarita, and from the "Shoals of *Dry Tortugas*" near the Florida Keys.[2] The men who originally settled the

---

*All quotations have been reprinted with their original spelling and punctuation.

rough, rocky island were surely deserters, escaped servants and slaves, early colonists, marooners, and shipwrecked sailors of many nationalities and ethnicities, particularly French, Spanish, Dutch, Flemish, Portuguese, and English (who briefly colonized Tortuga), plus some Scots and Irish. African slaves, Native Americans, and mulattoes inhabited the island as well, but the majority of the population, even if a small majority, was French. Later other settlers voluntarily moved to Tortuga from the settled islands and colonies of the Caribbean.[3]

The men of Tortuga sustained themselves by hunting on Hispaniola. Tortuga, however, was their refuge and redoubt from the Spanish and the first seat of the French government on Hispaniola, whose western third came to be known as Saint Domingue. Hunting was not a matter of mere survival, but of a profitable lifestyle, for there were markets for flesh, hide, and lard. Thus the boucanier was born.

The three principal, firsthand accounts of the lifestyle of boucaniers came from the filibuster, surgeon, and author Alexander Exquemelin and the French priests Du Tertre and Labat, the former a Jesuit, the latter a Dominican. All spent time among the boucaniers, Exquemelin much more so, for early in his life he was indentured to one. Not remarkably, their descriptions were nearly identical, and each filled in details the others lacked, although it seemed at times that Father Labat did not always know when he was being kidded. Boucaniers took their name from the Tupi (a language of native Brazilians) word for the grating on which flesh was cured slowly over a small fire: *boucan*. In French it became the verb *boucaner*; the site and hut where the curing took place was called *le boucan* (sometimes *deza boulan* or *ajoupa*), and *boucaniers* were the men who hunted and cured meat. The flesh was also called *boucan* and was described by the adjective *boucanée*. Boucan also referred to the celebration centered around the roasting of a pig or other animal. (A common misconception is that the word *bacon* derives from boucan. In fact, bacon's etymology is from Middle English, with Germanic origins.) The English, however, preferred the word *barbecue*, as in "barbecued pig," rather than boucan. Barbecue derives from *barbacoa*, a Spanish word probably derived from the Taino (a language of Native Americans in the Caribbean) word for grill or grate. The English also sometimes used the word *jerk*, as in "jerke porke," as well, although more often it referred to *sun-dried meat*. Jerk, or jerky, was derived from the Spanish *charqui*, from the Quechuan (a language native to South America) word for smoked or wind-dried flesh. The more common Spanish word for this dried flesh—wind dried, smoked, or both—was *tasajos*.[4]

*T*he French hunters on Hispaniola were of two sorts: those who hunted cattle for their hides and those who hunted hogs in order to smoke the flesh.

Exquemelin wrote that the cattle hunters were the true boucaniers, not the hog hunters, as did Father Labat. However, the restriction of the term solely to cattle hunters who produced hides, not boucan, made little etymological sense. It could simply be that because wild cattle were considered more dangerous (or noble) to hunt than wild hogs, the true boucanier was one who practiced the most dangerous (or noble) trade. Swine were swine, after all. Or perhaps the cattle hunters originally sold not only cowhides but boucan as well, or perhaps the hunting of cattle was the first remunerative trade of these wild men. Perhaps Exquemelin, having been the valet of a cattle-hunting boucanier, in the manner of a friendly rivalry was making a joke at the expense of his pig-hunting brethren. After all, he said, the cattle hunters wished to distinguish themselves from the pig hunters, whom they called *chasseurs* (hunters). It was unlikely these hunters limited their prey to only one of the beasts for trade, and never the other, over the course of years.[5]

*B*oucaniers lead a rough but healthy life, and aside from what they hunted and what they did with their kill, there was no difference in how they lived and looked.[6] Boucanier dress was functional, distinctive, and reeked of the abattoir. The sunburned, long-bearded men, some of whom wore their hair loose and unkempt while others tied or queued it, wore one or two simple shirts of linen or canvas that came halfway down the thigh, simple breeches, and a *casaque* or *caleçon* (an overgarment), over all of which was a belt of cowhide or alligator skin. Attached to the belt were a cartouche box (*gargoussier*) holding thirty paper cartridges of powder and ball, a sheath holding three or four Flemish knives used for skinning and butchering, and a bayonet or machete or perhaps a cutlass. Also tied around the waist was a length of light cloth used as a mosquito net when sleeping; when awake, boucaniers rubbed their faces with pork lard to keep the insects away. On their heads boucaniers wore the crown of a hat, the brim having been cut off except to a point in front to shield the eyes, virtually identical to a modern baseball cap. On their feet were shoes, if they could be so called, made simply by wrapping the feet in fresh pigskin or cowhide cut from hide of the leg, with the toes inserted at the hock. The shoes were secured with sinew and dried into shape. In general, all of the clothing was black with dried blood and thick with grease, so much so that the fabric could not be discerned.[7]

Boucaniers lived and hunted in small groups. They were found at Port Margot, on Isle des Boucaniers in Port Bahaya, on the *Savanne brulée*, near the embarcadero of Mirabalais, at Isle à Vache, at Le Fond de Isle à Vache (not to be confused with the isle itself), and at Samana at *la montagne ronde*, on the Spanish part of the island where, until at least 1676, a tiny French colony of hunters lived. Labat's boucaniers were two leagues inland from Cap Dona Maria, and more commonly boucaniers were found wherever the game was.

Each boucanier traveled with an *engagé*, an indentured servant referred to as a *valet* and who was required to serve for three years. Many hunters treated their valets brutally, beating them and working them mercilessly seven days per week: "Six days shall you kill bulls for their hides, and on the seventh shall you carry them to the sea." The hunters sold hides and pig lard to ships trading to Saint Domingue, and sold boucan and lard to ships and planters. Many planters hired hunters to provide meat.[8]

Boucaniers engaged in *matelotage*, a system in which two people hunted together, shared profits equally, tended to the other if injured, and watched each other's back. Matelotage was a custom of the sea, and the word itself was taken from *matelot* (sailor), for sailors paired up similarly for centuries, as did the *gens de guerre, les soldats camerades* (the men of war, the comrade soldiers). Partners shared supplies equally and kept nothing under key, considering it an insult to the other to do so. If one of the pair died, the other inherited everything unless the deceased were married, in which case both wife and partner were provided for.[9]

Cattle-hunting boucaniers did so with a pack of twenty to thirty dogs, using two to discover the beasts and the rest to keep the beasts from escaping. The dogs, which were also found running wild and whose puppies the boucaniers often raised, "typically have a long flat head, sharp muzzle, savage air, thin lean body . . . [and] are very swift at the hunt, and chase to perfection."[10] When the dogs discovered a bull, the master of the hunt remained on the ground while the rest of the party climbed trees to escape the possible wrath of the wounded bull. When the bull was shot and fell to the ground, immediately a boucanier or valet hamstrung it to prevent it from rising again in case it was not yet dead. Hunting cattle was a dangerous trade, for a wounded bull attacked if it could, trampling and goring the hunter.[11] Invariably, after they killed a bull boucaniers fed on its rich bone marrow.[12] A few boucaniers hunted as the Spanish did, running cattle down and hamstringing them, and did this so well that they rarely needed to shoot them. One, a mulatto named Vincent de Rosiers, shipped a hundred hides to France, of which only ten were pierced by musket balls.[13]

*H*ides were sold by size—one bull hide equaled two cowhides, which equaled three juvenile males called *couvarts* or *bouvards*—and were probably cured on Hispaniola as they were by logwood cutters at Campeche. The hunter stretched the hide on the ground, using thirty-six pegs "as big as a Man's Arm" to hold it taut, and let it dry, first on one side, then the other.

> When they are dry they fold them in the middle from Head to Tail, with the Hair outward, and then hang them across a strong Pole, so high that the ends may not touch the Ground, 40 or 50 one upon

another, and once in three Weeks or a Month they beat them with great Sticks, to strike off the Worms that breed in the Hair. . . . When they are to be ship'd off, they soak them in salt Water to kill the remaining Worms; and while they are yet wet they fold them in four folds, and afterwards spread them abroad again to dry. When they are fully dry, they fold them up again, and so send them aboard.[14]

Pig-hunting boucaniers hunted similarly with dogs, seeking feral swine they called *cochons marrons* (literally marooned pigs), and wild boars called *sangliers*, which were dangerous to hunt, for they too would gore the hunter if he was not careful. Pig hunters usually carried a staff with which to prod the boar and make certain he was dead. The cochons marrons were of medium size, black in color, and ran in packs of fifty to sixty. The boucaniers—or more likely their valets—hauled their kill to their boucan, where they carved the flesh from the bone and into strips one and a half inches thick and up to six feet long and smoked them on a barbecue over a low fire inside an ajoupa. They threw the bones and skin in the fire, believing they seasoned the meat. Often the flesh was salted for a few hours or even a day before it was smoked to help preserve it longer, particularly if it would be sold as provisions for voyages at sea. In this way it would keep for a year or more, although Exquemelin said it lost its good taste after six months. Boucan was hard and dry like wood, and was tied in bundles of one hundred pounds for sale. Brown and unappetizing, it turned red in warm water, could be cooked in any manner, and was said to be delicious. Boucaniers also rendered *mantègue* (*manteca*, pork lard) for sale or trade.[15]

The cattle hunters also hunted pigs, but only for food. They sometimes shot wild horses, rendering the fat into lamp oil, and sometimes cured the hides and smoked the meat as well. Some boucaniers raised hunting dogs and sold them. Some turned to planting and became *habitants* (inhabitants or planters), growing beans, sweet potatoes, and cassava for food, and tobacco, indigo, and sugar for trade. The tobacco quality was such that it was used primarily for chewing tobacco and dye. By the early 1670s there were at least two thousand planters on Saint Domingue.[16]

*B*oucaniers carried a long-barreled flintlock musket, which they named after themselves, (and cartridges as well), in use at least since 1651 and probably much earlier.[17] Called a *fusil boucanier* (or *boucanière*) in French and a "buccaneer gun" in English, its barrel averaged four and a half French feet in length (roughly fifty-seven English inches), and the musket itself was often more than six feet long. French calibers of the period were defined by the size of the ball, not the diameter of the bore. The boucanier's fusil shot a ball whose caliber was sixteen balls to the French pound, or roughly .65 inches in diameter. To allow windage for loading, the bore of the barrel averaged .75 inches in diameter. The musket was distinctive, not only for its exceptionally long barrel, but for its large club-butt or fish-belly stock (see Common Firearms illustration). Its lock was large and rounded; the hardware was brass or iron, although the butt plates on guns produced in the North American colonies were often leather; and the ramrod was lancewood. The long barrel was believed to give the musket greater range than shorter firearms, which were termed *giboyers* (hunters). French musket-makers Brachie (in Dieppe) and Gelin (in Nantes) were reputed to be the best, although the firearms were manufactured in other places as well. To better arm the French, from at least 1683 merchantmen traveling to the French islands of the Caribbean were required on pain of large fines to carry a dozen good quality muskets "with barrels of four and a half feet" (buccaneer guns), to be sold at fifteen livres apiece.[18]

Boucaniers and filibusters spent much time target shooting and maintaining their muskets, for their livelihood and even basic survival depended on their weaponry and skill. For sport they attempted to shoot oranges from trees with a single musket ball by hitting the twigs that held them, a practice that involved at least as much luck as skill, for muskets were not accurate at all by modern standards. Most boucaniers could probably hit a stationary man-sized target regularly at one hundred yards or so, but no farther. Nonetheless, buccaneers and filibusters were reputed to be able to hit an *écu* (or piece-of-eight, roughly the size of a modern silver dollar) at seventy-five yards, although in fact such a shot was impossible except by accident, given the relative inaccuracy of the smoothbore buccaneer gun and its imperfect ball. The men shot often and kept twenty pounds of the best powder stored in leather-covered calabashes at their boucan, enough for three shots per day if they stayed a year, as sometimes they did, and ten or twelve per day if they stayed three to four months, as they more typically did.[19]

Both the boucanier and the sea rover used an expedient method of loading, which gave them on average three shots to the Spanish one: they tore open a cartridge with their teeth, primed the pan, poured the powder in the barrel, squeezed the ball into the barrel (or perhaps spat it from the mouth), and banged the musket on the ground to seat the ball and powder. This procedure worked for several shots, until the barrel fouled sufficiently to require the use of the ramrod. The buccaneer gun found its way into the hands of Caribbean rovers, privateers, and navies in general, and until the mid-eighteenth century was the most highly regarded sea-service musket. So notable was the buccaneer gun that in 1670 Henry Morgan sent one to the governor of Panama, along with a cartouche box of thirty cartridges and a letter promising to retrieve the musket and cartouche box—the implication being by force of arms—within a year or two.[20]

Boucaniers settled their differences with a duel using buccaneer guns rather than cutlasses or pistols. The contesting parties stood a certain distance from each other, and the first to fire was determined by lot. The other, if still standing, then fired. The distance between the two parties is unknown, but given the boucanier's skill at shooting, was surely beyond fifty yards and was perhaps as many as one hundred. To ensure that skill, not chance, played the major part, the parties were probably limited to a single musket ball, not multiple balls or ball and shot. If a duel transpired without witnesses, a surgeon inspected the body for signs of treachery, looking for entry wounds in the back or sides, the absence of which suggested that the duelists faced each other full-front. Penalties were severe for shooting a man in the back, for shooting before he prepared his fusil boucanier, or for any other treachery: the guilty party was tied to a tree and shot in the head. This form of dueling was also practiced by both filibuster and buccaneer.[21]

*M*any of the early boucaniers and filibusters took false names, keeping their true names secret or sharing them only with close comrades. The practice was most common among the French, and Father Lepers provided a few examples: Vent-en-Panne (Becalmed), Passe-Partout (Passkey), Chasse-Marée (a fishing boat that brought in fresh catch), Brisegalet (*brise* means sea breeze, *galet* sea pebble), and Le Sage (the Wise or the Wise Man, which could have been meant seriously or as a joke) were such names.[22] Amusing as some are, the names were used by real men: François Grogniet used the nom de guerre of *Chasse-Marée,* and Vent-en-Panne was killed in action against two Ostend privateers. Le Sage was a Dutch filibuster. (Le Sage is also both a French and Dutch surname.) Exquemelin provided other examples: Alexandre, called Bras-de-Fer (Iron Arm); Michel le Basque; Montbars the Exterminator; Bartolomeo el Portugues; and Rock the Brazilian. Although most adventurers of the 1670s and '80s appeared to use their true names, others did not let their names be known for fear of prosecution for piracy: they "punished one of Waffe's sailors who asked the pirate captain's name," for "the commander owned himself a Jamaican, and said he had a good plantation there."[23] Others were simply better known by their nicknames: Jan Willems, known as Yanky; Nicolas Amon, known as Grénezé; and Pierre Santot, known as Pierre le Picard, for example. The French in the Caribbean at the time said that "you don't really know the people of the islands until they marry."[24]

*I*ndeed, these boucaniers and other adventurers did take wives. In the early days there were only a handful of women on French Hispaniola, but Governor d'Ogeron imported fifty who came to be known as *La Cinquantaine* (literally, the Fifty), after the Spanish lanceros of the same name. When one of a pair of boucaniers in matelotage took a wife, his companion was still received at the house—one wondered if they still shared and shared alike. If both men wished to marry the same woman, they decided the question by throwing dice, although the situation was probably rare, for according to Exquemelin a pair of boucaniers usually consisted of a leader and a follower, the latter yielding to the former in disputes. One witty boucanier leaned on his musket and told his wife-to-be that neither would ever ask the other about their pasts, that only the future mattered. Then, tapping the barrel of his musket with his hand, he informed her that if she was ever unfaithful to him, she may be assured his musket would not be—that is, it would not miss its mark (including an unfaithful wife). According to Father Lepers, these new "boucanières et flibustières" quickly learned to hunt cattle and pigs as their husbands did. They tested their shooting skills among themselves, and even dared to test themselves against the "old warriors," the male boucaniers and filibusters. They were, Father Lepers wrote, considered "heroines and Amazons." In 1693 Captain Laurens took as his second wife a woman born in Normandy. She was brought to Saint Domingue and had been twice married within the previous five years—one husband a filibuster and the other probably one—and twice widowed as well. Marie-Anne Dieuleveult (God wills it) was a "heroine" unafraid to put a pistol in her hand for self-defense or retribution. Women of all ethnicities and social classes of the New World were vastly underrepresented in written records of the period, although without doubt they played an active and significant role, one far greater than commonly accepted.[25]

The Spanish did not take this permanent intrusion of foreign hunters, pirates, planters, and wives passively. Instead, they carried on both guerrilla warfare and large-scale attacks against them, and the lancero was one of the most effective soldiers. Armed with a long lance, lanceros fought both mounted and afoot in the field, and manned barricades and bastions as well. Most lanceros were not as well armed as the Spanish professional soldiers, who had "leather jackets, leather or iron morions . . . harquebuses, lances, swords, and shields," although some were comparably equipped.[26] Typically, the mounted Spaniard in the New World was armed as one buccaneer described: "[T]hay had not all gunns, some launces, other Spade's [*espadas*, or rapiers]."[27] Originally said to be organized out of Santo Domingo into five companies of one hundred men each, lanceros were called *La Cinquantaine* by the French, for only half of each company took the field while the other half tended to their various affairs or trades. However, there were probably five hundred lanceros for only a short period of time. In 1663 the Flemish officer Vandelmof, a veteran of the wars in the Low Countries, was put in command of five hundred men recruited from Hispaniola and neighboring islands, for Santo Domingo alone could not provide so many lanceros from a population of less than three thousand, many of them women and children.[28]

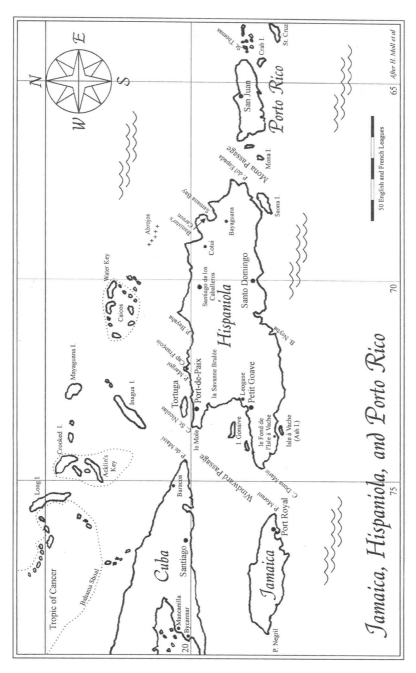

*Jamaica, Hispaniola, and Porto Rico*

BENERSON LITTLE AND COURTNEY LITTLE.

Landing at Gonaïves, Saint Domingue, the same year, the Spaniards intended a surprise attack, but the hunters were warned, barely in time but able to make some preparation. The Spanish located them in the gorge between Grand Fond and Petit Fond on the "Savanne brulée." Vandelmof led the attack. The boucaniers had no retreat, and so they stood and fought: Vandelmof was killed in the first discharge. The battle ended when the Spanish fled, leaving twenty-five of their dead behind.[29] The tactics of the boucaniers in this case were identical to those of buccaneers and filibusters who had thirty "Cartridges always fitted for our small Arms," which "they carry with them always, so they are never unprepared." Against mounted men they dismounted "the Front with a Volly of small Shot, which put a stop to their carreer and courages." ("Small shot" was "a Cartridge fit for the Bores of our Fuzees with a full Shot in it and 7 or 9 Swan Shot loose upon that"—in other words, a full load of buckshot on top of a musket ball.) Outnumbered by horsemen four to one in 1680, a party of thirty-five buccaneers fired only six at a time, to keep up a continual fire in order "to keep the longer from a close Fight." They fired so quickly and "scarce a shot . . . in vain" that "scarce two Vollies were fired before those that had discharged were ready loaded for them again, that he was happiest amongst them that got furthest behind; thus we battered them severely."[30] It was not simply a matter of rovers being better armed than the Spanish, for this was but one part of the equation. Buccaneers also knew how to handle their firearms effectively, how to employ associated tactics effectively, and how to maintain their muskets so that they *could* use them effectively.

Whatever their number at various times, and no matter the tactics of boucaniers, lanceros harassed and killed many of them, at one point forcing some to seek refuge on nearby islands for protection until France had a firmer hold on the western third of Hispaniola. Throughout the period lanceros remained capable of deadly incursions into isolated areas settled by the French. Between 1682 and 1684 there were "many massacres of hunters," although more and more the Spanish made their incursions by sea.[31]

Mounted or afoot were also *matadors*, or as some of the English called them from the word's literal translation, *cow killers*, for they too lived by the trade of butchering cattle for their hides and tallow. There were also hunters in general on the Main, called *monteros*, often equated with the French woodsmen and trappers of Canada, the *coureurs de bois*.[32] Many monteros and matadors probably were members of La Cinquantaine. If mounted on a trained horse, cow killers used a "Hocksing Iron" (a curved blade, or *croissant*, six or seven inches long on a fifteen-foot shaft) to hamstring a cow or bull, followed by a lance or long knife afoot for the coup de grâce. It was a dangerous practice, hunting cattle this way, and it was not unknown for a bull to kill two or three horses before being killed himself.[33] The hunters did not use muskets, although the French did sometimes refer to matadors as *boucaniers espagnols.*[34] They "are a sort of Vagabons that are saued from the gallowes in Spaine and the king doth send them heare."[35] Like the boucanier with his valet, the matador had black and mulatto slaves who also bore arms as necessary. The matador and his slave or servant used a lance when afoot for warfare as well as cow killing. It was longer than a half-pike, "nine or ten feet and sometimes longer," and its head was "very sharp, and soe brod that if they strik in the bodie it makes such a larg hole that it lettes the breth out of the bodie emediatlie."[36]

The preferred tactics of the lancero, matador, and montero were close ambushes by day and surprise attacks by night or in the rain, for such circumstances minimized the effectiveness of the boucaniers' firearms. Lacking these circumstances, they rarely attacked, but if they attacked afoot they fell to one knee if the enemy fired a single volley, then would "fall on" from a close range of twelve to fifteen yards; that is, they rushed in and attacked at close quarters or "handy grips" while the enemy reloaded. Their lances rarely missed their targets, and they were reputed "very expert in heaving or darting the Lance; with which upon Occasion, they will do great Feats, especially in Ambuscades."[37] The lancero, if nimbly mounted and on open ground, had a great advantage over the rover afoot and armed only with an edged weapon. Even a man afoot on open ground with his lance (or spear, javelin, half-pike, or pike) had the advantage of the rover armed only with a sword, or otherwise unable to fire his musket. Distance was the issue: to survive, the defender had to close with his enemy, avoiding the lance point as he moved closer. Typically, if the attack was directly from the front, the defender was able to counter it by making an inside parry with sword or musket while volting (pivoting) away from the point, then grasping the shaft of the lance with the unarmed hand, and quickly closing with the enemy, a difficult task if the lance was long.[38] Facing two or more lances, survival was practically impossible except for the fleet afoot. On open ground the Spanish enemies were held at bay with firearms, for "if you kep them out, then thay flie for it: but if thay come within you, then stand clear."[39]

When they were forced to defend themselves, boucaniers usually fired from cover and were adept at keeping up a constant fire by working in pairs, with one shooting cartridges of ball and shot while the other reloaded. In such circumstances Spaniards rarely charged them. Indeed, these musket tactics probably developed simultaneously at sea, where they worked well to suppress enemy fire, and ashore, where they prevented Spanish lancers from closing as well as suppressed enemy fire. However, in spite of these tactics of musketry, by attacking from ambush, by night, or in the rain, La Cinquantaine was able to reduce the numbers of boucaniers, at times even expelling them from many places. Unable to destroy all of the boucaniers, however, the lanceros began slaughtering wild cattle in the west, and this was perhaps their most effective strategy for reducing the population of boucaniers. Yet for this very reason the Spanish strategy backfired: the general French population of Hispaniola grew, because with less opportunity to hunt and a governor (d'Ogeron) wisely providing incentives to settle the coast, many turned to planting, which in turn provided the means for a stable population and economy. They also turned even more to raiding the Spanish at sea, causing more problems for the Spanish than hunting ever did.[40]

> If it were not for theas Cowkillers and Negros the spaniyards ware not abell to hould vp his hand against any ennemie, for the spaniyards are soe roten with the pox and soe lothegic that they cannot goe 2 mile but they are redie to die,

wrote Henry Whistler in 1655, referring to Spanish defenders on the Main.[41] His hyperbole of local Spanish pox and lethargy doubtless derived from hatred and perhaps some shred of truth, but other such men as he described—both slave and free, of all local ethnicities, and armed with spear or lance and a machete—were the common militia of Spain throughout the New World in the seventeenth century. There were professional soldiers armed with matchlock muskets and occasionally there was a well-armed cavalry, both often commanded by good officers. Many of the militiamen were "Greeks": well-paid soldiers from Mediterranean nations, whom some observers credited as being the best of Spain's professional fighting men in the New World, although others awarded the distinction to Biscayers. There were also local militias armed with firearms, although these arms were often poor-quality carbines, fowling pieces, and harquebuses.[42] But the backbone of the defense of the Spanish Main ashore was the man who labored in the fields and wild countryside, and his lance or spear. He was perhaps most dangerous defending his town or village: "[A buccaneer captain in 1680] went up corragiously with some brisk men with him, butt their was provided Mollattas and hunters with their launces which came to oppose him." The captain and three of his companions died at the hands of these fierce defenders.[43]

The English logwood cutters dealt with similar tactics, and in many ways these interlopers with axes corresponded to the French boucaniers, for both were frontiersmen whose skills and traditions were critical to piracy in the Caribbean. Both hunted for reasons of provisions and trade, one primarily, the other secondarily. They were strong, willful, independent, self-sufficient men accustomed to primitive living and the constant threat of Spanish attack. They survived profitably in a wilderness. They defended themselves against organized attacks and even made reprisals against neighboring Spaniards. They forged through a hostile environment of man and nature and were fit enough to attack and sack a city.

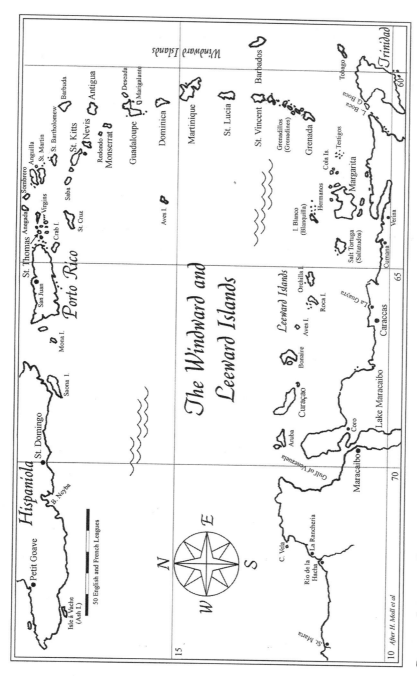

BENERSON LITTLE AND COURTNEY LITTLE.

While the boucaniers hunted on Hispaniola, the flibustier, anglicized as filibuster, roamed the seas. The word *flibustier* was derived from the French pronunciation of the Dutch *vryjbuiter* (freebooter), although some suggested it was derived from its counterpart and literal translation in English, *freebooter*, or even from both.[44] At any rate, a freebooter served for booty or *butin*— plunder, that is—and a filibuster sought plunder on or from the sea. In a narrow sense the term *filibuster* only meant pirates or privateers of the Caribbean derived from the French colonies therein who preyed primarily on the Spanish, except in time of war when they attacked France's other enemies as well. More broadly, the French used the word to indicate any Caribbean-based pirate or privateer, *flibustiers espagnole* or *flibustiers anglais*, for example.

Filibusters existed since the earliest days of French activity on Tortuga, and it was not long before filibusters and boucaniers banded together, first to expel a Spanish invasion force in Tortuga, then for protection in the form of reprisals against the Spanish, and finally in expeditions for which the sole purpose was plunder, with reprisal serving as a guise.[45] They stole not only from the Spanish but from the English and Dutch as well, and it was clear that many served in double or triple capacities, sometimes as boucanier, sometimes as planter, sometimes as filibuster. Many filibusters were former boucaniers: Jan Erasmus Reyning was first a hunter's valet before becoming a filibuster, Spanish guarda costa, Dutch privateer, and Dutch naval officer.[46] Exquemelin and the notorious L'Ollonois were also hunters' valets before becoming filibusters, as was the sieur Kercoue, who was engaged as a valet in 1674 to a boucanier for three years, then sailed as a filibuster for fifteen or more.[47] Raveneau de Lussan, noteworthy filibuster author, was likewise indentured to a cruel master, quite possibly a boucanier.[48] In fact, most boucaniers at some point probably joined with filibusters, and many were considered to be both hunter and filibuster. Often these men, in numbers up to ten, each providing his own arms, powder, and shot (as always they did), made short coastal raids in canoes, small barks, and other poorly outfitted vessels, cruising from isolated areas and often provisioned for only eight days.[49] Even in the 1680s some of these adventurers practiced a form of matelotage in which one remained ashore as a planter while the other went to sea as a filibuster, probably as a form of economic diversification. "The French are settled all round Hispaniola, but thinly, and plant only tobacco. They intend cruising chiefly, and are so mated that one stays and plants while the other goes abroad to seek booty."[50] Among themselves these men came to be known as the Brethren of the Coast (*les Frères de la Côte*), given their origin along the western coast of Hispaniola. For several decades this tripartite cooperation of brethren scourged the Spanish Main.

*A*fter the English conquest of Jamaica in 1655, English governors began granting commissions against the Spanish. Filibusters flocked to Port Royal, the principal port in Jamaica, and brought with them boucaniers, some of whom were hired by the English to help flush out Spanish guerrillas.[51] From the boucanier these new English-based Caribbean privateers and pirates took their name, anglicizing it as buccaneer. Like filibusters, buccaneers comprised of all sorts of men, not just sailors. Planters, fortune hunters, former slaves and indentured servants, romantic opportunists, gentlemen and their pretenders, debtors, the down and out, former Spanish prisoners, and others joined their ranks. According to both the accounts of the pirates themselves and records of Spanish interrogations, former slaves and former indentured servants made up a significant proportion of the buccaneer and filibuster population, not surprising given the vicissitudes they endured—sea roving must have seemed like heaven by comparison.[52] Some entered piracy as indentured servants or slaves of buccaneers and filibusters, and others, Spaniards especially, after being captured by pirates.[53] At times Caribbean sea roving was a family affair: Peter Harris, uncle, and Peter Harris, nephew, were buccaneer captains, and Pierre Ovinet and le Grand Ovinet, cousins, were filibuster captains.[54]

In the early years many buccaneers were former soldiers, survivors of the failed English attempt in 1655 to conquer Hispaniola, where disease, starvation, dehydration, and Spaniards killed many and incapacitated even more. But the man who bore arms effectively in spite of the constant fear of ambush and surprise attack, who remained ready to fight even when weakened from severe sickness, who went to extreme measures for survival, for example, by having a comrade urinate in his mouth to keep him from passing out from dehydration, and who survived and gutted his enemy in spite of all this was certainly physically tough enough to be a buccaneer.[55] One of these men, named Swan, was still with the buccaneers when he was eighty-four. Surrounded by Spaniards in 1685, he died refusing to surrender to his enemy.[56] Such acts of defiant courage and refusal of quarter were not uncommon, and the heroism was noted with great regard by sea rovers, transcending social, racial, and national boundaries. At Arica, Chile, in 1681,

> one Negro [buccaneer], who had his Leg shot off, being offered quarter, refused it, and killed four or five of their Men, before he was shot dead on the spot. This fellow had been a Slave, whom our Commander had freed, and brought from Jamaica.[57]

Before going to sea, buccaneers and filibusters drafted a *chasse-partie*, the name deriving from *charte-partie* (charter party) and from the hunt or chase (*la chasse*), and referred to in English as the articles or the articles of agreement. The charte-partie known among French merchant sailors was a contract between ship owner and merchant denoting the name and port of the vessel, the names of captain and *affréteur* (the merchant hiring the vessel), and also freight charges, interest, and various other conditions.[58] The chasse-partie of the filibuster was based on a tradition called the "Custom of the Coast" or the "Law of Privateers," an unwritten code that developed among the early adventurers and sufficed to settle most disagreements, although similar articles were often found among earlier rovers, including English pirates of the early seventeenth century.[59] The code was rigorously followed, although subject to interpretation, and the written articles of the chasse-partie, being derived from common consent, took priority.[60] The chasse-partie specified the intended cruise or raid and provided shares for each member based on his role, compensation for injury, reward for dangerous or exceptional service, and regulations of behavior. The articles also designated how provisions were secured and paid for, how much the carpenter received for making the vessel seaworthy, and how much the surgeon was paid for his medicines and service, assuming the ship was not outfitted by owners or investors. Compensation was based on the concept of "no prey, no pay." Shares were paid only if there was profit. Commanders were elected democratically, served only at the pleasure of the crew, and were deposed at any time by majority rule, with one exception: those who served under a lawful commission in time of war could not replace the commander listed therein, and often buccaneers and filibusters joined a commander simply because he had a commission.[61] All major decisions were determined by vote, and crew members were under no compulsion to serve for any given period—they could depart at any time, although they had to pay for food they took with them.[62] (See also appendixes A and B.)

In addition, if they had not already done so, each man paired with another and wrote and signed a "testament," either permanent or merely for the duration of the voyage, which stipulated the division of property and authorized the survivor to act as executor of the will and make decisions as necessary on the deceased's behalf. Also, each man agreed to look after the other if wounded.[63]

These sea rovers were exceedingly, almost purely, democratic in their practice of self-government. Although this form of democracy suggested social and political rebellion, if not an outright micro-revolution, it was also the only practical form of government among independent men in such circumstances. These adventurers were not, as some have suggested, communistic or near-communistic; personal material gain, after all, was their purpose. They believed in property, even if they often squandered it. Buccaneers and filibusters had no intention of putting their ill-gotten gains in any communal pot for the good of the whole, notwithstanding their generosity to their brethren in time of need. And while they considered themselves each other's equal, including the captain, they also considered themselves at least equal to all men and superior to most. As Governor Pouançay wrote: "They all consider themselves leaders."[64]

By the 1670s, ventures of piracy and privateering were often provisioned in port, rather than by raiding Spanish *crawls* (corrals), the latter being the circumstance under which Rock the Brazilian roasted men to death over open fires for refusing "to show him the road to the hog-yards he wanted to plunder."[65] Even so, hogs, cattle, goats, and sheep, wild or in corrals, remained important, particularly when provisions ran low or pirates could not enter ports.[66] Additionally, according to Dampier, crawls were found primarily in the Caribbean islands, not on the Main. Domestic swine ran free during the day to feed, but "at Night come in at the sounding of a Conch-shell."[67] Goats were found in great numbers on many islands, especially in the South Sea. In many places cattle and hogs were not as plentiful as they once were, nor were wild dogs, which ran in packs, attacked young cattle, and were generally shot on sight. Even wild Spanish horses were at one time so plentiful on Hispaniola that for sport Spaniards chased them into the sea to watch sharks devour them.[68] Still, wild horses, donkeys, and mules were plentiful enough, running in herds of two or three hundred, and they cost more to break than to purchase. There were more than enough hogs and cattle to sustain a moderate population of hunters on Saint Domingue: boucaniers remained active there into the eighteenth century, supporting filibuster expeditions.[69]

*U*sually there were no more than three to four hundred boucaniers on Saint Domingue at any given time, and for a time there were only one hundred. Even at their height there were never more than seven or eight hundred boucaniers, yet they provided both the initial foundation of the local French economy and the principal line of defense ashore, and significantly influenced the manner of piracy in the Caribbean.[70] Doubtless their independence influenced the form of articles or chasse-partie used among the Caribbean pirates, and their hunting and butchering skills, not to mention their population, were vital to early forays against the Spanish. But perhaps most important, their style of musketry, which consisted of individually aimed shots, often of ball and shot, intended to keep up a constant fire rather than volleys aimed at a mass target, became a trademark of the buccaneer and filibuster.

By the late 1660s, the process was complete and efficient: boucaniers and habitants routinely joined with filibusters to become *aventuriers*, and French adventurers joined English buccaneers and volunteers to engage in expeditions at sea and ashore. Many rovers and adventurers of the period (1674–88) were veterans of the great expeditions of which Exquemelin wrote, and many served under Henry Morgan himself, including the famous (or so destined) captains Bartholomew Sharp, John Coxon, Peter Harris, John Bennet, William Wright, Jean le Gascon, and John Watling. Jan Erasmus Reyning and Pierre le Picard served under the butcher L'Ollonois as well. These buccaneers and filibusters were heir to two bloody decades of practical experience in expeditions of privateering and piracy, great and small, along the Main.

They had two things in common, these buccaneers and adventurers, well noted by Exquemelin: the musket was their weapon, and their genius compensated for any lack in resources.[71] By these means alone did such men "from a small sloop take a small ship, and with it a greater one, and finally one of 24 to 28 cannons, with which will they take an even greater one," not to mention the towns and cities they sacked.[72] And they carried their prizes and booty into the great ports of the Caribbean pirates—but after 1673 the infamous Tortuga was no longer the main port of the filibuster.[73]

# 5 Petit Goave and Port Royal:
## Pirate Asylums and Sanctuaries

*A* visitor approaching Petit Goave, a small, rough town on the northern coast of the southwestern peninsula of Hispaniola, is first met off shore by the entrancing scent of orange and lime blossoms, in bloom year round and so plentiful that they weigh branches down and litter the ground with fruit. The oranges of the Caribbean "have a taste betwixt the *China* and *Sevil*, full of juice, and commonly extraordinarily large and refreshing. . . . This sort of orange in *France* is call'd *Bigarrade*"* (the sour orange), while the limes are those we call *Mexican, West Indian*, or *Key limes*.[1] Neither fruit is native to the Caribbean. Entering the comfortable harbor, about four thousand yards wide, our visitor observes the town and a tiny, almost inconsequential fort to the southeast. The shore is lined with palm trees, mosquito-infested mangroves, and other tropical foliage, and beyond it are rich green hills. One might even see a caiman swimming by.[2] Four hundred yards north of the town is an islet a few hundred feet across, "which is the usual Buriel-Place of the People of the pretended Reformed Religion"—Huguenots or other Protestants, that is, of whom a fair number are filibusters.[3] West in the harbor is the tiny Baye d'Acul, and at its mouth several tiny islets; beyond the bay itself to the west is the area called Acul. Our visitor's ship anchors near the center of the harbor, northwest of the disembogue of a small river and southwest of a shallow bank. The vessel is met by a pirogue

---

*All quotations have been reprinted with their original spelling and punctuation.

57

with twenty or so armed men, whose intention is to identify the ship and her purpose. Assuming all is well, our visitor goes ashore and is now quickly both fascinated and stunned.[4]

Fascinating were the filibusters, "men of all nations [and] the mélange of their different characters and their language," wrote one late seventeenth-century visitor.[5] And indeed, although more were French than any other nationality, they were also Dutch, Spanish, Portuguese, English, Irish, Scottish, German, and Flemish, and certainly most other European and Mediterranean nations were represented as well. Ethnically, they were white, black, Native American, mulatto, mestizo, other mixed bloods, and, according to one noted scholar, a few were even Asian.[6] They were everywhere, these adventurers, when ashore: the hunter with his bloody dress, buccaneer gun, and surely a dog or two; the filibuster with his brace of pistols, cutlass, and perhaps his buccaneer gun as well, not to mention his tales of adventure, pieces-of-eight, and pet parrots and monkeys. The parrots were a variety of New World and African—there were at least 136 species in the New World alone.[7] Many were trained to talk in various or even several languages.[8] True to the stereotype, pirates and other mariners were fond of them:

> The tame Parrots we found here [at Alvarado, Mexico] were the largest and fairest Birds of their Kind that I ever saw in the *West-Indies*. Their colour was yellow and red, very coarsely mixt; and they would prate very prettily; and there was scarce a Man but what sent aboard one or two of them.[9]

As for the appearance of the adventurers, we know the dress and accoutrements of the boucanier; the filibuster's were of the sea. In the tropical heat the sailor's "tarpaulins" were typically a shirt and wide sailor's breeches, and among the French and Spanish at least, an often brightly colored sash.[10] On their heads filibusters wore brimmed hats of felt, straw, or palm fibers (a "bast hat"), or perhaps a Monmouth hat, or a similar French knit hat, much like a stocking cap (the "tricorne" hat did not appear until the 1680s). Some of those who were no longer boucaniers might continue to wear their modified headgear, as perhaps did some buccaneers and filibusters: "privateer" John Hullock, captured along with several others by Spaniards, "cock'd up his little cropt hat, and told them he was the Captain."[11] (Hullock, who was not the captain, received better treatment, and afterward his fellow buccaneers referred to him in jest as "Captain Jack.") Some filibusters stowed a short pipe in their hatbands. Their hair was usually tied back, plaited, or tarred, for loose, long hair was dangerous aboard a ship, interfered with vision, and could be caught and drawn into a block, especially when "loosing, reefing, and handling the sails." It was not as great a hazard aboard small vessels.[12] The common rover was often barefoot, at sea and ashore (even attacking a town), and at sea in the tropics sailors often stripped down to their breeches.[13]

On a cruising voyage a rover carried a pistol or two, his musket, three or four ramrods, associated accoutrements, and a "good cutlass." He provided his own arms, powder, and shot. There was little or no room for a sea chest aboard small buccaneering vessels (if they were brought aboard, they were certainly shared), so the rover often went to sea with little more clothing than two shirts and a coat.[14] A filibuster with new clothes from a prize or from the profits of a cruise may have gone ashore dressed in a gentleman's laced coat, feathered hat, and shoes and stockings, or shoes but no stocking, or stockings but no shoes.[15] His skin may have been "pricked" with a design—*tattoo* was a Polynesian word not used by Europeans until the eighteenth century. Many seamen commonly bore such marks, and, like the French coureurs de bois, some rovers who lived among Native American tribes had "their Faces and Bodies with Figures wrought on them." Native Americans marked themselves permanently by pricking their flesh and pigmenting it with charcoal, vermilion, gunpowder, or a combination thereof; Europeans used gunpowder. Native American designs included patterns of "Scores or Streaks," leaves, flowers, and similar marks, and "Crosses [and] Names of Jesus" among some Christian Indians. English sailors were fond of the Jerusalem cross.[16] Some African and Native American rovers wore earrings, but there is no solid evidence that any European rovers wore them after the first half of the seventeenth century, although there are occasional cryptic hints: "[O]r was it the Gunpowder spot [a tattoo] on his hand, or the Jewel in his ear, that purchas'd your heart?" sneered Captain Manly in regard to a primping fop in Wycherley's *The Plain Dealer*, first performed in 1674.[17]

The sea rover's often flamboyant dress and appearance were certainly not a creation of the early eighteenth-century Anglo-American pirates, such as Calico Jack Rackam, Blackbeard, and Bartholomew Roberts. English pirates more than a century earlier were known for their spectacular dress, and such flamboyance was common in the late seventeenth century as well: Nicolas Van Horn, for example, commonly wore a "necklace of pearls of extraordinary size and inestimable price, with rubies of surpassing beauty."[18]

At Petit Goave filibusters drank, smoked, visited whores, played *passe-dix* (passage, played with three dice), and planned expeditions.[19] The atmosphere of imminent adventure was enticing, enough so that even visiting sailors and officers of the French Navy passed most of their time with the picaresque adventurers, telling sea stories and losing money to them at dice. In 1681 the comte d'Estrées, an admiral, lost ten thousand pieces-of-eight to the sieur de Grammont, one of the great filibuster commanders.[20] To come

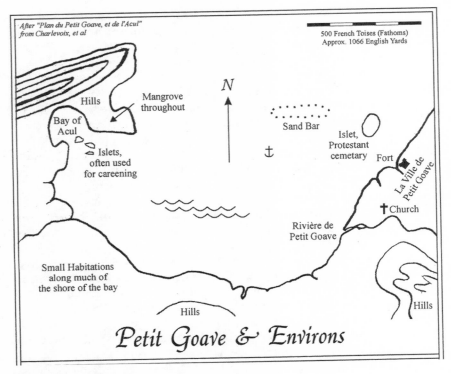

*After "Plan du Petit Goave, et de l'Acul" from Charlevoix, et al*

500 French Toises (Fathoms)
Approx. 1066 English Yards

N

Hills

Mangrove throughout

Bay of Acul

Sand Bar

Islet, Protestant cemetary  Fort

*La Ville de Petit Goave*

Islets, often used for careening

† Church

Rivière de Petit Goave

Small Habitations along much of the shore of the bay

Hills

Hills

*Petit Goave & Environs*

Benerson Little and Courtney Little.

from Europe and see for the first time men whose renown even in the seventeenth century was near-mythical could be nothing less than fascinating.

While the men of Petit Goave were fascinating, the women were stunning. Most of them were mulattoes, "nude except for a linen skirt." A visitor wrote that when he first saw them he was overwhelmed, incapable of ignoring the spectacle creating so much emotion within: their "free manner" made him weep and he wished for a "conquest" if time permitted. "They have much inclination for Europeans, whom the heat of the country renders so susceptible to love that they are incapable of letting any such occasion escape."[21] Perhaps the Europeans were susceptible to love, but doubtless they were more overcome by lust confused with love and plain, simple, overwhelming lust. Most men who went to sea without women aboard for more than a few days, much less weeks or months—and sometimes for only a few days—easily appreciated the visitor's sentiments at the sight of a beautiful half-dressed woman. What the visitor failed to remark on was the fact that the women, free or not, were the product of the slave trade, part of a system that classified people as part of a spectrum ranging from "property" to "nobility." However, few, if any, people gave that fact a second thought. Further, the average sailor going ashore was not inclined to question social conditions, for the desire to "get drunk and have sex" after being at sea tended to overwhelm. "We were all of us too wild and little considered the mercies we received, but took large liberty when ashore drinking and sporting as the manner of seamen generally is," wrote one sailor.[22] To this mental state add beautiful women walking topless on the shore, and it was easy to see how Petit Goave was viewed by some as paradise among the living. In an atmosphere of warm sea breezes blowing amid lust, violence, and plunder, what man would not be tempted to join these sea rovers—or at the very least, dream or write about them?

*P*etit Goave, which took its name from *goyave*, or "guava," was established as a town in 1663, although boucaniers had been there at least since 1659, and probably made boucans at the site periodically for many years prior.[23] In 1677 its population was six hundred, plus another two hundred engagés (indentured servants) and probably a fair number of slaves as well.[24] Many boucaniers and filibusters owned land, and when ashore, landowning filibusters tended to their holdings large or small, thus the need for engagés and slaves. Most rode wherever they went, for "in the mountains there are horses, mules, and wild donkeys, which we take when we want to. Thus, there is nobody so poor as not to be mounted."[25] Most houses in Petit Goave, as in most French towns on Hispaniola, were composed of posts stuck in the earth and mud walls (probably wattle and daub), although some houses had two stories, were built with boards, and had shingled roofs. There were also a few very fine houses in Petit Goave. In the Caribbean, lime trees were often planted close together to serve as fences or hedges. Most people in the West Indies slept in hammocks, and the same probably held true at Petit Goave. In the town were also storehouses near the water, for Petit Goave exported tobacco, indigo, hides, *roucou* (annatto, a dye derived from achiote), tallow, and even sugar, among other commodities, and also traded European goods to Spain illicitly. Boucan, however, was not usually exported, but was used to provision habitants and local vessels. Vital to the filibuster—at least he thought so—were the "many taverns" and "stews" (brothels) in town. By comparison, the first church was built in 1670 and another across the bay at l'Acul de Petit Goave in 1686, and in 1685 there were two Capuchins to tend to the parishioners of the "Religion Catholïque, Apostolique et Romaine."[26]

Much of the male population of French Hispaniola consisted of veteran filibusters and boucaniers, and thus the area, in theory, was well defended against an invasion. The French were well established on the west coast of Hispaniola, and by the early 1680s the French encroachment seemed permanent, although French plantations and trade lagged behind the English,

because the population was small. The English suggested the French population was three thousand in 1682, but unless the number counted only planters, it was too low. There were two thousand slaves alone, one thousand to
three thousand filibusters depending on how many were at sea (and who
was doing the counting), and a few years earlier an estimated two thousand
planters (one thousand of whom were probably filibusters), and surely that
number increased with time. The actual population was at least six thousand
and probably higher. The population had grown at a steady pace, owing in
large part to Governor d'Ogeron, from four hundred in 1665 to two thousand
in 1670 to four thousand or five thousand in 1677.[27]

Women made up a much smaller part of the population than men. There
were slaves, black and mulatto; free mulattoes; Native Americans; and Europeans, usually French, brought to become wives to hunters, filibusters, and planters. D'Ogeron began the practice of bringing women—the aforementioned
La Cinquantaine—to Saint Domingue, and more were brought later: one hundred were shipped to French Hispaniola in 1685, for example.[28] In addition, a
few women might have been disguised as men among the hunters and filibusters, for such women in dangerous places were not unknown yet sufficiently rare to be commented on when discovered. Captain Beare, pirate and
renegade, dressed his "strumpet," the daughter of a Port Royal tavern woman,
in men's clothing and sailed with her aboard his ship in 1687. Turning renegade, he even presented her as a noblewoman to the governor of Havana,
who attended their wedding. Aboard the letter-of-mart-ship *Hannibal* in 1693,
John Brown, a soldier of the Africa Company, was discovered to be a woman.
The captain gave her a private lodging and dressed her in women's clothing
"in recompense for which she prov'd very useful" in washing his linen, despite the fact that she had gone undiscovered for three months, and was as
willing and able to do a man's work as any in her company of soldiers. Aboard
the Spanish treasure fleet in 1698, a "woman being found aboard in man's
clothes, and there being no possibility of setting her ashore, she was left
among the other women." Certainly more went undiscovered.[29]

*P*etit Goave—"the retreat of the corsains"—was not yet a wealthy
town in terms of structures and facades, but some former engagés and
boucanier valets were rich, and by the 1690s many former adventurers had
become "fat seigneurs" who hardly moved the distance of a step except in a
coach and six and often failed to recall their humble origins.[30] Not all were
French, either. In 1681, for example, the English buccaneer Captain Wright
was well received and settled in Petit Goave, as well as a friend of the governor's and the Dutchman Laurens de Graff became a French citizen in 1685 and
a rich one to boot.[31] However, neither Petit Goave nor San Domingue in general were yet secure enough from attack that such wealth could not be taken

away in acts of open warfare or quick reprisal. San Domingue was not heavily fortified, on the theory that a lack of fortifications would force invaders to fight in the hinterland, the perfect battlefield for the boucanier and filibuster.[32] However, French settlements were left vulnerable to quick raids.

In 1676 a Dutch flotilla under the command of Jacob Binkes entered Petit Goave harbor under full sail. Anchoring at l'Acul de Petit Goave, the Dutch engaged French vessels at "musket shot" (two hundred to three hundred yards) for several hours until nightfall. The battle raged until the French ship *Dauphin* caught fire and exploded, killing her captain and twenty others. The crews of the other French vessels retreated ashore. The next morning the Dutch captured seven vessels and departed, not daring to go ashore. They left forty French casualties in their wake.[33]

Spanish attacks were far more common, often from the sea, and at times Spanish pirates ranged along the entire coast, attacking small settlements. With the assistance of a French traitor, they destroyed the small French colony at Samana in 1676 in reprisal for the sack of Cotuí by Samana boucaniers. The Spanish put both men and women "to the lance," but many escaped in the darkness, fleeing to Saint Domingue by canoe, only to return later.[34] In 1684 Spanish pirates in two pirogues with sixty men apiece captured a French ketch, part of La Salle's expedition to the Mississippi. A report in early 1685 noted that the coast was exposed both by land and by sea to Spanish incursions, and "in the past two years there have been several massacres of hunters, and frequent descents [attacks from the sea] in all the different quarters of the isle with the demi-galleys they have armed." The attacks included one repulsed at Le Cap, and a successful one at Leogane, where pirates seized merchandise and twenty slaves.[35]

During this period the government of Saint Domingue moved from Tortuga to Port-de-Paix across the channel, for Tortuga and its town and fort at Basse Terre were too isolated from the growing French settlements, and were no longer required as a redoubt against the Spanish.[36] But Port-de-Paix, the first French settlement on Hispaniola since Tortuga, served only as the seat of government. Petit Goave was the main port and chief garrison for French filibusters, the "most considerable in the colony," and had been since the early 1670s. Petit Goave became as important to sea rovers as Port Royal, if not more so.[37] It and San Domingue in general were home to almost half of the principal anti-Spanish sea rovers—a thousand or more in 1675 and up to three thousand a decade later—one-third of whom tended their plantations while the other two-thirds roved against the Spanish.[38] It was a base from which to launch expeditions against the Spanish, and, via its filibusters, it was a critical part of the local French economy. Perhaps more important, to the buccaneer and filibuster at least, San Domingue was the source of the cherished French commission, the document of legitimacy—or at least of enough semblance of legitimacy to keep a rope from a rover's neck. The French governor issued commissions: "It hath been usual . . . for the Governour of P. Guavres to send blank Commissions to Sea by many of his Captains, with Orders to dispose of them to whom they saw convenient." Filibusters and buccaneers walked the dirt streets of Petit Goave—"the Sanctuary and Asylum of all People of desperate Fortunes"—with impunity, having committed deeds and depredations against the Spanish without fear of arrest, much less of hanging.[39] Petit Goave had become the "Commission Port" of the pirates of the Caribbean, although some filibusters sailed from Tortuga and Martinique.[40]

𝓟ort Royal, Jamaica, southwest across the water, was undergoing an opposite transformation. It was once the great haven and inspiration of epic and largely legitimate buccaneering enterprises under Henry Morgan and others. However, peace between England and Spain was proclaimed in the Caribbean in 1671; buccaneers who afterward attacked Spanish ships or towns were pirates and thus subject to the authority of the law. It was more dangerous for a buccaneer engaged in piracy to walk the streets of Port Royal, and the days in which Rock the Brazilian strolled with "a naked cutlass on his arm," cutting or beating any he found offensive, were gone forever.[41] However, some merchants, planters, and at least one member of the "Grand Council" still outfitted, provisioned, or otherwise invested in the unlicensed expeditions of buccaneers.[42] In general, though, the buccaneer was considered detrimental to profit in Port Royal.[43] Although it was built by Spanish silver brought to Jamaica by buccaneers, the colony began to support itself with plantation exports and illicit trade with Spain. However, it remained common for buccaneers to plan and provision cruises under the guise of trading voyages, for example, although they were frequently planning such cruises elsewhere, to be safe. Even so, there were pirates in Jamaican waters. The richly laden English merchantman *Terra Nova*, for example, was approached the evening of her departure from Jamaica in 1688 by a sloop pretending to have a packet of letters from the lieutenant governor. The captain refused to send a boat or permit the sloop to lay the ship aboard (come alongside) on its starboard quarter, and so the sloop showed her true colors, firing two shotted guns at the ship, which returned the "salute" in kind. Without doubt the pirates knew of the rich cargo aboard.[44]

A visitor approaching Port Royal from the sea would first see the Blue Mountain in the distance, then the "Salt Pans which are round hills on the high land to leaward of Port Royal." Coming near the town, his vessel saluted any men-of-war at anchor near the keys (Sandy Key, Drunkard's Key, Gun Key, among others) south of the spit end that was Port Royal, and passed close under the guns of Morgan's Line and Fort Charles. He then was haled "to get into the harbour" itself, north of the spit, passing first a small cove called the Chocolate

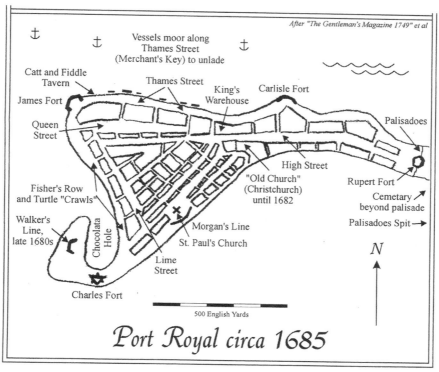

After "The Gentleman's Magazine 1749" et al

Vessels moor along
Thames Street
(Merchant's Key) to unlade

Catt and Fiddle
Tavern

Thames Street

King's
Warehouse

Carlisle Fort

James Fort

Palisadoes

Queen
Street

High Street

"Old Church"
(Christchurch)
until 1682

Rupert Fort

Fisher's Row
and Turtle "Crawls"

Cemetary
beyond palisade

Walker's
Line,
late 1680s

Chocolata Hole

Palisadoes Spit →

Morgan's Line

St. Paul's Church

Lime
Street

Charles Fort

500 English Yards

*N*

*Port Royal circa 1685*

BENERSON LITTLE AND COURTNEY LITTLE.

Hole, where men-of-war were careened, then the turtle crawls on Fisher's Row, and finally Fort James on the northwest point. By 1680, more than one hundred cannons protected Port Royal. After anchoring in the harbor, a visitor went ashore to a warren-like district of two-story, brick buildings, some with sash windows but most without, fronted by wharves on Thames Street, called "Merchant's Key" [quay], where "the largest ships . . . lay their broadsides to the wharf and load or unload from a plank on shore." The vessels were of all sorts and typically small, ranging from ten to one hundred and fifty tons. Larger ships were less common but easily accommodated.[45]

*A* visitor to Port Royal would be both fascinated and stunned by what he sensed: a town both cosmopolitan and frontier, reeking of the sailor, sex, rum and dice, and mercantile opportunity. Yet in 1700 Ned Ward described Jamaica as the "Dunghill of the Universe, the refuse of the whole Creation." Similar words were used by Henry Whistler in 1655 to describe Barbados: "the Dunghill wharone England doth cast forth its rubidg: Rodgs [rogues] and

hors and such like peopel are those which are generally Broght heare."Thus
was the reputation of pioneers, adventurers, and marginal sorts among their
"civilized," dependent, socially stable contemporaries. Nonetheless, one visitor described white Jamaicans as hot tempered, courageous, friendly, proud,
lazy, generous, and hospitable.[46]

As a buccaneer town and seaport on the edge of the world, Port Royal's
atmosphere was little different from Petit Goave's. Men, sailors especially, drank
and visited whores in taverns and fought in the streets. They gambled with
dice, some played billiards, and others attended cockfights and bull and bear
baiting (fights featuring dog attacks). The taverns, punch houses, and bordel-
los, often one and the same, and the women in them were notorious even by
the standards of the time. "Rum-punch-women," prostitutes, and others, with
reputed names such as Uncon the Green Dragon, the Catt and Fiddle, and the
Sign of the Mermaid, and were commonly observed engaging in "*Swearing,
Drinking*, and *Obscene Talk*." The "common sort of women [have] a proud
lazy stalking gait with them, swinging and dandling their arms about as they
walk and much addicted to a swearing obscene masculine talk and behavior
(at Port Royal especially)." It was a town where women "vie *Wickedness* with
the *Devil*" and "may be *Wicked* without *Shame*, and *Whore* on without *Punishment*." In other words, it was a town less hypocritical than many, a place
where women as well as men misbehaved outrageously and publicly.[47]

Exquemelin described the typical return of buccaneers and filibusters
to Port Royal and Tortuga with *bon butin* (good booty). Their clothing was
tattered, their faces pale, meager, and disfigured. But on their shoulders, backs,
or heads were large bags of pieces-of-eight, which they quickly put to good
use. First, they descended on the taverns, eating and drinking extravagantly,
throwing their glasses into the air after each shot of rum, and littering tables
and floor with the detritus of drunken celebration. Next, they bought expensive, flamboyant clothing, and in this splendidly sartorial and probably inebri-
ated state they visited houses of prostitution and gambling, where they lost
most, if not all, they had gained, yet it was no matter at all to them if they left
as they came, with only some clothing and their arms.[48]

*H*owever, Port Royal was more than the notorious and "principal place
for bucaneers or privateers and Spanish traders"; it was a town of significant
commerce. It supported the enormous export of Jamaican plantations, as well
as the local sloop trade—illicit but lucrative—with merchants of New Spain.
Vessels brought all sorts of goods to Jamaica, from butter, cheese, and flour to
Madeira wine. They departed variously with logwood and other dye woods,
sugar, cacao, cotton wool, indigo, hides, tobacco, tortoise shell, achiote, ginger, sarsaparilla, and "pimento" (allspice or "Jamaica pepper," called *pimento*

from its resemblance to peppercorns). "Many men . . . have their whole estates transported in ships, many ships and cargoes being worth one hundred thousand pounds." As such, Port Royal did not tolerate pirates who interfered with trade or with the colony's provisioning by "New England, New York, and Ireland, and . . . fishermen at the South Cays." All major trades existed in Port Royal, and those of faiths other than the Church of England were tolerated, including Presbyterians, Quakers, and Catholics—greed's blind eye can have a positive aspect. There was a large Jewish population, vital both to finance and to trade with the Spaniards, and in 1677 it had a synagogue as well.[49]

*I*n 1672 Denmark, seeking a foothold in the Caribbean in support of a venture into the slave trade, established a colony on St. Thomas and named its capital and port Christiansfort. In 1679 Nicolai Esmit became governor and began a soap-operatic reign of scoundrels and skullduggery: Nicolai was deposed by his brother Adolph, allegedly a former buccaneer captain, whose relief aboard a Danish vessel, Jörgen Iverson, the original governor of the colony, was murdered by mutineers in 1682. Gabriel Milan, who learned his trade under Cardinal Mazarin, replaced Adolph (with the assistance of an armed sloop sent by Governor Stapleton of the Leeward Islands), and before long both Esmit and Milan returned to Denmark as a prisoners. Adolph's English wife, Charity, pretended to be the relation of an English baron and pled her husband's case in Copenhagen. Under the Esmits the colony was notorious for outfitting and protecting pirates, among them the infamous Jean Hamlin of *La Trompeuse*; Captains Bond and Beare; some of the South Sea buccaneers; and near the end of the century, some of Captain Kidd's crew, along with the Mogul's ship and cargo. Hamlin even had a "private signal" for entering the harbor, as probably did other pirates using St. Thomas as a base.[50] So outrageous was Adolph Esmit—even his lies to his king were outrageous—that in 1684 King Christian V of Denmark ordered him to restore an English ship he seized and to restrain from similar acts, lest "the penalty of summary punishment of death" be carried out.[51]

The colony—pirates referred to it as a "Free Port," for all were allowed to trade there—was small, fewer than eight hundred residents in 1688, and of a mixed population of Dutch, English, Danes, Norwegians, French, Irish, Flemings, Germans, Swedes, Scots, Brazilians, Portuguese, blacks, Native Americans, and mixed races, most on small plantations.[52] The town was but a single long street, mostly warehouses and rude huts, although brick houses replaced the huts in the late seventeenth and early eighteenth centuries, and the harbor was eventually fronted by a small fort surrounded by a thick belt of prickly pear cactus.[53] Yet in spite of its size, St. Thomas saw plenty of swashbuckling action, most of it brought upon itself. In 1683 a small expedition sent by the governor of Nevis seized the English merchantman *Gideon*, captured by Capt. George

Bond of *Fortune's Adventure* in act of piracy. Governor Esmit pretended the ship was a wreck, and thus belonged to him by right of salvage, and "threatens vengeance against the English." Also in 1683 Capt. Charles Carlisle of the HMS *Francis* burned the pirate ship *La Trompeuse* in harbor:

> at 7 p.m. shoved off in the pinnace with nine men, towing another boat with five men more. The pirate discovered us before we reached them; we exchanged shots with them, and then boarded and took possession. The crew escaped. Fired her in several places, and lay on our oars close by, to see that none came off to put out the fire. When she blew up she kindled a great privateer that lay by, which burned to the water's edge.

The HMS *Francis* also burned a hundred-ton vessel filled with stores.[54]

The pirates vowed vengeance against Captain Carlisle. St. Thomas was a small colony, though, hardly able to make reprisals against England, France, or Spain, but perhaps her pirates were. Of all the assaults against St. Thomas between 1674 and 1688, only the attacks by the French in 1678 and 1688 were provoked by declared war. The colonists—that "nest of thieves that resorts to St. Thomas"—repulsed the attackers in 1678, but in 1688 the French sacked and burned the town.[55]

**N**orth of Cuba in the Bahamas was the island of New Providence, named after the original Providence Island settled with Puritan money and used as a base by English and Dutch pirates in the 1630s, later captured by the Spanish and retaken briefly by the English under Henry Morgan. New Providence was settled first by wreckers seeking Spanish silver from the sunken *Maravillas*, known as the "Old Wrack." Quickly the small island became a home for pirates as well. An English company raised money, established a small colony, and in 1677 appointed Robert Clarke as "Governor and Captain-General of the Bahamas," who in turn permitted reprisals against the Spanish and later granted unlawful commissions to English "privateers," some of whom attacked the Spanish in Florida. Governor Clarke, unable to forbear acting against the Spanish, was replaced by Governor Robert Lilburne, but too late. The Spanish grew weary of the depredations and, claiming reprisal for the French sack of Veracruz in 1683 and in spite of Governor Lilburne's supposed efforts to suppress piracy originating from New Providence, sent two hundred and fifty men (or one hundred and seventy in another account) under the command of Juan de Larco to attack New Providence in January 1684.[56]

Arriving at the small island of St. Andrews in two barcalongas (or piraguas, more likely) of forty and thirty oars, respectively, the Spaniards captured a sloop and used her crew of three as pilots. They sailed to New

Providence, waited overnight on the side of the island opposite the town, then attacked at dawn, catching most inhabitants in bed, and quickly dispatched with musket and cutlass those who were not. One hundred and twenty men attacked the town while fifty attacked vessels at anchor. A New England vessel of ten guns fled rather than fight, as did some of the residents, "about four hundred men that bear arms, and half as many women," having no appointed rally point. Governor Lilburne likewise fled through the backdoor of his house, unable, out of fear of being captured, to fire the warning gun out front, and hid in the woods with other residents. He made no effort to rally the populace and counterattack. Nonetheless, fourteen men on their own account did and drove "all the Spaniards before them," or at the very least killed one and wounded more, and according to one account would have driven the Spanish into the sea and retaken the plunder had they been fifty instead of fourteen. The Spanish killed few if any in the town and only three aboard the vessels they plundered, but many were carried away as prisoners to Havana, along with £14,000 "in plate and money" (£30,000 in another account) and a captured pink used to transport the booty. The Spanish pirates claimed to have a commission from Havana. Most survivors fled, many to South Carolina, others to the nearby island of Illa Terra (Eleuthera), vowing revenge: "Certainly these things will soon cause our mastiffs in the Indies to be let loose upon" the Spanish. In spite of the attack, two years later the island was settled again.[57]

Visitor and escaped, transported slave Dr. Henry Pitman provided a detailed description of the island eight months after its 1686 resettlement. New Providence consisted of a small town on the seashore and was protected by a small stockade fort. The inhabitants elected a governor and twelve men to serve as a council and make laws. Governor Thomas Bridges was a "very sober man, an Independent; and usually preached to the inhabitants every First Day of the week," first firing a cannon to give notice of his sermon. The inhabitants—pirates, wreckers, and self-proclaimed reformed pirates, among others— lived in fear of Spanish raids and armed the stockade with a cannon from an abandoned and burned pirate ship. Dr. Pitman suggested New Providence was no longer "a harbour for privateers, and a nest of robbers," but pirates and their goods continued to be received there, and most observers still considered its population to be "a kind of piratical and ungoverned people."[58]

$\mathcal{F}$or a brief period Nevis had a deserved reputation for supporting piracy. The center of English slave trade in the Windward Islands, Nevis was protected by seven forts, was constantly threatened by Carib Indians, and had a population of equal parts white and black. The colony also had a large Jewish population, yet was also known for its mistreatment of Quakers. Its capital, Charlestown, was as debauched as any port in the Caribbean. Sometimes called Mevis, it was "but a small island, yet one of the chief, . . . producing a great deal of sugar, ginger, and cotton wool."[59] In July 1686 Deputy Governor Sir James Russell renewed the governor's original commission to the pirate Captain Beare, in spite of official protests from a Royal Navy commander on a mission to suppress pirates, of whom Beare was one. Russell later granted Beare another commission for a Spanish prize, the *Soldada*, then sent him to St. Thomas to avoid capture by the Royal Navy. Beare, naturally, used his commission as a pretense to plunder the Spanish, and without doubt the deputy governor was complicit. The governor, Sir William Stapleton, pursued pirates in the past, including Captain Bond, but was in England at the time of Beare's renewed commission.[60]

The Province of Carolina was well known for supporting pirates, providing them not only a haven, but also a market for stolen goods. The notorious colony was known among privateers as Puerto Franco (French Port), owing either to the filibusters who consorted there, or the French attitude toward piracy, or both. In 1682 more than one hundred privateers were in Charleston, and a Spanish prize brought into the port by French and English pirates raised no eyebrows. Two months later the pirates "have allready spent most of it and are providing to be gone againe."[61] In Charleston the famous Grammont sold two hundred slaves taken at Veracruz in 1683, and the town provided both origin and refuge to Jacob Hall, an English captain present at the sack of Veracruz. In 1685 a "pirate full of plunder" sold its goods at Carolina, probably with the complicity of the government, and in 1687 a member of the government was accused of aiding pirates by provisioning the vessels and concealing stolen goods of pirates Chapman and Holloway. The pirates who rescued Dr. Pitman from Salt Tortuga were from Carolina. Captains Yanky and Jacob Evertson visited the colony in 1687, although they were not well received. To the north, pirates including Captain Wright used Accomac, Virginia, as a quiet respite, and even New England colonies such as Rhode Island and Massachusetts received known pirates and their goods. The reason for this support was simple: given the restrictions of the English Navigation Acts on trade, pirates brought much-needed goods and hard currency into local economies and governors' pockets, and it was difficult for a government across the sea to enforce its laws upon its colonies.[62]

The port of Willemstad on the island of Curaçao was not only the center of Dutch commerce in the New World, but also often a haven for sea rovers, or as the Dutch termed them, *zee-roovers*. During wartime it was a base for legitimate privateers (*kapres* or capers), Jan Erasmus Reyning being one of the best known. The Dutch, like the English, were a seagoing people, and "almost all among them are Seamen born, and like Frogs, can live both on Land and Water....They are in all manner *Aquatiles*, and therefore the Spaniards call them *Water Dogs*."[63] Willemstad, a haven for Dutch merchants and rovers in the Caribbean, had a good harbor, a strong fort, and a population that included Jewish merchants vital to the Spanish trade. Although the colony also produced sugar, wool, and hides, commerce with New Spain was its livelihood.[64] Even so, the Dutch had few qualms about receiving pirates and pirate goods, although they were circumspect in such dealings. They offered to buy sugar from pirates, for example, but advised the pirates to go to St. Thomas, and the governor of Curaçao would "send a Sloop with such Goods as [the pirates] wanted, and the Money to buy the Sugar."[65] In 1684 the governor of Curaçao not only refused to arrest the Spanish pirate Manuel Rodriguez, at anchor in port and certainly engaged in illicit trade, but later arrested and threatened to hang Captain Beare for capturing Rodriguez.[66] The Dutch had a reputation for valuing business above all else: "Jesus Christ is good," one of their proverbs said, "but trade is better."[67]

The Caribbean rovers also used "distant and secure creeks and holes" of the Caribbean for rendezvous, careening, provisioning, wood and water, and the occasional respite. Isle à Vache, the Isle of Pines, other Cuban isles, La Sound's Key, and many others served their purposes, as did the Bay of Campeche, the Bay of Honduras, and, usually, the Mosquito Coast.

$S$panish ports naturally supported Spanish pirates and privateers, Santiago de Cuba being one of the principal, given its location near the Windward Passage. Most other ports served similarly, including Veracruz, Havana, San Juan, and Santo Domingo.[68] Biscayers cruising from Spain brought their prizes into Cartagena and other great cities, and the Armada de Barlovento operated out of Veracruz, annually making its way through the Caribbean as well as escorting the New Spain fleet from Veracruz to Havana.

The sea rovers of the New World were not there primarily to settle and civilize colonies for the nations of their birth, even by acts of piracy. They sought plunder and did so bound to others by this common purpose. Although they were generally loyal to their nativity, they were more loyal to their comrades. Although they believed in honor and courage in battle, they did not engage in battle without a good reason—and that reason was plunder.

One example among many demonstrated this principal in action. Near the new city of Panama in 1680 (the original burned down during Henry Morgan's brief occupation), Capt. Richard Sawkins commanded buccaneers contemplating an attack on this bastion of the South Sea. In 1677 he captured the bishop of Santa Marta when buccaneers sacked the city, taking him hostage to Jamaica; in 1680 the same bishop was bishop of Panama. Via a Spanish merchant, Captain Sawkins sent the bishop two loaves of sugar in observation of their time together. Returning the compliment, the governor of Panama sent a gold ring, which Captain Sawkins dutifully put on his finger, and a letter. In one account written by a member of the expedition, the letter asked by what commission the men threatened Panama, for the governor wished to know to whom to make his complaint. Sawkins replied that "[we] will bring our commissions on the muzzles of our guns, at which time he should read them as plain as the flame of gun-powder could make them." A point well taken, indeed: the buccaneers had force of arms on their side. The cumbersome processes of law and diplomacy availed nothing in the actual moment of battle, for neither could stop a bullet in flight. But more illuminating was the remainder of the letter, as described by another buccaneer. The governor requested they "meete him on shoare with a hundred men to try their manhoods against one hundred of them." Captain Sawkins agreed, provided the Spaniards brought one hundred thousand pieces-of-eight with them, and then they would "fight him for the money, or Elce resolved to die in that Place." The governor wisely agreed to no such foolishness. Neither were buccaneers' fools. Although their self-image derived from their independence, fighting ability, and desperate courage, they fought only for profit or in self-defense. They fought duels solely for the sake of honor, but never battles.[69]

$I$n 1676 such battles on land and sea were on the rise, although often in consort with French or Dutch naval operations. The Dutch, under Jacob Binkes, captured Cayenne and Marie Galante from the French but were repulsed at St. Martin and lost three vessels near Nevis. Jan Erasmus Reyning was with Binkes, under a Dutch commission. The French, under d'Estrées, recaptured Cayenne from the Dutch, then sailed to Martinique. Meanwhile, Binkes recruited Carib Indians from St. Vincent and Dominica for an attack on St. Croix. The Spanish sacked the small but intrusive French colony at Samana. Captain Bennet was killed in action while attacking the "Honduras ship." Captains Wright and Lane, in command of several hundred pirates and Native Americans, sacked Segovia in Nicaragua. The French and English pirates, among them Bartholomew Sharp, were later badly defeated by the Spanish in Costa Rica. Rebellion still flourished in the New World: in Virginia, Nathaniel Bacon led a rebellion of discontented frontier farmers and burned Jamestown, but his reign was brief. Martin de Melgar of Havana attempted to salvage the silver treasure of the galleon *Nuestra Señora de las Maravillas*, part of the treasure fleet lost in 1656 on Los Mimbres in the Bahamas, near New Providence. Buccaneers, including William Dampier, sacked Alvarado after a long fight and were almost captured by Spanish armadillas shortly afterward.[70] Jacques Nepveu, sieur de Pouançay and nephew of Governor d'Ogeron, who built Hispaniola into a colony, was named governor of "Tortuga and the Coast of San Domingue," and was a strong supporter of *la course* (privateering)—of the "Golden Dreams" these rovers sought, or the capture of the rich produce of the great plantations and mines of the Spanish Main.

# 6 Muscovado, Indigo, and Urcas,

## Not to Mention Sweet Virginia

*A*n *urca*, often as large as seven hundred or eight hundred tons, sails annually from Spain to Trujllo and Puerto Cavallos in the Gulf of Honduras. Usually a registry ship (*navío de registro*, a vessel licensed to sail independently of the treasure fleet), in some years she is part of the Flota de Nueva España. She is always accompanied by a small frigate, the patache. The English refer to the "Honduras ship" as a *Spanish hulk*, the French as a *hourque*. In English, *hulk* originally described a large, unwieldy cargo vessel, but here it described an urca, a type of merchantman called a *flute* by the English, French, and Dutch: a flat-bottomed, round-bellied, pink-sterned cargo ship, ideal for lading and unlading large cargos in relatively shallow waters. The appellation is both descriptive and nominal, for the hulk, or *hourcre*, is not merely a great urca, but is also the usual term for the Honduras ship. The hulk and its patache spend weeks or even months unlading goods from Spain, then lading the produce of Honduras and Guatemala, much of it carried to Puerto Cavallos from bodegas (warehouses) in the Bahía de Amatique. Goods flow down Lake Izabal and are stored in bodegas where the lake meets the Río Dulce (where the small Castillo San Felipe de Lara stands to defend against pirates), and then the goods travel by sea or land to Puerto Cavallos. From 1603 to 1670 the Honduras ships lade at nearby St. Tomás de Castilla in Amatique Bay, called by buccaneers the "Gulph of Matique."* Afterward they

---

*All quotations have been reprinted with their original spelling and punctuation.

73

lade at Trujillo and Cavallos. The hulk is vital to this relatively isolated local economy and provides important goods to Spain. She is thus also a popular target of pirates and privateers.[1]

Urcas were an easy target to locate. Given the Caribbean sea rovers' intelligence of the Spanish Main, as well as their constant collecting and refining thereof, they were well acquainted with the Honduras ship. They knew approximately when she arrived, how long she took to unlade and lade, and confirmed their intelligence with interrogations of Spanish merchants and prisoners (whose various information they compared), which should have made the capture and plunder of the urca easy. The pirates needed only to wait at Roatan Island or among the Sapodilla Cays before seizing the fully laden ships. But few great tasks were ever as easy as they seemed. Some rovers new to the trade grumbled and whined when they discovered that pieces-of-eight were not "gathered as easily as pears from a tree," and found themselves mocked by veterans who would rather "perish than return without silver."[2]

The problem with the urca was foremost one of scale. The Honduras ship was usually very large and capable of effective broadsides and defense from closed quarters. She typically had a substantial number of crew, soldiers, and male passengers aboard to handle arms. If attacked she would withdraw her company within board behind barricaded bulkheads and batter away at her attackers, defying them to board and die. John Smith described the fighting aboard a ship defended by closed quarters, with boarding net, powder chests, loopholes, and cannon turned to fire inboard, as the most dangerous of all fights:

> I confess, the charging upon Trenches, and the entrances of a Breach in a Rampire [rampart], are Attempts as desperate as man would think could be performed, but he that hath tried himself as oft in the entring a resting Ship as I have done both them and the other, he would surely confess there is no such dangerous Service ashore, as a resolved resolute Fight at Sea.[3]

In open waters, where the hulk could maneuver with ease, the use of closed quarters was a particularly effective tactic, for it permitted the use of "great guns" while protecting the crew. If the pirates approached as if to board, the defenders briefly sallied on deck and hurled grenades and firepots at the attackers, then retreated again to closed quarters if the pirates managed to board. Buccaneers and filibusters seldom had a ship of sufficient force to engage large, well-armed, well-manned ships conventionally, but this was seldom their tactic anyway, both for means of economy and circumstance. Conventional engagements of broadsides only served to damage both predator and prey, and if the damage was extensive, left the former vulnerable to capture and the latter to recapture should a Spanish armadilla suddenly appear, ready and willing to fight on equal or superior terms. But in the case of the hulk, as in the case of many Spanish ships bearing wealth, a conventional sea fight was often the only option.

The crew of the Honduras ship knew that her annual timing and solitary course left her vulnerable—there were never more than two Honduras ships in consort, and one of them was small—and so crew members were prepared to speak to the Caribbean pirates in the only language they understood. But the rovers knew the urca's weaknesses. Besides knowing her location, they knew that if she was fully laden, her lower tier of guns might be useless on the open sea because they were too close to the waterline. To open the lower gun ports at sea risked the ship. They knew her decks might be so lumbered with cargo that she could not bring all of her cannon to bear. They also knew that if attacked at anchor she could not easily maneuver her great guns, and the crew had to haul the ship around on a "spring" (a cable that ran astern and attached to the anchor cable) to do so. Rovers had experience with ships in such circumstances, although they were not immune to risk. And often the Spaniards were prepared for them.

In 1676 Capt. John Bennet, an Englishman in consort with a vessel almost certainly flying French colors, bearing a French commission, and with a largely French crew, attacked the Honduras ship. Captain Bennet was an old hand at buccaneering: he sailed the fifteen-ton *Virgin Queen* on Morgan's expedition to Panama, and commanded a brigantine that captured the *Buen Jesus de las Almas* near Saint Domingue, among whose booty were 46,471 pieces-of-eight. He sought a similar prospect with the urca. To Honduras the Spanish hulk carried iron, steel, paper, wine, fine silk and other cloth, saffron, and oil, among other cargo. But Bennet and his crew were after the cargo she intended to carry to Spain: indigo, cochineal, and silver. Indigo and cochineal were dyes, blue and scarlet, respectively, the latter made from an insect that fed on the nopal prickly pear cactus. The hulk also carried cowhides, cacao, sarsaparilla (a vine whose bitter root had various medical uses, not to be confused with the sassafras or "sasparilla" tree of North America), jalap (a tuber with purgative or cathartic properties), and mechoacan (a variety of jalap). Therefore, pirates preferred to wait until the ship was laded for her return voyage.[4]

*F*or the most part ships did not carry commodities vital to sustain life from the New World to Europe in their bloated bellies—and the flute, or urca, certainly looked like a bloated belly. Rather, luxuries filled the damp wooden holds. Sugar, tobacco, and dyes drove the Western economy. Only silver used as a means of exchange might be described as a commodity, not a luxury, at least in terms of colonial goods shipped to the Old World. Some vital stores were shipped to Europe to support common needs—drugs, dried cod, and naval stores such as timber and pine tar, for example—but such shipments paled in comparison to the "vital luxuries."

The New World was a colonial world, a rural, agricultural engine intended solely to drive great European powers. The colonies were not an expansion of the state itself, but of the state's power, a critical distinction that one day led to revolution and the creation of new, independent states. The plantation was the primary means of production in the New World, and the process was almost industrial, relying on forced labor and a high degree of organization. For example, the cochineal insect was cultivated primarily on farms of cacti, producing the *grana fina* dye. Wild cochineal produced a weaker, less brilliant dye.[5] Many plantations were large, as might be expected, to maximize production. Jamaica had two hundred and forty-five sugar plantations, and a typical plantation could produce £1,000 per year, given an initial outlay of £5,000 and a thousand acres of land to cultivate.[6] In 1675 Jamaica was said to have ninety thousand acres under cultivation and thirty thousand persons, free and slave, working on the plantations, although similar numbers were provided in 1689 for the island's population: five thousand whites and twenty-five thousand slaves.[7] Even Jesuits and other priests operated sugar plantations, whose labor was provided by African slaves.[8] Further, nearly everyone in the New World was involved in plantations in some way, great or small. The only significant exceptions were Native American tribes, not yet destroyed, that remained free from the yoke of European invaders. The wealth of many merchants and planters was astounding. The marquis de Villette, visiting Cartagena in 1680, described a meal with a Cartagena "bourgeois." The table was set for twenty-two guests and the place settings were solid gold. The Spanish host owned two thousand slaves.[9]

However, most plantations were small and many planters eked out an existence without servants or slaves. In the early eighteenth century Captain Uring described the life of a small planter and his "middle-aged cleanly looking housewifely Woman" in Virginia:

> [T]hey were poor People, their House was build with Clap-boards, and the Chimney daubed within Side with Clay, to prevent it taking Fire; it consisted of one Room and a Closet; they had in the Room a Bed for themselves and two or three Chairs, and an old leathern Couch. . . . The Closet was made use of for their Kitchen Furniture, which consisted of an Iron Pot, a Frying-Pan, Two or Three earthen Dishes, Three or Four Pewter Plates, and as many Spoons.

The couple cultivated tobacco for trade and had an orchard and garden for food. They lived primarily on cornbread, kidney beans, and beef or pork. They baked their cornbread in a greased iron frying pan, as many people in the southern United States still do today.[10]

*F*or the English, and soon the French, sugar became the most significant crop. It was the principal Barbadian export and by the 1680s was the principle Jamaican export. To make sugar, sugar cane was crushed to remove the juice, and then the juice was boiled until it thickened, poured into wooden containers, and allowed to dry into the characteristic loaves of sugar. Molasses drained off as the loaves dried and was often boiled and distilled, along with the molasses skimmed off the surface of the boiling juice and the "Washings of the Boilers and Pots," into rum. Sugar loaves, when first dry, were a rich dark brown and the sugar tasted like molasses. They were referred to as *muscovado* or "brown sugar" (but bore no resemblance to modern brown sugar). Nine pounds of cane juice rendered one pound of sugar and one pound of molasses. If the loaves were further refined, the sugar was referred to as *clayed*, or white, sugar. The loaves were packed in large barrels, stored in "Rapp-Houses" in Jamaica, loaded onto sugar droghers—small sloops and other vessels—and transported to Port Royal.[11]

At Carolina the English produced "Rice, Pitch, Tar, Turpentine, and Skins," and at Virginia they traded hides, rice, pitch, tar, pork, Indian corn, and most important, tobacco.[12] Originally two varieties of tobacco were grown, sweetscented and Oronoco, the former mild, the latter strong. Planters germinated the seeds in seedbeds, transplanted the seedlings to the field, topped the plants after a month or so, and eventually cut the plants off at the base and left them to wilt in the field. The tobacco was hung in open-air buildings to cure, tied into "hands" after curing, packed in hogsheads, and shipped. Hogsheads of tobacco weighed between four hundred and eight hundred pounds.[13] The name "Sweet Virginia" notwithstanding, the tobacco "reputed the best in the World" came from Verina, near the town of Cumaná on the coast of Venezuela.[14] Tobacco from Gibraltar, called *Tabaco de Sacerdotes* (Priests' Tobacco) was also well-known.[15] Although recognized by many as a noxious and unhealthy habit that led to an early death not only of the smoker but also of those nearby, children especially—"tis a most Vile Abuse of Tobacco, for People by the Daily Smoking thereof, to Hurt themselves, and throw away their Precious Hours, and make a Chimney, or a Dunghill, of the Brain"— tobacco (smoked in pipes or cigars, chewed, or snorted as snuff) was extraordinarily popular owing to the stimulating, soothing, and addictive properties of nicotine, and thus tobacco made men rich. Moderation was recommended, but the advice was difficult to heed.[16]

Besides sugar and tobacco, all European nations in the Caribbean produced indigo and cotton. Indigo dye was made by cutting the indigo plant in short lengths, tying the cuttings into fagots, and letting them rot in cisterns filled with water. As the plants rotted, the entire mess was stirred several times. When the plants were completely rotted, the stalks were removed and the cisterns drained, leaving a mass that was molded into bricks of dye. The process of preparing cotton was simpler but labor intensive; it was picked by hand and put into a "sort of little Engines made with such artifice, that by the turning of a wheel, whereby they are put into motion, the Cotton falls on the one side, and the seed on the other." Workers then bagged the cotton for shipment.[17]

The cacao tree provided chocolate, an extraordinary food consumed passionately in a variety fashions by Spaniards. The fruit, or cod, was large and oblong, roughly three to five inches in diameter and six to twelve inches long; red when ripe; and grew directly from the trunk of the tree. Cacao was harvested both in the wild and on plantations twice a year. After harvesting, workers placed the cods in piles to sweat, then later opened them; removed the nuts, ranging from twenty to one hundred; and dried them in the sun. Planters in Jamaica grew cacao on "Cacao-walks" of five hundred to one thousand trees. Protection for the trees during the first two or three years of growth was provided by plantain trees or other trees, called by the Spanish *madres del cacao* (mothers of cacao), which were cut down when the cacao trees no longer needed their shelter. So valuable was cacao that "Cacao-Nuts are used as Money in the Bay of Campeachy."[18]

**M**ines were another great source of New World wealth. At the Isthmus of Darien were gold mines, and in Mexico and Peru were silver mines. Mercury—a deadly metal—was also mined and brought to Spanish colonies in *azogues*, or mercury ships, because it was vital to the process of refining silver. Miners and ore processors led a dangerous life. Mercury ore, for example, was mined, and the mercury was extracted from ore by placing it in a building with a perforated floor and a brass container beneath each hole. Firewood was stacked on the ore and ignited; the mercury melted and flowed into the containers, hardly a safe environment. Silver was mined by men who dug into mountains, using ladders for access and wooden supports to keep the walls and ceilings from caving in. Some mines were enormous—seven hundred Native Americans worked the Potosí mine. The process of extracting the ore was probably even more dangerous than mining it. Smelting required scarce timber, so an amalgamation process was used instead. Silver ore was pulverized; then mixed with water, salt or copper pyrites, and mercury; and stirred with shovels. Water was allowed to flow through the mixture and "wash" it; the silver and mercury settled to the bottom. Both were then scooped out with shovels by workers in bare feet, and placed in sacks so that the mercury drained off. In Mexico the process was called *patio*, for a stone floor was used, while in Peru stone tanks were used.[19]

Other trades were vital to the survival of the New World colonies, as well as to the health and wealth of Old World nations: fishing, hunting, ranching, farming, and shipbuilding. The variety of goods and commodities ferried from the New World to the old was staggering: hides and furs, dyes and dyewoods, tobacco, tortoiseshell, beeswax, cacao, cotton, sugar, ginger, achiote, vanilla, allspice, cod, naval stores, drugs, and of course, gems, pearls, silver, and gold. The list does not include goods and commodities produced for local use or consumption, foodstuffs especially. The goods waited to be taken by those willing to put forth the appropriate enterprise, courage, and effort—not to mention the ability to put aside any scruples. (See also appendix H.)

*W*e return to Captain Bennet and his attack on the Spanish hulk, filled, he hoped, with the riches of New Spain. To fight the ship at anchor was ideal, but he risked capturing her before the cargo was laded or, worse, unladed and carried away for fear of attack. To fight her at sea ensured the cargo was aboard, but also gave her room to maneuver. In all cases the action was difficult, for, beyond the difficulties associated with attacking a large, well-armed ship, some seventeenth-century texts described the flute as characteristically difficult to board.[20] The shape of its hull—with its narrow upper deck, bulging hull beneath, and severe tumblehome—kept the boarding vessel farther away than usual because the distance between the gunwales of an urca, or flute, and another ship "board and board" was greater than usual. In other words, boarders had a greater distance to leap from one ship to the other. For smaller vessels, the urca's height above the water was also a problem, because boarders could not leap directly from the forecastle into the waist, the preferred means of boarding. Attackers aboard a small vessel most likely boarded at the main chains, hauling themselves up and then aboard. However, not all flutes of the period displayed the characteristic hull shape, at least not to such an extreme. Many had wider upper decks than the flutes built for trade in the Baltic. However, a well-armed, well-manned flute of classic shape could indeed force attackers into a duel of great guns and broadsides, for boarding could be too dangerous until the defenders were sufficiently battered.[21]

The buccaneer's preferred method of fighting at sea was to engage at half-musket shot (from a distance of one hundred to one hundred fifty yards) or closer if only small arms were used. They used small arms to clear the decks and force gun ports closed, then came alongside and threw grapnels into the shrouds and onto the rails, and threw grenades and stinkpots onto the decks to clear them of men, destroy powder chests or cut their fuses, and create a fog of smoke in which to board. The attackers boarded, cut any remaining fuses to powder chests, then attempted to defeat the closed quarters, usually by hacking holes into the deck with boarding axes (the activity from which the boarding ax surely took its name) and throwing grenades and stinkpots into the breaches. Typically, rovers with a large crew were able to suppress the prey's fire, then quickly board, but if boarding was dangerous, they had no choice but to batter the ship with cannon fire. There are records of long, brutal engagements between flutes and frigate-built privateers or men-of-war. For example, the epic fights between the HMS *Chester* and the French flute *Loire* (one of whose passengers was Father Labat), and the moonlight battle between the flute *Profond*, commanded by the famous Duguay-Trouin, and a Swedish man-of-war that mistook the *Profond* for a Turkish pirate both lasted for hours.[22]

Desperate battles between Caribbean pirates and the "hulke" were common and often occurred at anchor. Exquemelin provided an excellent account of one such battle in 1667. Sailing the *Saint-Jean*, a flute captured at Maracaibo, with twenty-two guns (twenty-six in one account) and three hundred men, and in consort with a settee with a crew of about sixty, the pirate L'Ollonois attacked the hulk while four other small vessels sought the patache. However, the ship had been warned of the pirates and was prepared with forty-two guns (fifty-six in another account) and grenades, firepots, torches, and *saucissons* (various explosives and incendiaries) placed at the forecastle, quarterdeck, and poop. The battle lasted all day; the sixty or so Spaniards were heavily outnumbered but never flagged. "[T]he Spaniards defended themselves so well, as they forced the pirates to retire; but the smoke of the powder continuing thick, as a dark fog or mist, with four canoes well manned, they boarded the ship with great agility, and forced the Spaniards to surrender." Yet the action was not worth the courage and blood expended on either side: the ship was carrying only one hundred tons of iron ballast, twenty thousand reams of paper, and olive oil and bagatelles. Worse, the Spanish kept the patache upriver (probably the Río Dulce), out of the hands of the filibusters. Had L'Ollonois captured the hulk when she first arrived, her value might have been a million pieces-of-eight, and perhaps even more when laded for the return voyage.[23]

In 1683 Captain Van Horn, in his stout, well-armed *Saint Nicolas*, which had forty guns and two hundred and eighty filibusters, and in consort with a corvette commanded by Philippe Gombert de la Fleur, boarded the hulk *Nuestra Señora de Consolación*, which had forty-four guns and four hundred men at anchor, and then boarded her patache, the *Nuestra Señora de Regla*, which had half the hulk's strength. This action, which was not much of a fight, set up an eventual, even epic, confrontation with Captain Laurens, as discussed in chapter 19, that ultimately failed in its design: neither ship was yet laded with the cargo of indigo, cochineal, and silver the pirates sought, except for two thousand pounds of the blue dye. Van Horn had been unwisely precipitous.[24]

In late 1687 or early 1688, Captains Yanky and Jacob Evertson attacked a "hulke" in Puerto Cavallos. Yanky commanded a Dutch-built ship of forty guns, probably *La Fortune*, with a crew of sixty to one hundred men, mostly English, and Evertson commanded a "fine barque" of ten guns, sixteen patereroes, and fifty men. The battle in the bay lasted for eight hours until the rich urca finally struck her colors. Yanky's ship was in poor condition, and had he not captured the urca he might soon have been without a vessel at all.[25]

Attacking a hulk at sea usually guaranteed that her cargo was aboard, but made the attack difficult, as noted, and even a stout privateer or man-of-war could find itself in a desperate fight when engaged with a large, well-armed hourque. In 1696 the French *Gaillard* engaged *la Ourque* at sea seventeen leagues from Havana, broadside to broadside. The fight lasted four or five hours before the Spanish ship was defeated. Spanish losses were eighty killed and thirty wounded out of two hundred and sixty. French losses were "some" killed and thirty wounded. Even with a stout ship, the fight against a hulk could be brutal on both sides.[26]

At sea, in the Gulf of Mexico, Bennet and his consort also fought a hulk. In size and armament Bennet's vessels were no match for the large Spanish ship. It was smart to batter the great hulk first, but Bennet's small guns would have done little damage to the Spaniard's large, thick hull. Unfortunately, the details of Bennet's fight are lost, but not the outcome: "Two French vessels lately well beaten by a Spanish hulk in the Gulf of Mexico with the loss of 80 men, Captain Bennet killed in the engagement."[27] Doubtless, the hulk's great guns battered the smaller vessels mercilessly. Any of Bennet's Frenchmen who managed to board faced a deadly crossfire of ball, fire, and metal scrap, yet the distinguishing characteristic of the buccaneer and filibuster was their willingness to engage heavily defended prey at sea and ashore, if the risk was worth the outcome. They were willing to risk their lives on highly profitable ventures whose outcomes were not at all certain. For Bennet, however, the risk was greater than the means. He and his crew lost a prize cargo, and he and many others lost their lives. Yet Bennet was not the only man who lived a life of toil and danger—and unlike many other men, when successful, pirates shared in the spoils of their labor. Not all people in the New World enjoyed equality in the rewards of labor: one valuable cargo, exceedingly common to all colonies and highly sought by the Caribbean rovers, was missing from, or found only in small numbers on, the hulk: slaves, whose forced labor provided the muscle behind the plantation economy that produced the goods pirates stole.

# 7 Slaves, Monopolies, and Maroons:
## Africa on the Main

*N*ear Cartagena in 1677 a Scottish buccaneer captures the Dutch ship *Sun* loaded with slaves intended for trade with New World Spaniards, and kills the captain and several of the crew in the process. The cargo is valuable—nations go to war over the slave trade, for the economies of the New World have come to rely overwhelmingly on slave labor to produce the luxuries that drive the Old World economies.[1] Jamaica, for example, expects the Royal Africa Company to deliver five thousand slaves in 1684 and three thousand per year afterward.[2]

In theory, Capt. James Browne's Dutch prize is legitimate. He has a French commission, and France is at war with Holland. However, Browne's commission was signed by Governor d'Ogeron, who died in France two years earlier. Strictly speaking, then, the commission is invalid, and technically the capture of the Dutch ship is an act of piracy, but far more egregious acts are commonly overlooked. Captain Browne's circumstance not only raises the issue of the tenuous distinction between privateering and piracy—the twain are often difficult to differentiate—but also of the fragile balance between politics and profit. Browne lands the one hundred and fifty slaves at Jamaica, where willing buyers can easily be found. However, these slaves are designated for Spain, and England now not only sees Spain as a trading partner, illicit or otherwise, but also has a great stake in providing slaves to Spain. Now that Browne has, in an act of piracy obscured by an expired French commission, taken Spanish slaves from the Dutch and landed them on English territory, Spain may see this as nothing more than Jamaica's deliberate support of piracy. Thus Jamaican governor Vaughan must act decisively, for he intends to maintain good relations with Spain and also to vigorously suppress piracy. Yet in all of this posturing and wrangling, no one thinks at all of the human beings who have been reduced to mere property as slaves.[3]

That slaves were mere property was an accepted fact in this period. Indeed, a line from Henry Morgan's official instructions for his attack on Panama demonstrated exactly how slaves were viewed:

> [If] the Spaniards and Slaves are deaf to your proposals, you are then with all Expedition, to destroy or burn all Habitations, and leave it as a wilderness, putting the Men-Slaves to the sword and making the Women-Slaves Prisoners to be brought hither, and sold for account of your Fleet and Army.*

The next article, however, made it clear that Morgan was to act humanely toward persons, as opposed to mere property: "as our custom is to exceed in Civility and Humanity, endeavouring by all means to make all sorts of People sensible of your Moderation and good Nature, and your inaptitude and loathness to spill the blood of man."[4] Slaves, apparently, were not *men*, but property and could be destroyed to inconvenience the Spanish. Freemen could also be slaughtered with little thought of their humanity, but only after exhausting the conqueror's "good nature" and "loathness to spill . . . blood."[5] The view was highly hypocritical and reflected accepted rationalizations for treating people as property, a view many knew to be entirely contrary to Christian values or any fundamental sense of morality. For example, a 1685 entry in John Evelyn's diary noted that King James II wished that all slaves "in the Plantations" be baptized. Slave masters protested, "out of a mistaken opinion that they would be *ipso facto* free" if baptized.[6] Likewise in Barbados in 1676, due to "the Industry of the Quakers [in converting slaves]," the conversion of black slaves was forbidden for fear that baptism, "it was pretended, hazarded the Safety of the Island."[7] In other words, owners were well aware that slavery was an enormity, or at least wondered silently if the Christian God judged them harshly for owning slaves. They justified the condition of slavery by diminishing Africans as sub-Christian or sub-human, or both, and feared anything that might elevate them from their status, for under any reasonable moral code such elevation would render them free and even equal. The European subjugation of races

---

*All quotations have been reprinted with their original spelling and punctuation.

into slavery was a purely economic decision, overriding humanitarian values. Race was not the reason, but the excuse.

So slavery continued, with little protest with anyone, although occasionally some did speak out against the practice or attempted to rouse slaves to action. In Barbados in 1683, after the execution of a slave, one letter writer noted that "some foolish mischievous persons have scattered about [a] paper [intending to incite slaves] . . . forgetting that negroes are not able to read." The writer hoped that the authors of the paper were discovered and punished.[8] Novelist, playwright, poet, and spy Aphra Behn praised African slaves in her novel *Oroonoko*, published in 1688. Having lived in Surinam (and having led a "marginal" existence herself both as writer and imprisoned debtor), she described Oroonoko, her fictional enslaved African prince, as having "the best Grace in the World."[9] But to the white planter, blacks were not examples of virtue or grace, except in how they served their masters, and slave uprisings were a threat not only to life and limb, but also to economic prosperity.

*E*ach nation governed its own slave trade. Factories—forts and holding pens often garrisoned by company soldiers—on the African coast were vital, as were ships and crews to transport slaves. In England the Royal African Company held the slave monopoly, but interlopers (unlawful traders on a monopolist's territory) were common. Planters bought from anyone they could, for they simply wanted slaves at the best price. The French slave trade was monopolized by one of several successive *Sénégal* companies until 1684 when the company shared the trade with the *Compagnie de Guinée*. For the enormous number of slaves necessary to sustain its New World empire, Spain issued a monopoly privilege or contract called the asiento, sometimes referred to by the English as the Grand Assiento. Between 1674 and 1688 the asiento changed hands three times, and Dutch money and ships were behind much of the Spanish slave trade. Denmark and Brandenburg also entered the slave trade during this period.[10] All sold slaves to the Spanish colonies, and much English official correspondence of the period was devoted to the prospect of supplying the Spanish colonies with slaves, notwithstanding that often their "own planters are so in want of slaves that the last ship had more buyers than negroes."[11] In the 1680s, Spanish vessels even began to call at Jamaica for slaves.[12]

The process of trading slaves on the African coast is well known but bears repeating. Company ships traded directly with company factories, but interlopers had to be more circumspect. Labat described four categories of African slaves bought by Europeans: criminals whose death sentences had been commuted to banishment, prisoners of tribal wars, slaves owned by private parties, and those stolen solely for the purpose of being sold to Europeans. The last class made up the majority by far.[13] Another source of slaves were blacks, mulattoes, Native Americans, and mestizos, slave and free, captured and carried by privateers or pirates into other colonies, although pirates preferred to sell Spanish slaves back to the Spanish, given their inclination to rebel and escape.[14]

Africans themselves played an important role in supplying slaves, and most slaves were originally captured and imprisoned not by Europeans, but by Africans who sold them to white traders, who in turn promoted the capture and sale of Africans by Africans. However, were Africans not a critical part of the process, Europeans almost certainly would have taken slaves by force of arms. Slave traders and their local factories negotiated for slaves with *caboceers* (in general, village headmen; here, African slave traders or captains of slaves), providing gifts and bribes and bartering with "green Purpits [a type of cloth], Pewter Pots and Basons, small Knives, Guns and Powder," and also with brass pans, beads, iron bars, copper armlets, various liquor, old sheets, other fabric, casks of tallow, and miscellaneous small items such as mirrors. Often slavers also traded for gold dust, "elephant teeth," monkeys, and parrots. Slaves were inspected by the ship's surgeon before purchase, then ferried aboard canoes to the slave ship at anchor, where they were crammed tightly within and shackled. According to John Barbot, in 1698 a ship of one hundred tons carried as many as two hundred and twelve slaves (one hundred and two men, fifty-three women, forty-three boys, and fourteen girls), an incredible, unconscionable number on top of an already unconscionable trade. Slaves were usually fed with yams, and also with beans and Indian corn. Disease spread easily in the damp, overcrowded, festering conditions, and at times as many as one-half to two-thirds of the cargo of slaves died during the voyage. The slaver's crew, larger than the average merchantman's in order to prevent or quell uprisings, was armed and kept a constant watch over its cargo. A few slaves came from India as well: Dampier reported a New York slaver that arrived at the Coromandel Coast of India in 1689, seeking slaves taken prisoner in local wars.[15]

Once in the colonies, slaves were often given European names, for convenience and probably as well to acculturate—to alienate them from their native culture—the new arrivals. Examples of men's names from a 1696 English journal include Peter, London, Jack, Cesar, and Cajoe, and women's names included Hagar, Sarah, Bella, Susanna, and Quensa.[16] Spanish slave names were typically Spanish, as might be expected: Francisco, Chepillo, Hernando, Silvester, Santiago, and Beasero, for example.[17] Slave life was harsh, although plantation slaves were worse off than those who served in houses or in other capacities. In Cuba, "all the labour falls upon the *Blacks*," and in Peru, "they send the *Black* women to be got with child like cows, and if they prove barren they sell them."[18] Annual mortality among English plantation slaves was estimated at 10 percent.[19] Labat noted that among English slaves at Barbados the "overseers get every ounce of work out of them, beat them without mercy for the least fault, and appear to care far less for the life of a negro than for a horse," although the French treated their slaves no better. On the other hand, Labat also noted that "provided that they have plenty of children, work hard, and do not get ill, their masters are quite satisfied and ask no more of them"—but then, what more could their masters ask?[20]

$\mathcal{T}$he French *Code Noir* (Black Code), signed into law by Louis XIV in 1685 and enacted in Saint Domingue in 1687, provided slight legal protection for slaves. They required the consent of their masters before being allowed to marry, but could not be forced to marry. Masters had to furnish a minimum amount of cloth for clothing and a minimum ration of food (two and a half pots of cassava flour or three cassava roots of at least two and a half pounds each, or "equivalent things," plus two pounds of salt beef or three pounds of fish per week), and could not substitute rations with a day in which slaves worked for their own ends, to avoid providing the mandatory ration.[21] This last provision, however, was not always enforced, for Labat wrote of slave owners on Saint Domingue in 1701 feeding their slaves exclusively on sweet potatoes (which they dug themselves), and leaving them to their own devices to provide any other food.[22] Doubtless such practices existed before 1701. But even with the basic protections of the Code Noir, slavery remained slavery. Punishment against white masters for abuse of their slaves was rare, but not unknown. In 1670, for example, authorities relieved a French militia lieutenant of his office for mutilating his slaves and for "vexing" (abusing) his wife.[23] One suspects, however, that the loss of office did not prevent further mutilation and abuse.

Such abuse was common, and there can be no argument that the discipline and punishment of slaves were anything other than unconscionably cruel and often horrific. Labat rationalized the punishments, however extreme, as being necessary to "make the slaves fear and respect their masters, who would otherwise become the victims of their fury."[24] Slaves were whipped for slightest offense. A slave on Martinique who killed a white man's *bouriquet* (a small ass, or ass's colt) had "the leg cut" (was hamstrung) publicly at the gibbet as an example to others.[25] Slaves who ran away and were captured and returned to their owners could likewise be hamstrung.[26] Under the Code Noir, slaves could be whipped for carrying weapons, even a stick, except as authorized by their masters for hunting. Slaves from different plantations who gathered together, even for a wedding, could be whipped and then branded with the fleur-de-lis. A slave who struck his master, mistress, or their child in the face, or drew blood, was punished with death. A runaway slave captured after one month or more had his or her ears cut off and was branded with the fleur-de-lis on one shoulder. If the slave ran away again for more than a month, he or she was hamstrung and branded on the other shoulder. The penalty for the third such offense was death.[27] In Antigua in 1684 the government assembly proposed a reward of five hundred pounds of sugar for every runaway slave brought in alive, and two hundred pounds apiece for those brought in dead.[28]

Even a hint of rebellion brought terrible consequences. In Barbados in 1683, the rowdy behavior of several "bold insolent blacks" frightened local whites into believing that a slave uprising was in progress. An investigation revealed no such rebellion, and the blacks who caused the scare were "well whipped as an example." But one old slave warned his mistress that "some Christians, who were beating negroes, ere long would serve the Christians so." The old man was arrested, tried, sentenced, and burned alive.[29]

*B*ut slaves did rebel, and often successfully, enough so that in Jamaica there were at least two colonies of Maroons (runaway slaves, from the Spanish *cimarrones*, meaning "untamed")—the "Windward Negroes" in the Blue Mountains in the east and the "Cave Negroes" or "Leeward Maroons" in the cockpit country to the west.[30] By one estimate, there were fifteen hundred Maroons in Jamaica when the English captured the island from the Spanish in 1655. Between 1674 and 1688 in Jamaica there were at least four significant slave uprisings and more minor ones, as well as those plotted but never carried out, caught or betrayed in the planning stage.[31] Edward Barlow, writing of his voyage to Jamaica in 1678, described one of these, an uprising on Captain Duck's plantation. Eighty slaves rebelled, leaving the owner for dead and killing his wife and two other women. They took what arms they found, then attempted to rally slaves on other plantations to the cause, but failed—other slaves did not follow their lead. The English from surrounding plantations pursued the rebel slaves. Some they captured and put to death by fire, decapitation, or dismemberment, but many escaped to freedom, including the ringleader, Captain Duck's waiting man, who lived "a long time afterward in the woods."[32]

At Port-de-Paix on Saint Domingue lived a former slave named Padrejan (Padre Jean, probably originally Padre Juan), who had killed his Spanish master and fled to Tortuga out of fear of retribution. Granted his freedom by the French, around the year 1679 he recruited slaves to join him in a rebellion designed to kill any whites within reach, hoping that by doing so he could return to the Spaniards and be pardoned for the murder of his master. Twenty-five readily join him, and many were former Spanish slaves brought to Saint Domingue as booty from Spanish towns. Padrejan and his followers attacked and pillaged from Port Margot to Port-de-Paix, including the quarter coincidentally named Massacre, killing two dozen or more French. They were not strong enough to attack Port-de-Paix, so they retreated to Tarare Mountain and built a wooden fort to secure themselves. From there Padrejan sent his followers forth to recruit other slaves to their cause. Worried that the rebellion might spread, and knowing how difficult it would be to attack the escaped slaves in their stronghold, Governor Pouançay recruited thirty boucaniers who had come to Port-de-Paix from their boucan in Gonaïve. Quickly they attacked the rebel slaves in their stronghold, killing seven, including Padrejan. The rest escaped to Spanish Hispaniola; the pursuing boucaniers were unable to catch them.[33]

Slaves also routinely rebelled in the Spanish New World and Brazil.[34] Those captured after taking up arms against their masters were invariably put to death: in English colonies some were "passed through a cane mill" (rollers that crush the juice out of sugarcane stalks as they passed between them), others were burned, and still others were "put out to dry"—that is, "put into iron cages that prevent any movement and in which they are hung up to branches of trees and left to die of hunger and despair."[35]

Slaves also revolted at sea, although often unsuccessfully. Exquemelin described one such mutiny:

> For, being bound for Terra Firma in a ship that carried them to be sold
> in those parts, they killed the Captain and the mariners, with design
> to return unto their country. But, through their ignorance in marinery,
> they stranded their vessel hereabouts.[36]

Once ashore, he wrote, they were captured by Moskito Indians and enslaved again. (Some suggest the slaves were fleeing Providence Island after it was overrun by the Spanish in 1641.[37] De Lussan wrote that the Africans "were courteously received by the *Moustic Indians*," but his visit was two generations after the shipwreck, when a colony of "mulattos" of Native American and African descent was well established.)[38] In 1681, slaves attempted to rise against buccaneer Bartholomew Sharp and his crew, with the hope of killing them in their sleep. Santiago, the leader, was shot dead in the sea after the attempt failed and he tried to escape, and another was flogged.[39] In 1683 slaves captured by the pirate Jean Hamlin rose against their captors. There were sixteen pirates and twenty-two slaves, but the slaves were "beaten back with the loss of three killed."[40]

Edward Barlow, perhaps sympathetic because, as a sailor, he was familiar with the abuse of subordinates by superiors and the rebellion that abuse can breed, provided an apt description of the perceived causes of such rebellions:

> [F]or there are six blacks to one white, both in Jamaica and Barbados,
> and they live under so much torture and hardship that rather than
> endure it they will run any hazard, for they are very hard worked, and
> fed with anything they can get, especially those that work in the plan-
> tations.[41]

For the Caribbean sea rover, slaves were viewed primarily as plunder. Indeed, given the nature of slaves as property, piracy was inevitably wrapped up in the slave trade, and few buccaneers and filibusters of any nationality, race, or ethnicity were not at some point slave traders, even if they did not act on the scale of the slave-trading corporations. Many rovers owned slaves. Although most did not trade for slaves on the African coast, they did capture slave ships and, more often, captured slaves ashore (sometimes numbering in the hundreds and in one instance fifteen hundred) and sold the human cargo, a lucrative venture because slaves cost one hundred or more pieces-of-eight. On the other hand, most free persons of all races and ethnicities in the New World were in some way involved in the slave trade or slavery, even if only as a beneficiary of slave labor. Pirates often kept slaves of both sexes aboard as personal servants or to do the "drudgery," including much of the physical labor required aboard a ship—working the pumps, for example.[42] This was hardly surprising, given the Caribbean pirate's reputation for being a lazy sailor. Female slaves may have been kept aboard for sex as well, but direct evidence of this is rare, and in general Caribbean rovers preferred to keep their women ashore, where they could not be a divisive influence. One male slave, a shoemaker to buccaneers in the South Sea, was given his freedom at the end of the voyage.[43] The filibuster Captain Daniel even rewarded a priest, who said a celebratory mass aboard the pirates' sloop, with a slave because he had none to wait on him.[44] Pirates captured and sold far more blacks, mulattoes, mestizos, and Native Americans into slavery than they ever set free. However, sea rovers also brought freed slaves into their crews. The Jamaican slave freed by his owner, a buccaneer commander, and who died at Arica in an act of courage and defiance equal or superior to that of any of his white comrades was mentioned in chapter 4, and there were other freemen on South Sea voyages.[45]

*I*t was a curious hypocrisy, the duality of seeing men simultaneously as deserving slavery and freedom, yet it was common. Racism ranged from subtle to overt, and some people, biased against another race, nonetheless distinguished between the individual and the race itself, accepting the former under some circumstances, but never the latter. Such an attitude in buccaneers reflected a respect of courage, leadership, independence, and skill at arms—when it came to those values, race did not matter, or mattered much less than it normally would. The black buccaneer was an equal, but the black slave remained mere property. The real question was when the buccaneer recognized the slave as a man like himself, to be treated as his equal. Perhaps he acted on the recognition only when there was common ground and common purpose. It was unlikely, except for the fixated racist, that white buccaneers viewed blacks in general as an inferior race, for they faced them too many times on the battlefield, or fought at their side, and knew well their courage and ability. At the very least, white buccaneers and filibusters were more likely to accept other races as equal or near-equal than most other Europeans, but perhaps only as comrades in arms or allies and, in some cases, as wives. Sea rovers sought no utopia where all men were free. Again, they sought material gain by force of arms—and slaves were valuable plunder.

It is possible that there were black pirate captains in the Caribbean, but, if so, they are unknown. There are records of black militia captains and mulatto pirate or privateer captains in the service of Spain, and there was at least one well-known mulatto captain who served Spain's enemies as well. Diego Grillo, also called Diego the Mulatto, said to have been a slave in Havana, sailed the *Saint-Jean* under Morgan at Panama, attacked the Spanish ruthlessly, brought his prizes into Tortuga, and even defeated three Spanish vessels sent to capture or destroy him. But in spite of his skill and daring, in 1673 the Spanish captured and killed him.[46] Otherwise, buccaneer and filibuster captains and quartermasters were apparently white. Although pirates were more progressive regarding racial equality, they remained products of their time, and the lack of black captains in their ranks during the period 1674–88 is evidence to the fact. Captain Francis, a Dutch privateer in the Windward Islands in 1674, appears to have been the only mulatto captain sailing with the English, French, or Dutch in this period.[47]

Historians question whether white buccaneers and filibusters would even have served under a black or mulatto captain, but certainly there is precedent. Thirty years prior to Diego Grillo there was another Diego the Mulatto, who sailed under the famous Dutch captains Piet Heyn and "Pie de Palo" (Wooden Leg) Cornelis Jol and commanded a Dutch ship manned by a Dutch crew. Catholic priest Thomas Gage dined with Diego in 1637 after the famous captain and his crew of "Hollanders" captured the ship on which he was traveling. Diego's mother lived in Havana and Gage later visited her; "for her sake he [Diego] had used well and courteously in what he did."[48] White buccaneers or seamen probably served under Diego Grillo and Captain Francis as well. Spanish pirates and privateers very likely served under mulatto or "tawny" captains routinely. Some scholars have even suggested that the two Diegos were one and the same, and the argument is not unreasonable. Wyllem Blaufelt (anglicized as William Blewfield), associated with the Providence company in the 1630s and a Caribbean privateer from at least 1641, continued to cruise the Caribbean in 1663.[49]

**R**eturning to Captain Browne, he and his crew were arrested for piracy shortly after landing in Jamaica, although in many ways their arrest was a mere footnote in 1677, a year overwhelmed by acts of theft and violence. Englishmen were forbidden to serve a foreign prince, an act designed to prevent English "privateers" from hiding behind French commissions. Six buccaneer vessels, including those of Captains Coxon, Barnes, and La Garde, raided Santa Marta (Colombia), chased away Admiral Quintano and his counterattacking force, and returned to Jamaica with the governor and bishop as hostages for ransom. Soon after, more than three hundred of the English buccaneers involved in the Santa Marta raid accepted amnesty at Jamaica, annoying the French, whom they abandoned. The Spaniard de Melgar attempted to salvage a Dutch ship near the Florida Keys, then returned to the *Maravillas* wreck. Pirates attacked San Marcos de Apalache, Florida. The Dutch burned vessels along the coast of Hispaniola, a few Dutch privateers attacked the French, and the French and Dutch fought two major actions at sea and ashore. The comte d'Estrées was defeated by the Dutch at Tobago in a bloody fight early in the 1677, but later succeeded in capturing Tobago from the Dutch. Admiral Binkes and a large part of his Dutch force died when a French shot detonated the Tobago fort's magazine. Jan Erasmus Reyning attempted to rally the shocked, scattered survivors, then escaped with several others in a small boat, first to Trinidad, then to Aruba. Dutch naval power in the region was largely destroyed.

Captain Browne and his company were brought to trial. The chief evidence against them was Browne's expired commission, a hypocritical technicality brought forth by those who wished to make an example of him, Governor Vaughan, in particular. Vaughan was intent on bringing pirates to heel, although many Jamaicans opposed him. Browne and his eight men were condemned. The crew, English, French, and Dutch, were subsequently pardoned, but Browne's death sentence stood. Browne appealed to the Jamaica Assembly for a reprieve based on the Act of Privateers, under which privateers were being granted amnesty. Twice the Assembly appealed to the governor on his behalf and also sought a writ of habeas corpus from the chief justice. Governor Vaughan, however, was in no mood for legal machinations in Browne's favor, and, vexed by the Assembly's attempted intervention, ordered Browne's sentence executed immediately: Browne was hanged as a pirate. Thirty minutes too late an order was produced, signed by the speaker of the Assembly, requiring the observation of the writ of habeas corpus—Browne should not have been hanged, at least not so soon. Governor Vaughan, incensed by the Assembly's further challenge to his apparent authority, dissolved it. The slaves Browne stole remained in Jamaica.[50]

Vaughan was trying to suppress piracy, but slave trading, smuggling, and other marginal, if technically legal, acts continued with his approval. Sloops filled with slaves and illicit merchandise traded routinely with Spain, and many vessels were manned by those who were, or would be, pirates.

# 8 Contraband Cargaroon:
## The Sloop Trade

*I*t is a truism that no one likes taxes in any form, including customs duties and other laws designed to regulate or prevent trade in one's own goods, and perhaps none in history were better at evading taxes than the Spanish merchants of colonial America. William Dampier described how some of these merchants, on the arrival of the treasure fleet at Portobello, "pack up Money among Goods, and send it to *Venta de Cruzes* on the River *Chagre*; from thence down the River, and afterwards by Sea to *Portobel*."\*The privateers were well aware of this route and of the smuggled goods and coin, and in Dampier's words, "I have known a whole Fleet of [these] Periago's and Canoas taken [by buccaneers]."[1] If pirates knew of the route and cargo, then so did many Spaniards, but they pretended to know nothing. Smuggling was endemic along the shores of the Spanish Main and in many ways was not only a means to greater wealth for many, but also a means of acquiring necessary goods, for it was often a year, or two or three, between the arrivals of ships from Spain. Spain, like all European nations, attempted to control all trade in and out of her territories. However, the convoy system of the treasure fleets left Spanish towns often starved for European goods.

New World Spaniards had a variety of means to avoid or diminish taxes, duties, and prohibitions. Many converted gold and silver into personal jewelry; its links could be easily used as currency, in the Spanish style of "wearing

---

\*All quotations have been reprinted with their original spelling and punctuation.

93

wealth."This conversion extended to other furnishings as well.The comte de Forbin, accompanying the comte d'Estrées on his 1680 West Indian cruise of diplomacy and espionage, was fascinated by the size and weight of the serving vessel or platter at the governor's dinner in Cartagena. One of the Spanish guests informed him that it was forbidden by the viceroy and governors of the Indies to return to Spain with silver money, so Spaniards fashioned their silver into items not forbidden or not taxed so highly, such as serving dishes and goblets.[2] Again one was reminded of the Spanish slogan, "*Obedesco pero non cumplo*," meaning "I obey but I do not comply."

Many Spanish did more than avoid paying taxes or otherwise subvert the laws of commerce.They traded with pirates if they were able to. In the spring of 1680, buccaneers who captured several Spanish ships off Panama a few days earlier were approached by

> several Spanish merchants from Panama ... [who] sold us what com-
> modities we needed, buying also of us much of the goods we had
> taken in their own vessels.They gave us likewise 200 pieces-of-eight
> for each negro we could spare them of such as were our prisoners.[3]

There were numerous similar occurrences.

Strictly speaking, the Spanish in the New World were forbidden to trade with any other nation, excepting only slavers of the asiento. But if Spaniards were trading with pirates, they were certainly trading with other nations, even when at war with them.Thus the sloop trade was born, an illicit yet tacitly sanctioned and important trade between Spain and England, France, and Holland. Sir Thomas Lynch, governor of Jamaica from 1681 to 1684, wrote in 1682,

> We have much money, and a great quantity of hides, cacao, &c., im-
> ported by our trading sloops. We have about twenty of these, from
> fifteen to forty-five tons; they are built here, admirable sailers, well
> armed and treble manned, some carrying twenty or thirty hands, who
> receive forty shillings a month.They carry from here some few negroes,
> and dry goods of all sorts, and sell them in the islands, and all along
> the coast of the Main in bays, creeks, and remote places.[4]

Lynch also described the "trading vessels" as "from forty-five to fifty tons, six to eight guns, and fifteen to twenty-five men."[5] By 1689 one hundred of these sloops sailed from Jamaica.[6] *Sloopmen* was the common term for those who sought their livelihoods legally in sloops, whether as turtle or manatee fishermen, salt rakers, or traders to the Main.[7] Strictly speaking, Spanish trade with the English was exclusively in European goods and slaves, but in practice local goods were also traded, in violation of the Navigation Acts.[8] Nearly all of the English buccaneers who were granted amnesty as pirates ended up in the sloop trade or cutting logwood—at least until they returned to piracy.[9]

Half of the profit from a Jamaican sloop usually went to the sloop's owners and supercargo (owner's representative), and the other half to the owners of the traded goods. If nothing was sold, there were no charges for freight, thus the sloop's owners and supercargo were motivated to sell.[10] A large crew was necessary to defend against Spanish treachery in the trading process, as well as against pirates of any nationality, and cut into the profit of the sloop trade.[11] There was also the danger of legitimate seizure of "contrabanda goods" by authorities, an excuse often used by both the Spanish and the French. The main competitors of the English were the Dutch, who frequently undersold them and sailed more often in ships "of good force" from Holland than in local sloops. They had long been a supplier to the Spanish in the New World, originally under the guise of legitimate slave trading, although by the early 1680s the English had taken over the trade in European goods. The French also had a small sloop trade, but it was as efficient as neither that of the English nor the Dutch, and in general the French preferred direct action—the capture of Spanish prizes—to the more subtle act of smuggling.[12]

Much of the New World trade between England and Spain, and Holland and Spain, was facilitated by Jewish merchants, many of them Portuguese or descendents of Portuguese immigrants, whose role as merchants and bankers was amplified by their contacts among merchants throughout Europe and the New World. At Jamaica they had significant influence over much of the trade in European goods, and their role in the success both of the sloop trade and of Caribbean trade in general cannot be overstated.[13]

*F*ather Labat described the sloop trade as practiced by the English, French, and Dutch in the late seventeenth century. Using the pretext of a shortage of food, water, or wood, or of a sprung (cracked) mast, or of a leak in the hull that could not be repaired without unlading goods, the vessel's captain would send word to the local governor, along with a bribe. Treaties provided for exactly such pretenses; they permitted vessels to enter foreign ports in case of "storm, pirates, or other urgent need."[14] If the governor granted permission to enter the port and the cargo was large, the sloop typically entered port using the excuse of a hull leak. Goods were unladed into a warehouse, whose front door was dutifully sealed, while at night goods were traded out of an unsealed back door for local goods, such as indigo, cochineal, vanilla, and tobacco. When ready to sail, the vessel's captain explained that he did not have the funds to pay for the use of local services for repairs and asked to sell part of the cargo, to which the governor agreed. The entire "new" cargo was then sold, each purchaser pretending "that his share is the portion of the cargo which had to be sold to defray the cost of the repairs."[15]

According to Labat, smaller vessels anchored at night near the embarcaderos of small towns or at the mouths of small rivers and fired a few cannon shots to alert locals to their presence. A local canoe would inquire as to the nature of the vessel, then other canoes bearing merchants arrived by night to trade. Crews were on their guard, and never permitted more than a few buyers aboard at any one time, fearing the Spaniards might overpower and murder them, steal their cargo, and scuttle the vessel. Yet the Spaniards also had a right to be cautious, for pirates sometimes masqueraded as traders. Smugglers displayed their goods on a table behind a barricade, while the captain, supercargo, and entire crew, all well armed, saw to both security and hospitality. Payment was accepted only in cash or goods. The French called this process of negotiation and trade under arms *traiter à la pique* (trading by the pike). Those who came to purchase were treated to beverages, likely alcoholic, or such were at least offered, and the sloop fired a cannon to salute visitors of high rank or those who had distinguished themselves by making large purchases. Such formalities appealed to the Spanish sense of honor and deportment, and thus helped sales.[16] Local English sailors referred to this sort of cautious trade as "trading by stealth."[17]

Labat himself sailed aboard a Bermuda sloop, the *Aventurière* commanded by the veteran filibuster Captain Samson, intending to trade with the Spanish. The crew numbered fourteen including the cabin boy, in addition to the sieur de Portes Arson (the supercargo of St. Malo, trading from Martinique), Father Labat, and his teenage black slave. For trade the sloop carried silver in bar and coin, a bit of gold dust, many cases of *platilles* (cloth) from Brittany, plus silk stockings, hats, old thread, and other sundry items including three hundred pounds of pork lard and eighteen hundred pounds of *cochon boucanné*. Hats, Labat wrote, sold very well, especially gray hats with wide, flat brims, and satin hats, above all, fetched the best price.[18] Dampier likewise noted the popularity of hats, even old ones: an "old *English* Beaver thus ordered, would be worth 20 Dollars [pieces-of-eight]" in the Bay of Campeche, and Spaniards would, almost unbelievably, pay up to forty or fifty pieces-of-eight in some places.[19] Labat complimented the English and Dutch on their sales technique. He said they took a loss on a piece of fabric while convincing the same buyer to purchase lace just "like the grandees in Spain wear" — at six times the price it was worth.[20]

The *Aventurière*'s armament included nine muskets and a few pistols, plus cutlasses and a great many grenades. The sloop had two cannon but round shot (cannonballs) were not used. Instead the crew relied on bags of musket balls or scrap metal (known as *partridge* or *burrel*), which caused far more damage to men on deck, as well as to sails and rigging, than a single, small round shot fired at a larger, stronger hull would cause. There was one round shot aboard, and it was used only for crushing mustard seed to eat with boucan. Arms were vital. The *Aventurière*, for example, was chased by a pirate and escaped, only to fall into Spanish hands.[21]

Captain Uring described the sloop trade of the early eighteenth century, which was little different from the sloop trade of the late seventeenth century, other than the increased slave trade: "I went over in a Sloop, well mann'd and arm'd, to trade on the Coast of *New Spain*; and we carried with us a great Quantity of dry Goods, and about 150 Negroes." They sailed to Puerto de Garrote, several leagues from Portobello, for they would not have been permitted into the Spanish port in wartime or peacetime owing to Spanish mistrust. They sent one crewmember who spoke Spanish ashore to give notice of the cargo and location, and for six weeks they lay at anchor, trading with the Spanish, and neither the *guarda costa* nor Spanish pirates attempted to stop the trade. The Spanish bartered for goods and slaves, agreed on terms, then returned to town for money, and only after making payment were the goods and slaves delivered. One buyer agreed to buy seventy slaves and some dry goods, to be delivered between "*Chagre* and *Porto Nova*." Uring sailed his sloop to the meeting point, received the signal agreed upon from Chagres castle, and ashore found "Spaniards with several Asses and Mules laden with Gold and Silver, which we carried on board; and when the Money was found to be right, and all Things were adjusted, we landed the Negroes and dry Goods."[22]

Merchants in Panama received word of the slaves and goods Uring was trading, and ventured across the isthmus. To avoid the king's officers, they traveled dressed as peasants, with their money hidden in jars filled with meal. They "pretended they were poor People going to *Portobello* to buy some Trifles; but they for the most Part went through the Woods, and not in the Road, in order to prevent their being discovered." The Panama traders then returned, carrying their purchased goods in "little Packs, fit for one Man to carry, and we supplied them with as much Provision as was necessary for their Journey cross the *Isthmus* the *South-Sea*."[23] Traders on both sides were well acquainted with the procedure.

Sloops traded on the coasts of Cuba and Spanish Hispaniola, at Río de la Hacha and elsewhere along the Venezuelan coast, and also near Cartagena, and sometimes even at Cartagena, anchoring at the "Brew" eight miles from the great city.[24] They also traded "even where there are Governors, as St. Jago, St. Domingo, &c., for they are bold they are poor."[25] To trade at the great Spanish cities, however, required a cargo of slaves.[26] Near Río de la Hacha was the Native American village of Rancho-Reys, where Jamaican sloops traded for pearls, knowing that the Native American divers "secure the best Pearl for themselves" in spite of Spanish efforts to the contrary. The Dutch also traded along the coast of Venezuela, with as many as "three or four great Ships at a

Time on the Coast, each it may be of thirty or forty Guns."[27] The English, French, and Dutch traded at Trujillo in the Bay of Honduras for "sarsaparilla and other drugs, cocoa-nuts, bees-wax, &c." The Dutch also smuggled sugar from the English at St. Christopher, and the Spanish smuggled slaves from the English at Jamaica.[28]

*T*he dangers of the sloop trade were well known, and the Spanish did not always ignore the unlawful practice. Labat's sloop was seized by two armed boats of the Armada de Barlovento. The French priest barely avoided being killed by attacking Spaniards charged with adrenaline—a pistol pressed against his body misfired, and he parried a cutlass blow with his hand. Although technically, if only briefly, prisoners of the armada, the sloop's super-cargo and crew managed an illicit trade by night with their Spanish captors, selling their entire cargo, their old shirts, and all of their firearms except three muskets and two pistols. Captain Samson and his small crew were prepared to capture the governor of Puerto Rico's nearby bark, filled with goods and silver, and to set fire to the armada's fifty-two-gun flagship to prevent it from following, but Labat and de Portes stopped the planned attack.[29] In 1678 the Spanish seized an English sloop claiming to deliver letters to the local governor in Santiago, Cuba, then ordered it to depart after a search revealed trading goods and five slaves aboard.[30] In 1684 Spanish galleys and piraguas blockaded or attacked several turtling and trading sloops at Cuba; the English sent a man-of-war to relieve them, engaging a galley for two hours until it retreated into shallow waters where the larger warship could not follow.[31] There were numerous similar incidents, with an estimated ten to twenty English merchant vessels were captured by Spanish privateers, pirates, or the guarda costa annually.[32]

In addition to "trading by stealth," English sloops traded in the Bay of Campeche and Honduras for logwood. Spanish vessels traded openly at Jamaica in the 1680s, and there was a general colonial trade among the colonies of each nation. New England, for example, had a busy trade with the Caribbean English, not to mention a more curious business practice: as the governor of Nevis wrote, pirates were sometimes "fitted and protected by the godly New England independents."[33]

# Pirates and Puritans:
## The New England Connection

In August 1678 privateer Bernard Lemoyne, equipped in France, armed with a commission from Governor Pouançay at Saint Domingue, commanding the *Toison d'Or* (*Golden Fleece*), and in consort with Captain Pérou and perhaps others' vessels, cruises the south Cuban coast. In Matanzas Bay Lemoyne and his crew capture one Spanish and three Dutch trading ships. Sailing to Martinique, the seat of French government in the Caribbean, to have the prizes condemned, Lemoyne faces strident objection from two-thirds of his crew, who are English. Although recruited at Petit Goave, they want to carry the prizes to an English port. However, by sailing with the French they have obviously refused Governor Vaughan's offer of amnesty at Jamaica, as well as violated English law prohibiting service under a foreign commission, so the crew is forced to carry their prizes elsewhere. And so they do, to Boston, where they and their French captain are received with open arms. The reception is not surprising: the total value of the prizes, including a vessel lost on the New England coast whose cargo of any significant value was saved by the crew, is estimated at three hundred thousand pieces-of-eight.[1]

Sea rovers invariably ventured to New England, a maritime colony, whose Puritan merchants supported all forms of trade by sea. Puritans were involved in piracy and privateering since the 1630s, when they briefly colonized Providence (Santa Catalina) and Henrietta (San Andrés) in the Caribbean as bases from which to raid England's great, hated rival, Catholic Spain.[2] Also, between 1675 and 1676 New England endured King Philip's War, a bloody conflict that left the economy in shambles and the faithful skeptical about "God's Providence." The sudden influx of goods and silver was needed and welcomed, and any rationale was accepted by the colonists. Besides, the prizes were seized under a French commission and condemned in Martinique. Bostonians were merely providing a reasonable market.

New Englanders continued to support rovers throughout the period, and with fewer scruples as years passed, permitting the "refitting at the dock at Boston" in 1684 of the Spanish prize *La Paz* (*Peace*), which was renamed *La Mutine* and commanded by Captain Michel. She was captured near Cartagena by a French squadron commanded by Laurens, and her other captains included Michel, Yanky, Le Sage, Bréha, Blot, Grogniet, and an unidentified Englishman. Captured with her was the *San Francisco* of forty-eight guns. Laurens took her as his own and named her *Neptune*. His *Françoise* passed to Yanky, who renamed her *Dauphine*. The Spanish ship was rich with goods: "The Bostoners no sooner heard of her [the *Paz*] off the coast than they despatched a messenger and pilot to convoy her into port in defiance of the King's proclamation."* The filibusters purchased much of the "choice goods" in Boston, and thus "are likely to leave the greatest part of their plate behind them."[3]

In 1683 Captain Henley outfitted a ship in Boston and sailed for the Red Sea, seeking the Mogul's rich ships. Associated with him were the pirate captains Thomas Woolery and Christopher Goff, and in 1685 both Henley and Goff were proclaimed pirates. The pirates Graham and Veale briefly visited Boston in 1685, but were recognized as pirates who attacked an English vessel and were forced to put to sea. In the same year the pirate Jean Hamlin returned to the sea in a ship named after his first and notorious vessel: "The new *Trompeuse* was fitted and protected by the godly New England independents." Woolery returned to Boston in 1687 from "the South Sea," after burning his ship at New Providence. New England was confirmed as a pirate "retreat."[4]

𝓟uritans had a distinct reputation in both religion and trade, perhaps best described by the caustic Ned Ward:

> The Inhabitants seem very Religious, showing many outward and visible Signs of an inward and Spiritual Grace: But tho' they wear in their

---

*All quotations have been reprinted with their original spelling and punctuation.

Faces the Innocence of Doves, you will find them in their Dealings, as Subtile as Serpents. Interest is their Faith, Money their God, and Large Possessions the only Heaven they covet ... And it is a Proverb with those that know them, Whosover believes a New-England Saint, shall be sure to be cheated: And he that knows how to deal with their Traders, may Deal with the Devil and fear no Craft.[5]

Scholar Philip Ainsworth Means wrote that for the Puritans, money was "to be worked for enthusiastically, all to the Glory of God," and that, indeed, Puritans were "the establishers of [the United States'] present attitude toward business affairs," although certainly the Dutch of New York influenced it as well.[6]

*H*owever, New England was neither a single colony nor completely homogenous. Although more tolerant of nonconformist religions than Massachusetts, Rhode Island shared a similar reputation with the Puritan colony regarding its support of pirates, or privateers of dubious commission, based on Rhode Island's permissive coastline. There John Coxon threatened to bring his cargo of indigo stolen in 1679 from the Bay of Honduras, if he was not permitted to unlade the cargo at Jamaica, paying duties on it, of course—the pirates would be "well entertained" at Rhode Island.[7] In 1683 two pirate vessels, one of them commanded by Thomas Paine, were also well received at Rhode Island. Governor Cranfield of New Hampshire asked Rhode Island authorities to arrest them but was rebuffed.[8] New Hampshire and Connecticut were said to be clones of Massachusetts in government and religion. They followed the original Puritan colony in matters of politics, although the governors of New Hampshire did attempt to gain control of the assembly, a creature of Puritan congregational ministers influenced by their counterparts in Massachusetts.[9] The government of Massachusetts also gave aid and protection to Spanish prisoners who escaped a French pirate in Boston, for example, which prompted Governor Cranfield to inform the English government of Massachusetts's pandering to pirates.[10]

New York was not part of New England; not until 1674 was the colony finally free from Dutch political influence, thus colonists retained the morality and practices of Dutch traders. New Yorkers traded much, including in slaves, and also began financing piratical expeditions to the Red Sea in the last quarter of the seventeenth century. Pennsylvania (founded in 1681 by the Quaker William Penn) and New Jersey were also colonies distinct from New England and Puritan mores and manners. All Northeastern colonies, however, were distinguished to some degree from the rest of England's colonies by religion: the Northeastern colonies were often a sanctuary for independents and

dissenters, fully realizing the reality of the New World as a font both of opportunity and of rebellion.

Nonetheless, the term *New England* usually meant Massachusetts and
its Puritans. In a positive light, Puritans believed in representative government in both church and state. They built universities. They believed in strong
families and strong communities. They had a long history and tradition of
outright, even armed, rebellion against the English crown. On the darker side,
Puritans believed in social conformity and were perceived by many as religious hypocrites, not always practicing what they preached, and worried more
about appearance than substance. Having been persecuted, Puritans believed
in religious tolerance, which in practice meant they wished to be left alone
to exercise their faith, while enacting religious intolerance by taxing and limiting the rights of other faiths.[11] The doctrine of predestination inclined Puritans to an unwarranted faith in the wealthy and powerful, and their belief
that witches were the minions of the devil led them to hysterical persecu-
tions. In 1692 Puritans were responsible for an unreasonable and unconscionable witch-hunt, resulting in the deaths of twenty-four innocent persons:
nineteen were hanged, one was pressed to death, and four died in jail. Witch-
hunts were fueled by the belief that the devil, "exhibiting himself ordinarily
as a small Black man," was in New England because "New-Englanders are a
People of God settled in those, which were once the Devil's Territories." Therefore, New Englanders were enduring both the "Rebuke of Heaven" for their
"manifold Apostasies" and the infiltration of the devil. Or so Cotton Mather
believed.[12] In 1682 Edward Randolph, the king's agent, referred to the Massachusetts Corporation as "a faction whose Christian policy is to support themselves by falsehood."[13] In 1684 the king revoked the Massachusetts Charter,
and Increase Mather (Cotton's father) exhorted the freemen of Boston that if
they yielded to the king's declaration, "even as Ahab required Naboth's vine-
yard, their children would be bound to curse them."[14]

The Puritan reputation for religious hypocrisy and business acumen,
deserved or not, was well known among all who dealt with New England and
not even daily life was free from Puritanical scrutiny. Ned Ward wrote that if

> you Kiss a Woman in Publick, tho' offer'd as a Curteous Salutation, if
> any Information is given to the Select Members, both shall be Whip'd
> or Fin'd. It's an excellent Law to make Lovers in Privat make much of
> their time, since open Lip-Lechery is so dearly purchas'd. But the good
> humor'd Lasses, to make you amends, will Kiss the kinder in a Corner.[15]

This witty hyperbole was more wit than exaggeration, for Puritan laws
were strict—the "scarlet letter" was written into law: "Those guilty of adultery, male and female, to receive two whippings, not exceeding forty lashes

each, and to wear the two letters A D sewed on their upper garments." Fornication was punished by "injunction of marriage, fine, or whipping." Swearing, cursing, working on the Lord's day, and speaking "contemptuously of the Scriptures" were punished with fines, whippings, or often both. And although "Stealers of ships" in New Hampshire were "severely punished," the punishment was "not to extend to life or limb," doubtless a relief to all pirates.[16] Massachusetts, however, enacted severe laws against piracy in 1673 and in 1684 against those who assisted pirates, but the laws were often to little avail.[17] To be meaningful, laws must be enforced.

Sailors were usually exempt from such petty authority, or at least visiting pirates and privateers were, provided they kept to the "ordinaries and publique houses enterteinment" on the waterfront, where they commonly spent large sums drinking. There probably never was, nor is there likely to ever be, a busy seaport lacking the taverns and women that sailors seek when ashore, no matter the local moral culture. Mariners were tolerated in such places because they were a necessity. Even tavern keepers could not arrest sailors for nonpayment of their drinking debts, thus allowing ships to sail with their full crews.[18] Colonists probably realized that a sailor's character could not be altered anyway, at sea or ashore. New England, after all, was not only a Puritan culture but a quintessentially maritime one, with a history of privateering, a major shipbuilding industry (seven hundred and thirty or more locally built vessels were in New England waters in 1676), and provided a great trade to the English colonies, Europe, and even Guinea, Madagascar, and "Scanderoon" (Ýskenderun, Turkey, also called Alexandretta).[19] It was unlikely that a Puritan ever attempted to enforce a law against kissing in public against a filibuster or buccaneer whose hands were still red with blood and whose plunder aided in the financial salvation of the colony. The curious juxtaposition of pirates and Puritans was even noted by Nathaniel Hawthorne in *The Scarlet Letter*.

Puritan influence extended to the Caribbean and English buccaneers. Many of the early buccaneers were English soldiers recruited under Oliver Cromwell's "Western Design," which launched a failed attempt against the Spanish at Hispaniola, followed by the conquest of Jamaica. Certainly some of the recruited were Puritans, or had absorbed the Puritan ethos prevalent in Cromwell's army. The courageous and famous Capt. Richard Sawkins, a "generous man" who threw dice overboard in anger when he found buccaneers using them on a Sunday, was almost certainly an heir of the Puritan tradition.[20] Robert Clarke, "Governor and Captain General of the Bahamas," independent preacher, and granter of piratical commissions "to make war on the Spaniards of Cuba, St. Augustine, and others," was one of Cromwell's former officers and heir to the Lord Protector's Puritan and military traditions, as were many others in the Caribbean.[21]

*I*n addition to receiving various pirates and privateers for trading, New England also became home to many. One of the settled privateers, Samuel Moseley of Dorchester, Massachusetts, commanded the *Salisbury* Ketch, a coast guard with crew of forty-seven, along the New England coastline from 1673 to 1674 to defend against Dutch incursions. Moseley was admirably suited to the job, for he was reputedly a buccaneer or privateer at Jamaica. In 1675 he was commissioned to seek Dutch pirates who attacked English traders along the coast of Acadia. Sailing in consort with a French vessel, he discovered the trio: Peter Roderigo commanded the *Edward and Thomas*; Cornelius Andreson commanded the hired *Penobscot* Shallop; and George Manning, an Englishman captured by the Dutch who had taken up their cause, commanded the *Phillip* Shallop.

However, Roderigo and Andreson were legitimate privateers, not pirates. Roderigo, a "Flanderkin"; Andreson, a Dutchman; and John Rhoades had been officers under Hurriaen Aernouts of the Dutch *Flying Post-Horse* privateer, who attacked and expelled the French along the Acadian coast. Aernouts lawfully claimed Acadia for Holland, and before he departed for the Caribbean he commissioned Roderigo, Andreson, and Rhoades to manage the trade along the territory of "New Holland." Aernouts subsequently sailed with Reyning in an attack on Granada, but both were captured by the French. Unfortunately for the officers he left behind, English traders interloped on the Dutch-claimed territory. In turn, the Dutch officers "stole" sheep, ordered English traders at sea to strike "a Mayne for the Prince of orainge," and robbed them of "Beaver and Moose" pelts and skins. (To *strike amain* was to lower topsails, or mainsails if topsails were not set, to indicate submission or surrender.)[22] At one point, Roderigo beat Edward Youring, one of his English crewmen who objected to the theft of English goods. Youring was left ashore for a day "to be starved with could [cold]." In response to the attacks, the English accused the Dutch of piracy, and it was under this pretense that Captain Moseley engaged Roderigo, Andreson, and Manning. The battle was over quickly. The Dutch vessels were tiny, and Manning suddenly changed sides and engaged his Dutch consorts. Moseley bid the Dutch "a Mayne for the King of England," and Youring lowered Roderigo's mainsail three or four feet to indicate surrender, in spite of orders to the contrary. The two Dutch vessels, outnumbered by one French vessel, one English ketch, and Manning's newly conscripted Dutch shallop, were truly overwhelmed. Roderigo was convicted of piracy, but pardoned. Andreson was originally acquitted but later found guilty after the judges overturned the verdict. The eight remaining crewmen were also tried. Three, including Rhoades, were banished. The five others were condemned to death but were reprieved and banished on pain of death. They including John Williams, who had once served under Captain Morris, the famous buccaneer who killed Manoel Pardal Rivera, a famous Portuguese pirate in the service of Spain. In 1682 Williams was again in trouble for piracy, that time in Hartford, Connecticut.[23]

Moseley's story did not end there. King Philip's War began in 1675, and Captain Moseley led a company of volunteers, old soldiers, prisoners, and others against the Wampanoag leader. The privateer earned a reputation for both courage and cruelty; his hatred of all Native Americans, friend or foe, was implacable. He was a butcher of men. In the company he commanded, sometimes called "Moseley's Privateers," were several men condemned for piracy. Captain Andreson was among the condemned. However, Andreson was commended for his bravery in the field in both the pirate Moseley's company and Captain Wheeler's company as well and pardoned. Captain Roderigo served in Captain Scottow's company and similarly distinguished himself and was likewise pardoned. England never recognized the Dutch claim to "New Holland."[24]

*I*n 1678 King Philip's War officially ended with the Peace of Casco, although Philip had been dead for two years. Elsewhere in 1678, the activities of buccaneers and filibusters were significantly on the rise. Two hundred buccaneers and filibusters sacked Campeche. The sieur de Franquesnay raided Trujillo in Honduras and Santiago de Cuba. Other pirates raided San Tomás in Venezuela. The marquis de Maintenon in *La Sorcière*, accompanied by filibusters, attacked the Venezuelan coast, including the pearl fisheries at Margarita, and habitations at Trinidad. Charles Howard, the Earl of Carlisle, arrived as governor of Jamaica; Henry Morgan remained lieutenant governor, although he served in the capacity of governor for three and a half months. The Spaniard Martin de Melgar returned, for the third time, to the site of the *Maravillas* wreck, and Diego de Florencia searched for the wreck of the *Nuestra Señora de la Atocha*. The English returned the islands of St. Eustace and Saba to the Dutch, as dictated by the Treaty of Westminster. Jean Baptiste Du Casse, who later became one of the great filibuster leaders, forced the Dutch from their fort and factory at Arguin on the African coast, damaging the Dutch slave trade and improving that of the French. The French attacked St. Thomas but were repulsed. With the arrival of the comte d'Estrées and his fleet in the Caribbean, the English feared war with the French. Many English buccaneers abandoned the French, fearing to be accused of serving the enemy, although war was never declared between England and France. D'Estrées sailed for Curaçao but ran his fleet aground on the nearby Isle of Aves, a disaster for his planned expedition against the Dutch stronghold. He lost seven men-of-war, three patches, and one filibuster. Buccaneers and filibusters on the expedition included Captains Grammont and Paine. While careening shortly after running aground, Paine was nearly taken at Aves by the Dutch. He lost his ship but captured a nearby Dutch sloop with a good cargo. The sieur de Grammont, who had narrowly avoided being wrecked with d'Estrées and who was well known for his leadership and tactics in actions ashore, sacked nearby Maracaibo and occupied the city for weeks, burning two nearby villages and many habitations. He then returned to Petit Goave after suffering a loss of only twenty men. French privateer Bernard Lemoyne captured Dutch and Spanish ships at Cuba; a bad pilot ran his ship aground in New York. France and Holland signed the Treaty of Nymwegen, which granted that the nations retained lands in their current possession and guaranteed freedom of the seas in Europe, but nowhere else. France and Spain also signed the treaty, ceasing hostilities in Europe. A French slaver from Senegal wrecked at Martinique, but the crew, along with African and Arab slaves, were saved by Carib Indians.

"God's Providence," Puritans would have said regarding both the shipwreck and the "deliverance" of the slaver. However, the Christian faith in its several variations present in the New World was not the only influential religion on the Spanish Main.

# 10 Gods, Devils, and Castaways:
## Faith, Religion, and Superstition on the Main

*F*or the lubberly passenger aboard a merchantman traveling to the New World and subject to storms, tempests, and other vicissitudes of the sea; for the European settler encroaching on Native American lands framed by dark virgin forest; for the slave toiling in the field and not knowing how well or how poorly he will be treated from one day to the next, life in the New World is often dominated by a frightening sense of insecurity. For many, faith helps ward off this fear and even grants some sense of control in a world both bright and foreboding and whose workings often seem to make no sense at all. For most colonists and Native Americans, religion is an integral part of everyday life. Buccaneers and filibusters, however, tend to see the world differently. With wit, courage, arms, a vessel, and the will to use them all, they see themselves as masters of their own destiny. They see the world not as a place to work, hope, and pray, but as a place to seek, chase, and prey.

Among the writings of buccaneers and their contemporaries are few references to the religious practices of English Caribbean rovers: one captain threw dice overboard on the Sabbath, and another, with "common consent," kept the Sabbath for a short while until he was killed in action.[1] Religious practices were atypical, although not unusual, among buccaneers. Some observers noted violent disrespect for the Catholic faith among buccaneers sacking Spanish towns that led not only to increased enmity between the

English and Spanish, but between the buccaneers and their Catholic filibuster companions as well. The English buccaneers had "absolutely no scruples, when entering churches, against knocking down crucifixes with their sabers, firing guns and pistols, and breaking and mutilating the images of saints with their arms, scoffing at the veneration in which Frenchmen hold them."*[2] Filibusters did not destroy Catholic relics: they stole them instead and gave them to French churches.[3] Buccaneers even murdered a friar whose crime was likely not that he was a Spaniard, but a Spaniard who was a Catholic priest, and probably insolent too, for Protestant buccaneers often treated prisoners, including priests, fairly well.[4]

The French were more diligent in upholding the formalities and ceremonies of the Catholic faith, but such practices were largely limited to praying before attacking a Spaniard at sea "as if it were the most just war in the world, and asking God ardently for victory and silver," and as well to chanting the *Te Deum* or having a priest celebrate mass "with all solemnity" after the sack of a Spanish town or of the capture of rich prizes at sea.[5] Filibusters were known to fire a salute with cannon at the beginning of the mass and again before special prayers and hymns, followed by a shout of "*Vive le Roi!*" and in one case murdered a crewman who behaved disrespectfully during the *Sainte Sacrifice*, although insubordination was more likely the provocation.[6] Filibusters were also reputed to give money to their parish church after returning from a successful venture.[7] Exquemelin reported that rovers prayed before eating—filibusters recited the Canticle of Zachariah, the Magnificat, and the Miserere, while the "pretended reformers" (Huguenots, or most of the English and Dutch) read a chapter from the Bible and recited Psalms. Among buccaneers such acts of regular religiosity are noted as occurring only in the 1660s and may have been exaggerated by history, for buccaneers in later decades appear to have largely abandoned formal religious practice.[8]

In late seventeenth-century Europe, formal religion was tied inextricably to the state—James II of Britain was dethroned for his Catholicism and the possibility of a Catholic heir, for example—although its influence was diminished in some nations. In the Netherlands,

> 'Tis the University of all Religions, which grow here confusedly . . . without either Order or Pruning. . . . Their Country is the God they worship. War is their Heaven. Peace is their Hell: the Spaniard is the Devil they hate.[9]

Even so, with religion closely tied to most states, it was also tied to intolerance and violence. All major religions supported and promoted violence in

---

*All quotations have been reprinted with their original spelling and punctuation.

the national interest, and at times their clergy participated in force of arms. Father Labat, for example, directed cannon fire against an English man-of-war attacking Guadeloupe.[10] Religious institutions of the period often went beyond the violence of nationalism, practicing violence against those who profaned faith. The Holy Inquisition used torture as a tool for extricating confessions, and Puritans hanged Satan's minions in New England to appease God, or so they believed as they strangled their neighbors with the noose.

Slavery was also a form of violence: Catholic religious orders owned plantations whose labor was provided by slaves, and Catholic priests and Puritan clergy owned personal slaves. In 1681 the Reverend Cotton Mather bought "a Spanish Indian; and bestowed him for Servant on" his father, Increase. Tituba, well known from the Salem witch trials, and her husband John were also Native American slaves, almost certainly Spanish Indians, owned by the Reverend Samuel Parris.[11] "Spanish Indian" slaves were usually brought to New England by pirates or privateers.

The major Christian faiths engaged in figurative and often literal warfare against each other, and all considered Jews to be outcasts, except when they were necessary to finance commerce and warfare. Paradoxically, it was the violence and persecution among the major European religions that sent many people of faiths less dominant in their home nations, voluntarily and involuntarily, to the New World. The immigrants, including Huguenots, Mennonites, Puritans, Quakers, Jews, Catholics, Presbyterians, Covenanters, and Labadists, among many other religious "castaways," formed a cradle of religious freedom in the English and Dutch colonies. The Dutch granted the greatest freedom of religion, the Spaniards the least, actively excluding all but Catholics and Native Americans. Even buccaneers or filibusters who turned renegade and served Spain were required to convert to Roman Catholicism, or at least begin their catechism, as Reyning and Yellows did, however briefly, when they served Spain as guardas costas at Campeche from 1671 to 1672.[12] The French Code Noir restated the exclusion of Jews from French colonies and limited the rights of non-Catholics.[13]

Native American religions were perceived by many Europeans as devil worship, and European colonists, even those living beyond the bounds of New England, referred to Native Americans as devils. In Mexico, Spaniards linked Native Americans both to devil worship and to the devil's common disguise as an Indian.[14] Many Europeans believed that Indians could raise the devil. Labat wrote that the Carib Indians were "frequently tormented by the Devil," and that they erected a cross to protect themselves from him. But if fishing was bad, for example, they destroyed the cross, fearing the "Devil has punished them" on its account. Labat considered this reaction to bad luck in fishing mere superstition, as most Christians of any faith probably did—yet Puritans and other Christians held similar notions of the devil's involvement in cause and effect.[15] The Spanish, Portuguese, and French sent religious orders to establish missions among Native Americans, ostensibly to bring Christ to the uninitiated, but also to expand political influence, create allies against European and Native American enemies, and promote trade. It was clear that most Europeans did not understand Native American religion, and the few who did were typically those, other than clergy, who lived among them. Missionaries considered Native American religion to be inferior to the "superior" Christian religion. Much of the prejudice of Christians against Native America religions, and many African religions as well, derived not only from this patronizing paternalism, but from a failure to accept the animism and polytheism common to many unfamiliar faiths. Yet in spite of Spanish missionary zeal, many subjugated Indians who professed the Catholic faith still adhered to their ancient religions and "secretly adore carved idols that represent different sorts of animals with bizarre and unusual faces."[16] Thomas Gage described the "Christian" Guatemalan Indians' answer to questions of Catholic doctrine: not "Yes, it is so," but "Perhaps it may be so."[17]

African religions began to meld into new faiths owing to the mixture of tribes and peoples among plantation slaves, although the practice of religion was often impeded by slave owners who, fearing uprisings, limited the locations and size of slave gatherings. Some slave owners tried to convert slaves to Christianity, perhaps in the earnest belief that all people should be Christians but just as likely as a means of pacification by shared belief. Religion bound slave to master against a common enemy, but the connection was weakened by the circumstances of slavery. Labat noted that African slaves of the Islamic faith were thought to be dangerous because they could not be converted to Christianity.[18]

The merging of African with Christian and Native American faiths in a process known as *syncretism* created new Creole religions in the Caribbean, reflective of their African origins. Obeah was perhaps the earliest, followed in later centuries by Voudou, Santería, Espiritismo, and others. Deriving from the Ashanti and other Gold Coast (Coromantine) tribes, many of whose members were enslaved in Barbados, Jamaica, and French and Spanish islands, Obeah was common in the late seventeenth century.[19] Labat described practitioners as idolaters and sorcerers and claimed most had at least cursory knowledge of "magic, sorcery, and poison."[20] Europeans considered such fetishism and polytheistic practices as superstition, despite similar practices in their own Christian faiths. Almost certainly, Africans and Native Americans questioned, for example, how the Christian God and Jesus and Holy Spirit were not multiple gods, but a single one. One man's faith is another's superstition.

Superstition in general was common in the late seventeenth century. Some superstitions coexisted well with accepted religion—of witches and devils incarnate, for example—while others such as fortune-telling were considered, at least by Christians, works of the devil. That being said, fortune-telling and other forms of divination, as well as charms and spells, were popular among many of all faiths, although the deceits and tricks of practitioners were well known.[21] Belief in witches remained absolute among a minority of Christians, and witch hunts continued in spite of a trend toward disbelief, although they were largely confined to Europe. Along with well-educated advocates of the belief in witches were those just as well educated, but doubtless more enlightened, who spurned the notion. The French edict of 1682 largely abolished witch trials in France by relegating most "witchcraft" to the level of common superstition.[22] Caribbean sea rovers expressed neither concern for nor interest in witches or witchcraft, and even common mariners expressed little interest, other than in occasional petty superstitions. In the mid-seventeenth century, for example, a captain with "a mad fit on him" believed his ship haunted by a sorcerer, so he heated a marlinspike and drove it into the mainmast to "punish or kill the sorcerer." He was derided both by his crew and by the townsfolk of Dover for his madness and "whimsies."[23]

Stories of the unexplained were as popular in the late seventeenth century as they are now and, except for the addition of modern media, were for all practical purposes identical to modern stories.[24] Belief in spirits was common both among the educated and uneducated and among those who had traveled and those who had not. Samuel Pepys, the famous diarist and secretary of the navy under Charles II, discussed "Witches and Spirits" with a wine merchant and his sister, but did not write how serious the discussion was.[25] In 1667 Pepys, fearing thieves were in his home, ventured downstairs, firebrand in hand. As he did, his

> young gibb-cat [a neutered male cat] did leap down our stairs from top to bottom at two leaps and frighted us, that we could not tell well whether it was the cat or a spirit, and do sometimes think that the house might be haunted.[26]

However, in *The Further Adventures of Robinson Crusoe*, Defoe's famous Maroon made remarks contrary, if fictional, to those of Pepys:

> I have often heard persons of good judgment say, that all the stir people make in the world about ghosts and apparitions is owing to the strength of imagination, and the powerful operation of fancy in their minds; that there is no such thing as a spirit appearing, or a ghost walking ... in truth, there is nothing but shadow and vapor in the thing.[27]

Although reason was making progress in replacing supernatural and

superstitious beliefs in the late seventeenth century, many superstitions remained common. Horoscopes, for example, were popular among all classes
and levels of education, including common seamen and captains. The most
interesting feature of superstitions along the Spanish Main—carried there by
hundreds of cultures—was their similarity in spite of their variety of origin.

*S*eamen, just as many people who venture their lives in a struggle
against man or nature (in particular, serious athletes, adventurous risk takers,
members of combat forces, and those in other hazardous occupations), were
superstitious to some degree, and even those who claimed not to be tended
to adhere to the expected norms, if only out of habit, good manners, or that
hint of a doubt in the back of the mind. Many maritime traditions were based
on common superstition, yet their violation was tantamount to blasphemy or
apostasy. Even so, superstition did not interfere with plunder or commerce in
general—the lure of silver and gold was sufficient to overwhelm serious consideration of supernatural omens and fortune-teller predictions. To a pirate
seeking booty, there was no such thing as a "cursed treasure."

The journals of rovers and other mariners of the period make surprisingly little mention of superstition at sea, and the superstitions that were
mentioned were considered to be part of the nature of the sea, akin to the
sighting of an unusual or unidentified sea creature or atmospheric phenom-
enon (common today), or were associated with rights of passage. Passengers
aboard ships typically provided more description of superstition at sea than
did mariners in the late seventeenth century, although its role seemed limited to directing tradition or venting emotion. Superstition did not, for example, appear to force changes in courses or other decisions or routines at
sea. Superstitions of the sea usually addressed omens—the Portuguese, for
example, considered the *Corpo Santo* (Saint's Body) to be a bad omen—or
were bound with tradition.[28] The violation of tradition was itself an offense
tantamount to an evil portent, although any evil was likely to be committed
by the offended crew.

In 1684, for example, Mississippi explorer La Salle refused to permit the
ceremony of "ducking" at the crossing of the Tropic of Cancer, which rendered "himself privately odious" and caused "great Dissatisfaction of the inferior Officers and Sailors." In the ceremony, all who had not crossed the line
before were ducked in a tub of water (the English and Dutch ducked them
into the sea from a yardarm; the Spanish had a variety of customs, ranging
from hitting them with a rope's end to keelhauling). The arguments in favor
were custom (tradition, that is); an oath taken by all who were ducked, avow-
ing that they would not permit others to cross without being ducked; and
the money and liquor the crew received as payment from the uninitiated in

lieu of being ducked. Henri Joutel ascribed the crew's discontent largely to the latter argument. Money and liquor aside, the traditions had to be observed lest evil came to pass, whether by supernatural forces or by discontented crew. And La Salle's voyage was beset throughout by discontent and its associated evils. Almost certainly a superstitious member of La Salle's crew blamed La Salle's murder three years later on his breach of tradition.[29]

Modern superstitions include christening U.S. Navy warships with a bottle of champagne before launching and the ceremony of crossing the line (an initiation ceremony in which "Pollywogs"—those who have not crossed the Tropic of Cancer before—become "Shellbacks," similar to seventeenth-century practices. The failure to follow the traditions would cause most sailors and their officers to react superstitiously, the reactions ranging from the shaking of heads and muttering about the ship's luck, to sheer outrage and demands that the ceremony be performed. An unhappy crew, after all, can turn a ship into an unlucky one. Superstition bound into tradition was a reassuring routine that even superstitiously agnostic leaders acknowledged (or even manipulated) to lead effectively. Such traditions or superstitions also granted a sense, however slight, of self-will to the crew.

Other than omens and traditions, superstitions of sailors were thought to manage the wind, sea, and tide. Just as cursing was a safe way of venting anxiety and frustration that could otherwise have led to physical violence, so were superstitious behaviors. French sailors on a voyage to Port Royal, Acadia, in 1699 laughingly tied one of the ship's boys to a pump handle and flogged his bare buttocks "with a cat-o-nine tails made of rope ends, all quite new and full of knots" in order to veer (change the direction of) the wind. The boy was told not to scream for mercy, but to shout, "North-East, good wind for the Ship!" He was released only when he shouted, "North-East Wind!" For the sailors it was a welcome diversion that improved morale diminished by the contrary winds. For the "whipping boy" it resulted in the angry nursing of a welted bottom, and when he became an adult, his likely infliction of similar violence on another ship's boy. The observer, the sieur de Dièreville, did "not lay stress on such nonsense," yet noted curiously that indeed the "desired wind soon sprang up."[30]

Based on period documents, buccaneers and filibusters appeared less superstitious than their merchant-sailor counterparts, possibly owing to the sea rovers' greater sense of control over the courses of their lives. Superstition engendered a sense of control, and the Caribbean rovers had the greatest degree of independence and self-determination when compared to all other New World mariners and inhabitants. Nonetheless, even the greatest freedom, will, and ability could not overcome the dangers of man and sea. Men are mortal and the sea claimed many. Abraham Cowley wrote that in 1684, when buccaneers were chusing of Valentines, and discoursing of the Intrigues of Women, there arose a prodigious Storm driving us . . . further than ever any Ship hath sailed before South; so that we concluded the discoursing of Women at Sea was very unlucky and occasioned the Storm.[31]

The buccaneers were using their sense of humor, sexist as it may have been, to diffuse the tensions of their hazardous environment. Along the Spanish Main storms cast away many mariners. The sailor's irreverence and his apparent agnosticism in spite of his occasional practice of religious ritual— he never "consults Heaven beyond the Pole [Star], or the Pointers," for example—originated in the sudden violence of sea and, to a lesser extent, of armed men at sea.[32] "All Hands in a Calme to Pray or Pick Okum," went a saying, "but to work in a Storm, serve God serve Devil."[33] The sailor discovered that prayer did not help in a storm, nor was there time for it anyway— action was the only possible solution. Passengers prayed, but sailors served the ship in order to save their lives: in a storm, "one must be resolute, or find a grave."[34]

# 11 Lost Ships and Souls:
## Wrecks, Wrecking, and Wreckers

"Within the Torrid Zone are also violent Storms, as fierce, if not fiercer, than any are in other Parts of the World,"* wrote William Dampier in *Discourse of Trade-Winds*.[1] And so they were, those storms, and in conjunction with the many islands, shoals, and enormous coastline of the Main, not to mention human error, they sank or stranded many vessels. In January 1654, owing to darkness and one such storm, the *almiranta* (admiral, or a ship that was second in command) of the Galeones, the *Nuestra Señora de las Maravillas* (*Our Lady of the Marvels*), was struck by the *capitana* (flagship) and sank on Los Mimbres, now known as Mantilla Shoal, on Little Bahama Bank.[2] Mantilla Shoal remains dangerous today in heavy weather, modern vessels and navigation notwithstanding.

The loss of the *Maravillas* was not in itself unusual, but her manner of loss was. Most ships were lost when they foundered from the stresses of wind and sea, or owing to a storm or poor navigation, which caused ships to run aground or tear their bottoms on coral heads and become "bilged and lost."[3] As many mariners pointed out, the sounding lead (or modern depth finder) is the most important navigational tool, or at least as important as the compass. Collisions were rarer and occurred most often at night among ships in convoy, typically in bad weather, although human error—invariably inattention—was often the underlying cause. "Being at Sea, we make easy Sail,

---

*All quotations have been reprinted with their original spelling and punctuation.

that our Ships might have the liberty that Night to single themselves from Crowd of other Ships," wrote John Fryer of a voyage in 1672.

> [F]or Night hastening on (and in such a swarm of Vessels of greater bulk, not so readily manageable as smaller) ... we at length missed the *Masenberg*, on whom (it seems) a small Pink falling foul, had carried away her Head and Boltsprit, and 'tis to be feared disabled her this Voyage.[4]

Navigational errors and contrary wind and sea, and often both, contributed to many losses. Navigation was both science and art, but mariners lacked a means to accurately determine longitude at sea. Only latitude could be determined with reasonable accuracy, assuming conditions permitted the use of the appropriate instrument. The back staff and cross staff were instruments used to sight the sun or a star, but the quadrant (often very large) and astrolabe were also used by rovers. Whenever possible, a mariner used latitude sailing: he set a course that put him in the latitude of his destination, but well in advance of it. Upon arrival in the correct latitude, he proceeded along it until he reached his destination. The mariner thus always knew if he was east or west of his destination, compensating for his inability to accurately measure longitude. However, in many instances the Caribbean's tortuous navigation made latitude sailing ineffective: "The Sailor, when he would express the Intricacy of any Path-way, stiling it the *Caribbees*."[5] Often the mariner relied on dead reckoning at sea, piloting within sight of land, and the sounding lead. Nonetheless, the hazards of Caribbean navigation wrecked many vessels.

Edward Barlow wrote of the typical loss of "a pink, which was ... cast away and ship and goods lost, but all the men saved; by mistaking the entering in of the Gulf she ran upon the Bahama shoals." On another voyage the *Guannaboe*, aboard which Barlow served as mate, nearly ran aground on the "Roques" near the Bahama Shoals, "where we should have run into great danger had it been a longer night."[6] Errors and circumstances also put ships into danger without running them aground. "But our expectations were frustrate and we met with divers cross winds, so that our water and provisions began to grow short with us, and our ship being leaky, it began to go very hard with us."[7] Buccaneers in such circumstances in 1680 sold their rations of water at "30 pieces of Eight per Pint."[8] A privateer-sailor would pay six pence for a rat when provisions ran low, and a passenger six pence for a pint of water.[9] Prices rose as rations were depleted: "Nay, before the voyage did end ... a woman great with child offered twenty shillings for a rat, which the proprietor refusing, the woman died."[10] In such extreme circumstances some men hid extra food, if they had it, and ate in secret rather than share with their shipmates, following the proverb "The fewer the better chear."[11] But woe unto him who was caught! Buccaneers on short allowance—some did not drink for days—crossing the Pacific in 1686 caught a member of the company stealing food or water. He was "condemned ... to have three Blows from each Man in the ship, with a Two-Inch and a half Rope [circumference] on his bare Back," one of the few examples on record of buccaneers punishing one of their own in the manner of the navy or merchant service.[12]

In 1683 the sieur de Grammont and his filibuster crew aboard the *Saint Nicolas* were in danger of dying from want of water and provisions as they beat slowly to windward across the Gulf of Mexico, seeking to pass through the Bahama Channel on their way to South Carolina. They survived only through the good fortune of meeting the *Nuestra Señora de Candelaria* along the Florida Keys. The filibusters discovered her loaded with grain.[13]

*L*ightning was also a common danger at sea, damaging ships and setting them afire or detonating the powder in the magazine. Slaver John Barbot described two lightning strikes aboard a French man-of-war in 1682. The first struck the forecastle, passed through one of the doors and the ship's head, and injured a boy. The second bolt struck the mainmast "with so prodigious a noise, that the most undaunted sailors were seiz'd with horror, and some utterly stupify'd and void of sense." Barbot described a ball of fire the size of a man's fist "giving such a monstrous report" that it stunned him. The ship was filled with livestock, who made a "hideous shrieking and crying." The lightning passed through the topgallant mast and topmast, "shivering them as if they had been hew'd in splinters with tools." The tops were shattered and the sails "scorch'd and burnt." Worse, after the lightning, all but one of the ship's compasses deviated variously from seven to twenty-three degrees. If not for a spare, unaffected compass stowed under a bed, the ship and crew would have been in danger for they had "no load-stone aboard the ship, to touch the others again and render them useful."[14]

Most ships lost in storms foundered or ran aground. Dampier almost understated the situation when he described storms of the tropics as fierce. Both Dampier and Barbot described the most violent of storms as three sorts: norths, souths, and hurricanes. Norths, Dampier said, were "violent Winds, that frequently blow in the Bay of Mexico [and other places] from October till March." Souths arrived between June and August, and the greatest force of wind was from the south.[15] According to Barbot, norths and souths differed from hurricanes only in that norths and souths were "more constant to one point of the compass, or coming sooner in the year."[16] Inhabitants were well aware of the dangers of these storms, and planters of means always had a

> hurrican hut ... being built low, on large stumps of trees deeply fix'd
> in the ground, and commonly not above seven foot high, of strong

posts fasten'd to each other by cross-pieces of timber, with ropes cast over the roof to secure it from flying away.[17]

Also dangerous at times were "tornados." A tornado in the seventeenth century was not the violent vortex of wind we know today, but "a sudden, or violent storm of ill weather at sea"—a thunderstorm, in other words.[18] Curiously, some believed that firing two or three broadsides dissipated afternoon thunderstorms.[19] Many of these storms spawned waterspouts that snapped masts and yards and spun ships about, although Dampier suggested that the fear of them was their greatest harm. Some seamen suggested a cure for waterspouts:

> Therefore Men at Sea, when they see a Spout coming, and know not
> how to avoid it, do sometimes fire Shot out of their great Guns into it,
> to give it air or vent, that so it may break; but I did never hear that it
> proved to be of any Benefit.[20]

In a great storm a crew had little choice but to strike (lower) topmasts, lower fore and main yards "down a port-last" (to the gunwales), work the pumps continuously, and, depending on the violence of the storm, "bring to" or "lie a-trie" under the main course and mizzen, under the mizzen alone, under a "ballasted" mizzen (only part of the sail was used, "reefed" in other words), or even under a "main-bonnet . . . spread on our weather quarter."[21] Spaniards, however, reefed the fore and mizzen sails, which Dampier suggested put a great strain on a ship.[22] A crew might even set a sea anchor of "two Hassers [hawsers] on an end made fast to a Spare-yard, and a quoile of old Rope" to keep the ship's head to the sea.[23] If the storm was severe enough, the crew cut one or more of the masts "by the board," first cutting the shrouds that supported them. The rigging of a mast carried by the board during a storm had to be cut away immediately, lest the mast, dragging alongside, punched a hole in the hull and sent the ship to Davy Jones as the crew shouted, "A sieve! A sieve!"[24] Worst of all was to be in such a storm and near a lee shore, for disaster was almost certain. In a great storm a ship needed a safe haven, or sea room and a stout commander and crew.

The state of mind of those aboard, particularly of those who had never been to sea in a storm, could only be imagined by most. The sieur de Dièreville provided his impressions of a storm during a voyage in 1700, and like many non-mariner passengers writing of storms at sea in this period, he used verse to express himself:

> *The gale became more terrible,*
> *And ever higher rose the waves;*

> *Nature was by pressing danger racked;*
> *Night came, and fear redoubled, for*
> *In its obscurity, no one could tell*
> *Just where we were....*[25]

Edward Barlow described a storm during a voyage from Jamaica to London in 1681, and its effect on some of the passengers: "And coming into the latitude of 48 north, one day being under a fore course reefed, a great sea broke into our great cabin windows and broke them all to pieces, and filled the great cabin so with water that it beat down the nurse and little child, so that the little infant was almost 'drownded.'"[26] For passengers, most of whom never traveled by sea, the waiting was terrifying. Sailors at least had the distraction of action in time of danger, and the cry of "A breach! A breach!" roused them to action.[27]

Sailors worked like demons in a storm, not to "serve God serve Devil" nor to "find a grave," but to save their ship and souls. Under a stout, seamanlike commander, a crew worked what seemed to be miracles, keeping a ship afloat and under sail in the most extreme circumstances. In 1680, Capt. Cornelius Essex's barque was so leaky he "would [wold] his shipp Together with Two Hassers [hausers] to keep her together."[28] (*Wolding* was the tight wrapping of a line around a spar, or in this case the hull, to strengthen it, much like the whipping of a rope's end. Another term for the wolding of a hull was "swifted together with cables to keep her from sinking.")[29] In 1689 the merchantman *Terra Nova* arrived at Plymouth after a voyage from Port Royal, Jamaica. Crowds flocked to the shore to see the "wreck ship" whose Atlantic crossing was a miracle. The ship was jury-rigged fore and aft, having lost her head and cutwater, all of her masts and boats, and many of her fittings and much of her equipment. So violent was the sea that it "quite overset our ship, so that [after the storm was over] the main-hatches lay under water, and a man might have walk'd upon her starboard side without board, as he could before upon the main deck." Yet captain and crew stopped her many leaks, rigged new masts and spars (including a foremast from a deck beam strengthened with plank and wolded, and a fore-topmast from the whip staff), and even sailed her through another storm, a feat of extraordinary seamanship.[30]

But for those whose ship sunk in a storm, the fear for oneself, and even more for one's family and loved ones in the circumstances, was overwhelming. Anthony Thacher, a survivor of a vessel wrecked on rocks off the coast of Massachusetts in 1634 during a hurricane, remembered his children in the last moments before he was swept into the sea.

Now Called to my remembrance the time and manner how and when
I Last saw and Left my Children and freends. One was severed from

me Sitting on the Rocke at my feete, the other three in the Pinnace. My Little babe (ah poor Peter) Sitting in hiss Sister Ediths arms Who to the utmost of her power Sheltered him out of the waters, My poore William standing Close unto her. All three of them Looking rufully on mee on the Rocke, there very Countinance Calling unto mee to helpe them, Whom I Could not goe unto, neither Could they Come unto mee, neither Could the mercilesse waves aforde mee Space or time to use and meanes att all either to helpe them or my Selfe.[31]

All of Thacher's children were eventually swept into the sea and drowned.

In such wrecks, most aboard did not survive the immediate crisis. Boats— and there were no "lifeboats"—were difficult, if not impossible, to launch in storm seas, if they had not already been swept overboard, broken to pieces, or torn free if towed astern. If the number of passengers and crew was large, there may not have been enough boats anyway, and there were no life jackets. Thus most passengers and crew drowned—even a strong, experienced swimmer could easily drown in such seas—and if they did not, they had to contend with the dangers of exposure, dehydration, and hunger, as well as the complications of any injuries received in the wreck. Only fifty or so of the approximately seven hundred aboard the *Maravillas* survived, for example. In cold seas, hypothermia set in quickly among those immersed and was fatal unless victims were warmed quickly. Sharks and other dangerous denizens of the deep rarely rated as a significant danger in the immediate aftermath of a shipwreck, although they certainly fed on the bodies of the dead and on survivors foolish enough to consort with the dead.

Storms and human error also wrecked entire fleets. In 1684 a storm at Petit Goave cast twenty-five French merchantmen ashore.[32] In 1678 the comte d'Estrées ran aground at Aves. In spite of warning shots, his fleet followed him onto the reef, believing the cannon shots were not a warning but were fired in battle. With d'Estrées were buccaneers and filibusters, who, once shipwrecked, became drunk and stayed drunk for weeks. Forty Frenchmen were drunk aboard one ship, whose stern broke away and drifted off to sea with the filibusters aboard, still singing and drinking, never to be heard from again.[33]

In the Caribbean, most ships were lost in shallow water, and a few were filled with treasure. Although cannon were often recovered from wrecks and put to use again, the greatest salvage efforts were saved for those ships with riches of silver and gold. The Spanish made numerous efforts at salvaging treasure—called *wrecking* or *fishing*—from sunken Spanish ships. After the loss of the *Maravillas*, for example, Spaniards worked the wreck in 1657 and 1667. Annually from 1676 to 1679 Martin de Melgar worked the site.[34]

Unfortunately, Spaniards were not the only ones who knew the location of the wreck and sought its sunken riches, nor were the natural hazards of the sea and wrecks the only dangers to treasure seekers. Where there was wealth there were always men to seize it. Pirates knew of the *Maravillas* as well, and their violence could be as sudden and deadly as any storm. New Providence, established largely as a refuge for pirates and other treasure hunters—"dissolute fellows"—seeking silver from the "Old Wrack," the *Maravillas*, was their base.[35]

In 1679 Captain de Melgar, accompanied by a Spanish man-of-war of twenty-five guns, was working the site when filibusters attacked. In one account there was a running fight, the French fleeing from the Spanish until a cannon exploded and detonated powder charges on deck, killing thirty-six, including de Melgar.[36] The filibusters of Saint Domingue worked the site for two months, recovering 135 to 150 pigs of silver, whose value was estimated at two hundred thousand pieces-of-eight.[37] The French intended to return. For years off and on there were wreckers, buccaneers, filibusters, and outright pirates at the *Maravillas* site and seeking other sites, all grasping for the Spanish "pigs and sows of silver" taken by the sea.[38] Sir Thomas Lynch called the residents of New Providence "straggling people who receive such as come to dive for silver in a galleon wrecked on that coast."[39] Captains John Markham, Francis Townley, Captain Bréha, Jeremiah Conway, George Young, and Thomas Paine were pirates and wreckers, and the wrecking such men engaged in caused strain between the Caribbean governments of Spain, England, and France.[40] The fishers of the *Maravillas*, for example, "often get ten or twelve pound weight [of silver] a man," a sound inducement to fish the wreck and keep the Spanish away.[41] In 1684 William Phips, aboard the *Rose of Algeree* lent to him by Charles II of England, forced other wreckers from the *Maravillas* site and fished it himself. Obsessed with treasure, in 1687 he located the wreck of *Nuestra Señora de Concepción* and reputedly recovered £250,000 worth of silver. Phips was eventually knighted and made governor of Massachusetts, and held the office during the Salem witch trials in 1692.[42]

The divers who worked on the wrecks near Florida and the Bahamas were typically Native Americans from the nearby Bahamian islands or Florida Keys, many of them kidnapped or enslaved, although blacks were used as well.[43] Native Americans and Africans raised along the sea were generally excellent swimmers and, more important, comfortable in open water. African canoe men, for example, ferried passengers in and out of high surf, and if overset "are such excellent divers and swimmers, that they preserve the lives of those they have any kindness for."[44] Labat told of a sloop that foundered in a gale, and the only survivor was a Carib who remained afloat "for sixty hours without any assistance whatsoever," an entirely reasonable effort, albeit physically demanding, for a strong swimmer comfortable with his aquatic surroundings. He

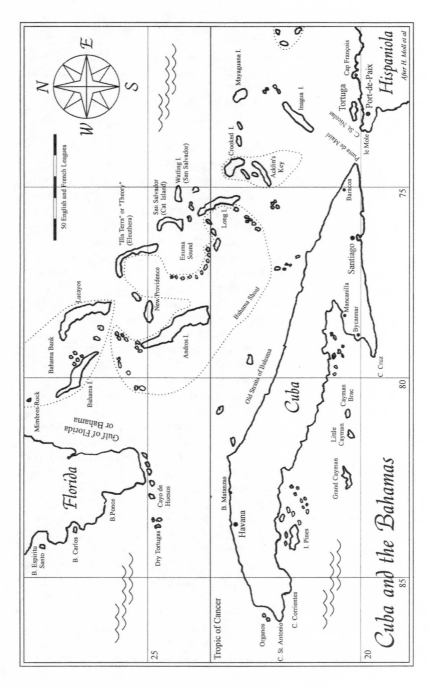

*Cuba and the Bahamas*

BENERSON LITTLE AND COURTNEY LITTLE.

described Carib mothers swimming with children at their breasts, and children swimming around their mothers "like so many little fishes." He also wrote of a Carib who attacked a shark in 1676 at St. Kitts. The shark had bitten off a bathing child's leg, and the Carib armed himself with two bayonets, drank two glasses of rum, and launched his assault on the shark, a twelve-foot hammerhead, stabbing it repeatedly in the belly. In half an hour the shark was dead.[45]

Many whites also swam and dived, and the notion that European sailors could not swim was false. Nonetheless, one captain observed "how deficient our common seamen in general are" in swimming. Europeans who fell overboard usually drowned, even if they landed uninjured in the water. A sailor "was hoisted into the Main [the sea], and perished, the Ship having fresh Way, and the Boats lying on Board; they threw over several Planks and Vessels, but he made no sign of contending with the Waves."[46] Perhaps only one in four to one in six common sailors could swim.[47] "He could swim very well," wrote Henry Teonge, chaplain aboard the HMS *Bristol*, of a sailor who intended to swim out and recover one of the ship's boats in 1678. The sailor scorned his companion who could not swim.[48] In 1685 two buccaneers swam to shore through surf too dangerous to row through and thought nothing of it. In the same year six filibusters failed to swim to shore through large surf, but the fact that they tried said much for their swimming ability.[49] A mid-eighteenth-century seaman aboard a privateer wagered that he could swim underwater to boats some distance from his ship. Instead, as a joke he swam underwater in the other direction, climbed through the stern lights, and hid, creating the impression he had drowned.[50] Some who could not swim found the ability in an emergency, as one seaman did in 1673 when attacked by Malay pirates: "*Daniel Wallis* leapt into the Sea, who could never swim before nor since; yet now he swam very well a good while before he was taken up."[51] On voyages, sailors swam for recreation: "We say a calm Sea, or *Becalmed*, when [it] is so smooth the Ship moves very little, and the men leap overboard to swim."[52] Swimmers used a variation of the breaststroke, probably much like that described in Thevenot's *L'Art de nager* (*The Art of Swimming*) published in 1695, with an English edition in 1699. It was not a dog paddle: "[I]nstead of swimming he could only paddle in the water like a dog, and was immediately drowned," wrote Teonge.[53] Floats made of inflated hide—goat, pig, seal, or horse—were also used, and were particularly helpful for long swims. Using inflated hides three slaves escaped from Tripoli to an English man-of-war in 1675.[54] Gulf Coast Indians swam through high surf with "a large Piece of Timber, which they threw into the Sea, plac'd themselves along both Sides of it, holding fast to it with one Arm, and swimming with the other."[55]

Anywhere there was water there was danger of drowning. Modern cardiopulmonary resuscitation (CPR) was not developed until the twentieth century, but various drowning remedies, even if they had limited effectiveness, existed in the seventeenth and eighteenth centuries. Henry Teonge, when chaplain aboard the HMS *Assistance*, described a curious procedure he observed used upon a drowning victim at Deal, England, in 1675.

> A traveller, in very poor clothes (coming to look on, as many more did), presently pulled out his knife sheath, cuts off the nether end of his sheath, and thrust his sheath into the fundament [anus] of the said Thomas Boules, and blew with all his force till he himself was weary; then desired some others to blow also; and in half an hour's time brought him to life again.[56]

While swimming ability was requisite for divers, they also had tools of the trade to assist them in their salvage. In the simplest form of wrecking, divers descended to the bottom and collected treasure, which was then hauled to the surface. Grapnels (boat anchors with four hooks) were used to tear decks to gain access to treasure below. A glass-bottomed bucket was used to see underwater from the surface. Major expeditions usually had a specially fitted vessel for salvage operations, with a windlass used to raise and lower a diving bell, and probably for any related tasks requiring vertical lifting or force. Diving bells ranged from the simple "Bermudia Tub" (a large cask fitted with weights to keep it submerged) to large bronze or wooden bells that could be refilled underwater with weighted buckets or, after 1690, barrels of air. Divers in a bell communicated with the surface via a line and pull signals, and stayed below for thirty to forty-five minutes at depths perhaps up to sixty or seventy feet.[57]

Free-swimming divers often made their descents by holding a rock or other weight. Divers could descend as quickly by hauling themselves headfirst or feetfirst down an anchored line, but this required more physical effort and consumed oxygen that would be better expended on the act of salvage itself.[58] Divers had to relieve the pressure in their ears, and probably did so by pinching the nose and blowing gently (the Valsalva technique), swallowing, or wriggling the jaw back and forth. Dive masks did not exist, but author Peter Earle pointed out an illustration showing goggles used by Mediterranean coral divers in the sixteenth century.[59] It is unknown whether seventeenth-century Caribbean divers used similar goggles and how well they kept out water, particularly at depth. As a diver swam deeper, goggles caused "eye squeezes" as the pressure increased and air volume decreased between the lenses and the eyes, turning the whites of the eyes a bloody red. Unlike face masks used for diving, the air space in a pair of goggles could not be equalized to the external pressure. (With a dive mask, a diver exhales slightly through his nose to equalize the pressure and prevent a possible face or eye squeeze.) Nonetheless, the lack of goggles was not a great impediment to underwater vision. In clear seawater on a sunlit day a diver could see reasonably well without a dive mask or goggles, although objects were blurred. To surface, divers swam, although if the depth was more than twenty-five or thirty feet, most probably hauled themselves up a line anchored for the purpose, to save their breath.[60] A Spanish illustration of 1626 appears to demonstrate a diver hauling himself to the surface.[61]

Currents and poor visibility make salvage difficult even in the modern age and in the seventeenth century could entirely preclude operations. Depth was another significant limitation: practically speaking, most experienced breath-hold divers swimming from the surface did not work effectively beyond sixty or seventy feet, although one hundred to one hundred and fifty feet was probably the extreme limit.[62] Diving bells, in common use since at least the sixteenth century, eased the burden of making numerous free-swimming ascents and descents and significantly extended the amount of time a diver spent underwater, for the diver returned to the bell for another breath rather than resurfacing. However, the use of bells was impractical beyond three atmospheres absolute (ATA), or sixty-six feet.[63] In a bell with a roughly equal diameter throughout, and four and a half feet of vertical space inside, and roughly the same width throughout (as in a large barrel), at the depth of thirty-three feet (2 ATA), the air volume decreased by half (Boyle's Law: gas volume is inversely proportional to pressure). In other words, seawater filled the bell halfway because pressure compressed the air inside. At sixty-six feet sea water filled two-thirds of the bell's volume, leaving only a foot and a half of air space in which to put one's head and breathe. A bell with six feet of vertical space would have two feet of air space at sixty-six feet.

Some Native American divers reputedly held their breath for fifteen minutes, but this was a gross exaggeration.[64] Most modern experienced breath-hold divers can remain underwater for no more than five minutes, if relaxed and minimizing physical exertion. For those engaged in underwater labor, two minutes is the practical limit, and one minute is more typical. Japanese *ama* and South Pacific breath-hold divers, for example, hold their breath for one to two minutes while working at depths up to thirty or forty feet.[65] Similar time limits are found among U.S. Navy SEALs and the former UDTs (Underwater Demolition Teams) engaged in hydrographic reconnaissance of landing beaches and associated obstacle clearance, although such operations are generally restricted to three and half fathoms and shallower.[66]

*H*ours of repetitive breath-hold diving subjected divers to a variety of stresses, including hypothermia (even in warm water) and dehydration, if precautions were not taken. A substantial diet was necessary, particularly in cold water, to help prevent hypothermia. Lengthy immersion in water caused the skin to macerate, and unless protective clothing was worn, skin abraded easily. Breath-hold divers who made dozens of one- to two-minute descents over the course of the day, even at depths of only ten to fifteen feet, were probably subjected to occasional temporary neurological disorders caused by decompression sickness, and some working at depths of thirty to forty feet probably exhibited mild symptoms of nitrogen narcosis as well.[67] Perhaps the greatest danger to breath-hold divers was hypoxia (lack of oxygen) of ascent, often known confusingly today as both *shallow-water blackout* and *deepwater blackout*. Increased partial pressure of oxygen in the lungs at depth permitted the breath-holder to remain conscious with a smaller volume of oxygen in the lungs than was possible at the surface or shallower depths. However, as the breath-hold diver ascended after consuming most of the oxygen in the lungs, the partial pressure of oxygen decreased to a level unable to sustain consciousness, and the diver could pass out and drown as a result. Breath-hold divers operating from a diving bell were subject to headaches from the buildup of carbon dioxide (a "$CO_2$ hit") and to hypoxia, and surely had a higher incidence of decompression sickness (the "bends") than did breath-hold divers operating from the surface. If divers operating from a diving bell made free-swimming ascents to the surface, they certainly knew not to hold their breath, but expelled the air from their lungs prior to ascent or exhaled continuously as they swam to the surface. If the diver held his breath as he ascended, the expansion of the air in the lungs could damage them or lead to death from an air embolism from ruptured alveoli.

Divers on the Phips expedition to the wreck of the *Concepción* in 1684 were often ill. Almost certainly this was partially because of the physical demands of repeated breath-hold diving over the course of day, combined with strenuous physical labor. Fatigue, ear squeezes, ear infections, and sinus problems, including sinus infections, are common complaints of working divers. However, many cases of illness were probably decompression sickness. Indeed, the likelihood of decompression sickness increases with fatigue and physical stress. Planter John Taylor reported that Indian divers ducked their heads back underwater for a "quarter of a minute" after reaching the surface, to not immediately receive "too much of the land air [lest] it would destroy them."[68] The resemblance of the practice to decompression is striking. However, without further research, or knowing the depth to which the divers momentarily descended after surfacing, it is impossible to do more than wonder if the practice reduced the incidence of the symptoms of decompression sickness, or, more likely, if it developed when divers first realized that their symptoms subsided when they dived underwater again.

Besides the stresses of underwater work, there were the dangers of the sea itself. Sharks were a rare but real danger, but certainly not as significant as modern novels, films, and television make them out to be. Divers were far more likely to be injured by coral, jellyfish and Portuguese men-of-war, scorpion fish, morays, stingrays, and barracuda. Dampier noted that Native American divers in the South Sea could have taken more silver from a sunken Spanish vessel but for the dangers of catfish and their venomous spines, which abounded in and around the wreck.[69] Breath-hold diving in support of salvage operations or treasure hunting was indeed a dangerous occupation, just as are modern commercial and military diving operations.

*A*nd like their modern counterparts, seventeenth-century divers were capable of more than treasure salvage and pearl diving. Such divers recovered "an anchor that weighed 600 pound, by tying a cable unto it with great dexterity and pulling it from a rock."[70] African divers at Acra helped a slave ship recover an anchor firmly wedged in the seabed, and black divers in Barbados inspected a ship's hull for damage.[71] Barlow described the capsizing of a four-hundred-ton merchantman in Port Royal harbor in 1680. The ship was top heavy, and "all the men running over on one side to do some work, she was fallen over and overset and sunk down to Rights" in nine fathoms of water, with the loss of a dozen men. Yet, "there being several good divers, with great cost and trouble, she not being laden, she was weighed again and recovered."[72] A diver aboard a ship was invaluable and not uncommon. The admiral and vice admirals of the Spanish treasure fleets each carried a diver, for example, "to discover where any Ship leaks."[73]

Divers, or more correctly swimmers, were also capable of attacking ships, albeit rarely, and can be considered the forerunners of modern special operations force "combat swimmers." In 1680 in the South Sea a swimmer

> with a couple of Seal Skins blown like Bladers, of which he made a float . . . in the dead of the night came under the Stern of our hip with a Ball of Pitch, Sulphur, Oakum, and such combustible matter, and struck it between the Rudder and Stern-port [sternpost], and set it on fire with a Brimstone match.[74]

Warned by the stench, the buccaneers put the fire out.[75] A swimmer attempted a similar attack on pirates in 1685 at Perico in the South Sea but was spotted before he reached the ship. He escaped by diving beneath the surface and swimming away.[76]

But there were no such swimmers to attack the filibusters on the "Old Wrack" in 1679, a busy year for pirates and others. France and Brandenburg made peace, as did Denmark and Sweden. Padrejan led his slave revolt on Saint Domingue. Raveneau de Lussan, who wrote one of the significant journals of the exploits of filibusters, traveled to Saint Domingue and was indentured for three years. Grammont sacked Puerto Principe. The comte d'Estrées returned to the Caribbean with a squadron of eleven vessels; his purpose, espionage and provocation. Nicolai Esmit was appointed governor of Saint Thomas and was deposed by his brother, Adolph. De Melgar, soon followed by pirates, fished the *Maravillas*. Captains Sharp, Coxon, Bréha, and others returned to Jamaica with five hundred chests of indigo, seized in raids on the Bay of Honduras, along with cochineal, tortoiseshell, money, and plate. Richard Sawkins, with a party of English and French rovers, plundered Santa Marta. The HMS *Success*, cruising Jamaican waters for pirates, captured Sawkins and arrested him—but soon the pirate was away to sea again. In reprisal for the seizure of his cargo of logwood and hides by Spanish men-of-war at Aruba in 1673, and after years of speeking restitution, Edmund Cook captured a Spanish bark loaded with cacao and money. From this *petite piracy* as Exquemelin termed it, not to mention murder (the Spanish captain and a priest were killed in the fight to take the bark), he turned to greater piracies. Peter Harris captured a valuable Dutch ship of twenty-eight guns in the south keys of Cuba. Governor Carlisle ordered the HMS *Success* to seek Harris as well, but the man-of-war was soon lost in fifteen feet of water. Cornelius Essex in the *Great Dolphin* plundered a Jamaica plantation, his men "riotously comporting themselves." He was captured by the HMS *Hunter*, and two of his crew were sentenced to death. Governor Carlisle prohibited logwood cutting and offered amnesty for pirates, including a "double proportion of land if they would plant." Captains Coxon, Essex, Sharp, Allison, and Mackett rendezvoused at Port Morant, Jamaica, for an expedition to the Isthmus of Darien, the beginning of the great expeditions to seek plunder in the South Sea.

But these pirates did not bury the treasure they stole, nor did any during the Golden Age, which some rightly claim should be called the *Silver Age of Piracy*. Rather, the pirates spent their shares when they returned home. Perhaps the only reasonable tale of buried treasure, and possibly apocryphal at that, was one told by Labat. Legend has it, he wrote, that a Spanish treasure galleon wrecked on Anegada Island, and the crew buried its treasure to keep it safe. Most survivors were lost at sea, and the few who lived to tell the tale did not know where the treasure was buried. In 1701 one man stayed "four or five months on the island, digging and sounding . . . but no one has yet discovered the real treasure."[77] Treasure maps were no more common, and the closest reference to a treasure map was that of a "private map" showing the approximate location of a sunken treasure ship.[78] Coins of silver and gold were not dug from the ground on the Spanish Main, but were taken by force of arms or from ships sunk in the sea.

Yet the lure of buried and sunken treasure was real. According to one witness in 1685, "While on a cruise on the north-east coast of Hispaniola they came on a reef on which they saw several ingots of silver and one of gold, and within forty feet of it the hull of a ship wedged in upright."[79] Such visions, real and imagined, inspired lifelong obsessions with riches beneath the sea.

# 12 To the Slaughter, Gentle Beasts:
## The Sea Turtle, Manatee, and Seal

*I*n the spring of 1680 buccaneers in nine vessels ranging from eight to one hundred and fifty tons sailed to Boca del Toro, where they refitted and provisioned, finding "plenty of fat tortoises [sea turtles], the pleasantest meat in the world."[1]* With the pirates were several Moskito Indian "strikers" whose primary duty was to spear "Fish, Turtle, or Manatee . . . one or two of them in a Ship, will maintain 100 Men."[2] Sea turtle was a popular provision for buccaneers and filibusters, certainly as popular as the hog—Captain Bréha forced English turtle sloops to provision his vessel in 1681, for example.[3]

Hardly a traveler or roving author in the tropics failed to describe the sea turtle, the most graceful of all sea creatures, also called the sea tortoise, which was vital to mariners and seaside peoples.[4] Its flesh was food and its fat was rendered into oil: fresh for cooking, stale for lamps.[5] The most commonly described sea turtles in the New World were the green turtle, the "Trunk-turtle" or "hooping" turtle (the leatherback), the loggerhead, and the hawksbill. In the Caribbean, the green turtle was "the best of that sort, both for Largeness and Sweetness," but its thin shell was used "only for inlays." The hawksbill was taken primarily for its shell, which was used for "Cabinets, Combs, and other things." It was "but ordinary food," and in some places where it fed on moss it was not as sweet, and its shell could be covered with barnacles. Dampier wrote

---

*All quotations have been reprinted with their original spelling and punctuation.

that some taken between Portobello and the "Samballos" (San Blas) Islands caused those who ate them to "purge and vomit excessively." The trunk-turtle was the largest (its body averaged sixty inches in length) and had a rubber-like skin resembling a shell. The trunk-turtle and the loggerhead were seldom eaten, their flesh being "very rank," although the loggerhead was taken for oil and some suggested it was the "second best" turtle for eating. The Galápagos giant tortoise, called "Land-turtle" and "Hecatee," was also slaughtered by buccaneers for provisions. The giant animal was said to be "so sweet, that no Pullet eats more pleasantly." An early eighteenth-century privateer compared its taste to that of buffalo. All sea turtles are threatened species today, but unfortunately not yet protected in all their habitats.[6]

The Cayman Islands were the prime turtle-fishing grounds of the seventeenth-century Caribbean. "[Cayman] is an island of no inhabitants, there being two of them, but the people of Jamaica come continually there to catch turtle or tortoise, which they take a-many of and carry to Port Royal, which they kill and sell by the pound for twopence and threepence per pound; and it is a good thing that helps the island very much, and is very good victuals, and sometimes in the year they salt it and keep it salted a long time."[7] The French hunted turtles at the Caymans as well, and mariners sometimes found their way by following the noise of swimming sea turtles, there were so many of them.[8] Buccaneers noted great quantities of sea turtles at Boca del Toro, on Salt Tortuga, among the islands of the Bay of Honduras, off the southern coast and islands of Cuba, and along the Mosquito Coast, but sea turtles were found in plentiful numbers throughout the Caribbean islands and "along all the Coast on the Main."[9] Observers of the period noted that sea turtles, depending on the species and location, typically laid eggs two or three times from April through August, although some laid as late as September, and others even in December and January.[10]

Turtles were most easily "fished" ashore when laying eggs. This technique of "turning turtle" was well described by surgeon James Yonge:

> All the men run suddenly, by moonshine, between the shore and them, and the turtles, hearing or seeing the men, run as fast as they can to seaward and the sailors turn them on their backs. From this posture they are unable to stir and so remain till next day, when the sailors come and kill them.[11]

Dampier, however, described a more circumspect approach:

> The manner of taking them is to watch the Bay, by walking from one part to the other all night, making no noise, nor keeping any sort of light. When the Turtle comes ashore, the Man that watches for them

turns them on their Backs, then hales them above the high-water mark, and leaves them till the Morning. A large green Turtle, with her weight and struggling, will puzzle 2 Men to turn her.[12]

The green turtle commonly weighed three hundred pounds, and could weigh up to four hundred pounds, so seamen or fishermen sometimes used handspikes to turn them.[13] When taken (or when, according to one observer, they see "you come with a knife in your hand to kill" them) turtles "sob and weep like a human person," but in reality, when "weeping," turtles were excreting salt from a tear gland as well as lubricating their eyes.[14] The sea turtle's three-chambered heart was believed to be "the heart of a fowl, of a beast, and of a fish."[15]

To take a sleeping turtle at sea, turtle fishermen rowed quietly until within reach of the creature.

When the boat comes near them we forbear rowing, only one man sculls softly while another, lying over the bow, suddenly catches him by the sides, and, ere he wakes, pulls him out of the water. If he spies you, he is gone presently, or if you have hold him in the water, he hath such force in the oars of his fins that you shall hardly pull him up.[16]

Moskito strikers took turtles at sea with a "Tortoise-Iron," a "square sharp Iron Peg . . . made 4 square, sharp at one End, and not much above an Inch in length." After quietly paddling as close as possible, the striker hit the turtle in the shell with a spear tipped with the iron. The iron, connected to the spear with a line, parted from the spear when the turtle was struck, penetrated the shell, and could not be withdrawn. Moskito strikers made the iron parts of their hunting implements themselves, and also made their own line from the bark of the mahoe tree (sea hibiscus).[17] When turtles were mating at sea, strikers speared the female; the male would not let go, and was hauled aboard with her.[18]

The sea turtle was vital as food not only to buccaneers, but to all coastal residents of the Caribbean. At Jamaica it was a "common Food there, chiefly for the ordinary sort of People" and slaves.[19] Jamaican turtle fishermen, who primarily turned turtles at the Caymans and at the islands off the southern coast of Cuba, loaded sea turtles, many of them alive, in the holds of their sloops prior to sailing. The turtles lived for up to six weeks without food or water, although Pitman noted that they only lived several days out of the water, and then only if protected from the sun.[20] At Port Royal, turtles were held in "crauls" or "crawls" (corrals)—"Wires made with Stakes in the Sea, to preserve them alive," that is, a "place of Salt Water of Depth and Room for them to swim in, pallisado'd or staked, in round above the Waters Surface."[21] Turtle hunters also used "crauls" where they gathered turtles, keeping them penned until they butchered them or until they stowed them in the sloop's hold.[22] Most turtles, however, were quickly butchered, salted, and "barreled" during the six to eight weeks the sloops lay at anchor until their holds were full.[23] A barrel of salted turtle sold for eighteen to twenty-five shillings at Port Royal. So desirable was sea turtle in the West Indies that it was imported from the Canary Islands.[24]

"We are fed by provisions from New England, New York, Ireland, and have fishermen at the South Cays; all these routes were interrupted and dangerous" by pirates, wrote Governor Lynch.[25] Colonel Molesworth likewise noted the importance of the turtle trade: "I believe that nearly two thousand people, black and white, feed on it daily" in Jamaica, and it "is what masters of ships chiefly feed their men on in port."[26] The sea turtle was a critical part of the care and feeding—and thus success—of the Jamaican colony, which relied heavily on imports, including food imports.

At Port Royal, sea turtle was

> most commonly baked in the under shell, (with spice, dry herbs and forced meat,) which they call the calipee; the other dressed they call the calipach. The flesh looks and eats much like choice veal, but the fat is of a green colour, very luscious and sweet.[27]

Another traveler wrote of "the Callope of the Turtle, pepper'd and salted, or roasted and baked," with the rest boiled with turtle eggs to make an excellent broth.[28] James Yonge suggested parboiling in water, salt, and vinegar to take "the fishiness of him," then stewing with pepper and herbs. "They eat very sweet and tender; the breast-piece, or callaper, hath a shell as thick as parchment which comes away in boiling, and the rest is as soft as piecrust and very sweet."[29] The English also ate turtle steaks, the French "boucaned" turtles in the sand, and all ate the eggs, which made good "*Fricasseys and Omeletts*."[30] The Spanish and Portuguese did not make as much use of turtle meat, although they did use it for provisions at sea, cutting the flesh into long strips and drying it for a week "in the wind after they have well salted it," then smoking it for a week. Spanish sailors boiled it with garlic.[31] Exquemelin noted that if one ate "nothing but [green] turtle flesh for three or four weeks, your shirt becomes so greasy from sweat you can squeeze oil out and your limbs are weighed down by it."[32]

The West Indian manatee, or sea cow, another species threatened today, was also hunted and eaten by buccaneers or more often hunted by their Moskito strikers. Manatee flesh was considered "extraordinarily sweet, wholsome Meat." Privateers roasted calves (a "most delicate Meat"), as well as the belly meat of adult manatees, but the "Tail of a young Cow is most esteem'd."[33] Fat was also rendered from the tail, stored in jars, and eaten with boiled cornmeal.[34] Manatees were sometimes hunted for their oil alone. Naval surgeon John Atkins wrote that "it has no fishy Taste, but is as acceptable a Treat as Venison to Cockneighs [Cockneys]."[35] Buccaneers used manatee skin for making loops, "which they make fast on the Sides of their Canoas thro' which they put their oars in rowing, instead of Tholes or Pegs." From the skin of the back of a bull or cow, they made "horse whips" that were used both on horses and "for punishing their Slaves."[36] One observer had "seen a Bar of Iron cut and dented" with one whip, and in Jamaica "Masters are forbidden and prohibited with it to strike their White Servants."[37] The manatee was also hunted for reasons other than food: some believed it "hath a stone in the Head which is a gallant Remedy against the Pains and Dolors of the Stone," and that its pulverized bones could be mixed with a liquid and drunk to "provoke Urine."[38] Similar beliefs persist and contribute to the manatee's demise even today.[39]

Moskito strikers hunted manatee with a harpoon from a canoe, striking the manatee and then following the float (similar to a large fishing cork) trailing on the surface until the animal tired. The strikers then pulled up the float and line, and let the manatee pull the canoe until the animal's "Strength is spent, [then] they hale it up to the Canoa's side, and knock it on the Head, and tow it to the nearest shore." Dampier wrote that he saw two Moskito strikers in a tiny canoe take two manatee a day for a week, none weighing less than six hundred pounds.[40]

A peaceful creature of two subspecies (the Florida and Antillian), the West Indian manatee was found both alone and in groups of up to twenty near the shore in shallow waters throughout the Caribbean, along the Atlantic coast of North America to latitude 40°north, and along the Atlantic coast of South America to latitude 8° or 10°south, although its principal range was within the tropics. The manatee was also capable of making deepwater passages. Primarily an herbivore, the manatee used its prehensile lips to grasp aquatic plants.[41] Dampier was familiar with the manatee in "*Blewfield's* River," as well as the "Bay of Campeachy, on the Coasts of Bocca del Drago and Bocco del Toro, in the River of Darien, and among the South Keys or little Islands of Cuba." He also heard of a few on the north coast of Jamaica and multitudes in the rivers of Surinam.[42] Said by some to be the origin of the mermaid legend, buccaneers made no such claim. If indeed the manatee was the original mermaid identified by sailors, it was surely as a joke after weeks at sea.

*B*uccaneers hunted other marine mammals as well. Seals, called *Seahounds* by the Dutch, provided "Seals-skins and Trane-Oyl" for traders and at times oil for buccaneers. By the late seventeenth century, their Caribbean range was limited: Dampier wrote that he saw them (the Caribbean monk seal) only "in the Bay of *Campeachy*, at certain Islands called the *Alceranes*, and at others called the *Desarts*."[43] Today they are extinct. At Juan Fernández Island in the South Sea lived the Juan Fernández fur seal, which Dampier noted had "fine thick short Furr; the like I have not taken notice of any where but in these Seas. Here are always Thousands, I might say possibly Millions of them." By 1965, due to massive overhunting the seals numbered only two hundred but are today much increased. Buccaneers were also familiar with the South American and Galápagos fur seals and with the harbor and gray seals on the Atlantic coast of North America.[44]

𝐵uccaneers at Juan Fernández also hunted sea lions for their fat, to be rendered into oil that Dampier said "is very sweet and wholesome to fry Meat withal" although typically the oil was used in lamps. A large male sea lion yielded a hogshead of oil. They also made dice from the animal's large teeth and occasionally ate the meat, an "indifferent good Food."[45] Buccaneer surgeon and author Lionel Wafer called them *Sea-Swine*, and wrote that those shot near the Río de la Plata "eat like Land-pork, except some Fishy taste it had."[46] Sea lions were found through much of the South Sea, and varieties included the California, Galápagos, South American, and Northern sea lions, although pirates probably had no contact with the latter. The sea lion, often a curious and playful creature, even to the point of playing pranks, could also be aggressive, nipping and biting in defense of its territory. Last, some pirates and other inhabitants of New Providence hunted whales when not engaged in piracy, wrecking, or searching for ambergris.[47]

𝑇he Moskito strikers who provisioned the buccaneer vessels at Boca del Toro with these beasts continued across Darien with pirates of admittedly dubious commission and pecuniary purpose. The Moskitos were one of the few tribes that managed to coexist with Europeans, perhaps because of the difficult access to their native lands on the Mosquito Coast. Most tribes were not so fortunate, and the best they managed was a tenuous and temporary coexistence, often by allying with one European nation against another, as even the Moskito and Darien (Cuna) did, both of whom were critical allies of the buccaneers.

# 13 The Beginning of the End:
## Native America Enslaved and Enraged

I n December 1679 five small vessels commanded by Captains Coxon, Essex, Sharp, Allison, and Mackett have set sail from Jamaica to cruise along the Isthmus of Darien, proving, among other things, that Port Royal remains a center of piracy, notwithstanding a pretended commission the expedition carries: "Let passes to goe into the bay of Hundoras, to cutt Logwood, from his Maj'ties Reall Subject the Earle of Carlisle."* Perhaps the buccaneers also carry a permission from the governor of Petit Goave, purchased for ten pieces-of-eight, to hunt and fish for three months, which they "contrived [by forgery] to make it last for three years."[1] They "wood and water" (take on fresh water and firewood) at Port Morant, then, capturing no prizes, plan an attack on nearby Portobello. Joined now by Captain Rose, a Frenchman, they rendezvous at Springer's Key. The wind is contrary, so they must make their way in fourteen or fifteen canoes and periagers, and quickly, before they are discovered. Leaving a sailing crew of roughly one hundred men behind, two hundred to two hundred and fifty buccaneers make their way toward Portobello, discovering Captain Lessone at anchor along the way. Eighty Frenchmen join the party, which soon comes ashore twenty leagues from Portobello at the "olde ruinated Port" called by the buccaneers *Puerta Pee* or *Port Scrivan*, and known by the Spanish as Puerto del Escribano. John Coxon is the expedition's "general," and Robert Allison leads the *forlorn*, as the advance guard is called.[2]

---

*All quotations have been reprinted with their original spelling and punctuation.

For three nights they march, hiding and sleeping by day. The men are ravenous and many are weak, having eaten little, and the feet of those who march barefoot have been cut and torn by the rough, rocky terrain. Three miles from Portobello they enter an Indian village. Although these pirates have recently received offers of aid by many local Indians, who, driven from the Pacific Main, have "a greate Antipothy against the Spaniards," the Indians in this village are not enemies of Spain, but a subjugated people who are now servant allies. "Ladrones!" (Thieves!) cries one villager (in one account not an Indian but a "Negro") as he races to warn the Spanish at Portobello.[3]

The runner arrives thirty minutes before the pirates do—their own "good boyes, You that are able to runn" cannot catch the swift Indian. The alarm gun fires and the town makes ready to receive the English and French villains, but by mid-afternoon Portobello is in pirate hands, most of its residents having retreated to the principal fort, the Glory (Fuerte Santiago de la Gloria). Although protected by two hundred or three hundred soldiers, the large Fuerte San Felipe on one side of the entrance to the bay, a "Block-House" on the other, the "small low Fort" of San Jeronimo in the town on the shore, and the Glory itself, Portobello's defenses are designed to repel an attack by sea, not by land. The following day two hundred Spaniards sally from the Glory, but the pirates and their superior musketry force them back. The rovers loot the town for another day, then depart—some by land, some by sea—missing by only a day a large Spanish force from Panama sent to relieve Portobello. The pirates lose none, and have but five or six wounded, half of them by fire from the two small forts of "Puerta Vella." An overladen canoe of the best plunder sinks, and the pirates share a relative pittance of one hundred pieces-of-eight per man.[4]

Besides illustrating a surprise attack on a Spanish town, the circumstances of this assault and the expedition across the Isthmus of Darien that soon followed revealed the status of Native Americans along the Main. Even within the literally narrow confines of the isthmus, where most Native Americans remained "free Indians," Native Americans were found in four capacities: unconquered, free, and able to ally with whom they choose; conquered but rebellious; conquered but allied to their conquerors; and, for all practical purposes, enslaved. With some exceptions, the Spanish kept subjugated Indians unarmed out of fear of uprisings and reprisals.[5] Our Caribbean pirates knew Indians in all of these states, but they saw them in more practical terms. There were Native Americans who were allies or members of the ship's company, guides, providers of material support, or slaves. And there were others who hindered or opposed them, often violently.

$\mathcal{T}$o most Europeans in the seventeenth century the Native American—the "Indian"—was entirely alien, an unknown savage lurking in a world of the savage unknown. And for European observers emphasizing the superficial, this view was understandable. In warm climes, for example, many Native Americans, men and women, dressed only in a "clout" (a cloth around the waist, covering the buttocks and groin) or in nothing at all. But European sailors aboard ships in the tropics also cared "not for any more than would slightly cover them."[6] Indians might "range about us, howling like Wolves and Dogs."[7] But Europeans shouted and made strange noises, from the screams of battle to the "Huzzah!" and *Te Deum* of triumph. Many Indians were horribly cruel to prisoners, with tortures as ingenious as any of the Inquisition, if they did not first kill their prisoners for the sake of convenience. They quenched hot iron instruments on the flesh of prisoners. "They break your teeth with a stone or clubs."[8] They burned fingernails with coals, then bit off them. "They cut off your stones [testicles], and the women play with them as with balls."[9] They burned prisoners alive. Europeans, however, also burned people at the stake, broke them on the wheel, strangled them by hanging or with the garrote, tortured and murdered them in the names of both faith and greed, and permitted their own poor to die of neglect.[10] Many pirates were known for their cruelty, and filibusters in the South Sea decapitated prisoners as an incentive for Spaniards to ransom towns and hostages.[11] Some Europeans pretended to be shocked by the Indian practice of "trophy taking"—Caribs used boucans to smoke the limbs of their enemies as trophies of war, and would "fill calabashes" with human fat, for example, and some North American tribes scalped their enemies or ate parts of their flesh.[12] But yet again, Europeans hanged many of their dead criminals and rebels in chains in public, or dismembered them and displayed the body parts for all to see, gristly trophies of a "civilized" justice system.

But the greatest differences between Europeans and Native Americans were not superficial—in European eyes, "wild" men and women were half-naked, painted, tattooed, feathered, and dressed in skins, for example—but cultural. The significant differences were in belief systems and the behaviors based on them, and some Europeans did try to see Native Americans in a balanced light.[13] Aphra Behn described them as representing "an absolute Idea of the first State of Innocence," a naive and patronizing view, but one more conducive to cultural exchange.[14] Yet even an understanding of Native American culture derived from common needs, fears, and passions—the finding of common ground—was seldom enough to override the simple fact that Native Americans occupied lands of rich resources on which Europeans encroached. Thomas Gage noted, albeit with a bias, that Spaniards were more earnest in conquering tribes whose land contained "the many mines of silver and treasures of gold which they know to be there."[15] Conflict was inevitable, and, unless the lands were not easily accessible, war followed, as did the eventual seizure of Indian lands by force of arms—conquest, in another word. Even before conflict came to blows with Europeans, disease ravaged many tribes, weakening or destroying them.

*W*hen they went to war with Europeans, in many ways Native Americans were at a disadvantage. Although their knowledge of the terrain was usually superior and their ambush tactics effective, their practice of warfare was often seasonal and their arms and numbers inferior to those of Europeans. Nearly all Native American tribes preferred the tactics of ambuscade and raid followed by a quick withdrawal to open warfare in the field because most tribes could not afford large-scale losses of warriors on the battlefield. Ambushes and quick raids were also highly effective tactics when facing an enemy superior in numbers and technology. However, Europeans learned to use similar tactics against Native Americans, and a successful assault on a tribe's town or village often reduced the tribe to subjugation or destroyed it. Native American tribes rarely remained unified in large numbers for long periods of sustained warfare against European enemies.

When Native Americans were introduced to European arms, they became adept at shooting the flintlock musket.[16] Many tribes, however, lacked firearms, and went to war with their traditional weapons. In 1702 more than one hundred Cuna, "very brisk young Fellows," allied themselves with English privateers, and each was armed with "two Lances, two Bows, and about twenty Arrows."[17] War clubs were also common. The bow (also used in Africa, Turkey, Tartary, Japan, India, Persia, and other areas) was a highly effective weapon, particularly at shorter ranges. A skilled shooter—as most Native American males were—could shoot far more swiftly than anyone armed with a musket, and were capable of shooting "ten or a dozen arrows in the time it takes to load a gun."[18] Accounts of Native American accuracy with the bow were common: "I went abroad with my Indian a-fishing, at which he was dexterous that with his bow and arrow, he would shoot a small fish at a great distance." Modern tests, however, suggest that arrows fired as swiftly as possible are no more accurate than musket fire.[19] Indians could also "tie balls of cotton to the points of their arrows and light them just before they shoot" to set fire to thatched roofs. However, this would require a large ball of cotton, probably saturated with a combustible substance, to prevent the flame from being extinguished in flight.[20] In wet weather, the bow was superior to the musket.[21] However, the bow lacked the effective range (killing range) of the musket, and an arrow was more likely to be stopped by cover or dense vegetation (a musket ball passed through an obstacle more easily than an arrow with its shaft and broad arrowhead) or to be deflected—certainly at longer ranges arrows were easily deflected.[22] Heavy leather coats or mail hindered or stopped arrow penetration, although at close range (up to thirty yards) arrows easily penetrated them. Exquemelin described Alexandre, called Bras-de-Fer (Iron Arm), demonstrating the superior penetrating power of the musket against the Native American bow from a greater distance. At shorter ranges, however, an arrow could pass through an animal, going in one side and out the other.[23]

At longer ranges the arrow lost velocity, became less accurate, and was more easily avoided; Indians were most accurate with the bow at ranges of less than fifty yards.[24] The bow also had a long learning curve that required diligent practice, and arrow making was labor intensive.[25] Muskets, unlike bows, were often loaded with "double ball," triple ball, or ball and seven or eight swan shot. A buccaneer carried thirty cartridges in his cartouche box (as opposed to the Indian's twenty or so arrows in his quiver) and could thus put one and a half to a dozen times as many projectiles in the air during a fight than could his Native American counterpart armed with a bow. The firing of multiple ball and shot in a single cartridge compensated for the inaccuracies introduced by longer ranges, and at close ranges it could injure or kill several men at one time. Indians, often allied with the Spanish, used the bow against buccaneers; for example: "Capt. Sawlkings was shott in the Head with an arrow, and one man more shot in the hand, butt both soon cured."[26]

Exquemelin described a filibuster at Chagres castle in 1671 who was shot

> with an arrow in his back, which pierced the body to the other side. This instantly he pulled out with great valour at the side of his breast: then, taking a little cotton that he had about him, he wound it about the said arrow, and putting it in his musket, he shot it back into the castle

where it kindled thatched roofs and blew up a store of powder.[27] Although this account may be largely true, the fire was probably kindled by grenades, thrown to great effect against the walls and on the roofs, as described in another account.[28]

*I*n the late seventeenth century, many tribes were defending themselves and their lands against encroaching Europeans. In New England King Philip's War ended, as had the attacks in Virginia and Maryland during Bacon's Rebellion by whites on the remaining Powhatan. In Florida, the Westo, Cherokee, and various Creeks, encouraged by Carolinians, began attacking the Guale, allies of the Spanish.

In the Caribbean, the Caribs—"a sort of Warlike Indians, delighting to rove on the Sea in Periagoes or large Canoes"—of St. Vincent and Dominica were engaged in warfare against the English of the Lesser Antilles and the Dutch at Suriname.[29] At Barbuda, "two hundred and forty, in six periagos" pillaged, drank "kill-devil or rum," and slaughtered several English, including three boys whose heads were dashed against tree trunks. The Carib attackers were armed primarily with bows, but also carried war clubs three and a half feet long. They had a few rapiers and backswords, a few braces of pistols, and forty muskets provided by the French and Dutch. The bows were six feet long, the arrows were three and a half feet long, and the arrowheads were barbed and often poisoned with manchineel (poison guava). Caribs sometimes cut the seizing, which held the arrowhead to the shaft, prior to shooting, so that the shaft fell off when the arrow struck its target, making the arrowhead more difficult to extract. The English retaliated in 1683, attacking both islands, burning three hundred houses and thirty-five pirogues, but killing only eleven Caribs, including Captain Tabary who led the attack at Barbuda.[30]

Caribs were known for their daring attacks ashore and at sea. In 1655,

> came of to vs a periago with 14 Ingons, they haueing all boes and arrowes, and one of our shipes commanding them to come abord they let flie a whole flight of arowes at our men as they stud vpon the ship sid, and wounded 5 men, and soe rune away frome vs, thayer bot going to swift for any shipp.[31]

The French often purchased Carib plunder, including slaves. Some of the New England tribes also engaged in sea-roving warfare, taking small English vessels at sea.[32]

One of the significant products of warfare between whites and Native Americans, or between tribes in wars provoked or urged on by whites, was a significant trade in Native American slaves. South Carolinians developed an alliance with local Westo Indians, encouraging them to attack the Spanish in Florida and enslave Native Americans who were Spanish allies. A Native American slave trade extended throughout the southeast region of North America in the late seventeenth century as the English, Spanish, and French attempted to expand and protect their holdings and spheres of influence. Much of the English trade was driven by surgeon John Woodward, once imprisoned at St. Augustine and later freed by the buccaneer Robert Searles in 1668.[33] Virginians likewise sold Powhatan prisoners, taken during Bacon's Rebellion, into slavery.[34] At the end of King Philip's War many Wampanoag prisoners, and those of other tribes as well, were sold as slaves and sent to the West Indies. Slavers believed the Native Americans would be less recalcitrant far from home, but in at least one instance they were wrong. Twenty "stout New-England Indians that were taken in the Wars there" were carried to Campeche to cut logwood. At the first opportunity, they killed the captain and marched off, "designing to return to their own Country by Land."[35]

Buccaneers and filibusters also traded in Indian slaves and attacked coastal tribes in Spanish territory, particularly in the Bay of Campeche, "where they plundered and brought away the Indian Women to serve them at their Huts, and sent their Husbands to be sold at Jamaica."[36] The women became sexual partners, some voluntarily, some by force. At an island at Cape Gracias à Dios buccaneers and filibusters contracted with Moskitos for women, each "buying" a woman "at the price of a knife or any old axe, wood-bill, or hatchet." The woman remained the pirate's servant for the time he was ashore, feeding him and providing sexual favors, although the pirate was forbidden to "commit any hostility, or depredation upon the inhabitants."[37] One buccaneer and logwood cutter on the Mosquito Coast kept a Native American woman as a slave, "who used to sleep with him and dress his Provisions, which he kept as his Wife." Nearby lived two other white men, who also each kept a slave as a "wife."[38] Others married Moskito women, and, according to Exquemelin, if a Moskito woman's pirate husband died while living with her, she would bury him with the same ceremony she would use for a Moskito husband, including disinterring the bones after a year, cleaning them, and carrying them with her for another year.[39]

*B*uccaneers' most common allies were the Moskito, who served as strikers, and the Cuna, who assisted them in attacks against the Spanish at Darien, and also aided them in crossing safely to the South Sea. As a pretense, buccaneers claimed to attack the Spanish under the authority of "our Emperour [Captain Andreas, a Cuna chief], under whose Commission we fought."[40] The Moskitos, whose homeland along the Honduran coast still retains their name, had been allies of the English since the Puritans established their colony at Providence Island in the 1630s, and Moskito "princes" even traveled to London.[41] At sea with the buccaneers the strikers dressed as their roving comrades did. Dampier wrote that they were a tribe of no more than one hundred males, and described them as loyal and honorable men who "behave themselves very bold in fight, and never seem to flinch nor hang back."[42]

Many of the native peoples of the Isthmus of Darien were known for killing interlopers, including pirates, but owing to John Gret, a Cuna boy kidnapped by Captain Wright at the San Blas Islands and raised by the Moskito, alliances were forged and buccaneers and filibusters could cross the isthmus to the South Sea with impunity.[43] Some rovers married into tribes, either by necessity from circumstances such as marooning or to seek a safe haven from pirate-hunting authorities. In 1702 near the Concepción River lived eight hundred "French pirates" (pirates, wives, and children) who had been there for at least a decade.[44] Others lived among the Moskito. Indians also served as common members of pirate crews, and some, like Pasqual Onan, served as captains or officers, at least among the Spanish. A "Spanish Indian" was among the company of buccaneers who crossed the isthmus in 1680; he "first took up Arms with Captain *Sawkins*."[45] One of King Andreas's "captains" and two or three of his men accompanied South Sea buccaneers in 1683 on raids up and down the Spanish Main. The captain was probably one of Andreas's sons, and his nephew was one of the company as well.[46] On this same voyage, buccaneers also kept Indian slaves, captured from the Spanish.[47]

Attacks by Spaniards on Native Americans in reprisal for assisting buccaneers and filibusters were noted, but few if any buccaneers or filibusters took up the Native American cause for its own sake, although many decried their treatment at the hands of both Spanish priests and laymen. The most notable exception was Monbars the Exterminator, who in the late 1660s led Native Americans against the Spanish, as much out of a desire for plunder as out of a desire, bordering on rage, to avenge the unjust treatment of the original inhabitants of the Spanish Main. Unfortunately, the story may be apocryphal or exaggerated.[48]

Only once did Native Americans expel the European conquerors from their lands. In 1680 Pueblo Indians revolted against their Spanish overlords, driving them from the Rio Grande Basin (now New Mexico). They were free Indians once more, until don Diego de Vargas made an *entrada* and ritual reconquest of the territory in 1692.

*A*lso in 1680 buccaneers under Coxon, Sharp, and others sacked Portobello and the English government at Jamaica issued warrants for their arrests. Hurricanes caused significant damage in Jamaica and the Leeward Islands. The fort at St. Thomas was completed, and the island's population grew to approximately one hundred and fifty whites and seventy-five blacks, mostly slaves. Charleston moved to its permanent site at the juncture of the Ashley and Cooper rivers in Carolina. The Spanish seized one of d'Estrées's support vessels. In retaliation, he sought reparations and the release of prisoners, by threat of force of arms at Santo Domingo, Santa Marta, and Cartagena. One of the released prisoners was Guillaume Champagne, a redoubtable filibuster imprisoned by the Spanish since 1668. D'Estrées also visited Petit Goave and met Grammont and his filibusters who sacked Maracaibo. The Spanish attacked Laguna de Términos and captured one hundred and sixty logwood cutters, but more than two hundred were away at the time of the attack, seeking the cacao mule trains. The English and Spanish signed a treaty and agreed to defend each other if attacked. Grammont, with Thomas Paine and William Wright in his company, sacked La Guayra (Caracas). Captain Townley gathered supplies at Petit Goave and returned to the site of the *Maravillas*, where he had been working for a year. The Spanish competed a fort, San Marcos de Apalache, on the headland at the juncture of the Toscache (St.

Marks) and Guacara (Wakulla) rivers at Apalache Bay on the Gulf Coast of Florida. Creek Indians and Carolina English began attacking Spanish missions on Jekyl and St. Catherine islands.

Capt. Bartholomew Sharp and others landed with three hundred men at Golden Island at Darien and met with Chief Don Andreas (a Cuna) to recruit people for an expedition. The commanders included Coxon, Essex, Sharp, Allison, Mackett, and Harris commanding vessels, as well as Captains Cook, Watling, and Springer in the capacity of common men. French captains Bournano and Rose abandoned the expedition, unwilling to cross into the South Sea. Most of the buccaneers on the expedition traveled by land, the rest by river. They sacked Santa Maria; blockaded Panama; attacked Pueblo Nuevo, Arica, and Ilo; sacked La Serena; and attacked shipping along the Pacific coast of the Americas. Coxon and seventy men parted company with the main force after a battle with an armadillo at Perico, and returned overland to the Caribbean. Coxon was briefly chased by the HMS *Hunter*, aboard which was Lord Carlisle, governor of Jamaica. In December d'Estrées made intimidating visits to Trinidad and the Orinoco, claiming reparations for Spanish depredations, and Brandenburg (German) privateers sailed to the Caribbean in search of Spanish prizes. Aboard the Brandenburg vessels were Dutchmen, Flemings, Brandenburgers, Danes, Russians, and Poles.

Piracy, especially for English buccaneers, had become more difficult in the Caribbean, and the South Sea lured away many. For those who sacked Portobello, the South Sea and its awaiting plunder was more appealing than a noose in Port Royal. Although the end of buccaneering and *la flibuste* was not yet in sight, and neither was the end of the free Indians of the New World near, the beginning of the end for both certainly was.

# 14 Tarpaulin Cant and Spanish Lingua: The Language of the Buccaneer

*S*hee fierd a Harkquebus att us, att which wee presented them with a whole Volley; she fier severall small gunns at us, and wounded 3 men. one of them after-wards died. wee laid her aboard and tooke her. She had about 30 hands in her, fitted out for an Armadillo to come downe to the Isle of Plate, to see what a posture we lay in,*

wrote a South Sea buccaneer, perhaps Edward Povey according to scholars Derek House and Norman Thrower.[1] The manuscript, left at St. Thomas and unedited for publication, provides excellent insight into buccaneer speech, showing us a lyrical language foremost of the sea, but also of armed conflict and adventure in general. It identifies the speaker not only as a mariner, but as a rover.

The language of sailors had always been unique and readily identifiable. Highly specialized, it dealt not only with the technology of the ship, but with her behavior in different environments, with the environments themselves—of sea, air, and land—and with the relationship of one vessel to others. Among

---

*All quotations have been reprinted with their original spelling and punctuation.

the often-multiethnic crew it was a unifying factor and a touchstone with which to learn a new language. A sailor's speech was one of his most recognizable characteristics, ranging from the strictly utilitarian terminology used to sail a ship to the relaxed speech of the sailor with his messmates or ashore in a tavern. Basil Ringrose provided an example of the former:

> We had a clear night the night before this day, and a strong gale, insomuch that this day we were forced to take in our fore-sail, and loosen our mizzen, which was soon blown to pieces. Our eldest seamen said that they were never in the like storm of wind before—the sea was all in a foam. . . . All the past night we had a furious W. N. W. wind. We set our sail a-drough, and so drove to the southward very much. . . . At noon we bent another mizzen.[2]

From John Smith we have an example of commands at sea:

> Let fall your Fore-sail . . . who is at the Helm there? coil your Cables in small fakes, hale the Cat, a Bitter, belay, loose fast your Anchor with your Shank-painter, stow the Boat, set the land, how it bears by the Compass[?][3]

In casual conversation, the mariner's speech was not only lyrical but metaphorical, as mildly lampooned by satirist Ned Ward, who seemed ultimately to have a deep regard for "Neptune's sunburnt subjects," some of whom he described as "jolly, rough-hewn, rattling topers, who looked as they'd been hammered into an uncouth shape upon Vulcan's anvil; whose iron sides, and metal-colored faces seemed to dare all weathers, spit fire at the frigid zone, and bid death defiance." He continued:

> I soon found by their dialect they were masters of ships:'Cheer up, my lads, pull away, save tide; come, boys.'Then handling the quart, being empty,'What, is she light? You, sir, that's next, haul the bar-line [bowline], and call the cooper's mate.' The drawer being come,'Here, you fly-blown swab, take away this damned tankard, and ballast her well. Pox take her, there's no stowage in her hold. Have you ne'er a larger vessel?'

And a seaman ashore seeking lodging: "'Ounds, mother, let me have a bucket full of punch, that we may swim and toss in ocean of good liquor, like a couple of little pinks in the Bay of Biscay."[4]

In another passage Ward captured the nuance, even if exaggerated, of the common sailor's argumentative boasting:

I'll tell you, there was my Master . . . an old Boatswain in one of his Majesties Ships, who was Superhanded, and past his Labour, and the Ambaraltie Divorc'd him from his Ship, and the King allow'd him a Suspension, and this Lubberly Whelp here says I talk like a Fool; and sure I have not used the Sea this Thirty Years but I can Argufie any thing as proper as he can.[5]

*R*eturning to the more practical parts of speech, the sailor's language included various chants to aid in hauling or heaving, although the term *shanty* or *chantey* (from the French *chanter*, to sing) did not appear until the nineteenth century. Few chants from the seventeenth century are extant, and most of those we know today are from the nineteenth century, with a few from the late eighteenth. However, simple examples do exist:"Haul, Cat, haul!" cried the boatswain.[6] And the coxswain:"Give the Boat more way for a dram of the Botel, who says Amends, one and all, *Vea, vea, vea, vea, vea, vea*," which means, as Smith put it,"they pull all strongly together."[7] And the most famous chant of them all, thanks to Robert Louis Stevenson, existed from at least the early eighteenth century, and probably much earlier:" . . . telling the master this *Yo-hope* of heaving up the anchor was a needless trouble, when they designed to burn the ship."[8] More musical than the chant was the cry of the leadsman:"tho' he should feel himself within half a Foot of Ruin, he'll sing ye forth his Soundings with as pleasant a Note, as Thief shall a Psalm at *Tyburn*."[9]

"Foul language" was another notable feature of the sailor's speech. Strictly speaking, there was swearing and there was cursing, the former being the use of "obscene" or profane language, and the latter being the use of profane language against someone. Although today the terms are usually considered synonymous, in the seventeenth century they were typically regarded as two forms of foul speech. Puritans punished swearing with a fine, cursing with a fine and a whipping, for example.[10] "Fuck!" and "Goddamn!" were examples of the former,"Goddamn you!" of the latter, although certainly they were often bound together. *Fuck* was an old English word, dating from at least the fifteenth century, with probable roots in cattle breeding or copulation in general, and was as prevalent in the "coarse speech" of the seventeenth century as it is in the present. Rake John Wilmot, Earl of Rochester, used it frequently in his poetry and both as noun and verb, no differently than it is used today, at least in regard to copulation.[11] It and other notable words of its ilk had a legitimate purpose, contrary to the opinion of the many who disapprove of such language. For example, when vented not at another but merely "to the heavens," it diffused anger and frustration that might otherwise lead to violence, for not all situations were amenable to more temperate means of anger management. Foul language also directed one's attention to faults or mistakes—especially life-threatening ones—better than could any other form of speech.

Boatswains past and present are well known for their foul language, and most have a knack for cussing at people, or cussing them out, without offending them, a valuable skill for getting things done. Sailors knew that "Oaths and horrid Threats, are but Wind . . . and they value no such Puffs, if they can weather a Beating."[12] It was only when such language became personally insulting and demeaning that seamen were likely to take serious offense. For the boatswain, "a damned thundering Fellow" who worked with rigging, heaving, towing, and other such tasks requiring the coordination of many elements, as well as the application of much physical labor, and whose tasks were subject to the rule of "shit happens," cussing—"embroidered Oaths and Curses"—was almost mandatory for completing the job. Foul language was a social lubricant with magical properties, for often work was suddenly completed after its application.[13] Not least of all, foul language contributed to group bonding, particularly in regard to socially marginal groups or those engaged in some form of rebellion or hazardous duty, or both: sailors, privateers, and pirates, for example. Not to be forgotten was artistic merit: a well-turned phrase of foul language was as deserving of appreciation as any and was often more useful. A fair amount of social disapproval was necessary, however, lest such language lose its natural force.

A boatswain circa 1700 expressed the need for this language best, at least from his point of view: "But, Zounds [God's Wounds], he'll cry, what would you have me do? A Man without Noise, is a Thing without a Soul, and fit for nothing but a Pissing-Post."[14] Henry Morgan, former buccaneer and lieutenant governor of Jamaica, was no stranger to such language. "In his drink Sir Henry reflects on the Government, swears, damns, and curses most extravagantly," even "so to the Assembly." He was formally accused by a woman of saying "God damn the Assembly," although another affidavit denied he made such a statement.[15] Offensive language—unlawful in this period in England and her colonies under a law passed during the reign of James I—was not limited to sailors and former sailors.[16] Most people cursed at times. The "common" women of Jamaica and Barbados were known, for example, as "great Swearers," especially (according to surgeon John Atkins) the Scotch and Irish.[17] As for reputations, Spanish sailors were reputed to curse as much as or more than any.[18]

Mariners were also reputed as "plain-dealers," as plainspoken men who spoke their minds and did not hide their feelings in polite prevarication. A line in John Gay's *Polly* (1729) explained it best: "Excuse my plain speaking, Captain; a boatswain must swear in a storm, and a man must speak plain, when he sees foul weather a-head of us."[19] Such plain speaking should come as no surprise, given the nature of the sea, for in this dangerous environment one must speak up as necessary or die. Such a habit, nay, requirement, was easily carried over into the more mundane aspects of life. Ego certainly contributed to plain speaking as well as the frustrations of a fatalistic environment, and perhaps also the fact that once at sea the sailor and his expertise could not be immediately replaced.[20] Mariners were also well known for their sense of humor, including "gallows humor" and for their bragging, "sea stories" and other exaggerations.

Alas, the pirate speech Hollywood has given us is little akin to the real thing. Even so, when a Hollywood pirate captain exhorted his crew with "Me Hearties!" he was repeating almost authentically a legitimate phrase found not only in Shakespeare's *Romeo and Juliet* and *The Tempest* (spoken by the boatswain in the latter), but also among real seamen.[21] "Come my Hearts, have up your Anchor, that we may have a good Prize," ordered an example of a seventeenth-century captain.[22] As for Long John Silver's "Shiver my timbers!"—in the language of the seventeenth-century sailor, timbers really could shiver, but the expression itself was probably from the nineteenth century.[23]

$\mathcal{M}$oving beyond the language of ship handling and the sea, Spanish was the most prevalent tongue in the New World and was vital to pirates for intelligence, deception, negotiation, and trade. It was also the language most often used with Native Americans, although if there was no common spoken language, whites and Native Americans communicated via a "dumb show," known today as *sign language*.[24] Dampier noted that many privateers spoke Spanish, although indications from other sources suggested that their fluency was doubtful, for "linguisters" (interpreters or translators) who had "the linqua att will" were commonly used.[25] Nevertheless, many pirates were reasonably fluent in Spanish, and at the very least most knew enough Spanish to engage in simple communication. Many were multilingual beyond Spanish and their native tongue. Laurens de Graff, for example, spoke Dutch, Spanish, and French, and possibly some English. Basil Ringrose was "both an ingenious man, and spake very well several Languages" including English, French, and Latin—but not Spanish. Dutch buccaneer and linguist Jacobus Marquess spoke fluent Spanish and several other languages, including English and Dutch. Bartholomew Sharp spoke Spanish as well as English, and probably knew at least a smattering of French, Moskito, and Cuna. Lionel Wafer spoke English, "the High-Land, or Primitive Irish Language" of the Scottish Highlands and Ireland, some Cuna, and probably some French, Spanish, and Latin as well. Rock the Brazilian, a Dutchman active in the 1660s, who spoke Dutch, Portuguese, and some Native American languages fluently, sailed with the buccaneers because he felt that English was easier to learn than French, which he did not speak well. He also spoke Spanish so well that he was often taken for one of that nation.[26] These pirates, and others as well, were also literate, in that they could read and write, although in general it seemed that more of these men were illiterate than literate.

The breadth of languages, regional variants, pidgins, and lingua francas among buccaneers and filibusters was surely as staggering as the great variety of peoples of the New World. The variants, not only among sailors but among local populations, gave rise to new accents, vocabularies, and usages necessary to life in a new world. As buccaneers and filibusters descended on the Spanish in the South Sea, language was vital to transcend or manipulate the various differences in peoples and their customs. Multinational and multiethnic crews had to work and fight together in spite of language differences; Spaniards had to be interrogated, used as pilots, and traded with; and Indians were needed as guides and allies: all things were hindered without clear communication. For the buccaneer, the addition of another tongue was as natural and necessary as knowing the difference between taking in, casting off, and letting go.

# 15 Armadillas, Galleons, and Canoes:
## Sea Battles in the Great South Sea

O n *Wednesday* early in the Morning we set out for King *Golden-Cap's-House*, (for so the *Buccaneers* called him, from a Wreath of Gold he usually wore about his head) as they Dignified *Don Andreas* with the Title of Emperor, and continued our Journey 'till about four in the Afternoon....*

wrote Bartholomew Sharp of the beginning of his march across the Isthmus of Darien into the South Sea in 1680.[1] Drums beat and flags waved.[2] Each of the five commanders had different colors: Sharp's was red, with white and green ribbons; Richard Sawkins's was red striped with yellow; Peter Harris's green; John Coxon's red; and Edmund Cook's red striped with yellow, with "a hand and sword for his device."[3]

This was the first of two major incursions that ravaged much of the Spanish Main in the South Sea, and left its population in fear or dread. For students of piracy or of independent military forces, these South Sea adventurers wrote numerous detailed journals—far more journals and information than are available on any other group of pirates in history. Basil Ringrose, Lionel Wafer, William Dick, Bartholomew Sharp, John Cox (not to be confused with John Coxon), and probably Edward Povey wrote of the first incursion, and William Dampier, Raveneau de Lussan, and Abraham Cowley the second.

---

*All quotations have been reprinted with their original spelling and punctuation.

Dampier's journal also included details of the first, and Wafer's of the second—Dampier, Ringrose, and Wafer were members of both incursions, and doubtless Ringrose would have written of the second as well, were he not killed in action. The details of these voyages, or even their mere summaries, are too vast to cover in a single chapter, and even an entire book can barely do justice to them. They are excellent examples of what man will do for the sake of greed and rebellion and what he will do to defend against them. Instead, we will look at several battles at sea, not only as examples of tactical improvisation and courageous persistence, but as metaphors for the piracies of buccaneers and filibusters: of daring to risk all, even one's life, in pursuit of material gain and in pursuit of that intangible, independence, even at the expense of others.

The first incursion began in 1680, the second began in 1683–84; the English pirate Thomas Peche had visited briefly in late 1675.[4] The first major expedition comprised buccaneers; buccaneers and filibusters composed the second, and much larger, expedition. The Isthmus of Darien, with assistance and protection from local Indians, was the first avenue of invasion, but both Darien and Cape Horn provided ingress for the second expedition. The brutal adventurers blockaded Panama, attacked shipping at sea, and raided towns and cities up and down the Pacific Coast of Central and South America. They returned from the first expedition via Darien or Cape Horn and its environs, and from the second via Nicaragua, Cape Horn, or a circumnavigation of the world. The South Sea lured not only buccaneers and filibusters, but others as well, to the dismay of the English and French governments. In addition to the first line of colonial defense, men whose labor was needed in the colonies deserted to these expeditions.[5]

Disagreements were common on the voyages. Commanders were often killed in action or deposed by their crews, and crews battled nature, the enemy, and themselves. Often victorious, the pirates also met at times with humiliating defeats. The first expedition's numbers diminished—through casualties, departures, and desertions—from more than three hundred to merely sixty, including slaves who did not bear arms, yet even the small party ranged freely in the South Sea. These were epic adventures of men operating independently of the state on territory reserved by the state, on the scale of major warfare, something hitherto unknown in the period.

The Spanish in the South Sea did not simply give up their cities and vessels to the invading buccaneers and filibusters, but fought back, using a variety of tactics ranging from deceit to shows of force to open battle. More will be said in chapter 18 of battles ashore. Battles at sea ranged from games

**Small English Frigate**

**Spanish Fragata or Galleon**

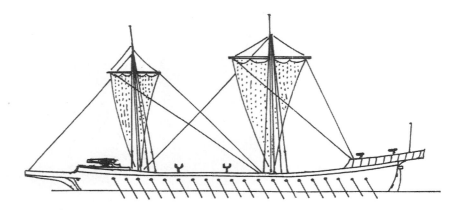

**Spanish Half-Galley**

**Tarteen**

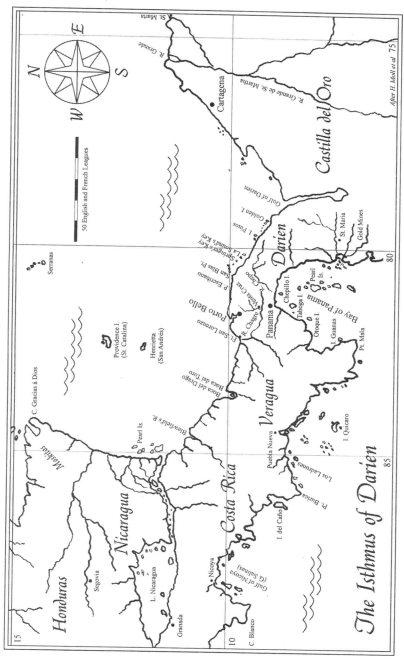

The Isthmus of Darien

BENERSON LITTLE AND COURTNEY LITTLE.

of cat and mouse (with none sure at times who was cat and who was mouse), to brief actions in which Spanish crews and volunteers were overwhelmed by buccaneer and filibuster firepower, to brutal battles that turned decks red and whose participants fought as bravely as any ever did, overcoming the grip of fear. During the first great expedition to the South Sea, battles were fought entirely with small arms on the part of buccaneers against Spanish ships often armed with cannon. However, by the second great invasion the rovers learned their lessons and brought ships of force into the South Sea, although often they fared no better than they did with small arms alone—the Spanish also learned their lessons well.

When word reached Panama of the buccaneer invasion in 1680, the viceroy dispatched an armadilla, or little fleet, of three small vessels called *Barcos de la Armadilla* to engage the invaders. Don Jacinto de Barahona, admiral of the South Sea, commanded the first, with eighty-six volunteer Biscayers. Don Francisco de Peralta, an Andalusian, commanded seventy-seven blacks in the second vessel. Don Diego de Carabaxal commanded sixty-five mestizos in the third. They had orders to give no quarter to the pirates. The buccaneers themselves numbered two hundred, although according to Ringrose, only sixty-eight, including King Golden Cap, actually engaged the enemy. Worse, their vessels were canoes and a piragua—and, as John Cox put it, the canoes carried six to fifteen men, and the crew "leaning on one side might overset the biggest." Owing to the cramped conditions, buccaneers could not load their muskets as quickly as usual and had to crouch or lie low in the canoes for cover.[6] Even so, the buccaneers quickly took advantage of the canoe's tactical assets, rowing into the eye of the wind and gaining the weather gage. Although the canoes lacked protection from Spanish fire, they moved swiftly windward where Spanish vessels could not follow them. Wrote John Cox:"[H]owever nothing daunted at the disadvantage of Fight, we made a resolution rather than drown in the Sea, or beg Quarter of the Spaniard, whom we used to Conquer, to run the extreament hazard of Fire and Sword." Carabaxal engaged the pirates first, sailing between two leeward canoes, firing on them both leeward and windward. The buccaneers returned fire, killing several Spaniards,"birding [firing with multiple shot] our Fusees as many as durst peep over Deck." Barahona engaged these and two other canoes next, but they killed his helmsman, causing his vessel to run "into the wind, and her sails lay aback." The buccaneers quickly rowed astern and opened fire, killing any who attempted to take the helm, and "put asunder his main sheet and brace." They maintained the position astern, for if they abandoned it the Spaniards could bring all of their arms to bear. They offered quarter to the Spaniards several times, which they "stoutly deny."[7]

Peralta engaged next, intending to relieve his admiral, but Captain Sawkins, as valiant a warrior as Peralta, engaged the Andalusian from his piragua.

Ringrose wrote: "Between him and Captain Sawkins the dispute, or fight, was very hot, lying board on board together, and both giving and receiving death unto each other as fast as they could charge." Seeing Peralta desperately engaged, Carabaxal tacked to relieve his admiral instead, who waved him on with a handkerchief. The buccaneers, fearing they would be driven from the stern of the admiral, sent two canoes to engage Carabaxal, which they did with such ferocity that they drove him off, killing so many of his crew that he barely managed his vessel well enough to escape. Then the buccaneers closely engaged Admiral Barahona, slipping under his stern and wedging his rudder so it could not steer. They killed Barahona and the new helmsman. Two thirds of the valiant Biscayers were dead or wounded; the vessel surrendered, and Coxon took command because Harris was shot through both legs.[8]

Meanwhile, in the bloodiest of three bloody battles, Sawkins was thrice beaten from Peralta's vessel by a "valiant defence." Other canoes attacked, and suddenly powder blew up on deck, killing and wounding many, even launching some into the sea. Peralta leaped overboard and "in spite of all of our shot, got several of them into the ship again, though he was much burnt in his hands himself." Under cover of the smoke, Sawkins laid the vessel "on board" and captured it. Ringrose wrote:

> I went on board Captain Peralta, to see what condition they were in, and indeed such a miserable sight I never saw in my life, for not one man there was found but was either killed, desperately wounded, or horribly burnt with powder, insomuch that their black skins were turned white in several places, the powder having torn it from their flesh and bones.

The fight lasted a few hours in the morning. Of the seventy-eight men aboard Peralta's vessel, only twenty-five survived, and of those only eight were not so wounded that they could still bear arms. Buccaneer casualties were eleven killed and thirty-four "dangerously" wounded. The courage of Peralta and his men earned the respect of the buccaneers, and although Peralta remained their prisoner and pilot for some months, they treated him with extraordinary courtesy.[9]

In nearby Perico harbor, the buccaneers captured the four-hundred-ton *Santissima Trinidad*, the same galleon commanded by Peralta when Henry Morgan captured Panama. The galleon, then lightly armed, escaped with much of the wealth of Panama. After they captured the galleon, the buccaneers made it their flagship, although it carried not a single cannon, nor would it during the entire subsequent voyage. They took several other vessels as well and made Sawkins their admiral. Coxon, called *coward* by some and "houted at by the Party," returned overland to the Caribbean.[10]

$\mathcal{N}$o other engagements matched the magnitude of the armadilla battle during the first invasion, although there were other fights at sea. "On Tuesday night about nine a Clock, we stood to the Westward and saw a Sail; the Trinity then cast us off, and gave chase, and in a short time came up with her," wrote John Cox of the sighting of a Spanish vessel in the South Sea in August 1680.

> [S]he was a small Man of War, fitted out of *Guiaque* or *Wyake* [Guayaquil] by a parcel of merry Blades, Gentlemen, who drinking in a Tavern, made a vow to come to Sea with that Vessel and thirty Men and take us; but we made them repent their undertaking.[11]

For half an hour the thirty-five Spaniards, of whom twenty-four were "Old Spain Men," put up a sharp fight with only thirty-one firearms and no cannon, doing "very great damage in our rigging, by cutting it in pieces."[12] The buccaneers were no less diligent: their musketry disabled the Spaniards' maintop halyards and killed the helmsman, at which point the Spaniards surrendered, for none dared take the dead helmsman's exposed place at the tiller. Bartholomew Sharp commented little about the capture, except to note that the vessel was fitted out to capture the *Trinity*, that her commander was a former governor of Guayaquil (don Tomás de Argandona, a noted mariner whose family included several other noted commanders), and that three buccaneers were wounded in the engagement.[13] In fact, only two were wounded by Spanish bullets. The third, Robert Montgomery, was wounded "by the negligence of one our own men, occasioned by a pistol which went off un-advisedly." Montgomery died two weeks later of his wounds.[14] Cox wrote that the number of Spanish dead was unknown because the battle was fought at night; William Dick did not recall how many Spaniards were killed; and other buccaneer authors did not mention Spanish losses.[15] Dick, however, noted that the Spaniards "in a true blue Spanish bravado had undertaken to take or destroy us with that little tool and only 30 or 40 men."[16] In his waggoner (chart book) Basil Ringrose noted slyly that "the Governour of this Guayaquill came out with Soldiers in a Ship to fighte us but wee kept him from Returning for Some months."[17]

Of the Spanish prisoners, several were "persons of quality." The next day, all were interrogated, and some provided detailed intelligence of Spanish armadillas, fortifications, and men under arms. That same day the buccaneers shared 3,276 pieces-of-eight captured aboard the vessel and murdered a friar, the vessel's chaplain—*punished* was the word they used. They threw him overboard before he died. Only Basil Ringrose mentioned (and deplored) the murder, but gave no reason for it. Other Spanish prisoners appeared to be well treated, all things considered. One of them, Nicholas Moreno, was kept as a pilot for nine months.[18]

*T*he buccaneers also attacked a three-hundred-ton merchantman, the *Rosario*, intending to employ the typical tactic of musketry to suppress enemy fire, kill officers and helmsmen, and cut the rigging, forcing the vessel to surrender or permitting the buccaneers to come alongside and board. "Using our fusils, we made so great a fire upon them, that they were forced to close up their port-holes, and bear up to the wind," wrote de Lussan of the common tactic.[19] Povey gave a similar account of the tactic used to capture the *Rosario*: "[W]e fired severall small Armes before they called for quarter, butt calling, was presently granted and not a gunn fier'd. her capt. was shott downe in takeing of her."[20] The captain, Juan Lopez, was killed by one of the first three shots. The buccaneers looted the ship and abandoned it, leaving seven hundred pigs of silver aboard, believing them to be only pewter. The most vital cargo included seven jars of wine, one hundred of brandy, and a *derrotero*, or book of Spanish sea charts.[21]

*T*he second great expedition into the South Sea differed in three respects: it was composed of multiple small expeditions that combined into larger ones; two ships of force were brought into Spanish waters; and both filibusters and buccaneers participated in significant numbers. Captains included Cook, Eaton, Swan, Davis, Grogniet, Townley, and Read. But the Spanish also had ships of force, often heavily armed, and although they were cautious of closing with the buccaneers and filibusters, they galled them with cannon fire. They kept them at a distance, although they killed few of their enemy. "[N]early all his [Swan's] ship was razed; he had had a number of canon-shots near his water-line, and though his quarter-master had had his head shot off by a bullet, only three had been wounded," wrote de Lussan, who also noted that the pirates considered this standoff form of warfare and reluctance to board to be cowardice.[22] But not all pirates in the South Sea sailed vessels armed with a cannon, and there were pirates who fought only with a musket and grenades against cannon.[23] Otherwise, engagements at sea were the same as they were in the 1680–81 incursion. One advantage the rovers had in the South Sea was the foolish method the Spaniards used to load their great guns in these waters. "Nay, they have not the sense to have their Guns run within the sides upon their discharge, but have Platforms without for the Men to stand on to charge them; so that when we come near we can fetch them down with small shot out of our Boats."[24]

*I*n spite of the number of buccaneers who fled to the South Sea, piracy increased in the Caribbean. In 1681 Henry Morgan attacked the pirate Jacob Evertson at Jamaica and diligently pursued other pirates. Evertson, however, escaped and joined Captain Yanky somewhere in the Caribbean. The South Sea buccaneers attacked Arica, Ilo, and Huasco. Fifty-two men parted company, including Dampier and Wafer, and returned to the Caribbean. Wafer was burned by gunpowder and left to recover among the Cuna. Dampier sailed with Captains Tristian, then Archemboe, then in the company of Wright and Yanky, and was with them when they sacked Río de la Hacha. The pirate Thomas captured a Jamaican vessel, but was himself later captured and charged with piracy. Sir Thomas Lynch was appointed governor of Jamaica. The English pursued Captain Laurens. Nicolas Van Horn, a Dutchman of Vlissingen (or perhaps Ostend), purchased the *Mary and Martha* at London, renamed her the *St. Nicolas*, and by Christmas was at Cadiz. His French factor (agent) could not get a license to trade with the Spanish in the New World, so Van Horn sailed away, abandoned his factor, and enraged the Spanish by making reprisals. In the same year, Lancelot Blackburne, who would become archbishop of York in 1724, traveled to Nevis. As a cleric, rumors abounded that among his many purported vices was Caribbean piracy. Numerous interlopers landed slaves at Jamaica. Caribs attacked Antigua and Barbuda. Brandenburg privateers cruised the Caribbean. The *Trinity*, commanded by Sharp, set sail for the North Sea but failed to find the Straits of Magellan and so sailed around Cape Horn.

Piracy was becoming uncontrollable, and when one captain was killed in action or captured and hanged, others were ready to take his place. Piracy was indeed a dangerous profession, and a good surgeon was as valuable as any member of the ship's company.

# Battle Wounds and Belly Timber:

## Chirurgery, Physic, Diet, and Health

16

*A*nd Brave vallient capt. Peter Harriss was shott in his cannoe through both his leggs, bordeing a greate shipp ... [H]e [Captain Peralta] told us on his word the Trinnity was the best in the South Seas, soe wee pitched on her for Admirall, putting capt. Harriss aboard that was wounded,*

wrote Povey.[1] Capt. Peter Harris was sorely in need of a doctor to tend to his shot and shattered legs after the fight with the armadilla, and there were several among the company. "The Doctors cutting of[f] one legg . . .," continued Povey.[2]

So vital were surgeons and their instruments and medicines that the criticism of John Coxon's "desertion" included not only his perceived cowardice in action, but his taking of the best surgeon (of at least six) with him when he departed, not to mention critical instruments and most of his medicines, for the surgeon would not leave them. The buccaneers who remained were initially unaware that Coxon had taken most of his medicines with him, and they were sorely needed for the forty or fifty wounded buccaneers, twenty of them Coxon's own men.[3] Sharp and others excoriated him:

---

*All quotations have been reprinted with their original spelling and punctuation.

*Coxon* not content with going off as aforesaid, and moreover to carry the best of our Doctors and Medicines with him, would have tempted others to do the like with him, and particularly my self who could not hear of so dirty and inhuman an Action, without Detestation.[4]

While one of the surgeon's duties was to keep the company healthy (a duty reserved in common society for the physician), his skill was vital for preserving life and limb after the body was injured, often in horrible trauma. In an age lacking antiseptics and antibiotics, the surgeon's skill was critical. As for the forty or fifty wounded men, all but two survived, a testament to their surgeons' skill.[5]

Surgery was primitive in the seventeenth century, although its gross instruments and procedures were virtually identical to those used today—cut the flesh, saw the bone. Diarist John Evelyn described an amputation in 1671:

I saw the chirurgeon cut off the leg of a wounded sailor, the stout and gallant man enduring it with incredible patience, without being bound to his chaire as usual on such painfull occasions. I had hardly courage to be present. Not being cut off high enough, the gangreen prevail'd, and the second operation cost the poore creature his life.[6]

At sea, surgeons routinely dealt with broken bones and cracked skulls, hernias, and the various cuts, lacerations, and contusions that came with handling a vessel. Wounds of battle included the lacerations from splinters and edged weapons; the penetrations of musket balls, small shot, partridge, and splinters; and the crushing (and sometimes decapitating) injuries of falling blocks and spars and flying round shot. If a surgeon was not available, in a pinch one could stuff an eye socket with oakum, use candle tallow as a salve for burns, and use a mixture of brandy and butter as a liniment for bruises.[7]

On the physic side, surgeons treated the common and uncommon ailments of man, including smallpox, malaria, and yellow fever. Among sailors on long voyages, scurvy—"growing Scorbutick"—was a common problem, although by the late seventeenth and early eighteenth centuries it was known that with "Oranges, Lemmons, all Sorts of Greens and Roots, the Sailors find much Relief at it against the Scurvy."[8] Sexually transmitted diseases were routine. One might believe these "diseases of Venus" were more common when vessels were put into port often, opportunity being what it was, but even a single short stay during a voyage could infect an entire crew.[9] Mercury was the standard cure. Sea surgeons carried a medicine chest stocked with medicinal concoctions such as "Oleum Hyperic," or oil of Saint-John's-wort; "Linimt. Arni.," or arnica liniment; and "Pulv. Jalap," or pulverized jalap root.[10] Some were efficacious, others probably relied unknowingly on the placebo effect, or still others did harm. The chest included soporifics such as opium or laudanum, which in addition to their purpose of pain relief, some individuals took to sleep when mosquitoes were bad or when sleep was otherwise difficult.[11] The surgeon's favorite remedy, however, was bleeding, which he even used when a wound, in his opinion, had not bled enough.[12] Sanitation aboard ships consisted of washing the decks, steaming decks below with vinegar, or burning tar or tobacco between decks.

Blacks and Native Americans were often consulted for cures. Dampier, for example, was treated successfully for the guinea worm by a black healer who charged a white rooster for his fee. (He also healed a horse of a "gall'd Back," or skin sores.)[13] Notwithstanding the remedies of surgeons and tribal healers, many rovers treated themselves or their comrades with various diets. Sea turtle, particularly the green turtle, was believed to drive "out any such gross Humours." Sickly Jamaicans sometimes traveled to the Caymans and lived on turtle "to have their bodies scoured by this Food, and their Distempers driven out." Dampier sarcastically suggested that Spaniards did not eat turtle because, being "pox'd," it would make them "break out loathsomely like Lepers" as it drove out disease.[14] Moskito Indians also considered turtle meat a valuable treatment for many illnesses and afflictions.[15] Iguanas, a "flesh much esteem'd by Privateers," were fed to sick men, for "they make very good Broath," although the flesh had to be boiled well, lest it made one sick.[16] Likewise, rice boiled with coconut milk was fed to the ill, for it "is accounted by our Doctors to be very nourishing."[17]

*T*aken as a whole, buccaneers were probably not paragons of health. At the very least, they had habits not conducive to long life, not counting their hazardous profession. Most used tobacco regularly, drank heavily, were often "pox'd" and sunburned, and the Caribbean rover's diet contained much meat, often heavily salted and fat. Even so, the diet of pirates was not nearly as terrible as some claimed. Typically, they ate better than common seamen, because most of their voyages were not long, and they had fresh, high-quality provisions looted from ship or shore. Besides their common provision of boucan (salt pork), salted sea turtle, and salted manatee, they ate fresh sea turtle, manatee, pork, goat (especially good with cabbage), beef, iguana, various fowl, limpets, mussels, oysters, and various fish including shark but especially jewfish (Goliath grouper) and dolphin (also called *dorado* or *gilt-head*, today most commonly known as *mahimahi*).[18] According to Dampier, a jewfish was so-called because it was a "clean Fish, according to *Levitical Law*," often eaten by the Jewish population of Jamaica. Buccaneers sometimes salted jewfish and carried it as provision.[19] Pirates did not turn their noses up at fruits and vegetables, even rejoicing when part of their plunder was "garden herbs, roots, and most excellent fruit."[20] Lime juice was routinely consumed in rum punch, and buccaneers ate or drank "Chocolate with Sugar to sweeten it."[21] "Dumplings" or "dough-boys" (described as "cakes of bread") made of flour and water, boiled and eaten with manteca (pork lard), butter, or oil, was the typical bread of buccaneers.[22] *Biscuit* was the term for what was later called *hardtack*, and rusk was also a light biscuit, much like toasted bread and easy to eat.[23] Cassava (manioc), corn (maize), and wheat flours (eventually full of "Vermin, Maggots and Spiders") and their breads were common in various forms.[24] Burgoo, a typical dish of English sailors, was rare among the Caribbean pirates because it required oats.[25] Ashore, potatoes, sweet potatoes, and plantains often substituted for bread. The Spanish allowance for the crews of the Armada de Barlovento consisted of biscuits, water, poor jack (dried fish), beans and peas, cheese, olive oil, vinegar, and wine. Three days of the week, bacon and rice substituted for the fish.[26] However, common Spanish pirates and privateers provisioned with boiled coarse cornmeal (polenta or yellow corn grits, in essence) ground in a large wooden mortar and pestle, pork, and plantains.[27]

In more extreme circumstances, rovers ate almost anything, including alligator, horse, mule, seal, various sea birds, monkey, penguin, rattlesnake, dog (a Spaniel in one case), rat, leather, tallow, and anything else that could reasonably be digested.

According to Exquemelin, filibusters and buccaneers ate two meals per day, the first around noon (cooking began at ten in the morning), the second probably late afternoon or early evening. Crews ate in "messes" of seven men, and the captain ate no better than the rest of the ship's company. Indeed, any crewman could exchange the food on his plate for that of the captain. They ate as much as they pleased, but if rations ran short, meals were reduced to one a day. This practice of eating as much as one desired was surely modified on long voyages, for the rationing of provisions was critical. Further, three meals a day was common among both buccaneers and filibusters from 1674 to 1688, reduced to two a day if provisions ran short.[28] Typical fare among the filibusters was boucan boiled in a "copper" filled with freshwater or seawater, and, like Spainish diets, boiled meal, usually cornmeal (maize, "Bled d'Inde"), seasoned with fat and grease dipped from the copper of pork.[29]

The physical fitness of the various populations was difficult to determine in broad generalities and impossible to measure. Native Americans, however, were routinely described as both healthier and more fit than Europeans, or for that matter, any others in the Americas.[30] The average person of most populations on the Main, excepting only the very wealthy, was far more physically fit than the average person today, given the need for daily physical labor in the seventeenth century. Walking, for example, was far more common. As for the Caribbean sea rovers, their physical strength was fairly good, given the need for manual labor in the handling, provisioning, and general upkeep of a vessel, as well as the various other physical labors they undertook—logwood cutting, for example. Their cardiovascular endurance was also fair. The buccaneers who attacked Portobello marched sixty miles in three nights, over rough terrain and paths, no mean feat even for modern special operations forces, although there were stragglers on such forced marches.[31] Three miles from Portobello a Native American ran to warn the city, and buccaneers chased him. (Even in the seventeenth century, runners trained for the task by running regularly.) He arrived half an hour before they did.[32] Assuming the runner covered the distance in fifteen minutes or so, the buccaneers, weighed down with arms and ammunition, many of them barefoot and with feet cut and torn, covered the distance in forty-five minutes, or at four miles an hour. That was not a bad pace for men in their condition, easily comparable if not superior to what most soldiers today can manage with boots, and the feet inside of them uninjured. Overall, buccaneers and filibusters were ideally suited physically and mentally to their purpose:

> We had also a great Advantage above raw Men that are sent out of England into these places . . . besides the danger of their Lives in so great and sudden a change of Air: whereas we were all inured to hot Climates, hardened by many Fatigues, and in general, daring Men, and such as would not be easily baffled.[33]

In 1682 Jamaica had a shortage of these men, many of whom had gone "privateering," and of working men in general. Even slaves were in short supply. Elsewhere, La Salle discovered the mouth of the Mississippi, having traveled down the great river from the north. Brandenburg entered the slave trade. Captain Sharp and his crew returned to the Caribbean in the *Trinity*. They took their leave in various places, and the handful remaining abandoned the *Trinity* at St. Thomas. Many traveled to England, including Sharp, Dick, and Cox, who were arrested, charged with piracy and murder, and acquitted. Buccaneers and filibusters raided the Florida coast for Native Americans to use as divers at the *Maravillas* site and captured seven vessels bound to or from Havana. In February pirates captured the *Nuestra Señora de Candelaria* in the Florida Keys. In March, Van Horn plundered the cargo of the Dutch West Indian ship *Aletta* for goods to trade on the African coast, where he took on a cargo of six hundred slaves. In Jamaica, more than one hundred slaves rebelled at the Gregg plantation. Filibusters attacked San Marcos de Apalache in Florida. In June, a French pirate arrived at Charleston with forty men—three-fourths of them English, the remainder French—with a Spanish prize and one hundred prisoners in tow. Approximately one hundred pirates or privateers were actively operating out of South Carolina. In June, filibusters raided Florida *ranchos*, then burned the large Hacienda de la Chua. Captain Bréha was fishing at the site of the *Maravillas*. Pirates made a small raid at Tindall's Point on the Chesapeake. Captain-General Clark of New Providence was issuing unlawful commissions to attack the Spanish, and John Coxon was one of the recipients. Filibusters were very active, including Captains Picard, Pennon, and Guernsey. The governor of Jamaica forbade logwood cutting, although ineffectively. A French Huguenot named Paine arrived in Jamaica with a stolen cargo, although he claimed it as his own, and pretended to be seeking asylum as one persecuted for his faith. His ship, *La Trompeuse*, was subsequently captured by a pirate who made it the vessel of a piratical rampage. English frigates were dispatched in pursuit.

In the summer, Laurens captured the *Francesa*, originally a French prize. As a ship of the Armada de Barlovento, it was loaded with goods as well as the payroll for Puerto Rico and Santiago de Cuba, and the capture caused a financial crisis and enraged the Spanish. The filibusters shared seven hundred pieces-of-eight per man. Wright and his company arrived in Virginia and settled temporarily on the eastern shore at Accomac. John Coxon, back in good graces with the English government, was sent by Governor Lynch to the Bay of Honduras to arrest the English logwood cutters; en route he suppressed a mutiny. Returning to Jamaica, he was hired by the governor to convoy a Spaniard to Havana. Near year's end, Van Horn arrived at Santo Domingo with three hundred slaves to sell to the Spanish, but warned of his behavior at Cadiz, the Spanish confiscated one hundred and sixty-five of his slaves for restitution and in reprisal for Laurens's capture of the *Francesa*. The new governor of St. Thomas, Jörgen Iversen, was murdered en route to the island; Adolph Esmit remained in office, supporting piracy. Pirate George Spurre cruised off the coast of Jamaica, probably recruiting, provisioning, and seeking Spanish traders, and pirate Thomas Paine was commissioned by Governor Lynch to hunt pirates.

These "daring Men," as Dampier called them, braved the dangers of land, sea, and enemy in the pursuit of riches. While their means of achieving their riches were varied, the men did share one commonality: much of their plunder was spent on sensual pleasures.

# 17 The Torrid Zone:
## Sex and Romance on the Main

*S*ailors have always been stereotyped as lusting after "strumpets and whores"* when ashore, and indeed, the stereotype is more fact than fiction. Exquemelin noted that buccaneers and filibusters gave "themselves to all manner of debauchery with strumpets and wine."[1] In 1692 the entire crew of a French privateer, including a *mousse* (ship's boy) of fifteen or sixteen, was afflicted by the *vénériens* over the course of three days, providing one of many concrete examples of what sailors had on their minds when they went ashore and of the consequences of passion overriding common sense. Bawdy houses were the natural habitats of various forms of the "French pox."[2] However, sailors' lust was not limited to exotic women or "loose" women, but to women in general—all were fair game. Prostitutes were simply closer to the embarcadero and the most easily had.

Many sailors and sea rovers made little distinction regarding race when selecting partners for several reasons: the lure of the exotic, the "when in Rome" philosophy, and the women available. In the Caribbean colonies of England, France, and the Netherlands, availability carried weight because men far outnumbered women (a factor that also contributed to prostitution). Further, the distance from the various European social orders allowed men and women of different races more freedom to engage in sex and other social relationships, including marriage. Unfortunately, that same freedom also

---

*All quotations have been reprinted with their original spelling and punctuation.

165

permitted the exploitation of women slaves and indentured servants. Wrote one scholar: "West Indian slave societies were characterized by distorted social relationships and unchecked male sexual tyranny. From the latter, female servants received insufficient protection."[3]

Black women were considered the most exotic of the Spanish Main, and some observers remarked on them with extraordinary fascination, in particular on their perceived overt sexuality compared to European and Creole women. The Spaniards were "lying, as they do, so promiscuously with their Negrines and She-slaves," wrote Dampier, but his account was surely an anti-Spanish sentiment tinged with prudery and legitimate moralizing (given the master-slave relationship, such liaisons morally constituted rape) and racism and hypocrisy, because English slave owners certainly did likewise.[4] Thomas Gage, an Englishman and Catholic priest who lived among the Spanish in the New World in the first half of the seventeenth century, described a Spanish slave owner, perhaps much like many slave owners of any nation, who routinely forced himself upon his female slaves, including those who were married, and even bought female slaves solely for sex.[5] That being said, "[n]ot all relations between slave women and males in authority can or should be construed as sexual abuse," according to one scholar.[6] Another scholar noted that some slave owners freed their "slave mistresses" or their children by these mistresses, or both, or otherwise displayed "some measure of love and responsibility toward his illicit black family."[7] Gage revealed his own personal conflict of faith and lust (in his case, remarkably like a Puritan's) in his description of black women in Mexico City, running to three long paragraphs, fragments of which are excerpted here:

> Nay, a blackamoor or tawny young maid and slave will make hard shift, but she will be in fashion with her neck-chain and bracelets of pearls, and her ear-bobs of some considerable jewels. The attire of this baser sort of people of blackamoors and mulattoes . . . is so light, and their carriage so enticing, that many Spaniards even of the better sort (who are too prone to venery) disdain their wives for them. . . . Their bare, black, and tawny breasts are covered with bobs hanging from their chains of pearls. . . . Most of these are or have been slaves, though love have set them loose, at liberty to enslave souls to sin and Satan.[8]

The average sailor's reply to this prudish tirade would be along the lines of "Thank God for these women!" and his single thought when observing one of them: "What a woman!" (If French, "Quelle femme!") The similar lustful and typical fascination of the French officer at Petit Goave has already been noted in chapter 5. Many blamed the tropics for such behavior, believing heat to incline one to idleness and excessive sexual proclivities.[9]

There was, however, a more romantic, marital, even familial side to the sailor, buccaneers and filibusters included. Most sailors married, many to foreign women, including those of other races, during long voyages. At Santa Helena in the South Atlantic, Dampier wrote,

> [M]any of the seamen got Sweethearts. One young Man . . . married, and brought his wife to *England* with him . . . and several other of our Men, were over Head and Ears in Love with the *Santa Hellena* Maids [who] are but one remove from *English*, being the Daughters of such. They are well shaped, proper and comely, were they in a Dress to set them off.[10]

Buccaneers even chose Valentines on St. Valentine's Day.[11] Bartholomew Sharp (or Basil Ringrose—both used the same superlative) noted briefly of "the Lady call'd Donna Joanna Constanta, about 18 Years of Age, Wife to Don John—and the beautifullest Creature that my Eyes ever beheld in the South Sea."[12] Rovers also married and had children.[13] Filibusters often married black or mixed race women (much like those described by Gage) at Saint Domingue, many of whom were carried there as slaves from Spanish colonies.[14] The buccaneer Captain Beare ran away from Port Royal to Havana with his occasionally cross-dressing inamorata and married her. In the South Sea, Dutch buccaneer and linguister Jacobus Marquess deserted his comrades for the sake of a "Mustees" woman.

> [T]he woman lieing on borde one or two nights, was very familiar with one Copas a dutch a man, who formerly had saild with the Spaniards . . . but was mainly Inamoured with thiss women, makeing her severall presents of some Vallew.

Marquess pretended to go hunting but deserted instead, taking with him two hundred pieces-of-eight and leaving behind "2200 ps. 8/8 besides Jewels and Goods."[15] During the filibuster occupation of Guayaquil,

> several of our men made friends with the ladies among our prisoners and, without being violent, solicited their favors and made them lose . . . whatever aversion they may previously have had for the French nation before they knew them.

Raveneau de Lussan himself was almost seduced away by the "widow of the local treasurer," who suggested they hide in the woods until the filibusters left, then they could marry and he could have "her husband's office in addition to her own extensive holdings." Doubtless the length of the cruise and the great distance from home tempted men to accept such offers. In spite of the temptation, however, de Lussan declined, for ultimately he did not trust the Spanish.[16]

Spaniards by reputation and behavior were romantics, if jealous ones, some confusing jealousy with love or romance. Tales of romantic assignations abounded, in church, at the theater, covered by a mantle in the streets, and even secretly and dangerously at night. Tales of lovers' deaths, often owing to mistaken identity, were also popular. In one, a jealous woman dressed as a man to eavesdrop on her lover. In another, she invited him to choose between poison and a dagger as punishment for his infidelity. More positively,

> *Spaniards* are so kind-hearted to one another in Love Affairs, that if a Man meets his Mistress in a place where he has no opportunity of conversing with her in private, he need only go into the next House, and request the Master (whether he knows him or not) to give him the opportunity of talking with a Lady of his acquaintance in private in his House, and he is sure twill scarce ever be refus'd.

On the physical side, if the baronne d'Aulnoy was to be believed, "after a Spanish Lady has granted the last Favour to her Lover, she will shew him her Feet, as a Pledge of her Passion to him."[17] Notwithstanding Spanish romance, Carlos Fuentes remarked that a "puritanical streak and an outbreak of debauchery existed during [Spanish] colonial times" and that "[s]exual cruelty can be easily exercised in societies of strict social separation"—and in societies of strict patriarchy.[18]

There is little information on how wives, sweethearts, and prostitutes perceived the men who roved in and out of their lives. Perhaps they felt as Moretta in Aphra Behn's comedy *The Rover* did:

> Nay, to love such a shameroon, a very beggar; nay, a pirate beggar, whose business is to rifle and be gone; a no-purchase, no-pay tatterdemalion, and English picaroon; a rogue that fights for daily drink, and takes a pride in being loyally lousy? Oh, I could curse now, if I durst. This is the fate of most whores.[19]

Sex itself in the seventeenth century was little different from sex today, and most of what we tend to think of as modern has actually been practiced for ages. Bathing, oral hygiene, antibiotics, and contraceptives, including practical condoms, are the major differences. Sex then, as now, was potentially hazardous, bringing with it the possibility of disease—including potentially fatal ones—for either party, and of pregnancy for the female (we have forgotten how dangerous childbirth could be). Such potentials rarely diminished sexual desire and practices, however. Alcohol and its abuse were common among Europeans and contributed to the number of sexual liaisons, as did closely shared living spaces, bedrooms especially, in a household.

The Earl of Rochester described French kissing, although he did not use this term, and the practice was surely universal. Both conventional and unconventional sexual practices abounded. The female orgasm in general was not neglected, and many believed that it facilitated conception, although some men may have neglected it for this very reason.[20] Pornography, both written (the *École des Filles*, for example) and illustrated ("bawdy pictures" or "postures"), was well known and the latter well represented.[21] Dildos were imported from Italy to London and other cities.[22] Male transsexuals were known and sometimes obvious. In the first years of the eighteenth century, Governor Edward Hyde of New York dressed in public as a woman and even sat for a portrait dressed as one, his hands hidden in gloves and made to look small and feminine.[23] Cross-dressing women were known in life and on stage.

Homosexuals probably made up the same proportion of the general population as they do today, and buccaneer and filibuster populations probably reflected this. There was only one brief mention of homosexuals or homosexual acts in all of the journals of the buccaneers, that of Captain Cook being accused of sodomy by his servant:

> This day, likewise, William Cook, servant to Captain Cook, confessed that his master had oftentimes buggered him in England, leaving his wife and coming to bed him; that he had also done the same in Jamaica, and once in these seas before Panama.[24]

For this offense, which may have been a false accusation, or personally or politically motivated, or all of these, Captain Cook was put in irons, along with his servant, who was found "with a paper will all our names in it, which it was suspected he designed to have given to the Spanish prisoners." The accusation apparently did not sully Captain Cook's reputation, for he soon served again as a buccaneer commander. In the Royal Navy, however, such accusations put a man on trial for his life.[25]

Birth control methods included *coitus interruptus* and probably some form of the rhythm method, based on hearsay and experience. Certainly manual, oral, and anal sex were used to prevent pregnancy in addition to their other roles in sexual practices, despite their classification as "sodomy" by most religions.[26] Aside from the latter three methods, contraceptives had poor results. Antonia Fraser pointed out that women in general in the seventeenth century were "in a state of virtually perpetual pregnancy."[27] Vaginal sponges existed, but were used primarily by prostitutes as protection against the "pox." Condoms were available, at least in the great European cities. Made of sheep's gut and secured with a ribbon around the testicles, they were used primarily to prevent sexually transmitted diseases. "Morning-after" remedies were also available but were certainly quackery. A variety of well-known abortion practices involved physical exercise or potions, although it was unknown how well they worked, if they worked at all, or how many women availed themselves of them.[28]

Supposed aphrodisiacs included chocolate (said to give men endurance and make women willing), avocados (they "provoke to Lust," and the word itself derived from the Nahuatl [Aztec] *âhuacatl*, meaning testicle), and "Spanish *flies*" (an extract of a blister beetle, used to arouse cattle). Spanish fly was also considered a cure for impotence in spite of its dangers to humans: "[it] so heated the old man's reins [loins], that next morning he bragg'd to us, that he never had a pleasanter night."[29]

Adultery and premarital sex was as common as it is today. Diarist, navy secretary, and husband Samuel Pepys chased every woman he could, for example, and often successfully. Restoration comedies, with their references to prostitutes, cuckolds, promiscuous or prudish (or both) men and women, and sex in general, abounded. Some of the plays were extraordinarily bawdy, hilarious, and insightful.[30] Puritans and other religious or social conservatives were typically strong advocates of sex, as long as it was confined to the marriage bed. Parents, particularly of the upper classes, appreciated the property value of virgin brides and so demanded absolute chastity of their daughters, no matter how many mistresses the fathers may have had, nor how many virgins the fathers may have debauched. Divorce was not unknown, although difficult or sometimes impossible to obtain, depending on society and circumstance. Captain Laurens divorced his first wife, for example.

*W*here there was sex, there were children, not only from men and women of the same race but of different races. Genes invariably crossed all social and racial boundaries, and genetic testing was not necessary to prove this fact. One needed only to watch sailors of any ethnicity ashore in any port in the world or to note the variety of ethnicities in the New World or of Spanish racial categories. Children, however, were rarely mentioned in the journals of rovers or of mariners, except where they played a role in an incident aboard a vessel: a child nearly drowned, or boys were kept as servants, or a Native American family visited, or a mixed race woman taken aboard as a pilot brought her "three or four small Children" with her.[31] This lack of mention may be because children, like pregnant women, were ubiquitous and thus unexceptional. Rovers commonly avoided mentioning them in their accounts of cities sacked, although children, their mothers, and the elderly were assuredly the most afflicted by these violent invasions, for battle was but one part of a sacking. For the buccaneer and filibuster, however, it was the most critical and most dangerous part. Although his own distant children may have been on the rover's mind while he attacked a city, sex was seldom on the mind of any man at whom shots were being fired. His mind was on survival, teamwork, and the tactics and violence necessary to ensure victory.

# 18 *Ladrones! Ladrones!*
## *Towns Plundered, Lives Violated*

*M*y *Padrone* had also been Prisoner at the *Havana*, on the Island of *Cuba*, and often told me how both that Place and *LeVeracruz*, might be surprized by the *English*; and recounted to me how a Number of Bucaniers surprized, took and plunder'd the Latter,\*

wrote Captain Uring.[1]

Veracruz was the major Spanish port in the Gulf of Mexico, the home of the ships of the Armada de Barlovento, the home away from home of the Flota de Nueva España, and the point of departure for Mexican and West Indian goods exported to Spain.[2] In typical New World Spanish style, "the Streets of *Veracruz* are streight as a Line; the Houses are handsome and regular; the Fortifications next the Land inconsiderable, but the Front of the Town next the Sea forms a Semicircle, with a little Fort at each End." The men of Veracruz were reputed to be haughty and jealous of their wives. The women were expensively and well dressed, and both sexes were accused by the French and English of being "sloathful and averse to Labour, fond of State and Ease." Houses were well furnished with "pictures and Images of Devotion . . . [and] Purceline and *China* Goods." Caged cardinals were in many homes , and "they often tame and teach [them] to sing like a *Canary* Bird." Usually the city

---

\*All quotations have been reprinted with their original spelling and punctuation.

171

resembled only "a village of fisherman," but nearing the arrival of the flota, its wealth extended beyond its churches "magnificently adorned with Plate," and its population increased. Fort San Juan de Ulloa, by whose name Veracruz was often called, was half a league away across the water and "only serves to secure the port and ships," but not the city itself. The city's wall was only "about six spans high," sections of it were often buried by the sand, and the bastions and redoubts were far apart.[3]

On May 17, 1683, two fleets came over the horizon. One of them, the flota, was a few days away and expected. The other, a pirate armada, was much closer on the horizon, and the city was unprepared for its arrival. After all, given Veracruz's size, fortifications, and population, who would dare attack it, except perhaps a great fleet in time of war? But such complacency is often the deadliest of all of the martial vices.

*S*panish towns and cities were usually defended by one or more types of fortifications: barricades or breastworks, palisades (tall fences of poles or stakes), stockades (walls of vertical logs), and stone forts that ranged from small to enormous. Larger forts, whether of palisade or stone walls, were typically defended by cannon, although those great guns were not always well mounted or well maintained and often numbered no more than a dozen. In the field, Spanish defenders rarely formed in ranks and invited battle on open ground, and when they did they seldom engaged beyond skirmishing unless their enemy was obviously inferior in number. The general Spanish tactic against sea rovers was to attack from ambush, or as buccaneers called the tactic, *ambuscade*, either by close assault with spears or with musket volleys, preferably (and wisely) from behind a breastwork. Mounted soldiers and volunteers also attacked from ambush. When a town or city was attacked, Spaniards usually defended from a fortification and, if the pirates were repulsed, harried them as they retreated. The Spanish used fire as a weapon at times, setting fire to savannahs or woods in order to hinder the pirates' advance.[4]

Raveneau de Lussan quoted a captured Spanish letter regarding tactics against the invading pirates:

> When you find them advance within the shot of your arquebusses, let not your men fire but by twenties, to the end your firing may not be in vain; and when you find them weakened, raise a shout to frighten them, and fall in with your swords, while Don Rodrigo attacks them in the rear. I hope God will favor our designs, since they are no other than for his glory and the destruction of these new sort of Turks. Hearten up your men, though they may have enough of that according to your example; they shall be rewarded in heaven, and if they get the better, they will have gold and silver enough, wherewith these thieves are laden.[5]

The Spanish intended to shoot in small volleys to keep up a constant fire, perhaps having learned the tactic from the buccaneers and filibusters. However, most lacked the discipline, training, or experience to load and fire independently, unconventionally, and accurately as their enemy did. At Panama in 1671, their intended tactics were entirely conventional: "and that coming within shot, the three first Ranks should Fire on their Knees, and after this [dis]charge, they should give place to the Rear to come up and Fire."[6]

Pirates routinely captured Spaniards for intelligence purposes, and the Spanish also captured pirates for the same reason:

> Use your endeavors to take one or other of the enemy, to the end we may now what they design to do. . . . Order the cattle to be drove away from the seaside, and put them into a place fit to lay an ambuscade, to the end that the enemy, severing from another, according to their usual manner, in order to kill them, it may be so much the more easy for you to secure some of them. . . . Especially interrogate the women [who have been prisoners of the pirates], that you may know whether they have met with some weak fellow that hath made any discovery unto them,

advised a Spanish officer.[7]

Two major weaknesses hindered the Spanish in their tactics, even when well devised according to good intelligence. Many inhabitants of New Spain and Peru were unaccustomed to warfare.[8] Most were merchants, planters, and various workers, slave and free, not veterans of bloody battles. Worse, many were intimidated by their enemy. Although there were notable exceptions, in general the Spanish who defended the New World were not of the standard of the famed Spanish *tercios* who fought in Europe. In his defense after the sack of Panama in 1671, Governor de Guzman wrote that he had two sorts of men serving under him: "valiant Military Men, and faint hearted cowards."[9] This state, of a combination of veterans willing to fight and of unskilled men often unwilling to fight, plagued Spanish defenses in the New World.

Spanish arms were typically inferior in quality and number. Dampier reported on the "want of small Fire-arms" among the Spanish, "for they have but few on all the Sea Coasts, unless near their larger Garrisons."[10] De Guzman noted that their "firearms were few and bad, in comparison of those the Enemy brought: For ours were Carbins, Harquebusses and Fowling pieces, but few Muskets."[11] At El Realejo, Nicaragua, in 1687 reportedly there were only two hundred firearms for six hundred men, and at Campeche in 1672 there were only a handful.[12] In 1671 Colonel Beeston reported that the Spanish soldiers at Cartagena were armed "only with match Locks, in the use of which they are likewise very un-expert."[13] Even at Veracruz, whose armory had approximately four thousand firearms in 1683, most were *arcabuzes* (harquebuses).[14] At La Guayra there were four hundred muskets and six thousand arrows, demonstrating just how much the New World Spanish relied on arms generally considered obsolete in European warfare.[15]

The Spanish term *mosquete* (musket) indicated a sturdy matchlock musket of heavy caliber, which by the second half of the seventeenth century was light enough not to require a forked rest. Spanish harquebuses of the period were small-caliber matchlock muskets, although the term was also sometimes applied to light wheel-lock muskets. Muskets fitted with flintlocks or Spanish *miquelet* locks were generally termed *escopetas*.[16] Carbines (*carabinas*) were short, light muskets, and the Spanish versions, usually described as *de chispa*, were fitted with miquelet locks. Pistols were only common among the professional military in the Spanish New World: civilians were forbidden to carry them, and masters of ships ensured that passengers did not have them.[17] Even the 1674 order permitting Spanish privateers in the Caribbean included specific authorization of the use of pistols for boarding.[18]

Matchlocks had advantages over flintlock muskets, according to a 1721 French text: they were often of larger caliber, causing more damage, and they seldom "missed fire," as flintlocks did.[19] However, matchlock arms, even if loaded from paper cartridges, were slow to load relative to flint arms, although a well-trained shooter using a streamlined loading sequence was capable of firing three times in a minute, equal to the average, trained flintlock shooter.[20] The lighted match used to fire matchlocks was a nuisance and could be dangerous, igniting dry fields or even powder flasks when handled carelessly, and at night the match embers were visible, making ambushes and concealment difficult.[21] To carry their ball and powder, the Spanish used the traditional bandolier with individual charges of powder in small wooden containers, along with a priming flask, ball bag, and a powder flask for extra powder, although for speed in loading, trained soldiers often kept several musket balls in their mouths.[22] Owing to the dangling wooden chargers, bandoliers were noisy, making stealth difficult. During the conquest of Jamaica in 1655, land crabs alarmed English soldiers, for "thay did heare a nois like the ratling of Bandaleares."[23]

Buccaneers and filibusters, however, armed themselves with flintlocks, preferably the fusil boucanier. Even the English and French militias demanded flintlocks, and by the early 1680s they were ubiquitous among everyone but the Spanish. In 1682 Barbados acquired at least five thousand flintlock muskets of the "Tower standard," and two years later militiamen were required to "appear with firelocks [flintlocks], or [they] will be fined as though they appeared without arms."[24] Cartouche boxes were used by sea rovers and

English and French militias, and buccaneers fighting on the move could be followed by "the tracks of our Feet and tops of our Cartridges.[25] In general, flint arms were preferred for *la guerre de campagne* (on campaign)—exactly the sort of warfare practiced in the New World.[26]

The most common shot for all firearms were musket balls and swan shot, often in combination, but "tumbled" shot (somewhat square shaped), slugs, and other small shot were also used.[27] Pistols were loaded, perhaps commonly, with multiple shot.[28] If lead shot was unavailable, shooters loaded with anything at hand: in 1687 some of Henry Pitman's companions loaded their muskets and blunderbusses with bottle glass, having left their bag of musket balls behind.[29] In the South Sea Spaniards sometimes fired poisoned musket balls, killing filibusters with them, for which their surviving comrades chastised the governor of Panama in a letter for his "breach of law and practices of clean warfare."[30] In the same letter they reminded the governor of the severed heads they recently sent him—apparently the decapitation of hostages when ransom was not paid on time was not a breach of the same magnitude. Although the pirates considered poisoned bullets a perfidious practice, the Spanish claimed they recovered musket balls "all chewn and gnawed with the teeth" from the bodies of their own dead. They sent "some to all the Governments thereabouts to create in them abhorrence of all these villains, and one here [at Jamaica] to be shown to the Governor that he might report to the King the villanies of his subjects."[31] Such musket balls caused greater internal damage than a smooth round ball and were considered contrary to the laws of war. (The teeth marks on some of the "chewn" musket balls recovered from various battlefields may not have been made by a patient "biting the bullet" during surgery, as is often claimed, but were intentionally deformed and fired at the enemy.)

In spite of these vulnerabilities, there was a core of "Old Spain Men," including Biscayers, plus Greeks, mulatto hunters, slaves, Native Americans, and merchants and planters, who fought fiercely and courageously. They adapted their inferiority in arms and their lack of a well-trained militia to the tactic of ambush and defense. Their conventional tactics were sound as well—assuming they faced a compliant, conventional enemy. However, these conventional tactics were often hindered not only by their execution, but by the uncooperative pirate adversary. Spanish tactics in the New World were best at luring the enemy into ambush, defending from fortifications, stalling while waiting for reinforcements to arrive, and taking advantage of disorder. Given the mix of a few professionals and many amateurs, these were certainly the most viable objectives.

*I*n buccaneer and filibuster tactics the fundamental principal was to attack by surprise, usually at dawn, to gain the maximum effect of numbers and firepower and to deny the inhabitants the opportunity to escape or hide their wealth.[32]

> Thither we went in two Barks with thirty Men in each, and had ten or eleven kill'd and desperately wounded in taking the Fort, being four or five Hours engag'd in that Service, in which time the Inhabitants having plenty of Boats and Canoas, carried all their Riches and best Moveables away,

wrote Dampier of an attack on Alvarado near Veracruz.[33] Hand in hand with a surprise attack was the principle of never attacking a large town or city after it was alarmed.[34]

Attacking at dawn provided the concealment of prior darkness in which to approach, and light in which to engage the Spanish, or to consolidate control if the pirates attacked at dawn's approach. Dawn was also the time at which the defenders' physical and psychological rhythms were at their lowest ebb, and most inhabitants were in bed. Specific tactics of rovers included never attacking fortifications with cannon from the sea—pirate cannon were too small and too few, and their vessels were vulnerable to the larger guns of fortifications. The forts at La Guayra, for example, were armed with forty-four cannon, four of which were twenty-four pounders, and another four of which were eighteen pounders, guns that made short work of the typical Caribbean sea-roving vessel.[35] Instead, rovers assaulted towns by land, by surprise at their gates if possible, or by engaging weak points at the walls or palisades. Whenever possible, fortifications were simply bypassed. Caribbean pirates rarely brought cannon or patereroes ashore to use in their engagements.

When engaging fortifications, buccaneers and filibusters used musketry to suppress fire from the walls while grenadiers moved forward under a cover of musketry and gunpowder smoke (which was very dense owing to the properties of black powder) and attempted to clear a portion of the walls with grenades. However, smoke also obscured the target, diminishing the attackers' accuracy. If successful, the attackers scaled the walls with ladders prepared for the purpose or used muscle and axes to breach a palisade, stockade, or sally port. Once inside the fortification, they engaged the Spanish at longer ranges with muskets, at closer ranges with muskets and grenades, and at close range with pistols and cutlasses. Pirates flanked barricades and breastworks by fire and maneuver as ground forces do today:

> At last some of ours got to the End of their biggest Breastwork, which galled us most and then we plyed them well with small Shot [a musket ball and seven or eight swan shot]. . . . This kept them in play till our Men in the Front began to Storm the wall.[36]

The practice was dangerous, however, if the barricade was well manned and those who flanked it were few. Against cavalry or lanceros, if outnumbered and without cover, rovers moved into a circle and fired a few at a time to maintain a constant volume, as described in chapter 4. The same tactic was also used when pirates were outnumbered by foot soldiers on open ground. The preferred tactic against cavalry and lanceros was to engage them at long range and disperse them or, failing that, to fire from cover among trees or dense vegetation, although the Spanish sometimes charged bravely into those areas.

To prevent or give warning of ambushes, buccaneers and filibusters marched with a group of "forlorn" or "forlorn hope" in the vanguard. The men who made up those *enfants perdus* (lost children) were usually volunteers, or had been selected by the throw of dice, and rotated duty every morning while on the march. Although buccaneers sometimes took the field with "drums beating and colors flying" as conventional armies did, they did not typically appear in *battalia* order, as they did at Panama, or engage in conventional volleys.[37] Instead they worked in pairs, one aiming and firing from the knee from cover, while the other reloaded, maintaining a constant fire designed to break the will of undisciplined troops to fight. Even at Panama in 1671 firing lines of rovers and volunteers in conventional order did not break the charge of Spanish cavalry. The task was accomplished by two hundred boucanier and filibuster skirmishers, who fired in their independent manner in pairs "so their fusillade never paused."[38] The tactic also helped dissuade the enemy from charging or otherwise coming to a close fight. However, pirates fought in ranks as necessary, although in an ad hoc fashion at times. In a street, for example, one rank fired (probably a ragged-aimed discharge, as opposed to a volley on command), then the next moved forward and fired, and then the third, each rank taking ground as they moved.[39] But if opposing fire became too heavy, they sought cover and fired independently. The accuracy of the second and third ranks was reduced when firing from confined areas, because the amount of smoke produced by black powder made viewing the target difficult until the smoke dissipated.

In the open, these rovers dropped flat to the ground when a Spanish volley was fired until the Spaniards realized the practice and began to fire low after the rovers were on the ground. However, these tactics were general principals only: pirates adjusted their tactics based on the situation, and the tactics were indeed unconventional: "[W]e were very well prepared to receive them, but the way of fighting practised by these men did so much astonish ours, that we could not make that resistance we had promised ourselves we should do," wrote the governor general of the province of Costa Rica in 1686. In another letter he warned: "Take good measures, for those devils have a cunning and subtlety that is not in use amongst us."[40]

Pirates frequently had an advantage in leadership, being led by men like the sieur de Grammont (who may have been Henry Morgan's tactical equal). Such men were well experienced in land warfare, and they led from the front and by example, rather than from a position in the rear that permitted a better overall sense of the battle but was poor for inspiring men. The frontal leadership position had its disadvantage: many pirate commanders were killed in action. However, many Spanish commanders also led and died from the front like their enemy's leaders.

From 1674 to 1688 buccaneers and filibusters attacked dozens of Spanish towns and cities and sacked many of them, battering much of an already battered Spanish population and economy. Many coastal inhabitants lived in constant fear of attack, which affected the psychology of these proud people— their hatred of the French, English, and Dutch pirates was often bitter and easy to appreciate, although there were many in the New World who had good reason to hate the Spanish as well. A few brief descriptions of various attacks on Spanish towns illustrates exactly what the attackers, defenders, and innocents faced in the circumstances of battle and its aftermath.

$\mathcal{N}$ot long after the French disaster at Aves in 1678, the sieur de Grammont attacked Maracaibo with seven hundred men. Grammont was a gouty, fighting French gentleman, most of whose forty or fifty years were spent as a corsair or filibuster. He was "well-made," olive skinned, black haired, "with the look of a warrior." Neither age nor gout slowed him down, and he led from the front. He was also impious and irreverent; could be cold blooded; was excessively fond of wine, women, and dice; and had "the secret of gaining [the filibusters'] hearts and insinuating himself into their spirits." He was beloved by the filibusters of Saint Domingue, and at Maracaibo they gladly obeyed his every command.[41]

The bottleneck of the great lake on whose shores the city rested was protected by the Fort de la Barre with twelve cannon and a few patereroes. The fort controlled access in and out of the lake, something Henry Morgan discovered all too well in1669. Grammont offered quarter to the fort's outnumbered defenders, but they refused to surrender, so his filibusters worked to construct ladders and open a trench from which to attack the fort. When they had built enough ladders, his men demanded to attack, but Grammont, wishing to minimize losses, made them continue to work on the trench. When the defenders realized an assault was imminent, they chose discretion as the better part of valor and surrendered. Grammont permitted the fort's commander to keep his sword but disarmed his men. Leaving a garrison of seventy filibusters behind, Grammont sailed into the lake only to find Maracaibo deserted and the town of Gibraltar a place of little resistance or wealth. The filibusters captured a large ship too old and battered to put to sea, and

Grammont sent pirogues to capture a twelve-gun frigate. For several months the filibusters scoured the countryside for plunder. They were repulsed at Mérida, Venezuela, and burned Gibraltar in revenge. At one point the Spanish, in two parties of fifty, attacked two groups of filibusters of nine men each. The pirates defended themselves vigorously, killing ten or so of each party, and forced one group of Spaniards to flee by deliberately loading and firing wadding into the reeds concealing the Spanish, setting the dry plants on fire. In all, Grammont lost only a few men and returned with a moderate amount of plunder.[42]

*I*n 1680, four leagues off the coast of La Guayra, Grammont and 183 men debarked into seven pirogues at night and proceeded ashore. The force landed half a league to the east of the city, then used axes to render their pirogues useless, because Grammont had too few men already and could leave none behind to guard the craft. The pirates marched on the city at dawn, capturing the sleeping watch. With "drum beating and flag flying" they entered at the east gate and attacked the closest fort, assaulting it twice with grenades before its defenders surrendered. Mounting the French flag on its rampart and giving three shouts of "*Vive le roi!*" they intimidated the other fort into surrendering. The city was theirs, the only real defense having been that of the eighty or so men of the forts' garrisons. Besides signaling their vessels into the harbor and plundering the city, the filibusters disabled the cannon, razed the forts, and destroyed stockpiled arms and munitions. But their stay was not long. Grammont lost six men in a massive Spanish counterattack from Caracas that forced him to withdraw to his vessels in the harbor, and he was wounded in the throat by an arrow. Worse, his ship was wrecked in a storm, and he lost the treasure aboard.[43]

*C*ampeche was sacked twice, first in 1678 by buccaneers who landed at night two leagues from the town and attacked at dawn. The townspeople were expecting the return of Spanish soldiers, and so took no notice of the pirates afoot until it was too late. The only defense was from the fort, which the buccaneers breached after a "furious Attack" in which they turned two parade-ground cannon on the gate.[44] After first being repulsed at Mérida, Mexico, to the north, filibusters led by Laurens and Grammont sacked the town in 1685, but only after an initially stout resistance. Spanish accounts stated that when the filibusters landed two leagues from the town, they were ambushed and initially forced to retreat, but Exquemelin mentioned no such repulse. At any rate, the pirates advanced on the city in two groups—Laurens from the road along the shore, Grammont from the hinterland. The town itself fell quickly, and the Spanish destroyed their own frigate in the harbor, although the French suggested it burned accidentally during its cannonade of the filibusters. Using ten cannon captured from the bastions on the city walls, the invaders cannonaded the principal fortification, whose garrison eventually withdrew at night during a cease-fire for negotiations, fearing a filibuster attack. In all, it took several days to fully secure the town. For almost two months the pirates plundered city and countryside.The filibusters briefly attempted to march north to attack Mérida again but were stopped by a large Spanish force at the village of Xampolol, where nineteen pirates, including two of their leaders (the brave Garderies being one of them), were killed, and in this both French and Spanish accounts for once agree. One of the Spanish commanders, Además de Baldraque, killed "many pirates" in the action.When Spanish merchants and authorities failed to pay a ransom, Grammont decapitated several captives at Campeche, and in one account Laurens intervened to spare others. Exquemelin, however, suggested it was Grammont's humanity that spared the rest. Finally, threatened by a relief force on the march, the pirates departed, burned the city, destroyed the fort, and, because it was the day of St. Louis, celebrated with musket and cannon fire, probably with drum and trumpet music, and with an enormous logwood bonfire.[45]

*I*n the South Sea, Guayaquil was also attacked by pirates twice, first in 1684 by Swan and Davis, among whose company was William Dampier, and again in the same year byTownley and Grogniet, among whose company was Raveneau de Lussan.The first attempt failed owing to the escape, apparently contrived by a pirate, of the Native American prisoner guiding them. The buccaneers, knowing the town would have been warned by the escaped prisoner, observed it from canoes in the river, then departed.[46] The Spanish described the second attackers as French, English, Dutch, and Flemish, with Spaniards, NativeAmericans, mulattoes, and others. As usual, the pirates were guided by those who knew the city well, this time by turncoat locals. Approaching from the sea in canoes, they headed up river, intending to land above the city, but an ebb tide prevented them. Hacking their way toward Guayaquil, a filibuster lit his pipe in spite of orders and gave away their presence.The Spanish attacked from behind a barricade, killing several filibusters and halting their advance. Believing the pirates were on the run, the Spanish left the barricade and attacked sword in hand, which was their undoing.The filibusters routed them from the field, followed them to the city (whose walls were but a few feet high), and with grenades pressed them from fort to fort. The Spanish made a second courageous assault sword in hand, but the filibusters, with losses, beat them back again. Running out of powder, the pirates renewed their effort and late in the evening captured the last fort.They put their prisoners in the largest church, looted the city, and departed.The Spanish claimed to have killed more than fifty pirates in the action and wounded a dozen or more (the filibusters acknowledged nine dead and twelve wounded), but claimed to have lost only thirty of their own in the action. The Spanish said their dead included women, because the pirates considered it inconvenient to guard them, and don Lorenzo de Sotomayor, who was shot in the head because he said there was no more silver with which to ransom the city, the pirates having already found it all.[47]

*A*t Arica, the South Sea embarcadero of Potosí silver, buccaneers were twice repulsed. The first time in October 1680 they discovered that not only was the entire countryside alarmed and armed (*al armas!*), but that the surf was too high to safely land their boats. The buccaneers returned to the *Trinity*. Their second attempt on Arica was for "revenging" the previous rebuff and an act of desperation. A new captain, John Watling, wanted to prove himself worthy of command by putting plunder in the hands of his buccaneers, and so he led an attack on Arica in spite of evidence that the town was fortified and waiting. And indeed the Ariqueños were ready for them, but the buccaneers formed two parties of forty men each, one to attack the fort and the other to attack the town. Exposed to a devastating fire from the breastworks at the town, the parties joined together but came under fire from the fort's cannon. Seeing their salvation in the town itself, they flanked and captured the main barricade and took many prisoners. They came under fire from other barricades and from defenders on rooftops. The pirates captured three more barricades, and, according to Cox, they gave the defenders no quarter. Many Spaniards fled to the fort, strengthening it. For an hour the pirates set up a hospital for their wounded, put their many prisoners (whom they could barely manage) under guard, and, recalling Henry Morgan at Portobello, marched to the fort behind some of the prisoners, hoping the Spanish would not fire on them. Instead, the defenders fired both on the buccaneers and on their own, and worse, some of the prisoners in the vanguard ran to a sally port and entered the fort. Worse still, when the buccaneers attacked the fort with their mere ten grenades, they found the powder bad and the grenades ineffective.[48]

The buccaneers, who could no longer manage their prisoners, retreated to the town to find the Spanish closing in on them on horse and afoot. Captain Watling was "shot into the Reins [loins]," and both quartermasters were killed, leaving none in line to command. Bartholomew Sharp was entreated to lead (he had been recently deposed as captain by a vote of the company for putting his own interests first), and he did. They retreated in good order in a circle, "not one Man of us offering to run," protecting their wounded in the center and keeping up a constant fire. They moved slowly to the seaside three miles away, where their canoes awaited. By torturing one of the captured, wounded buccaneers, the Spanish discovered the signal to bring the *Trinity* into harbor. They lit fires to create two pillars of smoke to draw the ship under the dozen guns of the fort, where the sea breeze would have left it embayed if it had entered the harbor. The ruse almost worked, but the *Trinity's* sailing crew spotted the buccaneers' canoes as they took to the sea. The pirates claimed to have lost twenty-six men, all but three of them—the surgeons who were taken prisoner—killed in action, or wounded and later "knocked in the head" by their Spanish captors. They also claimed, based on subsequent Spanish statements, to have killed more than seventy defenders and wounded one hundred to two hundred, and that the Spanish spared as many as ten of the captured buccaneers. But casualty figures cited by adversaries seldom agree. The Spanish claimed to have found twenty dead pirates in the street and to have captured another nineteen, most of whom they hanged. They put their own losses at twenty-three dead and a few more wounded. For the buccaneers, the hero was not Captain Watling, who led a desperate, valiant, foolish attack, but Bartholomew Sharp, who led the embattled buccaneers to safety. For the Spaniards the hero was not the governor who urged his men on from the safety of the great hill called El Morro, but the *Alfarez Real de Arica*, don Gaspar de Oviedo, who organized the defenses and led his men in battle.[49]

Arica was not the only place where buccaneers and filibusters were repulsed multiple times. Cumaná, according to William Dampier, was "the only Place in the North-Seas they attempted in vain for many Years; and the *Spaniards* since throw it in their Teeth frequently, as a Word of reproach or defiance to them," although Sir Christopher Myngs sacked the city in 1658.[50] Between 1674 and 1688 only one in four pirate attacks were repulsed or called off, suggesting a strong ability in intelligence gathering, planning, and execution, as well as the ability to choose targets wisely. (See appendix G.)

*W*e now return to Veracruz. We have already briefly met Nicolas Van Horn, the privateer-turned-slaver who defrauded and angered the Spanish and had part of his cargo of slaves seized in recompense. Van Horn complained to Governor Pouançay of Petit Goave, who provided him with a commission (which Van Horn suggested to the English was only a commission to take pirates), men, and Grammont as his lieutenant. Soon, Van Horn precipitously captured the Honduras ship and its patache before they were fully laded, infuriating Laurens to the point that he refused to speak with his fellow countryman. Perhaps owing to Grammont's intercession at Roatan Island, Laurens, Van Horn, and Grammont decided to attack Veracruz. Considering their resources, this was as audacious as the attack on Panama was—but the way was much easier, because Veracruz lay on the coast in the Gulf of Mexico.

Two filibuster ships captured from the Spanish approached within sight of the city but raised few eyebrows because the flota was expected. That evening the filibusters landed eight hundred men and marched to the city, guided by those who were formerly prisoners in the city, including, according to Dampier, an Englishman named John Russel.[51] Laurens led the enfants perdus, with Charles Roinel as his ensign carrying French colors. Immediately they captured the two main bastions at the water's edge, Laurens leading the attack against the southern bastion.[52] According to Luke Haughton, a participant in the attack, one of the gates or bastions (probably one of the forts captured by the *enfants perdus*) was seized by Spanish-speaking filibusters (probably Spaniards) dressed as locals. One climbed the ladder to the bastion, pretending to "beg Fire of the Centinel to light his Pipe." He promptly shot the sentinel dead, and at this point the attack commenced, some say after three shots were fired as a signal.[53] Others reported the sentinels were asleep.[54] Grammont led the main body to the plaza or parade ground, meeting little if any resistance, and three discharges of musketry followed by a charge routed the few defenders.[55] Filibuster casualties were light.[56]

Quickly the attackers went from house to house, gathering prisoners and plundering, facilitated by former prisoners who knew their way around. Some took the opportunity for private revenge: one filibuster, a former inhabitant, murdered his wife, and others murdered don Pedro Estrada of the Holy Inquisition, recalling their harsh treatment at his hands while they were his prisoners.[57] By one account, Captain Spurre, an Englishman, discovered the governor in hiding.[58] Overall, there was little resistance except for a few officers and soldiers, including Juan Morfa, the Irishman who turned renegade at Tortuga so many decades past. Briefly he and his servants put up a stout resistance, but realizing it was hopeless and only endangered his family, he submitted. For his resistance he was viciously abused by pirates, including Laurens, and his wife died, probably from heat and other stresses, during the occupation.[59]

The attackers imprisoned four thousand or more inhabitants in the largest church, La Merced, largely without food or water for three days. The heat was intense and suffocating, and prisoners died from the stress. The pirates put barrels of gunpowder at the church, telling their prisoners they would detonate them if more plunder was not provided—and so it was. In response food and water was provided to the prisoners. Outside, the streets were littered with corpses and dead animals. On the fourth day, aware that the well-armed flota was nearby, the filibusters transferred plunder and four thousand prisoners to ships, and moved them to the Sacrificios Island, a barren bit of sand, where over eight days more prisoners succumbed to heat and dehydration while awaiting ransom. As at Campeche, Laurens prevented Grammont from killing prisoners.[60] When they left, the pirates took fifteen hundred blacks and mulattoes, slave and free, to sell as slaves. The assault was physically brutal, and its effects were economically and politically devastating. Spain's response was war, and the Armada de Barlovento began to actively seek pirates on the sea.[61]

*A*ttacks on towns and their aftermath were brutal, both to combatants and inhabitants, including women, children, and the elderly. Pirates sometimes burned the towns they sacked. Some attackers assaulted and raped women, although there were not as many complaints of rape on record as one might expect, probably because the rape of slaves was unrecorded. Nonetheless, even Ringrose recorded that seven or eight buccaneers sacked the isle of Gallo and carried away "three white women in their company," their intentions toward the women certain.[62] The same men were later ambushed by the Spanish, and all but one was shot dead.

The journals of the South Sea buccaneers were somewhat circumspect on the subject of torture, although "interrogations" were well recorded.[63] Raveneau de Lussan specifically mentioned torture practiced on a Spaniard who had been following the filibusters at a distance, "making mouths" and reviling them as he did:"[W]e made him make a grimace in good earnest. We questioned him according to our usual ceremony, that is to say, by putting him on the rack, about the place where we were."[64] Exquemelin listed several means of torture, including *the rack*, although the term was synonymous with torture among pirates.[65] The tortures inflicted by the notorious Hamlin were probably typical:"they tortured the mate, the doctor, and all the rest of the men, squeezing their thumbs and privy members in vices, hanging them up in the brails by their hands tied behind them; and so found out what riches they carried."[66] Flogging was also common, and murder to inspire others to talk was not unknown. The tortures were not invented by sea rovers— mankind had long known how to inflict severe pain on its own. Caribbean rovers, for example, applied the sailor's term *wolding* to a torture in which a victim's head above his eyes was wrapped with line that was subsequently tightened until, according to Exquemelin, the eyes began to bulge. But this torture was original only in its name; the forehead tourniquet was long used in Europe for extracting confessions.[67]

There were other brutalities, enormities beyond rape and torture. Often neither side provided quarter, and both sides killed prisoners in reprisal or out of mere malice. Filibusters decapitated hostages when ransoms were not paid as agreed or as demanded. One can only imagine the terror of hostages throwing dice to determine who lived and who died, and for the losers, the even greater terror of waiting to be murdered by decapitation, not to mention of the act itself. Almost as terrible was the fear and suffering of the inhabitants at Veracruz who suffocated in the church or were exposed to sun, hunger, thirst, and the terror of the unknown for days.

Few people today know of the sack of Veracruz, the personalities involved, or the horrors suffered by the inhabitants. One exception is found in a popular song, although most people do not realize that it refers to the sack of Veracruz. In the seventeenth century the guitar was popular in both Old and New Spain. In 1674, for example, Gaspar Sanz published his great opus, *Instrucción de Música Sobre la Guitarra Española*, parts of which are heard today in Rodrigo's *Concierto de Aranjuez*. The guitar was also the instrument of the Spanish balladeer, who wrote and sang songs about everything from true love to spurned love to pompous fools, the latter typically in witty satire. According to the folklore of Veracruz, shortly after the sack of the city a local musician composed a song ridiculing those who pretended to prepare to drive off the attacking pirates. The Mexican folk song, of a musical form permitting improvisation, is known today throughout much of the world thanks to singer Ritchie Valens: "La Bamba."

*A*lthough the sack of Veracruz was the most significant attack by pirates from 1674 to 1688, it was not the only significant event of 1683. In January, Grammont and others, including Captain Bréha, blockaded Cuba. Soon after, Bréha sailed from New Providence, along with Jeremiah Conway and George Young, seeking a Spanish wreck on the Organos Bank off the coast of Cuba. Interrupted by the Spanish, they returned to New Providence and the *Maravillas* wreck and recruited Paine, Markham, Woolery, and Cornelison for an attack on St. Augustine in Florida. They captured the watchtower in Matanzas, Florida, but St. Augustine was prepared for them, so they sacked the villages of San Juan and Santa Maria, Florida, instead. Captain Du Chesne sacked Tampico, Mexico, in the spring. Governor Pouançay died, and the sieur de Franquesnay was appointed interim governor of Petit Goave and ineffectually attempted to suppress French piracy. Jamaican governor Lynch sent a frigate to pursue pirates and sent Coxon to find Yanky, offering both of them money, pardons, and commissions, and offering Yanky naturalization as well, to pursue the pirate Hamlin, whose depredations against English shipping had become infamous. Spanish rover Juan Corso was active off the coast of Jamaica. At Saint Domingue Edmond Cook seized Captain Tristian's vessel in retaliation for an earlier affront by the French, then soon after captured a French merchantman laded with wine and a small frigate of eighteen guns, and sailed to Virginia. Dampier and Captain Davis were in his company. After the sack of Veracruz, the Armada de Barlovento captured six pirate vessels, including the *Nuestra Señora de Regla*, but Captain Tristian and his crew escaped. The sack of the city prompted new Spanish raids on Saint Domingue, which in turn the French used as an excuse for more raids against the Spanish. At the end of summer, Cook sailed from Virginia in the *Revenge*, Dampier and Abraham Cowley in his company, as well as some of Wright's former crew. At the Guinea Coast they captured a Danish ship with forty guns, renamed her the *Batchelor's Delight*, and set sail for the South Sea. In December Laurens, Michel, Yanky, Le Sage, and Bréha blockaded Cartagena and captured the *San Francisco* and the *Nuestra Señora de la Paz*. Grammont finally arrived at Petit Goave, having almost starved owing to delays caused by beating against prevailing winds. Saved by the capture of the *Nuestra Señora de Candelaria* and its cargo of grain, Grammont sailed for Carolina to sell his cargo of captured slaves. Spain declared war on France, and Grammont, Laurens, and many other filibusters received legitimate commissions to attack the Spanish.

The following year Pierre-Paul Tarin, seigneur de Cussy, arrived at Saint Domingue as governor. At Jamaica Governor Lynch died and was replaced by Hender Molesworth. Adolf Esmit was replaced as governor of St. Thomas by Gabriel Milan. Captain Michel sailed the *Paz* to Boston. Yamassee Indians allied with the South Carolina English and threatened the Spanish in Florida. Privateers operated out of South Carolina, attacking the Spanish under the guise of the Spanish-French conflict. Captain Eaton joined Captain Swan in the South Sea. The Spanish sacked New Providence. Captain Thomas Jingle captured the *Plantanera* in the Florida Keys. In March, the sieur de Bournano, along with Captains Grogniet, Blot, Vigneron, and Petit, was on the coast of Trinidad and at the Gulf of Paria. Captain Phips, commanding the *Rose of Algeree*, arrived at the *Maravillas* wreck. Buccaneers and wreckers sacked Tampico after growing weary of seeking treasure at the *Maravillas* wreck, but the Spanish captured 104 of them. Captains Brouage and Michel captured two Dutch ships in the service of the asiento, the *Stad Rotterdam* and the *Elisabeth*, angering the Dutch. Laurens captured a Spanish vessel and its English prize, and returned the English vessel to Governor Lynch of Jamaica. While provisioning with turtle at the Caymans, pirate Joseph Banister was captured by the HMS *Ruby*. At Cuba, Captain Bréha forced English turtle sloops to fish turtles for him. Peter Harris (nephew of the Peter Harris wounded at Perico) sacked Santa Maria on the Isthmus of Darien, then crossed into the South Sea. Laurens, among whose company was Raveneau de Lussan, was almost attacked by the filibuster Captain Rose. Many filibusters, including de Lussan, crossed into the South Sea. Eaton broke consort with Cook and headed across the Pacific, but Cook and Swan joined forces. La Salle arrived at Petit Goave, where some of his crew deserted to the filibusters, and some pirates, including the German-born English gunner John Heins, joined La Salle. The Spanish captured one of his vessels, a ketch laded with supplies. In August, war between France and Spain ended. Near the end of 1684 Captains Brouage, Pedneau, and others returned from an expedition on the Orinoco River.

None of these expeditions, no matter how successful, were without conflict within their ranks, and certainly those who sacked Veracruz were no exception. The filibusters, with their thousands of suffering prisoners on Sacrificios Island and the thousands of very tangible silver coins in their greedy, grasping hands, also experienced personal conflicts, which were settled according to custom, one on one.

# 19 Honor With an Edge:
## Dueling and Swordplay on the Main

"One could say that seldom were so many brave filibuster captains assembled together,"* writes Exquemelin of the sack of Veracruz.[1] Courage notwithstanding, the aftermath has been brutal. Yet not all is sheer violence and abuse, nor is all said and done after the city is taken and plundered. There are moments of near humanity and of arguably justified revenge and just deserts as well.

Captain Laurens's opinion of Captain Van Horn's character and competence is not improved by the success of the raid. If Exquemelin's description of Laurens is correct—as not only "intrepid in danger" but also "impatient, hot-headed, and much-addicted to swearing"—this is no surprise.[2] Van Horn himself remains abhorred by many of the French "for his insolence and passion," and Laurens remains outraged at Van Horn's premature capture of the Honduras ships months before, an act that cost Laurens and his crew thousands of pieces-of-eight.[3]

Accounts differ as to how the next event transpires. We know the filibusters have thousands of prisoners on Sacrificios Island, and that the filibusters await a ransom. According to a modern account based on period Spanish sources, Van Horn becomes enraged when the Spanish fire upon the filibusters who are fetching flour to feed the captives. In response he intends to decapitate a dozen captives as a warning that no further violence will be

---

*All quotations have been reprinted with their original spelling and punctuation.

189

tolerated. Laurens, hearing of this, storms ashore to stop the incipient butchery and violation of good quarter, venting his temper, doubtlessly colorfully, on Van Horn.[4]

Exquemelin, however, writes that nothing in particular is known about the actual cause of the dispute on the island, only that an English buccaneer reports to Laurens that Van Horn has said something insulting about him. "Will you affirm this?" Laurens asks of the buccaneer, who replies, "Oui." They confront Van Horn and he denies the charge. The buccaneer, however, maintains the accusation and Laurens believes him.[5]

A letter from Sir Thomas Lynch to Sir Leoline Jenkins suggests a source for the insult. According to Lynch's information, when the flota arrived off Veracruz, Van Horn

> pressed the Captains to attack the flota and offered to board the admiral himself, but Laurens would not, either because he had got enough, or from jealousy of Van Horn ... for taking the Spanish ship and for calling him coward.[6]

Van Horn, whom, like Laurens, few would have dared call *coward*, may have called his countryman one for refusing to attack the flota. Even so, another English account, as well as a Spanish version recounted by an Arab traveler, claim that Laurens and Van Horn quarrel "about the dividend" of plunder.[7] A French account simply notes that they "had a difference."[8] Whatever the catalyst, the festering animosity between the two Dutch commanders is brought to a head.

All accounts agree on what happens next.

"Voilà," says Laurens, drawing his sword. "Here is what will avenge the injury you have given me."[9] Van Horn draws his sword as well, and on the beach at Sacrificios Island off Veracruz is the most significant duel among the pirates of the Caribbean, matching in drama even the fictional duels of Capt. Peter Blood against Captain Levasseur in Sabatini's *Captain Blood*, and of Charles de Bernis against the notorious Captain Leach in Sabatini's *The Black Swan*. Only the damsel in distress is missing.

Dueling—formal combat between two persons for the sake of honor, and usually unlawful—was fairly common among buccaneers and filibusters, probably as common as it was among the other dueling classes: a man may have fought a duel, or a few, over an entire lifetime, or he may have fought none at all.[10] Some men were prone to fight fairly often, and others never. Although dueling among buccaneers and filibusters was common enough to be mentioned in general terms in several contemporary sources, only two duels between pirates were specifically noted in the principal buccaneer journals of 1674–88.[11] During the course of a long buccaneering cruise, for example, only one duel may have been noted, although there could have been occasions for several more unless cooler heads prevailed. "Here it was that our quartermaster, James Chappel, and myself fought a duel together on shore" was all that was noted in the case of one duel.[12] Dueling, after all, was antithetical to good order among combat forces, and duels were not fought aboard ships but ashore, thus limiting their opportunity and providing time at sea for the adversaries to come to terms again.

The author has found no record of a duel fought between buccaneers or filibusters for command of a ship or expedition, although the duel between Van Horn and Laurens was popularly seen as such by some Spaniards at the time.[13] However, David Van der Sterre, the seventeenth-century biographer of Jan Erasmus Reyning, claimed that Rock the Brazilian and Reyning fought a duel aboard ship (Exquemelin, however, never mentioned Reyning at all), and described a challenge from Reyning to another to determine command, although the latter refused.[14] Such duels were otherwise unknown among buccaneers and filibusters, and in the case of dueling for command were entirely unacceptable under the "Custom of the Coast." Command was determined democratically, and captains served at the consent of the crew. In Reyning's case, the shipboard duel and the challenge for command may have reflected Dutch practices, but more likely they were literary exaggerations or even inventions by Reyning's biographer. Regarding buccaneer arms, on at least two of the very few occasions on record of disagreement degenerating into assault or affray (as opposed to a duel) among buccaneers, they used firearms, not swords: John Coxon fired on Peter Harris ashore, possibly with a musket, and Bartholomew Sharp discharged a pistol at Richard Hendricks at sea.[15]

Rovers of the noblesse and bourgeoisie—persons of quality—fought duels as well. Before he became a filibuster, the sieur de Grammont fought a duel as a youth, pushing his blade thrice into an officer who sought his sister's hand. The officer died from his wounds.[16] The comte de Forbin, a French corsair, naval officer, and former *mousquetaire* who discovered his own aggressive qualities at the age of ten when he disemboweled an attacking dog, mortally wounded the chevalier de Gourdon in the belly and throat, and was himself wounded in the side.[17] The common filibuster and buccaneer, being of the "vulgar sort," as the upper classes referred to them, probably fought duels only with other filibusters and buccaneers or with others of the vulgar sort. In 1694 a sailor serving as a trumpeter (and a "most dissolute wicked wretch") aboard the slaver *Hannibal* quarreled with a sergeant at Cape Corso Castle, Africa. The sergeant issued a challenge, the trumpeter answered it, and "both lugging [lunging] out, it was the serjeant's chance to be thrust through the belly." Later in Barbados the trumpeter signed aboard a vessel pretending to be a trade vessel but intending piracy in the Red Sea.[18] Dueling proclivity seemed as much based on temperament as social class.

The Spanish and Portuguese temperaments reputedly inclined them to duel incessantly (if they did not first attack each other with daggers), and when dueling failed, to assassinate. Indeed, some implied that assassination was more common than dueling among some of the Spanish, and that many quarrels passed directly to assassination.[19] Some Italians had a similar reputation, relying as much on the vendetta as on the *duello*.The Highland Scots did likewise, dueling for honor but also thinking nothing of ambushing an enemy as he walked along a path through the glens.The English in Ireland, in particular soldiers and aristocrats, and the native Irish gentry, or what soon was left of them, dueled as well.[20]

The European working classes tended to use fists, knives, cudgels, or quarterstaves to work out their differences, often owing to class restrictions on the wearing of swords. Dutch sailors, and the Dutch working class in general, were fond of the knife and settled disputes in a fashion nearly identical to a formal duel.[21] Sailors in England did not wear cutlasses when ashore, but often carried cudgels instead.[22] In the Old World perhaps only in the Highlands of Scotland did men of all classes routinely bear arms. Among the Spanish and Portuguese, however, it was reported that nearly every man esteemed himself a hidalgo or better, and so wore his cloak and carried his rapier and poniard, even when "a barber come to shave a man."[23]

The buccaneers and filibusters, however, claimed equality with all men, and thus believed dueling was a right by virtue of courage and independence, not birth.They were like Wycherley's plain-speaking sea captain in his 1677 play *The Plain Dealer*: "I weigh the man, not his title."[24] In general in the English and French Caribbean, both the gentry— including former "Newgate birds" and their French counterparts—and the "ordinary or sea-faring people" fought duels.The only difference was in the arms they used: sword or sword and pistol for the gentry, and musket or cutlass for the buccaneer.[25] Buccaneers and filibusters also bore arms when ashore unless forbidden by a local governor, which was a rare thing indeed in the Caribbean.[26] The routine bearing of arms ashore surely increased the likelihood of dueling.

"They seldom want courage," wrote Francis Rogers of the Creole Jamaicans, both the gentry and seafaring sorts, "being too forward in duelling on very slight occasions, standing much on their honour and scorning base litigious actions."[27] They preferred the field of honor over the courts of law.They preferred "satisfaction by way of Challenge, as t'other by way of Writ," although each of these arenas was well represented by both honor and knavery.[28] The difference, at least in the mind of the duelist, was that the field of honor was much less often the refuge of a coward than were the courts of law, particularly of a rich coward.[29]

Pretexts for dueling—"to measure the length of my sword"—included a just cause or any insult to honor.[30] Based on a review of firsthand accounts, they included political or religious differences, or both; competition over a woman; drunkenness (often a factor); calling a man a dog, coward, liar, or cuckold, or otherwise impugning him; national rivalries; differences of opinion on any subject; gambling and gambling debts; and simple incompatibility of character. Specific instances ranged from the dislike of a sister's suitor to the extortion of one's pay as a soldier to the theft of a man's "bread winner" prostitutes.[31] Sometimes there were underlying motives, long simmering. Sometimes there were none, only the passion of the moment.

*G*iven that the sword in one form or another was mandatory on the battlefield, not to mention the typical choice of weapon in duels among soldiers and aristocrats, and often among sea rovers as well, the ability to handle one well was vital. "[I]n the wars and places of most danger it maketh [a man] bold, hardie, and valient," wrote George Silver in 1599, stating a fact understood for centuries.[32]

Training in the sword was and is unique among arts, sciences, or finished skills, particularly because the individual lesson reigned, master and student facing each other. Group instruction was useful only for true beginners, and occasionally for footwork, tactics, and simple drills. In the individual lesson the *maître d'armes* (master of arms or fencing master), or teacher, played a complex and simultaneous role of professor and adversary to the student, leading him to grasp the skill and independence required to face an enemy alone, sword in hand. Lessons were coupled with practice against many adversaries or they were useless.

The language of fencing was unique as well. Then as now, it was an amalgam of Italian, French, and bastardized Latin vocabulary, with other terms thrown in for good measure in the language in which it was taught. It was a language as complex as that of the law, but more honest. It had words for various guards and parries such as *tierce, carte, seconde, falloon,* and *demi-cercle.* It included *pushes, passes, voltes, demi-voltes, lunges,* and *flanconnades,* as well as "Strokes, Chops, Thro's, Flirts, Slips and Darts." It had *counter-cave-ating thrusts* and *mountanos,* as well as *bottes, batters,* and *binds.* The language of fencing was the language of adventure.[33]

*T*o better understand the sword duel, some knowledge of swords and swordplay of the period is in order. Swords were of three sorts: those designed solely or primarily for thrusting, those for cutting, and those for cutting and thrusting. Of the thrusting swords the smallsword, a light, quick sword descended from the rapier and often called a *rapier*, began to predominate among the French, English, and many of the Dutch. Its hilt was small, providing little protection to the hand. Recommended blade length varied, but thirty-four to thirty-six inches was not uncommon. Its shape was often triangular or "hollow," and these triangular blades typically lacked cutting edges. A smallsword with a much wider *forte* (the third of the blade near the hilt) was called a *colichemarde*. "Spanish tucks" were considered the best blades, but too heavy unless shortened, and so German blades were recommended. The ideal balance point was two to three inches from the hilt, and the blade should have been well tempered and strong, but not brittle, and fairly stiff. The blade may have been straight or had a bend near the forte or foible, up or down, as suited the swordsman.[34]

The Spanish, Portuguese, some Italians, and some in the Spanish Netherlands carried the true rapier—"a very long sword . . . and a Ponyard [poniard]." It was popular among Spanish soldiers and seamen: Captain Fitzgerald, a renegade Irishman and Spanish pirate, used his to murder an English sailor who refused to serve under him.[35] The rapier (*espada ropera* or *spado*, as the English called it) was primarily a thrusting sword but could also make shallow cuts. Often cup-hilted (*tazza* in Spanish) with long quillons, its blade was commonly more than forty inches long. Indeed, a visitor to Spain made a questionable claim that some were so long "the Scabbards of these Swords have a Spring, which opens them on the side with the least touch, no Man, except a Gyant, being able to draw them otherwise, by reason of their excessive length."[36] Whether or not the claim was factual, the hyperbole was certainly fair, for the blades were often a foot or more longer than smallsword blades. Indeed, the rapier's advantage and disadvantage were in the length of its blade. Last, what in modern terminology is called a *transitional rapier*— a lighter rapier but not yet quite a smallsword—was used and perhaps was more prevalent than the smallsword in the New World.

Swords designed primarily for cutting and used by Europeans were of three sorts. Broadswords were heavy, straight, double-edged swords intended for use from horseback, although Scottish Highlanders used them effectively afoot. Heavy backswords (swords sharpened only on the fore edge) are included in this category. A poetic term for a sword in general, the scimitar was an Islamic curved sword. Similar was the saber, a curved sword descended from the scimitar and made popular by Hungarian hussars (light horsemen said to take their name from their battle cry of "Husa!").[37] Last, the cutlass and hanger were shorter swords with straight or slightly curved blades, the former for maritime use (longer swords were difficult to use in the confines of a vessel), the latter for infantry and hunters. The cutlass was the common sword of pirates and privateers, including the Spanish. Although all of these swords were intended for cutting, they could also be used for thrusting. Curved blades had a natural slicing action, while straight blades were used in a chopping or draw-cut fashion. Heavy swords were capable of lopping off heads and limbs, not to mention cleaving skulls and torsos almost in two, but the wide movements required of such cuts left the swordsman vulnerable if he missed, and were best made from horseback or with a shield for protection. For this reason, swift, shallower cuts were the norm, and a wise swordsman made wide cuts only when a safe opportunity presented itself.

Swords designed for both cut and thrust included light, double-edged swords called *sheering swords*, often used by infantry; smallswords fitted with wide, sharpened, triangular blades; and light backswords.[38]

These three types of swords, thrusting, cutting, and cutting and thrusting, distinguished three sorts of swordplay, although for convenience they were usually considered as two, thrusting and cutting. A skillful swordsman was adept at both. In general, the thrust was believed to be more dangerous than the cut. A thrust to the chest or abdomen often killed, sooner or later, while a cut, unless delivered with great force, could more often be mended. "But still the Small Sword hath great odds of the Broad, for the Small Sword kills, and you may receive forty cuts and not be disabled."[39] Further, the thrust was considered more difficult to parry, because a cut could be parried simply by placing one's own sword in its path and blocking it, but a thrust had to be intercepted and deflected by a moving blade. Thrusting swords were more commonly used for self-defense and to "answer the call of honor," while cutting or cut-and-thrust swords were mandatory to "answer the call of duty" in battle, owing to the variety of weapons and adversaries. After all, who wanted to parry the thrust of a half-pike or Spanish lance with a smallsword? Even so, in 1692 Governor Du Casse of Saint Domingue, a capable soldier and fighting sailor, requested "espées à la connismaq" (colichemardes), as well as sabers and bayonets, to aid in fighting Spanish lancers and spearmen.[40]

*T*here were also distinct schools of swordplay. For the smallsword or "transitional rapier," the developing French school and its variations were most popular among swordsmen, relying on a good parry and riposte for defense. Dutch and German schools (sometimes considered as one) often used a high-hanging or *falloon* (from the pronunciation of *Walloon*, a term for an inhabitant of the Low Countries) guard, had a tendency to *time* (to thrust at an opening created by a movement of the adversary's hand or foot), and had evident Italian and French influences. Dutch fencing in the Spanish Netherlands was influenced by the Spanish, but was nonetheless an independent school. There were several Italian schools, some relying much on their rapier origins, while others still used the rapier. The Spanish had two schools, *la verdadera destreza*, or true skill, and a more conventional school, although to the author they are indistinguishable except for the former's academic and philosophical emphasis on geometry, which was lampooned by some.[41] A dagger in the opposite hand was typical of Spanish swordplay, although the rapier was also used alone. The swordplay of all of these schools was well developed and effective.

The English, German, and Dutch had distinct native schools of broadsword and cut-and-thrust play, as did the Scottish Highlanders. Although there was a limited range of useful technique with a sword, its application and learning it were complex. The Highland form was based on the broadsword and *targe* (shield). In battle "after one general discharge they attack them with sword in hand, having their target on their left hand," although duels were often fought with broadsword alone.[42] The Highland form was highly effective: a Highland dragoon "having reproch'd a Dutchman for cowardice in our late fight, was attack'd by two Dutchmen, when with his sword he struck off the head of one, and cleft the skull of the other down to his chin."[43]

Swordplay was popular not only as a subject of study, but also as a spectator sport. Prize-fighting "stage gladiators" were common and popular enough that in 1709 a prize fighter could tour "most Parts of the West Indies, viz., Jamaica, Barbados, and several other Parts of the World."[44] Nor was swordplay solely the province of gentlemen, soldiers, and fighting sailors. Some West Indies slaves were known as swordsmen:

> I have seen some of these *Portugal Negroes*, at Collonel *James Draxes*, play at Rapier and Dagger very skilfully, with their Stookados, their Imbrocados, and their Passes: And at single Rapier too, after the manner of *Charanza*, with such comeliness ...they were skilful too, which I perceived by their binding with their points, and nimble and subtle avoidings with their bodies. For, in this Science, I had been so well vers'd in my youth, as I was now able to be a competent judge.[45]

Wealthy Spaniards often had retinues of six to twelve liveried black slaves armed with rapiers.[46]

Modern accounts of the degree of formal swordplay study among sea rovers are conjectural, but they doubtless possessed adequate skill in the cutlass, and some buccaneers and filibusters were surely as exceptional as soldiers. Fencing schools, formal and informal, abounded in the Old World and were known in New—even New England had a "fencing school." There are records, albeit few, of training and exercise in the sword among privateer sailors of the late seventeenth to mid-eighteenth centuries, and the aforementioned trumpeter and soon-to-be pirate seemed right at home in a duel, thrusting sword in hand.[47] Rock the Brazilian was said to have been adept at all weapons, both those of Native Americans and Europeans.[48] Such knowledge and skill required a great deal of study and practice.

*S*wordplay in the duel and on the battlefield must also be distinguished. A duel was fought between two individuals on open ground with plenty of room to maneuver, with certain rules of behavior, and, often with witnesses. The duelist needed to concentrate solely on defeating his single adversary. However, on the battlefield or when boarding a ship there were many enemies with various arms and who attacked simultaneously; according to few if any rules; usually on a littered field or cluttered deck with limited room to maneuver or engage in precise, stable footwork; and with no third parties to see honor done. Tactics and technique were more restricted in battle than in a duel, and the fencing was often simple, fast, aggressive, and ugly.[49] Also, the sword, while vital to defend against many threats, could not defend a man against all threats in battle—no man is an army. The combat-experienced swordsman knew to heed the warning "Nullus Hercules contra duos," sometimes expressed as "Ne Hercules quidem contra multos" (Hercules is no match against two [or against many], except perhaps one at a time).[50]

Between the duel and battlefield was the affray, or street fight. It had elements both of the duel, in that the affray was often a combat between two individuals, and of the battlefield, in that often any sort of violence was acceptable, there was limited room to maneuver, and there could be multiple adversaries to deal with simultaneously.

There were also differences between "school play" and practical swordplay. All preparation for combat or warfare was only a simulation; no training ever exactly duplicated the conditions of combat. Unfortunately, training sometimes introduced actions detrimental to fighting ability. For example, in the seventeenth century many masters introduced a penalty for students who attacked as their adversary was attacking, causing a *contretemps*, or a double touch in which each man was hit.[51] While the penalty inclined a fencer to avoid attacking into an attack, it also rewarded him in spite of a double hit when someone attacked as he did, and did nothing to ensure that he could defend against this foolishness, whether done on purpose or by accident. Other such rules were introduced for reasons of safety. For example, there was no mask or other protection for the face, so practice was modified to protect the eyes. "Playing for prizes"—sport fencing—introduced other artificialities such as the restriction of the target area by making the arms and legs off-limits.

Further, because there was little risk in the school, a fencer could use an unsound technique with *sharps* (real swords). The wise man who ventured his life in a duel or on the battlefield kept his swordplay simple. He may have had a broad technique, but he avoided actions that lacked a measure of safety, no matter how elegant, flamboyant, or theoretically sound they were. When it came to arms, knowledge was written in bloody and often fatal experience. The goal in a duel or in battle was to stay alive and "sleep in a whole skin," not to earn a point in the school, or *salle*, by fencing elegantly or according to conventions of attack, or by hitting a moment before being hit.[52] The goal was to hit without being hit, to give and not receive. It was to take risks, yet not be rash. Aggressive patience was vital, yet paradoxically so was the courage to seize the moment *without hesitation.*[53]

$\mathcal{H}$owever, not all who wore swords were schooled in swordplay, or at least not all were well schooled—and even the well-schooled pirates had weaknesses. George Silver pointed out quite rightly in 1599 that a fencing master (and by inference a swordsman) should be tested by fencing "three bouts apeece with three of the best English Maisters of Defence, & three bouts apeece with three unskillful valient men, and three bouts apeece with three resolute men half drunke."[54] In a real fight an adversary may have been a "rude and forward ignorant rambler" or foolishly believed that in fencing "the quicker the better; run 'em down, run 'em down; no matter for parrying."[55] Worse, "some men care not . . . if they receive a thrust, if it be not immediately mortal, so that they can but give one."[56] Or an enemy may simply surprise his adversary with an ignorant attack or response, or have an unorthodox style that tended to work because it was unfamiliar to the average fencer. The only solution was to never assume, to train under many circumstances with as many and as wide a variety of adversaries as possible in order to never be surprised, and to always keep one's wits. Luck was ever present as well, or bad luck as the case may have been, and the assumption of rational or reasonable behavior on any battleground was a foolish and often fatal one.

$\mathcal{W}$e now return to Laurens and Van Horn on the sandy shore of Sacrificios Island. The drama was based not on colorful Hollywood action, but on the simple fact that one man might kill another. The audience's breath was bated. The drama was real. However, nothing is known of the engagement itself, not of *en gardes* or technique or tactics, not even of swords used, although cutlasses were the most likely.

The end, however, is known: Laurens cut to Van Horn's wrist, putting him *hors de combat*, or out of action. Van Horn was wounded, although "nobody thinking it to be but a slight wound" in one account, or at least not a mortal wound, and he should have soon been himself again.[57] Yet he never was. Soon he died, probably of gangrene, a common result of dirty wounds.[58] Perhaps he was poorly attended by his surgeon, or not at all. The crews were in ill spirits, partly from the divisiveness after the sack of Veracruz, partly from an unknown contagion that broke out among the filibuster fleet.[59]

"He died of a *coup* which his enemy gave him," wrote Exquemelin in epitaph, although the original French was more elegant—"On porte un coup" (one "carries" a thrust or cut to his enemy).

Their combat took place on the Cay of Sacrifice, two leagues from
Veracruz, and Van Horn was buried on Cay Logrette, which is but
three leagues from Cape Catoche, in the province of Yucatan, some
two hundred leagues distant from Veracruz, or thereabouts.[60]

It was perhaps both ironic and appropriate that Sacrificios was named
for a temple where Native Americans once performed human sacrifice. Writer
al-Mûsili seemed to delight in the fact that the "heretical chief" Van Horn was
killed by a "Spaniard," as he called the Dutchman Laurens, even if he was a
pirate.[61]

Perhaps Van Horn was a cruel, drunken, bombastic, pompous man until
his death, but there was never any doubt of his courage. According to
Exquemelin, "in the heat of combat" he would range from bow to stern, his
eye on everything, fearing nothing, not even the shot of musket and cannon
passing nearby. He believed in courage and "rewarded well all those who had
it."[62] To die from a duel was perhaps a fitting end to his courage; to die from a
festering wound while surrounded by an ill-spirited crew was perhaps a fitting end to his cruelties.

# 20 Clean Bottoms and Lost Souls:
## Keys, Cays, Isles, and Inlets

*L*ate in the night of July 5, 1685, James, Duke of Monmouth, pretender to the throne of England, and his ragtag army of untrained volunteers were defeated by Royalist forces at Sedgemoor on the island of Great Britain. The event was an interesting footnote to the spectacle of British history, noteworthy for the folly with which the abortive rebellion against King James II was undertaken; for the brutality of the debauched Colonel Kirke and his dragoons toward rebel prisoners; for the vituperation of the infamous Lord Chief Justice Jeffreys who presided over the "Bloody Assizes" in which many were hanged, disemboweled, beheaded, and quartered; and for John Ketch's mangling of Monmouth's decapitation. Monmouth himself felt the ax blade's edge. "I fear it is not sharp enough," he said just before he lay his head on the block. The executioner struck five times before Monmouth's head was severed from his body.[1]

The brief rebellion was also noteworthy in a small way for one of its accidental participants, Dr. Henry Pitman, who ventured out of curiosity to view the rebels and their commander, found himself trapped between two armies, and was eventually constrained by his conscience to tend the "many sick and wounded men miserably lamenting the want of chirurgeons to dress their wounds."[2] But most of Pitman's patients were rebels, and charity to a rebel was treason. Lord Jeffreys, between his rants about "Presbyters,"* hanged

---

*All quotations have been reprinted with their original spelling and punctuation.

more than three hundred rebels, but Dr. Pitman, whose trial was by chance later rather than earlier, avoided the noose. Instead, he was transported as a convicted traitor and indentured slave. His adventurous curiosity and Hippocratic humanity gave rise to an odyssey that, two and a half centuries later, inspired Rafael Sabatini to write *Captain Blood*, an epic of romantic love and romanticized piracy about a surgeon transported from England to Barbados, from one island to another, and then to yet another.

Islands and hidden coves were much of what we commonly associate with the Caribbean: isolated places of sun-washed, water-lapped shores lined with palm trees or mangroves. Without them the Caribbean would lose much of its romance, and it was partly for this reason that the term *the Spanish Main* came to indicate not only the mainland of Spain in the New World, but the waters and islands of the Caribbean as well. The names and associations of these islands and coves hint at history and adventure, often over-romanticized today but still imbuing our imaginations. There is Watling Island, purportedly named for buccaneer John Watling; La Sound's careening key; and Roatan Island, the common rendezvous for pirate expeditions in the Bay of Honduras. There is Serles Key, named after Robert Searles who sacked St. Augustine in 1668 and at Panama let the *Trinidad* escape with much of the wealth of the great city, and there are the appropriately named One Bush Key, Water Key, and the Isle of Pines. There is Blewfield's Bay, where Wyllem Blauveldt careened and repaired his vessels manned with Moskitos, Dutch, and English. Of course there is Tortuga, the original haven of buccaneers and filibusters, and St. Thomas, another true pirate haven. And there are also Sacrificos Island, where Van Horn received his mortal wound in a duel; Cayo Logrette, where he was buried; and many more.

𝒫irates had several uses for the many islands; rendezvousing and provisioning were two of the most common and most important. However, some served two other purposes as well. The first, although prosaic, was *careening*, a process vital both to a vessel's speed (necessary for pursuit and escape) and to its general seaworthiness: not only was a clean hull faster, but a rotten one would sink the vessel sooner or later. In general, quiet, sheltered beaches without rocks or other material that could damage the hull were required to careen a vessel—"a clean sand" or "a smooth sand indifferently hard" worked well.[3] A large tidal range was also helpful. The crew haled the vessel ashore and moored it, for example, by making "fast our cable to the trees, and the other Anchor in the offing [toward sea]".[4] Next, the crew "unrigged" the vessel, then off-loaded her cannon, shot, sails (first ensuring they were dry), spars, stores, cargo, and ballast. They built "a house on shoare to put our Rigging and saile in," as well as to store powder, if unladed, and other stores.[5] Her ballast, invariably foul, was typically deposited where the tide would wash over it and clean away much of its filth. With the tide out, the vessel was "haled over" so that one entire side of her hull was exposed, from gunwales to keel, using baulks of timber to support the hull as necessary. A "Greate shipp" was "haled down" with the assistance of a smaller vessel. To clean the hull, the crew burned off pitch and light marine growth using dry reeds or grass, or, in at least one instance in the early eighteenth century, papal bulls.[6] Using scrapers they "scrubbed" the hull, removing barnacles and other heavy growth. Once the hull was clean they made any necessary repairs to loose or worm-eaten sheathing or damaged hull planking, because the teredo worm (the common shipworm, or a bivalve mollusk that used its shell to burrow through wood) was endemic in the tropical waters, and ate through hulls. Sometimes the crew sawed new sheathing boards, "ripping" off the old, and "clapping on" the new, having first caulked the seams. The crew protected the hull with one or more layers of tallow, pitch, lime (obtained by burning seashells), tar, or other substances, then, with the assistance of the tide, hauled the vessel over to expose the other side. Often part of the crew cut firewood and filled water barrels while the rest cleaned the hull. Moskito strikers hunted turtle, manatee, and jewfish, and the crew salted and barreled it. Ideally, a careening place supported both careening and provisioning, and the entire process of "making clean" and provisioning could take six weeks. Twenty days was considered fast indeed to careen a frigate in a harbor, although a disciplined privateer crew could do it in two weeks on an island shore. In the Caribbean, the island of Aves, Springer's Key, the Isle of Pines, and Blewfield's were favorite careening places, as was Gorgona island in the South Sea.[7]

For buccaneers and filibusters, security was a primary consideration when careening. A vessel in such a state was vulnerable, and an enemy needed only stand off and shoot holes in her, or even send a boat ashore to burn her, although a beached vessel was easily defended against an attacking boat.[8] A cautious captain mounted his cannon ashore to defend the approaches. In 1686 the English frigates *Falcon* and *Drake* attacked the pirates Banister and La Garde careening two ships at Samana, but the rovers had mounted their cannon in two batteries ashore. For two hours the frigates were "warmly entertained ... from the batteries, and with small shot from the ships," but the frigates prevailed, beating both ships "almost to pieces," at the price of ten killed aboard the *Falcon* and thirteen aboard the *Drake*.[9]

$\mathcal{T}$he other purpose of small islands was more poetic, at least to the reader sitting comfortably in an armchair: marooning. Most often, persons were marooned accidentally, for example, by going ashore to hunt, getting lost, and being left behind. Will the Moskito was accidentally marooned when ashore hunting goats for provisions, and Spanish armadillas forced the *Trinity* to pull up her anchors and put herself in a posture of defense.

Others were marooned by shipwreck or even occasionally as refugees, as was the case with Dr. Pitman. Sentenced to indentured servitude on Barbados, he detailed in his journal the abuse of indentured servants. Many planters considered them poor workers, worth less than slaves, and so they worked them hard and fed them poorly for the few years they owned their labor. "Spiriting" or "kidnapping" as a means of securing indentured slaves was common: spirits and kidnappers "promise them great wages and good fortune" to lure them aboard ships where "they cannot get away . . . nor send the least note to any of their friends to come and get them clear."[10] Others were criminals, vagrants, defenseless, poor, or even rebels like Dr. Pitman, all forced into servitude by the courts of law. Many, however, were transported voluntarily because they could not afford the cost of emigration. As a convicted criminal, Dr. Pitman's indenture was ten years (some served even longer), but most indentures were shorter—three to ten years for the English, with four being the most common term, and three for the French. Rebelling against his mistreatment (he was whipped once and left in the sun until his master's wife took pity on him), Dr. Pitman devised a plan of escape and convinced a debtor to purchase a small boat, which they and several others provisioned and put to sea one night. Sailing Southwest (the only practical course) for Curaçao, they ended up instead on Saltatudos, or Salt Tortuga, constrained by their leaky vessel to go no farther. They met a handful of pirates who claimed to be rebels, too: "if the Duke of Monmouth had had 1,000 of them, they would soon have put to flight the King's army." Pitman bought an Indian slave from the pirates to hunt and fish for him and his companions, but in the end the rovers did not honor the purchase. The marooned rebels lived mostly on sea turtle, fish, lobster, and whelks until their eventual rescue.[11]

The marooned had much to fear. Physically, a person was most vulnerable when alone, for there was no one to watch one's back, to tend to one in illness or injury, or to keep one from maddening solitude. Along much of the Spanish Main there were caimans, alligators, and crocodiles to fear, as well as poisonous serpents. There were Spaniards who would enslave a captured pirate or interloper, if they did not kill him first. There were Indians, some of whom helped the marooned in need, but some of whom tortured and killed him. And there were other dangers just as likely to kill the marooned: dehydration, starvation, and disease. To survive, one had to rely solely on one's wits, especially on any past experience living off the land. The allure of sandy beaches, lapping water, and peaceful solitude became sinister. A person marooned alone over long periods could temporarily lose fluency in his own language.[12] Not surprisingly, because of this physical vulnerability, one's mental health was expected to diminish as a consequence, yet many were mentally the least vulnerable when alone—having no one else to rely on, they must do, or die.

Some, however, were not marooned by accident or by choice, but by others, usually those with whom they sailed. For the Caribbean pirates, death as a punishment was commonly reserved for murder, often for the man who killed another unfairly in a duel or otherwise killed a shipmate without good reason, and for such a crime he was shot in the head. For all other serious crimes a crew could, by consent of the company, maroon a malefactor on a "desert isle." They permitted the condemned his musket, pistols, and cutlass, and if the notion took them, they might return seven or eight months later to see if he was alive.[13] A man might even be marooned simply because he disagreed with his shipmates: "One Daws, another South Sea man . . . was not aware of the design [of piracy] when he embarked, and opposed it so strongly that his mates put him ashore on an island to starve, from which he was only saved by another privateer [pirate]."[14]

$\mathcal{R}$escue by pirates was not surprising because pirates were endemic, going places others seldom did, with a freedom few ever experienced. In 1685 piracy remained unrestrained in spite of contrary policies by state governments. Laurens and Grammont sacked Campeche, and the Armada de Barlovento attacked them as they sailed away. Spanish interrogation of captured French pirates revealed a French colony somewhere on the gulf, and Spanish pirate Juan Corso set sail to seek the purported French colony at Espíritu Santo (present-day Tampa Bay, Florida), and raid it. The debtor and pirate Banister in the *Golden Fleece* made a daring escape from Port Royal, running a gauntlet of blazing cannon. The filibuster Du Chesne's ship was captured while careening on the north shore of Jamaica, but Du Chesne escaped and joined Banister. Filibusters crossed the Isthmus of Darien to the South Sea, but Laurens declined to join them. The South Sea lured many pirates, leaving piratical activity in the Caribbean somewhat diminished as compared to previous years. South Sea pirates sacked Paita, Peru, and Leon, Nicaragua. Three "privateer" sloops departed Carolina, destination unknown. La Salle arrived at Matagorda Bay, Texas, thinking it was the mouth of the Mississippi. At Guanaboa, Jamaica, maroons and rebel slaves attacked the plantations of the widow Grey and Major Price. The attackers were one hundred and fifty strong. In England the Battle of Sedgemoor foreshadowed political changes to come. The French began to voice complaints about their own filibusters and pirates and considered measures against them.

The following year filibusters under Grammont attempted an attack on St. Augustine, but his lieutenant Nicolas Brigaut and fifty men were ambushed at Matanzas. They reportedly held out for three days against three hundred

Spaniards. Laurens sacked Tihosuco and marched on Valladolid in Mexico, but turned back just shy of the city. The Carolina sloops that sailed the previous year captured a stout Dutch ship, but otherwise their cruise was unprofitable. Pirates were active at the Cape Verde Islands. The pirate Woolery, with the pirate Goff aboard, sailed to New Providence and was rebuffed by the governor, so he burned his ship at Andrew's Island and found passage to New England. Coxon returned to cutting logwood, claiming to have given up piracy. An English ship captured one of the Spanish galleys that attacked New Providence, and it was refitted at Jamaica to chase pirates. The HMS *Dartmouth*, seeking a Spanish pirate in San Juan, Puerto Rico, barely escaped the port's one hudred and fifty cannon. Captain Yanky captured a Spanish ship with a cargo worth fifty thousand pieces-of-eight, and Captain Laurens wrecked on a reef near Cartagena and lost his ship, but still captured his prey and escaped. Captain Swan crossed the Pacific, stopping at Guam, then the Philippines. Captain Davis returned to the North Sea via Cape Horn. Marcos Delgado marched from Apalache to an area near modern Montgomery, Alabama, searching for La Salle. One of La Salle's vessels, *La Belle*, was wrecked and lost at Matagorda Bay. Three Spanish galleys manned with St. Augustine Spaniards and allied Native Americans attacked plantations south of Charleston, then destroyed the new Scottish colony at Port Royal, Carolina. Charleston prepared to retaliate, but the new governor, James Colleton, ordered the expedition disbanded. Governor Milan of St. Thomas was relieved and shipped to Denmark, along with Adolph Esmit. Christopher Heins governed in the interim.

As for the intrepid Dr. Pitman, he was eventually rescued by pirates, whose captain treated him courteously but whose name Pitman did not provide. Based on the consent of his crew, the captain took only the doctor aboard; Pitman's companions were left behind, but with supplies to assist their needs. They too eventually made their way off the island, and they too ran into pirates. But those pirates were not the sort Dr. Pitman sailed away with. They were Spanish pirates, bent on plunder and revenge.

# 21 Cannon, Sword, and Garrote:
## Spain Strikes Back

The sack of Veracruz was the straw that broke the back of Spanish lethargy regarding pirate hunting. Spain sent the Armada de Barlovento on its most successful campaigns. In 1685, Spain created the Armada de Vizcaínos, a Biscayan armadilla of four ships intended to cruise for Caribbean pirates, which eventually sent Blas Miguel on a mission of revenge against Laurens and Petit Goave. Biscayers and other Spanish *corsarios* used the excuses of piracy and war with the French to attack more French, English, and even Dutch trading vessels.[1]

Following the sack of Veracruz, the heavily armed, stoutly manned Armada de Barlovento set sail, including the *Nuestra Señora de Burgos* and the *Nuestra Señora de la Concepción*, of six hundred and fifty and five hundred and fifty tons, respectively. The fleet captured the French sloop *Prophète Daniel*, the one-hundred-and-thirty-ton French *Concordia*, the English sloop *Margarita*, and another English sloop off Hispaniola as well. A fifth prize was lost off Puerto Rico. More detrimental to the filibusters, the Spanish retook the *Nuestra Señora de Regla*, the patache captured earlier by Van Horn at Honduras and which the pirates referred to as the *Reglita*. Captain Tristian and ninety men reportedly escaped the capture at night in a single boat, carrying their silver with them, but leaving behind their plunder of slaves and goods. The armada took one hundred and ten prisoners. In the spring of 1684 buccaneers (many of them treasure hunters) in three ships and eight sloops were piloted to Tampico by Richard Carter and guided into the city by four

Native American slaves captured at Veracruz and later sold at New Providence. The buccaneers then sacked the town. An armadilla of three vessels sailed from Veracruz and captured the frigate *Presbyter* laded with plunder, including wheat, fish, sugar, clothing, and church ornaments and silver. The armadilla also captured a small sloop and took a total of 104 pirates prisoner. Authorities sentenced eleven to death at Veracruz, and executed their sentences with a garrote, three of them as heretics who refused to convert to Catholicism. However, after the garrote used on one prisoner broke twice, he was rescued by a Spanish curate who intervened, shouting, "This man has offered himself to the Virgin, and God does not wish that he die."[2]

The *Nuestra Señora de Regla*, newly returned to her Spanish owners, was sent to Spain and returned late in the year with a cargo of wine and other goods, only to find herself again attacked by filibusters, this time south of Cuba by Captain Bréha commanding the barque *Diligent* with ten guns and one hundred men. The fight was brutal, and the Spanish resistance was fierce, leaving eight or nine filibusters dead. Yet in the end, the patache returned to the French. In another twist of fate, Bréha and the fleet of pirates returning from the sack of Campeche sailed into the path of four vessels of the Armada de Barlovento between the Alacranes and Cabo Catoche, including the *Burgos* with fifty-six guns and the *Concepción* with fifty-two. The pirate vessels scattered, but two were trapped. One, a barque-longue loaded with slaves and other plunder, engaged but was captured. She was so shot up that she was no longer seaworthy and was burned. The other was Bréha's *Regla* with a mere twenty-two guns, ten patereroes, and one hundred and fifty men. The filibusters fought but were no match for the more than one hundred great guns and perhaps as many as nine hundred men of the armada. The pirates asked for quarter, and all one hundred and thirty of the survivors were taken prisoner. The Spanish used a garrote to execute six prisoners, including Bréha, for attacking Campeche, and hanged four other French pirates for being both pirates and heretics who refused to convert. The rest were intended for the galleys of Spain.[3]

Spanish privateers and pirates, local and Biscayan, played a critical role in the war against the pirates, largely by harassing English, French, and Dutch shipping (some of whose crews were or had been pirates) and in general by making reprisals on sea and land. On the smaller scale, the tactic was to attack anything and everything not Spanish, naturally with a mind to profit.[4] Of these attackers, Juan Corso was the most famous. Among his many prizes were three English vessels at Honduras, another at Jurabán, two more from Jamaica, and many small trading and turtling sloops. At one point he was almost captured by an English rowing galley, built to chase Spanish pirates, but escaped. Later, the governor of Trinidad de Cuba threatened to kill the English buccaneer Cornelison after Corso captured his trading sloop, for Cornelison had been lieutenant aboard the English rowing galley. In general Corso carried his prizes into Santiago de Cuba, but ranged much of the Caribbean and would bring prizes into any convenient Spanish port. Corso was known for his cruelty, including the murder of captured seamen, whom he would otherwise put to work as oarsmen. He tortured prisoners into confessions, even false, that they traded with the Spanish, so that he could condemn their vessel and cargo.[5] So successful was he that the French seriously considered destroying Santiago de Cuba to deny him his principle port.[6]

Learning of a French colony on the Gulf Coast through interrogation of Denis Thomas, one of the crew of Bréha's *Reglita* and also a deserter from La Salle's expedition, Corso set sail in 1685, intending to discover and destroy the settlement. His vessel was a well-manned pirogue or half galley, well suited to exploring the many inlets, coves, and harbors of the Gulf Coast, and his mate was Jorge Nicolás (Giorgio Nicola) of Venitia (either Venicia, Venice, or the surrounding region of Venetia). At Tuxpan, Mexico, the expedition was joined by Capt. Pedro de Castro, another famous pirate. They rowed and sailed to Tampico, and then headed for Apalache, but a storm forced them south and ashore near Espíritu Santo. The galley was put to sea in haste due to weather, inadvertently stranding twenty-five men ashore, and was soon aground again at Punta Brava (present-day Cape San Blas, Florida)—and that time permanently. The vessel was wrecked and her crew cast ashore, where most died from starvation or at the hands of Native Americans. De Castro and thirty-five men reportedly survived, many if not all "by rendering the cut-up corpses in the stewpot . . . without wasting even the heads."* Only three of those marooned at Espíritu Santo and two of those shipwrecked at Punta Brava were ever rescued.[7]

$\mathcal{D}$r. Pitman provided the best account of a Spanish pirate's routine, as told to him by John Whicker, one of those who escaped with him to Saltatudos. In 1687 Whicker, his companions, and one pirate stole a four-ton boat from other pirates, sailed from Saltatudos to the Isle of Ash (Ile à Vache), and hauled it into a creek to dig a well because they were short on water. The isle, populated by a few boucaniers, often served English and French turtle hunters and pirates and should have been a safe haven. A sloop flying English colors and a commission pendant arrived and anchored. Hailed, she answered, "From Jamaica." The refugees from Saltatudos anchored nearby, and were immediately boarded by two canoes of Spaniards "all armed as pirates." From the frying pan into the fire, the men were taken, stripped naked, and imprisoned

---

*All quotations have been reprinted with their original spelling and punctuation.

in the sloop's hold on "ballast stones, or atop of their water casks." For nine days they were fed only a half pint of Native American corn per day, until they arrived at Santiago de Cuba, where their ration of boiled corn was increased but not otherwise improved. For clothing they were given "a rag sufficient to cover our nakedness," but no shoes, hat, or shirt. Their captors worked them as slaves. Ashore they carried water and cut firewood, and at sea they pumped the sloop, washed the Spaniards' clothes, and "beat corn in great wooden mortars; with Negroes, with naked swords, always standing by as overseers."[8]

Having information that a Dutch trading vessel lay beyond Cabo Cruz near the town of Byan (possibly Bycannar), the sloop went to sea with three of their captives aboard as slaves. One of the English captives fell gravely ill, was not permitted to be carried to the hold, but was left to suffer on deck day and night, and was thrown overboard without ceremony or weight to sink him after he died. Failing to find the Dutchman, the sloop returned to Santiago, careened, and set sail again, "bound to the north side of Hispaniola, to take Frenchmen." They met a Jamaican sloop bound for the "Old Wrack" (Phips's *almiranta* on the Abrohos, whose location was revealed after Phips departed with much of her treasure), and ordered the sloop's captain to "hoist out his canoe, and come aboard." The captain wisely refused and sailed away, apparently having a much swifter sloop. The Spanish pirate sloop then weathered Cape Myceze (Punta de Maisí), sailed to Baracoa, provisioned and made repairs, and set sail again. Off Mole St. Nicholas, Saint Domingue, the pirate captured an English sloop bound from Jamaica to New York, then chased a French sloop that put up a running fight until nightfall. The French resistance—seven or eight men, almost certainly filibusters, against thirty-five Spaniards (a dozen others manned the prize) aboard a sloop mounted with eight cannon and six patereros—was so spirited that the Spanish swore they would kill them all when they captured them. Instead, as soon as it was dark the French ran their sloop aground at Mole St. Nicholas and escaped; the Spanish carried the sloop off the next day. Whicker, his companions, and the English prisoners were carried into Santiago again, where by good fortune the Duke of Albemarle's diplomacy eventually freed them.[9]

*I*n January 1684 Spanish pirates sacked New Providence and attacked Laurens's plantation on Saint Domingue in 1687, carrying off more than one hundred slaves. But the most significant Spanish assault on French or English soil was an attack on Petit Goave itself in 1687. Although ostensibly protected by its filibuster populace and a small earthen fort, eighty-five Spanish pirates stormed ashore from a piragua and a boat or brigantine in 1687. They were "as many whites [and] mulattos as Indians and blacks," and were commanded by Blas Miguel, a Corsican and "the chief and author of these excesses and enterprises," and his twenty-year-old lieutenant, Pasqual Onan, a

Native American from Campeche. Miguel was said to be intent on avenging his brother's death at Laurens's hand during an encounter with the Armada de Vizcaínos in May. The pirates seized the small fort, pillaged the town, burned many houses, killed men, and according to the French, raped and murdered women. But rather than departing after sacking Petit Goave, they decided to plunder nearby habitations, giving the French time to rally. Soon the attackers retreated to the fort, surrounded. There sixty Spaniards surrendered, having no chance of holding off the French onslaught for long—twenty-five of their number were already dead. Refusing quarter and fighting to the death en masse were fairly rare in warfare (but certainly not unknown), and by surrendering the Spaniards hoped to escape, or at least prolong their fate. Some soon discovered that they would never see another dawn, for the French put them immediately to the sword.[10]

Interrogated, Miguel claimed to have commissions from both the viceroy and the commander of the Castillo de Morro at Havana, who was standing in for the governor, but to have left them in the pirogue. He also claimed impossibly not to know that France and Spain were at peace. The next day a council of war of thirteen passed judgment on the remaining forty-four, taking into account that the attackers gave no quarter and had no commission. The following day part of the sentence was executed: forty-two men were hanged. Miguel and Onan had one day's respite more, but they could not escape their fates: they were broken on the wheel alive and decapitated, and their heads were displayed on the gallows where their dead crew still swayed in the tropical breeze.[11]

Breaking on the wheel (*rouer* in French) was a common and brutal method of killing malefactors among the French. "Death by torture" described it best: the condemned was bound with his arms and legs outstretched, often to a wheel although this was not necessary. In the West Indies a cross was sometimes used upon a scaffold, which probably provided a better view. Father Labat witnessed one such execution: the condemned mounted the scaffold, kneeled, prayed, then undressed and stretched out on the cross. With a hammer the executioner then broke each of the long bones in the condemned man's arms and legs several times. If the condemned was fortunate, a priest might cover his face with a handkerchief during the excruciating process as Labat once did. The executioner ended the agony—if the condemned was not already dead from the trauma—by strangling him with a rope, first permitting a priest to ask the condemned for a last act of contrition.[12]

Of all of the Spanish actions in pursuit of pirates, or pretending to pursue them and taking other vessels instead, one stands out not only as one of the greatest Spanish-versus-pirates engagements, but as one that fits the classic image of pirates' sea battles. Recalling that the filibusters scattered the day the Spanish captured Captain Bréha and his *Reglita*, we turn to Laurens and his *Neptune*. Three days later Laurens and his crew, aboard their forty-eight gun ship, found themselves face to face with two vessels, the *Nuestra Señora del Honhón* (formerly the *Leon Coronada*, an English ship captured by Juan Corso, turned into a guarda costa, then taken up by the Armada de Barlovento), and a patache of eight guns, the *Sevillana*. Laurens pursued, but before long he sighted the fifty-six-gun *Burgos* and fifty-two-gun *Concepción*. With them also was the *Reglita*, but she was undermanned. Laurens was outgunned, outmanned, and outnumbered. The next morning he realized his only chance of escape was to engage, and so he did.[13]

According to Exquemelin, Laurens had the bravest man in his crew standby with a lighted match to fire the magazine, should it appear they would fall to the Spanish. Significantly, taking advantage both of what the French said was the Spaniards' understandable unwillingness to board (and what the Spanish said was Laurens's superlative ability to maneuver his ship and prevent their boarding), and of the Spaniards' poor coordination and communications, Laurens controlled the engagement, maneuvering as he pleased, engaging defensively, preserving his ship and men, but battering the enemy as opportunity arose or was created. Both sides fired broadside after broadside, so many that the *Burgos* was claimed to have fired 1,600 cannonballs—enough for as many as sixty broadsides. Unfortunately for the armada, the Spanish were plagued by bad powder and perhaps poor guns as well: one exploded and killed several men. At one point Laurens, pistol in one hand, cutlass in the other, maneuvered the *Neptune* directly between both great Spanish ships, fired starboard and larboard broadsides, followed by discharges of musketry, and engaged each ship simultaneously. Exquemelin claimed the first discharge of muskets killed or wounded forty-eight between the two Spanish ships. During the engagement Laurens was wounded and, in his account, was carried below to the surgeon, but when he heard his cannon slow their rate of fire, he took to the deck again to rally his men. Of the same incident, Exquemelin wrote that when Laurens was wounded in the thigh he fell but quickly arose, claiming, "It is nothing." When night came, the filibusters made repairs and waited for the fight to begin again at dawn, but at sunrise the Spanish were gone, surprising Laurens, who knew the Spanish forced the French prisoners to assist and believed they would certainly be waiting to continue the engagement. Exquemelin, doubtlessly exaggerating, claimed Laurens dismasted the *Burgos* with a cannon he aimed and fired himself, after which he "escapes gloriously within sight of his enemies." The French lost only eight men and had twice as many wounded.[14]

*B*y 1687 tensions in Europe, and thus in the New World, were on the rise. The Armada de Vizcaínos arrived in the Caribbean and was engaged by

Laurens, but escaped. Blas Miguel's brother was killed in the action. In the South Sea, the privately funded Armada del Nuestra Señora de Guía was formed to protect against the incursions of pirates and traders. On the North American continent, mutineers murdered the explorer La Salle; one of them was a German-born buccaneer named Heins. Across the Pacific, Swan's crew mutinied and he was replaced by Captain Read. Governor de Cussy fortified Ile à Vache, and Christopher Monck, Duke of Albermarle, was appointed governor at Jamaica. Phips recovered extraordinary riches from the wreck of the almiranta on the Abrohos, and when he left, dozens of vessels went to fish the wreck. Blas Miguel sacked Petit Goave, but he and his men were captured and put to death. Pirates Woolery and Beare were active in the Caribbean, and pirates Yanky and Evertson considered English service, but could not accept the stipulation that they destroy their ships, being foreign built. Carolina pirates in their Dutch prize headed for the South Sea, but foul weather turned them back. Off Brazil they captured a Portuguese merchantman, the *Grand Gustaphus*. The pirates parted company; the French in the *Gustaphus* sailed to Petit Goave, while the English remained aboard their Dutch prize. They rescued Dr. Pitman, sailed to the recently repopulated New Providence, burned their ship, and fortified themselves on a nearby island, but Captain Needham, commissioned to arrest pirates, beat them out of the fort, set it ablaze, and captured the pirates. The suppression of privateering continued, and many buccaneers and filibusters turned to logwood cutting, planting, or the sloop trade—or else they were no longer called *privateers*, but became branded as *pirates*.

# 22 Yo Ho, Yo Ho— A Pirate's Life for Me

*I* f any single buccaneer or filibuster came close to matching the modern, idealized, romantic image of the swashbuckling pirate, it was Dutchman Laurens-Cornille Baldran, "sieur de Graff, escuyer, lieutenant de roy en l'isle de Saint-Domingue, capitaine de Frégate légère, chevalier de Saint-Louis," or more simply, "the great pirate of Petit Guavos." An expert in the techniques and tactics of warfare at sea and ashore, courageous in battle, usually merciful to his Spanish enemies (perhaps because he served with them for years), and skilled with the sword, he was said even to be accompanied by violins and trumpets when ashore. Naturally, as the image required, he was tall, handsome, blond, and had the finest mustache "in the Spanish style"* (a handlebar mustache). "To resolve, to attempt, and to accomplish, these are all the same thing to him," wrote Exquemelin.[1]

Although aligned with the French when the governor of Petit Goave, de Franquesnay, attempted to suppress la flibuste in 1683, Laurens considered serving the English, even to the point of negotiating arrangements such as the transportation of his first wife, Françoise Pretuline de Gusman (Petronila de Guzman), from Tenerife. But Laurens sought French citizenship instead after the arrival of Governor de Cussy, a strong supporter of the filibusters' trade. For having killed Van Horn in a duel, Laurens was granted a royal pardon and citizenship as well. Among his many subsequent experiences, he

---

*All quotations have been reprinted with their original spelling and punctuation.

was made a French officer, divorced his first wife in order to marry another, conducted successful raids against the Spanish and English on land and sea, blockaded the north coast of Jamaica, was once forced to retreat after engaging the HMS *Drake* near Jamaica, captured an English man-of-war sloop after a battle that lasted many hours, was reprimanded after a successful English attack on Saint Domingue in 1695, and was almost sent to trial in France for dereliction of duty. According to Lepers, his second wife, Marie-Anne Dieuleveult, was captured by the English and Spanish and carried first to Santo Domingue, then to Veracruz, where memories of her husband's attack were still vivid. Nonetheless, she was eventually repatriated to Saint Domingue. Laurens later served as pilot to Pierre LeMoyne d'Iberville on the French expedition to the Mississippi and Gulf Coast.[2]

Novelist Rafael Sabatini admitted to appropriating Henry Morgan's tactics for his eponymous pirate hero, Captain Blood. But in character, Peter Blood was more akin to a taciturn, sardonic Laurens de Graff, and without doubt Sabatini appropriated Laurens's tactic of sailing between two Spanish men-of-war and engaging them simultaneously, and lent it to his hero. Laurens was larger than life, as heroes are supposed to be, although accompanying vices inappropriate to the twenty-first century, such as torture, slavery, or the murder of prisoners (of which the English, French, Dutch, and Spanish were all guilty) are ignored or diminished by those who demand a Hollywood image of the pirate, Laurens included.[3]

Many buccaneers and filibusters served other nations at times, but most, unlike Laurens—a Dutchman in the service of the French, who had also served the Spanish, and considered serving the English—did not entirely abandon the nation of their origin. With few exceptions, the English pirate sailed with the French but he retained some loyalty to England, as pirates of other nations remained somewhat loyal to their nativity. From this perspective, Jan Erasmus Reyning may have epitomized the Dutch freebooter; the sieur de Grammont, the French filibuster; Juan Corso, the Spanish corsario; and Bartholomew Sharp, the English buccaneer. Nations were always most fond of their own, even if adopted.

Sharp, who may well have been called "Bat" for short—Povey wrote his name as "Batt. Sharpe," and the French referred to him as "Betcharpe"— exemplified the strengths and weaknesses of the English buccaneer, and served as a more typical example of the pirate captain during the period of transition. He had a classic buccaneer history, beginning, he said, in 1666 at the age of sixteen. Doubtless he served under Henry Morgan. With Coxon he attacked the bodegas at Honduras for indigo and other goods in 1679. He was one of the commanders at Portobello the same year, and in the South Sea afterward, where his attitude and success at dice alienated many of his crew. In 1682 he was tried for piracy and acquitted by a London jury, which refused to convict in spite of the evidence against him. Soon after, he was commissioned as a naval officer and assigned to the *Bonetta* sloop (which later accompanied Phips to the "Old Wrack"), but he never took command. William Dick wrote that Sharp snuck out of England, stealing cattle at Romney Marsh as he went. In 1684 Sharp, sailing under a commission to seek pirates, seized the frigate *Resolution*, originally a Spanish prize, from the pirate Henley; renamed her *Josiah*; and made her his. In 1685 he sailed with the French at Campeche and sold Native American slaves, taken at Campeche, at New Providence. He assisted the governor of Bermuda in suppressing rebellious residents, including Monmouth rebels. Accused variously of crimes and misdemeanors and served with writs, Sharp was said to have "lit his pipe and wiped his breech with them." The following year Sharp was arrested by the governor of Nevis, tried once more for piracy, and again acquitted in spite of the evidence against him. In 1688 he was "commander" of Anguilla, and in 1699 he was under arrest at St. Thomas, the pirate's nest, "for misdemeanours." After this we hear no more of this picaresque pirate.[4]

One of the distinguishing features of buccaneers and filibusters, no matter their piracies, was the general, although seldom absolute, restriction of their plundering of the Spanish. Like Sharp, they served as independent sea rovers or as agents of their governments as it suited them, although they preferred some semblance of legitimacy that combined the former with the latter, for this kept a noose from the neck. Never did they claim to be pirates—but that began to change.

*I*n 1683 Jean Hamlin, a Frenchman, who captured two sloops and then stole the ship *La Trompeuse* (*The Deceiver*) from a French Huguenot, conman, and thief named Paine, embarked on a piratical rampage. He captured an English ship, informed the crew he was a pirate, tortured some, "pressed" some (forced them into service), plundered the ship, and let it go. He next captured several other English vessels, then sailed to the Guinea Coast, and captured eleven slavers and three boats, plundering them all. At Cape St. John the pirates divided the spoil, and quarreling, separated into two companies, part remaining with Hamlin, part choosing to serve under an Englishman named Morgan. Hamlin's usual tactic was to fly English colors and commission pendant as if he were an English man-of-war, come alongside as if seeking a salute, and fire a broadside. Indeed, Hamlin's strategy and tactics were identical to those of the early eighteenth-century Anglo American pirates who flew the black flag: attack weaker merchantmen, preferably by ruse. More significantly, Hamlin and his crew referred to themselves openly as *pirates*, not buccaneers, filibusters, or privateers.[5]

Throughout his piracies he was sheltered and protected by the governor of St. Thomas, although after his return to St. Thomas, the HMS *Francis* burned his ship and the hulk of the South Sea galleon *Trinity* as well. Some of Hamlin's crew volunteered to serve Captain Le Sage, others Captain Yanky. Soon, though, the governor of St. Thomas sold Hamlin a sloop with which he captured a Dutch frigate of thirty-six guns, renamed her *La Nouvelle Trompeuse* (*The New Deceiver*), manned her with sixty of his old crew and sixty new men, and continued his depredations. Reportedly, the ship was outfitted in New England. He captured a Portuguese ship and carried her into St. Thomas, where he forced some of her Dutch crew to serve with him, while the governor of St. Thomas forced some of the captured crew to draw lots and hanged the losers. Hamlin, who could rightly be called the first of the true pirates of the Golden Age—only the black flag was missing—was never taken.[6]

*A*lthough many buccaneers, filibusters, and outright pirates escaped the noose, not all did, and the dangers of the course they followed shortened many of their lives. Of commanders alone, many died in their capacity as leaders. Richard Harris, remembered for his bravery at Perico against the Spanish armadillas, died of gangrene after the amputation of one of his legs.[7] Richard Sawkins, revered by all, was killed in action "corragiously" leading his men around the flank of a barricade well manned with spearmen.[8] John Watling, commanding at Arica, was shot dead through the "reins" (the loins or kidneys).[9] Captain Yanky died in 1688, perhaps of wounds received in the battle for the hulk, and Captain Tristian was killed by the Spanish in 1692.[10] Edmond Cook died of an illness off Cabo Blanco in the South Sea, and Captain Swan was drowned by natives in the Philippines.[11] Captains Townley and Grogniet also died in the South Sea, each of wounds received in action.[12] John Banister was turned over to the HMS *Drake* by Moskito Indians, and hanged from a yardarm in sight of Port Royal. At the same time a boy named Lewis was hanged by his middle from the mizzen peak of the HMS *Drake*. He was pardoned and grew up to be a notorious pirate. Captain Spurre died in 1684, cause unknown. His wife, her corrupt lawyer, and the Jamaican government wrangled over his "piratical goods."[13] Shipwrecked Juan Corso died "of a weakness that he suffered in the breast." His companion commander Pedro de Castro survived longer, but was never heard from again.[14] Pierre l'Orange was hanged at Veracruz and his head spiked on the pier, and likewise Captain Bréha was put to death there.[15] Nicolas Brigaut was put to death by the Spanish at St. Augustine, and in 1686 the sieur de Grammont was lost with all hands in a storm near the Azores Islands.[16] John Bennett was killed in action against the Honduras ship; Nicolas Van Horn died of gangrene from the wound he received in a duel; Blas Miguel and Pasqual Onan were broken on the wheel. John Coxon, however, died quietly in 1698 among the Moskito, "he having long traded with them in a sloop of his own."[17]

Others survived longer, but the final days of many are unknown. Robert Allison sailed as a pilot with the Scottish Company of Darien in 1698.[18] Jan Erasmus Reyning served variously as a Dutch privateer, slaver, and naval officer, and John Beare, the renegade English pirate who served Spain, took up arms with the French in the 1690.[19] Thomas Paine, who seemed to have sailed with all of the major Caribbean pirates at one time or another, defended Rhode Island in 1690 against a French flotilla commanded by Pierre le Picard, a noted filibuster and one of Paine's former comrades in arms.[20] Paine, like many of his buccaneer and filibuster contemporaries, became semi-respectable. Similarly, the pirate Goff was commissioned in 1691 to cruise for pirates and privateers off the New England coast.[21]

As for Captain Laurens, he died in 1704, not in battle, but of disease or natural causes at Cap François on Saint Domingue. Some historians and Gulf Coast residents claimed he died and was buried at either Biloxi, Mississippi, or Old Mobile, Alabama, but almost certainly he returned in 1698 "with the marquis de Chateaumorand to St. Domingue," to his wife and wealth. He sailed as pilot, not colonist, on d'Iberville's Mississippi expedition, and had no need to remain. However, other filibusters did go as settlers, leaving buccaneer and filibuster blood in both the soil and subsequent generations. Upon his death, Laurens left "goods worth an estimated 190,000 *livres*, including a sugar plantation in the Quartier Morin, with five copper boilers and more than one hundred-twenty slaves" to his widow, Marie-Anne, and his eleven-year-old daughter, Marie-Catherine. He did well by piracy, and piracy did well by him.[22]

Of the buccaneer authors, Alexander Exquemelin returned to Europe in 1674, and became a surgeon first in Amsterdam, then in Honfleur. He returned to the Caribbean in 1697 (and perhaps one or more times prior to this) as a surgeon aboard de Pointis's expedition against Cartagena.[23] Cox, Povey, Cowley, and de Lussan disappeared from view soon after their South Sea piracies. William Dampier was cruising the Philippines and East Indies in 1688, first with Captain Read, who replaced Captain Swan, then aboard an East Indiaman. Three years later he was in England again, completing his first circumnavigation. He had several adventures ahead of him, including command of a ship of the Royal Navy on a mission of exploration, command of a privateer to the South Sea, and service as pilot to the South Sea under privateer Woodes Rogers. Basil Ringrose was killed in action in Mexico in 1685, along with fifty of his comrades. Lionel Wafer, after arrest and incarceration in the Jamestown, Virginia, jail for piracy (along with Capt. Edward Davis, for which neither stood trial), later provided intelligence on the Isthmus of Darien for the Scottish Company of Darien, which intended a colony there in 1698.[24]

By 1688 the dangerous potential of unrestrained piracy on a large scale, as proved by Jean Hamlin, was surely obvious. Only war, and nothing else, prevented this great scourge from emerging in force. England ousted James II, crowning William III of Orange and his English wife Mary, daughter of James II, king and queen to rule jointly. Strictly speaking, war did not begin until October 1688 in the Palatinate (southwest Germany) and not until 1689 in Caribbean, but for all practical purposes Europe was already at war, or in violent preparation for it. Spain aligned with the "Grand Alliance," which included England, the Netherlands, and most other European states as well, and buccaneers had to withhold attacking their natural enemy. One war followed another, but warfare merely postponed the rise of unrestrained piracy for three decades. Even so, eighteenth-century piracy, whose practitioners were known as "Enemies of all Mankind," had its origin in the late-seventeenth-century buccaneers and filibusters, and flowed in its early years from the English colonies of North America to the Guinea Coast of Africa to the Red Sea, and back again. In Jamaica, Sir Henry Morgan died, his timing perfect, at the end of an era.

The buccaneer and filibuster pirates of 1674–88 differed from the pirates who followed a generation later in that they saw themselves as adventurers, as soldiers as well as buccaneers or filibusters, as men who fought on sea *and* land, and as men who had little if any tangible support of the state even while they claimed nominal allegiance to it. Never again were independent ventures of warfare for profit undertaken on the soil of the New World on a such a scale. The infamous Anglo American pirates—Blackbeard, Bartholomew Roberts, Calico Jack, and their ilk—preyed almost entirely on weak merchantmen at sea. Not for them were attacks on great cities or rich, well-defended men-of-war, and a single frigate was often enough to send them scurrying.

It was hard to claim virtue among men who pursued wealth by unlicensed force of arms and who were considered by many to be "only beasts of prey," yet in many ways the buccaneers and filibusters merited such accounting. They made long-term alliances with Native American tribes. They not only provided medical care to their entire crews, but also significant disability compensation. They were ahead of their contemporaries in accepting social differences, at least while they were part of the same company of men: each member of the crew, no matter his race, nationality, or faith, was entitled to an equal share of plunder and an equal vote in council, the latter of which even the United States did not begin to accept in practice until the late twentieth century. Further, these pirates often displayed magnanimity toward their captured enemies. Laurens, for example, set the wounded Spanish captain of the *Francesa* ashore after a fierce sea fight, with a servant and surgeon to attend to him, and South Sea buccaneers praised the extraordinary valor of Captain Peralta and treated him with extraordinary civility as their prisoner. They were not, however, democratic utopians seeking independence from the state. They sought wealth by force of arms, and many returned to the state, often becoming planters or traders. Some assisted governments in suppressing rebellion. Even the egalitarian principal of "one man, one share" neither restricted wealth nor made all men equal. A captain who owned a ship, for example, could grow quite wealthy: Van Horn reportedly received thirty shares for his *St. Nicolas* after Veracruz. If pirates sought a utopia, it was one where piracy was without penalty, a place where they could raid, plunder, drink, gamble, and whore to their hearts' content—in other words, the Spanish Main.[25]

But the importance, virtue, or value of those pirates extended far beyond their limited, if unique for its time, acceptance of race, religion, and nationality; far beyond the civilized, respectful mercies they granted to some of their enemies; far beyond their democratic organization in pursuit of plunder. These men were the first line of defense for the English and French colonies in the Caribbean, and they provided significant financial support in the form of plunder to the colonies, with the French in particular continuing their significant economic support into the early eighteenth century. The men battered the tired Spanish empire, diminishing its hold over the New World. They explored places unknown to most Europeans other than Spaniards. They provided valuable military and economic intelligence to their governments, and much scientific, geographic, and hydrographic information as well. Indeed, one has to consider that Saint Domingue might have remained Spanish if boucaniers had not developed tactics against lanceros and hunters, and Jamaica might have returned to the Spanish were there no buccaneers, for on such small but vital details does the world turn.

Although we may remember the buccaneers and filibusters more for their infamies than for their virtues, in the end it is their courage, plain speaking, and independence we respect; their egalitarianism, leadership, and teamwork (in spite of great ego) we appreciate; and their marginal origins, self-sufficiency, and self-determination we understand. But most of all, it is their audacity and their freedom from common society we truly admire, notwithstanding their often great cruelties and other failings.

*B*efore the first shots were fired in his famous battle with the Armada de Barlovento, Laurens exhorted his crew with a speech epitomizing the principal characteristic that rendered these buccaneers and filibusters capable of such deeds: their wits and courage in adversity. In Laurens's own words (according to Exquemelin),

You are too experienced to not understand the peril we are running, and too brave to fear it. It is necessary here to be cautious of all yet to risk all, to defend and attack at the same time. Valor, deception, fear, and even despair must all be put to use on this occasion; where, if we fall into the hands of our enemies, nothing awaits us but all sorts of infamies, from the most cruel of torments to, finally, the end of life. We must therefore escape their barbarity; and to escape, we must fight.[26]

None have ever said it better.

Yet it was the common buccaneer whose simple words best captured the true face of buccaneers and filibusters and their effect on the Spanish Main: "Wee makeing in all, in mony, Plate and Plunder, about a hundred peices of Eight a man att Puerta Vella, peopple was Eagar for more Voyage."[27]

Mostly they were of common origin, these uncommon men, the buccaneers and filibusters, these marginal souls cast upon and seizing a new, marginal, marvelous, naked world. For good, for bad, by force of arms they took their eminent place in the history of a rebellious New World—the buccaneer's realm.

# Appendix A
## The Chasse-Partie

This appendix has been compiled from the following sources (abbreviations used follow in parentheses): Exquemelin, *The Buccaneers of America*, 1678, translated from the Dutch (D1678); Exquemelin, *The Buccaneers of America*, 1684, English edition (E1684); Exquemelin, *The Buccaneers of America*, 1699, English edition (E1699); Exquemelin, *Flibustiers*, 1699, French edition (F1699); Ringrose, "Buccaneers of America," 1684 (Rr); Dick, "Brief Account," 1684 (Dk); Pitman, "Relation," 1689 (Pt); de Lussan, *Voyage*, 1689 (dL); Dampier, *New Voyage*, 1697 (Dp); Cox, *Adventures*, 1684 (Cx); [Povey?], "Buccaneers on the Isthmus," 1682 (Pv); Wafer, *Isthmus of Darien*, 1699, (W); Labat, *Voyages aux isles*, 1722 (Lb); "Extract of Letters of the King to M. de Blénac," 7 May 1680, in Saint-Méry (XIV); *Calendar of State Papers 1681–1685, 1685–1688* (CSP). Exquemelin's works generally refer to the 1660s through 1680s; Pitman's refer to the late 1680s; de Lussan's refer to the mid- to late 1680s; Dampier's refer to the 1680s; Cox's refer to the early 1680s; Povey's refer to 1680–82; and Labat's refer to the late 1690s and early 1700s. French texts generally use the terms *écus* and *piastres* instead of pieces-of-eight (see also appendix F). For convenience, pieces-of-eight are indicated below by $. The articles are provided in the general order found in the texts, but may have varied according to the *chasse-partie*.

All voyages were based on the condition of *No Prey, No Pay*, sometimes referred to as *No Purchase, No Pay*. In other words, with a handful of exceptions, compensation was based on net profit alone (D1678, E1684, E1699, F1699, Lb). When towns were attacked, rovers who actually made the attack and those who remained behind guarding the ships shared equally in the plunder (Dk).

If the captain owned the vessel, the company decided how much he should be compensated for its use. Typically this was four or five shares above

223

his usual two, but if the ship was large, it may have been as many as ten (in the case of Swan's *Cygnet*, one hundred and forty tons) or even more (reputedly thirty for Van Horn's *St. Nicolas*, four hundred tons) (D1678, E1684, E1699, CSP). Or instead of shares he may be given the first prize taken, but must then burn the "meaner" of the two vessels (F1699, Dp). The crew decided whether or not to keep a new prize, if they were cruising without a commission, and sometimes even if they had a commission (D1678, Dp). If the captain's vessel was lost, the company must remain with him until they took another. If the vessel was owned by the crew, the captain might receive the first vessel taken as a prize, in addition to his common shares (F1699). The quartermaster was typically first in line to command a prize (Dp). However, pirate "admirals" or "commanders in chief" appear to have had some authority to appoint commanders of prizes (dL, Pv, Rr, Dp, Dk).

The company decided how much the carpenter or shipwright who "careened, mended, and rigged the vessel" should have, if the vessel had not been outfitted by an investor. This was typically $100 to $150. In general, if the carpenter was a member of the crew, this money was paid in addition to his usual share and prior to division of shares (D1678, E1684, E1699, F1699). If the ship was outfitted by an investor, this money was not paid by the company, but by the investor (Lb).

The company decided how much to pay the surgeon for his services, instruments, and chest of medicines. Typically, this was $200 to $250 in addition to his usual share, depending on the size of the vessel. This money was to be paid prior to the division of shares, and was to be paid whether or not a prize was taken (D1678, E1684, E1699, F1699). If the surgeon was not satisfied with silver, he could have two slaves (F1699). If the vessel had been outfitted and provisioned by an investor, the surgeon was not paid by the company, but by the investor (Lb).

Money was drawn from the common stock for provisioning, typically about $200 (D1678, E1684, E1699, F1699). This provision generally referred to meat provided by a hunter (D1678). If the vessel was outfitted and provisioned by an investor, the provisions were not paid by the company, but by the investor (Lb). Exquemelin noted that gunpowder for the great guns was purchased fresh "from all of the crew," although sometimes "the captain advances the powder himself," and spared the crew the expense if powder was taken from a prize. Most likely, powder for the ship's guns was another expense of provisioning, drawn from the common stock. Buccaneers and filibusters provided their own individual arms, powder, and shot (F1699, et al.).

Compensation for wounds received was stipulated and varied according to sources. For the loss of the right arm, $600 or six slaves. For the loss of the left arm, $500 or five slaves. For the loss of the right leg, $500 or five slaves, and for the loss of the left leg $400 or four slaves. For the loss of an eye, $100 or one slave. If a man lost the use of a limb, he was compensated as if he had actually lost it. For a wound to the body that required a cannula (a tube, usually of gold or silver, used to drain an infected wound, often in the chest), the injured party received $500 or five slaves (D1678, E1684, E1699).

The French editions of Exquemelin's *Buccaneers of America* listed less compensation. For the loss of an eye, $100 or one slave. For loss of both eyes, $600 or six slaves. For the loss of the right hand or arm, $200 or two slaves. For the loss of both hands or arms, $600 or six slaves. For the loss of a finger or ear, $100 or one slave. For the loss of a foot or leg, $200 or two slaves. For the loss of both feet or legs, $600 or six slaves. For a wound requiring him to *porter une canule* (wear a tube), $200 or two slaves. If a man lost the use of limb entirely, he was compensated as if he had lost the limb. The injured man chose silver or slaves (F1699).

The articles for Morgan's expedition against Panama in 1671 provided $1,500 for the loss of both legs, or fifteen slaves, at the choice of the injured party. For the loss of both arms, $1,800 or eighteen slaves, at the choice of the injured party. For the loss of a leg, right or left, $500 or six slaves. For the loss of a hand or arm, right or left, $500 or six slaves. For the loss of an eye, $100 or one slave. For the loss of both eyes, $2,000 or twenty slaves. For the loss of a finger, $100 or one slave. If the injured was treated with a cannula, $100 or one slave. Compensation was paid prior to dividing the booty into shares (F1699).

Labat described yet another typical set of articles of compensation. The wounded were provided, above and beyond their shares, one dollar per day, up to sixty days, for nourishment while in the hands of the surgeon, who was obligated to tend to them and furnish their medicines. Those who lost an arm or leg, or whose arm or leg was rendered useless, received $600 for each limb lost. Those who lost a thumb or index finger of the right hand, or an eye, received $300. Those who lost any other digit of the hand received $100. Those who had to bear a cannula were compensated as if they had lost a limb and received $600. Labat also wrote that those who had a wooden arm or leg, and lost it as they might lose a real one, were compensated as if the limb were real. However, in this case it seems very likely that the filibusters Labat consorted with were "pulling his leg" (Lb).

De Lussan's filibusters, based on the "local practices out of the South Sea," provided $1,000 for those who were crippled and $600 for those "inconvenienced" (dL).

If no prizes were taken, the company had to seek until they had plunder enough to compensate the injured (Lb). The injured was compensated even if it meant there was no booty left to be shared. The surgeon was responsible for determining the extent of injury (dL).

$\mathcal{T}$he *chasse-partie* also rewarded valor or espying a sail that turned out to be a prize. The man whose initiative caused the capture of a prize—that is, who sighted a sail that was taken as a prize—was rewarded with $100, although according to Labat the reward was an additional half share, probably limited to booty from the prize he sighted. Morgan's articles for the attack on Panama included the following: $5 for each grenade a man threw onto an enemy fort. For the man who captured a prisoner who provided useful intelligence, $100. For the man who captured the enemy's flag on a fort, in order to raise the flag of the buccaneers, $500. He who captured an important officer in battle, at the risk of his own life, was compensated according to the merit of his action (F1699). De Lussan reported that the "ensign" who first planted the colors (ensign) upon the fort at Guayaquil would receive $1,000 (dL).

The division of spoils was done by shares and paid only after all other monies were paid, particularly compensation for injury. "[W]ee sheard our Puerta Vella voyage," wrote one buccaneer (Pv). That is, they distributed the plunder according to the articles, typically soon after the capture of a vessel or the sack of a town. Items of great value that could not be divided, such as jewels and large pearls, were sometimes auctioned among the crew. Payment was required in coin or other easily divisible items of value, and the proceeds were added to the common stock of plunder (dL). If the voyage was made under a lawful commission, 10 percent of the gross profit was paid to the governor (Lb). If an investor (called in French an *armateur, bourgeois,* or *propriétaire*) outfitted and provisioned the ship, typically one-third of the net profit was for him, and two-thirds for the company, after the governor, surgeon, carpenter, hunter, and wounded were paid (Lb). However, a letter from Louis XIV to the French governor-general in 1680 provided for the usual 10 percent for the crown *for prizes by sea,* but for a full third (33.3 percent) to be divided between the governor-general and the governor of the island granting the commission *for plunder by land* (XIV). In such case by land, the percentage of profit due to investors is unknown. Among many European privateers of the period, two-thirds was commonly assigned to investors and one-third to the company. Perhaps an additional third was assigned to the investors for expeditions by land, although it is difficult to see how these sea rovers would have tolerated the extreme reduction in their usual profit.

As for division of spoils among the crew, articles varied according to the following: five or six shares for the captain, two for the master's mate, and "other officers proportionable to their employment" (E1684, E1699). However, two shares for the captain and one for all others seemed more common (D1678, Pt, CSP). The shares allocated in the English editions of Exquemelin may be due to translation error, or may reflect the practice of the English as opposed to the French. Even so, a third allocation from French sources provided one share for every man, except for officers (captain, quartermaster, surgeon, pilot), who were rewarded a "recompense" or "gift" by common consent (F1699, Lb). This generally amounted to three shares for the captain, sometimes four; two shares for the quartermaster; and one and a half shares apiece for the surgeon and pilot (Lb). Boys were typically compensated with a half-share (D1678, E1684, E1699, F1699, Lb). (So ingrained was this practice of equal shares that the buccaneer Heins, an accessory to the murder of La Salle and others, afterward "demanded his share of the effects he had seize'd upon." Joutel, *Last Voyage*, 123.)

When plundering a ship or town, most accounts stated that a man must swear he had not concealed any plunder (D1678, E1684, E1699, Lb), or "not to wrong anyone" (Pv). If he broke this oath, he was banished forever from the rovers (D1678, E1684, E1699). Labat said the offender lost all of his share in the voyage and might even be "degraded"—that is, marooned on a desert isle, or at least banished from the vessel (Lb). Some articles limited harsh punishment to those who had concealed more than a piece-of-eight or sixpence (Lb, D1678).

By custom, the shares of a dead man passed to his partner, and if he was dead or could not be found, they passed to the deceased's heirs. If the heirs could not be found, or if he had none, his share was donated to the poor or to the church (Lb). However, in the case of a large share, a crew might instead share it among themselves, as apparently they did after Van Horn's son, who inherited his father's shares, died (CSP). The French commissions to "hunt and fish" were inheritable and passed from commander to commander upon death, or sometimes theft (Dp).

*A*rticles of discipline were also included in a chasse-partie, although they were most often handled according to the "Custom of the Coast," "local practices out of the South Sea," or the "Law of Privateers," all of which were general terms for the customary practices of sea rovers. The filibusters with whom de Lussan cruised the South Sea eventually added "regulations condemning anyone to forfeit his share of our loot if convicted of cowardliness, rape, drunkenness, disobedience, larceny, and failure to obey orders" (dL). Dampier's party of buccaneers crossing the Isthmus of Darien "gave out, that if any Man faultred in the Journey over Land he must expect to be shot to Death; for we knew that the *Spaniards* would soon be after us, and one Man falling into their Hands might be the ruin of us all" (Dp). However, Lionel Wafer did fall out, from injury, but was by no means shot—the regulation seemed more of an incentive than absolute law (W). In some cases, a straggler did not receive his share of plunder nor compensation for injury (dL). One expedition of buccaneers crossing the Isthmus toward Panama gave word that "no man, on the loss of life, should fier a gunn in the woodes, least some Indian Rogues or other should betray us" (Pv). A buccaneer caught stealing in time of severe food or water rationing might be whipped three times by each member of the crew (Dp). Regulations added to the articles during the course of a voyage were called *ordonnances* by the French (dL).

When vessels sailed in consort with each other, as often they did, articles stipulated how plunder would be shared among crews, although these articles were sometimes included in a separate document, as was usual among conventional privateers. For example, Morgan's Panama articles stated that any ship taken at sea or in harbor was to be shared among the entire fleet, up to the value of $10,000. If the prize was worth more, the first vessel to board the prize received an extra $1,000 to be divided among its crew, and the remainder was divided equally among the entire fleet. This division was made for each $10,000 in value of the prize. One suspects that in practice the first vessel to board a prize worth $10,000 or more was awarded 10 percent of the value, over its standard share of the prize (F1699). These articles were typically negotiated and drafted by the quartermasters of the vessels and approved by the crews. In one case, the French and English negotiated to sail in consort, and if they captured another vessel, fifty of each nation would be placed aboard until a second was captured, and then they would throw dice for the choice of vessel—but the English demanded that the first vessel go to them, so no agreement was made (dL).

Conflicts between law and custom sometimes arose between vessels in consortship. In 1681, Captains Wright and Yanky, sailing as consorts, argued over the capture of a prize. Yanky claimed it, having first boarded and captured the prize. But Wright had a commission, under which Yanky sailed for protection, and engaged the prize first and so claimed it. Wright argued his commission, Yanky the Law of Privateers. Put to a vote, Wright lost: Yanky got the prize. Wright then burned his tartan and took Yanky's former vessel (Dp).

Other issues possibly settled in the articles but more probably "according to the Custom of the Coast" included votes in council, how council was handled, and how officers were elected. The captain apparently had two votes (making him the tiebreaker, in essence), all others one (Pt). All hands had a vote in all matters, according to all sources. However, often only the "chiefest" or elected representatives actually signed their names to a document, for example, "subscribed a Paper to make *John Watling* commander."

Such statements also suggest that modifications were typically proposed in writing (E1684, Cx).

In the language of the buccaneer, one "agreed with" the chasse-partie or the captain and his articles, as in "Agreed with him for his ship at ten shares, himself at two, and his boy at half a share" (CSP). The articles were signed by the captain and five or six principals selected by the crew to sign on their behalf (F1699). Or "all of them, or the chiefest, do set their hands unto" (E1684). The size of the company probably determined whether all or only a few signed the articles. Buccaneers "made articles" and signed them each time a new captain was elected (Rr).

# Appendix B
## Buccaneer Organization

### Officers, in Order of Rank and Shares

*Admiral, Vice Admiral, Commander in Chief*: Buccaneers often used these military terms to describe their commanders. A buccaneer admiral was one who had more than one vessel under his command, but remained a ship's captain as well. *Admiral* and *commander in chief* (or *command't in chiefe*) were often used interchangeably; commander in chief was considered appropriate because the nature of buccaneering included attacks both at sea and ashore. These titles did not typically confer additional shares.

*General*: The buccaneer in overall command ashore was often referred to as the *general*.

*Captain (Capitaine)*: His authority was tactical, not strategic. The captain commanded in battle and his authority there was absolute. Outside of battle, his authority was moderated, and consent of the company was typically required. As a leader he was expected to develop the strategy of a cruise, although its implementation was subject to the consent of the company, and might be altered by vote at any time. The captain was also responsible for overseeing ship handling and other matters of routine. Buccaneers expected their commanders to be courageous in battle and lead from the front, and expected leadership not only in battle but in general. If sailing under a legitimate commission that named him as captain and defined the cruise or expedition, he then had more authority over the management of the cruise, but remained subject otherwise to the chasse-partie. His personality and character could make or break a cruise, but not even reputation and force of character could always keep a crew of Caribbean sea rovers together.

*Quartermaster (Quartier-maître)*: Second in the hierarchy of the Caribbean sea rovers, according to the Law of Privateers, the captain's lieutenant, liaison with the rest of the company, and ambassador when negotiating with other buccaneer or filibuster crews. The quartermaster was often given command of a significant prize: "the Company's Quarter-Master, was made Captain by consent of all the Company; for it was his Place by Succession."

*Master (Maître, Maistre):* One who sailed and navigated the vessel under the captain's direction. A ship's master must be a consummate seaman. A standard officer among buccaneers, although not listed by Exquemelin.

*Master's Mate (Contre-maître):* Assistant to the ship's master. The title was listed in the English versions of Exquemelin's *Buccaneers of America* (but *master* was not).

*Pilot (Pilote):* One who had special knowledge of a coastline or harbor. Among buccaneers and filibusters, a pilot might be one of their own, including any of the other officers, or a prisoner working under compulsion or for pay.

*Boatswain (Maître d'équipage):* Managed all rigging and cordage aboard a vessel, called the crew to their watch or quarters, supervised work gangs, and, aboard merchantmen and men-of-war, carried out punishments. He wore a silver whistle as his badge of office. The boatswain was not listed as an officer in published lists of articles, but was noted in various buccaneer and filibuster journals. Pronounced *bos'n.*

*Carpenter (Charpentier, Maître de hache):* A sea artist who made repairs to all that was wood aboard a ship.

*Hunter (Boucanier, Chasseur):* Hired to provision small buccaneer and filibuster vessels with meat. He may or may not have been a member of the vessel's company.

*Striker:* a Moskito Indian signed to "strike" turtle, manatee, and fish for provisions during a buccaneering cruise.

*Surgeon (Chyrurgeon, Chirurgien):* The surgeon's skill in both physic and chirurgery were vital to buccaneer success. He was also responsible for determining the extent of a man's injury in regard to compensation for said injury. Surgeons, when captured by the Spanish, were often spared.

*Cooper (Tonnelier):* Responsible for preparing casks and barrels used for provisions, especially salt pig and turtle. Coopers were not listed as officers among buccaneers, nor did they appear to receive extra compensation, but their skill was vital in provisioning. There were a few references to coopers among the rovers.

*Musician:* Seamen or adventurers who played a musical instrument in addition to their other duties. There was no reference to additional compensation for this duty aboard buccaneers or filibusters, although some did serve in this capacity. The pirate who rescued Dr. Pitman had trumpeters, for example, and fiddlers and trumpeters attended Captain Laurens ashore, although in this case they may not have been part of the ship's company.

*Ship's Boy (Mousse, Gromette):* A boy, probably younger than seventeen and as young as nine. The *Coutume de la Mer* (1647) described a seaman as being seventeen or older, although a *page* (akin to a midshipman) was described as younger than eighteen. Ship's boys served in menial capacities; learned to hand, reef, and steer (and doubtless many vices as well); and at least in the early days of Caribbean sea roving (1660s) had the job of lighting the fire to burn an abandoned vessel or prize at sea.

## Organization at Sea

The crew was divided into two watches as was common aboard ships: larboard (port, the left side) and starboard (the right side), with the quartermaster probably handling one, the master the other. (Aboard merchantmen, the master ran one watch, the first mate the other, sometimes with quartermasters assisting.) Watches were four hours long: first watch from 8 p.m. to midnight; middle watch from midnight to 4 a.m.; morning watch from 4 a.m. to 8 a.m.; forenoon watch from 8 a.m. to noon; afternoon watch from noon to 4 p.m.; look-out watch, or first dog watch, from 4 p.m. to 6 p.m.; last dog watch from 6 p.m. to 8 p.m. The dog watches of two hours each ensured rotation of the watches, so that crew members did not stand the same watches day after day. At four o'clock, eight o'clock, and twelve o'clock, eight bells were struck, then one bell at the first half hour afterward, and one bell more for each half hour after that, until eight bells. For example, the bell was struck four times (two pairs, or couplets) at 6 p.m., and the bell was struck three times (a pair followed by a single strike) at 1:30 a.m.

In spite of the democratic nature of buccaneers and filibusters, organization was mandatory lest the sea or enemy on the sea kill all. Certainly there were various seamen acting as petty officers or warrant officers, although not called by these names, to serve variously as carpenter's mates, boatswain and boatswain's mates, gunner and gunner's mates, and so forth. A vessel could not otherwise sail and fight. However, discipline was lax among the Caribbean rovers during the routine at sea, and sometimes they were so drunk that they had to "stand out to sea" (sail into the open ocean) at night to avoid running aground. On another occasion, pirates were too drunk to board a Spanish vessel and captured it only after they sobered up.

## Organization in Action

In battle, buccaneer organization generally reflected the practice of privateers and men-of-war. In chase aboard the typical small vessels of buccaneers and filibusters, the crew lay on their bellies under cover until it was time to engage at close range, except for the few required to command and sail the vessel. Once the fight commenced, the captain's place was on the quarterdeck or poop, or if there were neither, astern near the tiller where he could see all and conn the helm (direct the steering); as necessary he ranged the entire vessel. The quartermaster might be at the helm, on the forecastle, or commanding the working of the guns. The master and mate managed the sailing of the vessel, as did the bos'n, with a small part of the crew to lend a hand. Among a small crew the bos'n had other duties—to pass the captain's word, for example. In general, the master was at the captain's side to hear his orders, and the mate or bos'n was on the forecastle to assist in working the vessel. Aboard vessels with small crews the master and mate might manage the guns or have other duties.

Aboard a vessel armed with cannon, part of the crew handled small arms, grenades, and swivels on deck, and small arms and grenades in the tops, and the other part the great guns. A small cannon was easily managed with a gun crew of two to four men, and each gun crew was responsible for two cannon: the starboard and its larboard opposite. Ship's boys carried cartridges from the magazine to the guns, and probably also served as runners or messengers, much as midshipmen do aboard men-of-war. Duties in battle—the *quarter bill*—were determined beforehand, put in writing, and posted.

The buccaneer carpenter's primary purpose was to plug shot holes at or beneath the waterline. The surgeon tended the wounded as necessary with bandage, tourniquet, and saw. His space was in the lazaretto or in the hold aboard small vessels. In a fleet consisting mostly of small vessels, he placed his surgery in one of the larger vessels.

# Appendix C
## Captains and Their Vessels

*T*he following is but a sampling of privateer, buccaneer, filibuster, and outright pirate captains of the Spanish Main from 1674 to 1688, of which something about their vessels is known. Many of these captains almost certainly commanded vessels not listed here. Further, the information below is limited only to their known vessels. Many of these captains were rovers for many years, even decades, beyond the dates given for command of vessels. The term *guns* is shorthand for *great guns*, and refers to cannon. *Patereroes* and *swivels* are small swivel-mounted cannon, either breech or muzzle loaded.

*Allison, Robert* (also *Alliston, Alleston, Allisson*). English, commanded a sloop of eighteen tons, no guns, and twenty-four men at Portobello in 1680, and prior to crossing Darien.

*Amon, Nicolas* (called *Grénezé*). French, commanded a sloop at Campeche in 1685.

*Andrieszoon, Michel* (also *Michel, Mitchel, l'Andresson, Landresson*). Dutch, in 1683 commanded *le Tigre* of three hundred men and thirty or thirty-six guns, although in late 1683 she was listed with twenty-six guns and one hundred and eighty men. In 1684 he commanded *la Mutine*, formerly the Spanish *Paz* (*Peace*) of forty-four guns, described in early 1685 as of fifty guns but later in the year as of thirty-six guns and one hundred and twenty men—some of the larger number may have been swivels.

*Archemboe* (also *Archaimbault*). French, commanded an eight-gun privateer of forty men at the Samballos Islands in 1681. In 1683 he commanded a vessel of ten guns and eighty men, perhaps the same as in 1681.

*Banister, Joseph* (also *Bannister*). English, commanded the thirty-six gun *Golden Fleece* in 1685.

*Barnes*. English, in 1676 commanded a Dutch privateer of twelve guns and one hundred and fifty men.

*Beare, John*. English, in 1686 commanded the *James*, a small frigate, probably the former Spanish *Soldada*.

*Bennet, John*. English, in 1676 sailed a brigantine, later the *Buen Jesus de las Almas*, a prize.

*Bernard, Antoine* (also *Bernal, Antonio*). French, commanded the sloop *Prophète Daniel* (sometimes cited as the *Prophète Samuel*) of Martinique, of thirty-five tons, two guns, two patereroes, and seventeen men, in 1683.

*Blot*. Dutch according to one source, in 1683 commanded a vessel of fifteen guns and one hundred and fifty men. In 1683 and 1684 commanded *la Guagone* (or *Quagone*), a Spanish prize of eight guns and ninety men, perhaps the same vessel.

*Bond, George*. English, of Bristol, in 1683 sailed *Fortune's Adventure* out of St. Thomas, a Dutch ship purchased from the governor, probably the same vessel described as a "small ship" of one hundred men. Previously he commanded the ship *Summer Island* of London.

*Bournano, le sieur de* (also *Bernanos*). French, in 1684 commanded the *Schitié*. (The name was perhaps derived from *schijt*, Dutch for *shit*, or from a French spelling of the English word. This would not be without precedent—Drake fought the *Cacafuego* or *Shitfire*, for example).

*Branley*. English, in 1685 in the South Sea commanded a small vessel of thirty-six men (English and French).

*Bréha, le capitaine* (*Pierre Bart*, also *Abraham*, *Pedro Bot*). French, commanded the barque-longue *Diligent* of eight guns in 1683, and in 1684 commanded the barque-longue *Fortune* (or *Diligent*, perhaps the same vessel) of one hundred men and fourteen guns. In 1684 recaptured the *Nuestra Señora de Regla* (the *Reglita*), but in 1685 after the sack of Campeche, armed with twenty-six guns and one hundred and fifty men, the vessel was recaptured again by the Spanish, along with its captain and crew.

*Brigaut, Nicolas*. French, at Campeche in 1685 and at St. Augustine in 1686 commanded a galliot captured at Campeche in 1685.

*Brouage*. French, briefly commanded de Graff's *Neptune* in 1684.

*Connoway, Morriss* (probably *Morris Conway*). English, commanded a small prize bark in the South Sea of seven men. The Spanish captured the crew and killed all but one.

*Conway, Jeremiah* (also *Conaway, Canoe*). English, in 1683 commanded the *Prosperous* a small, six-gun frigate of twenty-eight men out of New Providence.

*Cook, Edmund* (also *Cooke, John*). English, in 1680 prior to crossing Darien commanded a bark of thirty-five tons, no cannon, and forty-three men. Briefly commanded a one-hundred-and-eighty-ton ship or bark in the South

Sea, later given command of the *Mayflower* prize but the crew refused to serve. In 1683 captured Tristian's bark and a French ship laded with wine at Petit Goave. In 1683 commanded the ship *Revenge* of either eight or eighteen guns and fifty-two men, a converted prize. Later in the same year captured a Danish ship of thirty-six or forty guns, renamed her the *Batchelor's Delight*, and transferred to the prize.

*Corso, Juan* (also *Corzo, Cora, Costeau*, "*Corsario John*"). Spanish, in 1684 commanded an armadilla of two or three piraguas. At one point he captured two English ships, renamed them *el Leon Coronado* (*Crowned Lion*, a frigate of 335 tons) and *el Leon*. The former became a guarda costa vessel for Campeche, and later a ship of the Armada de Barlovento, renamed *Nuestra Señora del Honhón*. The piragua seemed to be his typical vessel, although he apparently commanded a half galley, also referred to as a galliot or barque-longue, in the search for La Salle.

*Cox, John*. English, commanded the *Mayflower* prize, a ship of one hundred tons (one source referred to it as a "Barque"), during Sharp's South Sea voyage, until the ship lost her bowsprit when, in tow, she collided with the *Trinidad*, and it could not be replaced.

*Coxon, John* (also *Coxen*). English, commanded a ten-gun privateer of one hundred men at Samballos in 1680. At Water Key the same year, the vessel was described as of eighty tons, eight guns, and ninety-seven men. In 1688 commanded a barcalonga of eighty-eight men (eighty English, five Dutch, three French).

*Davis, Edward* (also *David*). Dutch, succeeded to command of the *Batchelor's Delight* after the death of her captain, Cook, in 1684. In 1685 commanded the same ship, "fort belle," with thirty-six guns and 156 men.

*Deane, John*. English, commanded the *St. David* in 1676.

*Dedran* (also *Defran*). French, in 1684 commanded *le Chasseur* (the *Hunter*) of one hundred and twenty men and twenty guns. See *Pedneau*.

*Dumesnil, le sieur*. French, in 1684 commanded *la Trompeuse* (the *Deceiver*, note the feminine case) of one hundred men and fourteen guns.

*Eaton, John*. English, commanded the *Nicholas* of London, with twenty-six guns, in the South Sea in 1683.

*Essex, Cornelius*. English, sailed a bark at Portobello in 1680.

*Evertson, Jacob* (also *Everson, James*). Dutch, in 1681 commanded a sloop of seventy-six men (seventy English, six Spanish), and from 1687–88 a "fine barque" of ten guns, sixteen patereroes, and fifty men.

*Fitzgerald, Philip* (also *Don Philip Hellen*). Irish, commanded a twelve-gun frigate out of Havana in 1675.

*Francis*. Mulatto, a privateer serving the Dutch, commanded a ship of twenty guns and one hundred men in 1676.

*Gombert, Philippe de la Fleur.* French, sailed a corvette under Grammont and Van Horn.

*Graff, Laurens de.* Dutch, in 1679 commanded a Spanish prize of twenty-four to twenty-eight guns, which he renamed *le Tigre.* Later captured the *Francesa,* a frigate of twenty-six guns and ten patereroes, from the Spanish, who previously captured it from the French. At Veracruz in 1683 commanded the *la Françoise (Francesa)* of thirty guns and two hundred men. In 1684 commanded the *Neptune,* formerly the Spanish *San Francisco,* of fifty-four guns and 210 men; the *Françoise* became Yanky's ship. In 1684 the *Neptune* was listed variously with forty-four guns, and in 1685 with forty-eight guns and three hundred men. Briefly commanded the prize *Cascarille* in 1685, then returned to the *Neptune.* Laurens variously was the captain of at least seven or eight different vessels, not including any he might have commanded while serving Spain. Pouançay noted that prior to capturing the *Francesa,* Laurens commanded a small sloop, then a small ship, then a larger one, then one of twenty-four to twenty-eight guns (probably *le Tigre*).

*Grammont, Michel de* or *le sieur de* (also *Granmont, Agrammont*). French, in 1684 commanded the *Hardy* (formerly Van Horn's *Saint Nicolas*) of three hundred men and fifty-two guns.

*Grogniet, François* (called *Chasse-Marée,* also *Gronet, Grognier*). French, commanded the *St. Françoise* (or *St. Joseph*) of seventy men and six guns from 1683–84. In 1685 commanded a ship of six guns (rated for sixteen) and six swivels. In the South Sea in 1685, commanded a vessel of 308 Frenchmen, but no cannon.

*Guernsey.* French, in 1682 commanded a vessel named *la Trompeuse.*

*Hall, Jacob.* English, of Bermuda, according to various sources commanded a small frigate, or a small bark, or a brig of eight guns at Veracruz in 1683.

*Hamelyn, William.* English, in 1676 commanded a Dutch privateer, perhaps the sloop *Betty,* in the Windward Isles.

*Hamlin, Jean* (also *Hamlyn, Hamelin*). French, commanded *la Trompeuse* of thirty or thirty-two guns and six patereroes. Later commanded *la Nouvelle Trompeuse,* a Dutch frigate of thirty-six guns and one hundred and twenty men.

*Harris, Peter.* English, at Boca del Toro in 1680 commanded a captured Dutch frigate of thirty-two guns. The same ship was described at Water Key in 1680 as of one hundred and fifty tons, twenty-five guns, and 107 men; one source states twenty-six guns.

*Harris, Peter* (nephew of the previous, also *Pitre-Henry*). English, in 1684–85 in the South Sea commanded a small bark of one hundred men, most of them English, and no cannons, formerly commanded by Henry More.

*Henley, Thomas.* English, of New England, in 1684 commanded the

*Resolution*, formerly the Spanish *Baldivia*, until Bartholomew Sharp took it from him.

*Hewet*. English, probably the commander under whom Dampier served in 1676–77. If so, he sailed a bark with a crew of thirty.

*Jocard*. French, commanded *la Irondelle* at St. Domingue in 1684.

*Johns, Samuel*. A New Englander, commanded the *Isabella* in 1684. This vessel was probably also the *Presbyter* (*Presbíteros* in Spanish records), a small frigate captured by the Spanish at Tampico in 1684.

*La Garde* (also *Lagarde*). French, commanded the *Subtile* of two guns and thirty men in 1684. In 1685 commanded the brigantine *le Galant* of four guns and six swivels. In the same year, his vessel was also referred to as a *bateau*.

*Larco, Juan de*. Spanish, commanded a piragua of forty oars in an attack on New Providence in 1684.

*Lemoyne, Bernard* (also *l'Moin, Lemoign, Lemogne*). French, in 1678 commanded the *Toison d'Or* (*Golden Fleece*).

*Le Sage, François* (also *Lesage*). Dutch, at Veracruz in 1683 commanded a barque-longue and lost it on the Cuban coast after the sack of Veracruz. In 1684 commanded *le Tigre* of thirty guns and one hundred and thirty men (sixty of whom served under Hamlin), passed to him by Andrieszoon.

*Lescuier* (also *L'Escuyer, Lequie*). French, commanded a vessel of six cannon and five swivels in 1685.

*Lessone* (also *La Sound*). French, commanded a "greate shipp" in 1680 at Portobello.

*Mackett* (also *Maggott*). English, in 1680 commanded a sloop of fourteen tons and twenty men at Boca del Toro.

*Marcus, Peter* (also *Pedro Marcus*). Dutch, commanded the ship *White Lamb* in 1679.

*Markham, John* (also *Marquaim, Marguain*). English, in 1686 was listed variously as commanding a large barque-longue of eight guns or a small ship of twelve guns.

*Martin, Alonzo* (also *Anthonio*). Italian, in 1686 commanded the frigate *la Virgen de Populo y San Antonio de Padua*, built and armed in Santo Domingo, of twelve guns, eight patereroes, and eighty men.

*Miguel, Blas* (also *Bras, Miguel Curro*). A Corsican serving Spain, in 1687 commanded a piragua at the attack on Petit Goave.

*More, Henry*. English, commanded a small prize bark in the South Sea under Captain Knight.

*Morgan*. English, probably commanded a Dutch West India Company prize of twenty guns, manned with some of Hamlin's former crew (Morgan included).

*Nevil*. English, probably sailed a bark of thirty men in 1676–77.

*Onan, Pasqual.* Native American serving Spain, in 1687 commanded a brigantine at the attack on Petit Goave.

*Orange, Pierre l'* (also *Pedro Naranjo*). French, sailed the *Dauphin* of two guns at the time of the sack of Veracruz.

*Paine, Thomas* (also *Payne, Pain*). English, in 1678 commanded a privateer of six guns, lost it to the Dutch at Aves but captured a Dutch sloop. At Darien in 1681 commanded a vessel of ten guns and one hundred men. In 1683 sailed the *Pearl*, of eight guns and eighty men.

*Pedneau.* French, in 1684 commanded *le Chasseur* (the *Hunter*) of twenty guns and one hundred and twenty men. See *Dedran.*

*Pennon.* French, in 1682 commanded a Spanish barque.

*Peterson.* English, arrived at Rhode Island in 1688 in a barcalonga of ten guns (possibly swivels) and seventy men.

*Petit.* French, in 1684 was listed variously as commanding *le Ruzé*, a boat (*bateau*) of forty men and four guns (probably patereroes), and *le Subtille* of forty men, probably the same vessel.

*Picard.* French, in 1682 commanded a brigantine.

*Read.* English, succeeded to command of the *Cygnet* in the Philippines after a mutiny removed Captain Swan.

*Riet, Willem.* Dutch, in 1683 sailed the *Tyger* out of Curaçao.

*Robert, William.* English, commanded the sloop *Margarita* in 1683.

*Rodriguez, Manuel* (also *Rodrigo*). Spanish, in 1684 sailed a "ship."

*Rose, Jean* (also *John Row*). French, commanded a twenty-ton barcalonga at Samballos in 1680, with a crew of twenty-five; another source indicated a brigantine. The vessel carried no cannon. In 1685 he commanded a tartan of six guns, two swivels, and sixty-four men.

*Santot, Pierre* (called *Pierre le Picard*, also *Pearse Hantot, Peckar*). French, cruised 1685–87 in the *Cascarille.*

*Sawkins, Richard* (also *Sawlkings*). English, at Water Key in 1680 commanded a bark of sixteen tons, one gun, and thirty-five men, although at Boca del Toro in 1680 he was listed as commanding a small brigantine of four guns. Commanded the *Trinity* in the South Sea until his death.

*Sharp, Bartholomew* (also *Betcharp, Botcharpe, Batt. Sharpe*). English, at Water Key in 1680 commanded a bark of twenty-five tons, two guns, and forty men. In the South Sea he commanded first a small bark, then briefly the "Lima ship" of one hundred tons captured off Panama, then the galleon *Trinity* of four hundred tons but no guns, formerly the *Santissima Trinidad*. From 1684 onward he commanded the frigate *Josiah*, formerly Henley's *Resolution* (the Spanish *Baldivia*), of ten guns, eight patereroes, and one hundred men.

*Spurre, George.* English, commanded a sloop and sixty men in 1682, and perhaps the same Jamaica sloop at Veracruz in 1683.

*Swan, Charles.* (also *Swann, Suan*). English, in the South Sea in 1684 commanded the *Cygnet of London*, of one hundred and forty tons, sixteen guns, and twenty men (all English, soon much increased); a merchantman turned pirate.

*Tocard, Jean* (also *Tucker*). French, commanded a six-gun privateer of seventy men at Samballos in 1681. At Veracruz commanded a small prize captured by de Graff. Later commanded *el Padre Ramos*, passed to him by Yanky.

*Towers.* Dutch, sailed a ship of thirty or forty guns.

*Townley* (also *Touslé, Thouslé*). English, commanded a small vessel in the South Sea in 1685 with one hundred and ten Englishmen and no cannon.

*Tristian* (also *Tristan*). French (one source suggests Dutch), in 1681 at Darien sailed a bark or barque-longue, later seized by Cook. In 1683 commanded the *Nuestra Señora de Regla* (the *Reglita*) of twenty-four guns (or twenty-two) and ten patereroes. The Spanish recaptured the ship after Veracruz, but Tristian escaped. In 1686 commanded either a large barque-longue of eight guns, or a small ship of twelve guns.

*Van Horn, Nicolas* (also *Van Horne, Van Hoorne, Banoren*). Dutch, in 1683 commanded the *Saint Nicolas* of forty guns and four hundred tons, formerly the English merchantman *Mary and Martha*. In 1683 captured the patache *Nuestra Señora de Regla*, a fragata of one hundred and fifty tons, having burned her larger consort, the *Consolación*; the *Regla* passed to Tristian. In European waters Van Horn commanded a French privateer disguised as a fishing boat, and later a privateer ship.

*Verpré.* French, in 1684 commanded the *Postillon* of two guns and twenty-five men.

*Vigneron.* French, in 1684 commanded the sloop *Louise* of four guns and thirty men. In 1685 his sloop carried only two swivels.

*Vigot, Guillaume.* French, commanded the one-hundred-and-thirty-ton *Concordia*, probably a pink, of twelve guns and forty-three men in 1684.

*Watling, John.* English, briefly commanded the *Trinity* (see *Sharp, Bartholomew*) in the South Sea.

*Wright, John.* English, in 1681 at Darien sailed a barcalonga of four guns and forty men.

*Yanky (Jan Willems, John Williams, Yankey, Janquais, Jean Quet, Junqué, Hianquêe*). Dutch, commanded a barcalonga of four guns and sixty men (English, Dutch, French) at Darien in 1681. Commanded the frigate *el Padre Ramos* of eighteen guns and one hundred and fifty men in 1683 at Veracruz. In 1684 received de Graff's *Françoise* and renamed her *la Dauphine*, of one hundred and eighty men (forty-eight of whom formerly sailed with Hamlin) and thirty guns. From 1686 to 1688 he commanded a Dutch-built ship of forty (or forty-eight) guns and sixty to one hundred men, probably a prize captured from the Spanish.

*Young, George* (also *Younge*). English, in 1683 commanded a sloop of eighteen men out of New Providence.

# Appendix D
## Roving Books and Authors, 1674–1699

1674    Alexander Exquemelin returned to Europe from Tortuga.
        William Dampier arrived in Jamaica.

1675    Elias al-Mûsili, a Chaldean priest from Iraq, traveled to New Spain
        aboard the treasure fleet. The manuscript of his New World travels
        was not published until 1905.

1677    Exquemelin was in Amsterdam to study surgery.

1678    *De Americaensche Zee-Roovers* by Alexander Exquemelin was pub-
        lished in Dutch in Amsterdam.
        Dampier, having spent a year at the Campeche logwood trade, re-
        turned to England.
        Edward Barlow, who would write and illustrate a journal of his many
        sea voyages, sailed as second mate aboard the *Guannaboe* merchant-
        man from England to Jamaica. Barlow's manuscript remained unpub-
        lished until 1934.

1679    *Americanische Seeräuber*, a German translation of Exquemelin's
        work, was published in Nuremberg. Exquemelin was a member of
        the Surgeons' Guild in Amsterdam.
        Raveneau de Lussan arrived at Saint Domingue and was indentured
        for three years.
        Barlow returned to Jamaica aboard the *Guannaboe*, this time as chief
        mate, in company with the *Loyal Merchant*.
        William Dampier, returning to Jamaica, was a passenger aboard the
        *Loyal Merchant*.

1680    The comte de Forbin (who later served alongside the famous corsaires
        Duguay-Trouin and Jean Bart) and the marquis de Villette arrived in

the Caribbean as part of d'Estrées's Caribbean cruise, and visited
Petit Goave. Both of their memoirs were published in the eighteenth
century.

Barlow returned to Jamaica aboard the *Cadiz Merchant* as second
mate.

Buccaneers under Bartholomew Sharp and others attacked the Spanish in the South Sea. The expedition included William Dampier, Lionel
Wafer, Basil Ringrose, Edward Povey, William Dick, and John Cox. One
account of the expedition, believed to be Povey's, was published in
1923 in Jameson's *Privateering and Piracy in the Colonial Period*.

1681	*Piratas de la America*, a Spanish translation of the Dutch edition of
Exquemelin's work, was published in Cologne.

Barlow sailed again to Jamaica aboard the *Cadiz Merchant*, this time
as chief mate.

Dampier and others departed the South Sea.

Bartholomew Sharp, William Dick, and John Cox were tried in London for piracy, but acquitted.

1683	Dampier returned to the South Sea as a buccaneer. Abraham (or Am-
brose) Cowley was a member of the same expedition, but claimed
not to have known at first that its intention was piracy.

Al-Mûsili returned to Spain aboard the treasure fleet.

1684	The *Buccaneers of America* by "Alexander Esquemeling" was pub-
lished in London, based on the Spanish edition. Also published was
*The History of the Buccaneers*, based on the Dutch edition. Henry
Morgan sued both publishers for libel and won. The *Buccaneers of
America* included a chapter by William Dick (W. D.) on the South Sea
expedition of Sharp and others.

Philip Ayers published *The Voyages and Adventures of Capt. Barth.
Sharp and Others, in the South Sea*; John Cox was the anonymous
author of the title work. The volume also included relations of
Morgan's attack on Panama, Beeston's visit to Cartagena, and the
French sack of Veracruz.

Ringrose returned to the South Sea aboard the *Cygnet*.

1685	A revised edition of *The Buccaneers of America* was published, and
included Basil Ringrose's account of the South Sea expedition.

Raveneau de Lussan joined the second great South Sea expedition.

Dr. Henry Pitman, whose odyssey inspired Rafael Sabatini to write
*Captain Blood*, was convicted of treason for treating rebels wounded
in the Monmouth uprising and was transported as a slave to Barbados.

1686   *Histoire des aventuriers flibustiers qui se sont signalez dans les Indes* by "A. O. Oexmelin" was published in Paris. Exquemelin was identified as a French surgeon from Honfleur, France, and was involved in the publication of this edition. This and later French editions included much information on French and Dutch filibusters (Grammont, de Graff, and Van Horn, among others), sadly lacking in any of the English-language editions, past or present.
       Basil Ringrose was killed in action in Mexico.

1687   Dr. Pitman escaped from Barbados, only to be marooned on Salt Tortuga. He was later rescued by pirates.

1688   Lionel Wafer and two companions were arrested in Virginia and held at Jamestown on charges of piracy in the South Sea, but were never brought to trial. Part of Wafer's booty helped found the College of William and Mary in Williamsburg, Virginia.
       A second edition of the *Histoire des aventuriers flibustiers qui se sont signalez dans les Indes* was published in Paris.

1689   The first edition of de Lussan's *Les Flibustiers de la mer du sud* was published.
       *A Relation of the Great Sufferings and Strange Adventures of Henry Pitman* was published in London.
       In Tonqueen (Vietnam) Dampier mailed a packet of letters via Edward Barlow, now mate of the *Rainbow of London*.

1690   A second edition of de Lussan's *Les Flibustiers de la mer du sud* was published.

1691   Dampier returned to England, completing his first circumnavigation.

1694   Father Jean Baptiste Labat, a Jacobin, arrived in the West Indies. His *Nouveau voyage aux isles d'Amerique* was published in Paris in 1722 in six volumes.

1695   A third edition of de Lussan's *Les Flibustiers de la mer du sud* was published in Paris.

1697   Dampier's *A New Voyage Round the World* was published in London in two editions. It detailed his participation in the second great South Sea expedition, as well as his subsequent journey around the world. Exquemelin returned to the Caribbean as a surgeon with de Pointis's expedition against Cartagena, and perhaps previously.

Dr. Giovanni Francesco Gemelli Careri, an Italian, crossed the Pacific aboard the Manila Galleon. An account of his travels around the world was published in 1700.

1698    Wafer's *New Voyage and Description of the Isthmus of Panama* was published in London.

An anonymous relation of de Pointis's expedition was published in Brussels and one by de Pointis himself was published in Amsterdam. A third edition of Dampier's *New Voyage* was published.

Gemelli Careri crossed the Atlantic aboard the Spanish treasure fleet. Dampier dined with now-famous diarists John Evelyn and Samuel Pepys. Dampier and Barlow provided navigational intelligence to the Council of Trade and Plantations.

1699 and on

Another edition of *The Buccaneers of America* was published in London. Virtually identical to the 1684 edition in most respects, it included minor, but often critical, alterations and additions, as well as translations of de Lussan's book and of the sieur de Montauban's account of his privateering escapades.

Dampier's *Voyages and Discoveries* was published in London, comprising three works: *The Supplement of the Voyage Round the World*, *The Campeachy Voyages*, and *The Discourse of Winds*, and a fourth edition of his *New Voyage* was published (and other editions in 1703, 1717, and 1729).

William Hacke's *A Collection of Original Voyages* was published in London, and included the journals of Sharp and Cowley.

The third edition of the *Histoire des aventuriers flibustiers qui se sont signalez dans les Indes* was published in Paris, and included a chapter on the sack of Cartagena.

For details on the various editions of Exquemelin's and Dampier's books, see the introductions to Exquemelin, *Buccaneers of America* (1678); Exquemelin, *Buccaneers of America* (1684); Exquemelin, *Flibustiers*; and Dampier, *New Voyage*, as listed in the bibliography. Ringrose's *Buccaneer's Atlas*, edited by House and Thrower, provides excellent detail on the various editions and manuscripts of the accounts of Sharp's South Sea voyage, as well a detailed summary of the South Sea voyage under Sharp and others, not to mention a complete and annotated copy of Ringrose's South Sea atlas.

# Appendix E
## A Boucanier Barbecue

"Sund. Our Men feasted on shoar with Barbakude, Goats and Fish, &c.," wrote John Cox, former commander of the *Mayflower* prize in the South Sea. An ancient tradition even in the seventeenth century, smoking or grilling meat on a barbecue, or barbacoa, was common both as a means of preserving food as well as cooking it. Today, purists distinguish between barbecuing and grilling: the former is slow cooking over several hours or more, the latter quick. However, for the Caribbean adventurer in the late seventeenth century, *barbecue* referred to the grill or frame upon which food was either smoked slowly in order to preserve it, or cooked for immediate consumption.

The typical barbecue, or boucan, among most Caribbean adventurers was simple and casual: food on the barbecue—pork, beef, goat, manatee, fish, or anything else available—and plenty of rum punch to drink while it cooked, and for that matter, while it was eaten, and then well into the evening. Turtle could be cooked in the half shell, staked up near the fire. Among the boucaniers, however, were rules, traditions, and procedures, described in detail by Father Labat.

Now let us explore how to create a traditional boucanier barbecue.

First, the barbecue or boucan. Cut plenty of firewood, stack it so it will burn well, then light it. While the wood is burning, pound four forked sticks the diameter of one's arm and about four feet long into the ground to form a rectangle roughly four feet by three feet. Set sturdy crosspieces in the forks, then lay sticks lengthwise and crosswise to form a barbecue or grill. Tie the barbecue at each intersection with liana (any woody climbing vine of the tropics).

Next, the pig. Boucaniers preferred the sanglier, or wild boar, but today even a whole domestic pig is often difficult to obtain. Lay the pig on its back on the barbecue. Use sticks to keep the belly cavity open. Make a marinade of lime juice, salt, and crushed allspice (called *pimento* or *piment* from its resemblence to peppercorns—*pimentas*), and rub the cavity well. Next, lay hot coals beneath the barbecue, and add wood or coals as necessary while the pig cooks. The coals must be carried with tree bark, for all instruments of metal, other than a knife, are forbidden. While the pig is cooking, use a *brochette*—a sharp stick—to pierce the flesh within the cavity, but do not push the brochette through to the outside.

Third, the table. Lay it with ferns and large leaves—boucaniers did not use tablecloths or plates. Cut enough brochettes so that each person has two. Fill a large calabash gourd with the mixture of lime juice, salt, and allspice, and another with gravy. Fold cachibou leaves into bowls, securing the corners with liana. When the pig is served, guests will use these for a mixture of gravy and lime juice, salt, and allspice to taste. Provide a calabash for each person to drink from, and ensure there is enough liquor to go around. Labat described wine, but without doubt rum was served as well, either straight up or as rum punch: lime juice, muscovado sugar, and rum.

Fourth, the hunt. While the pig is cooking, hunters shoot birds to be placed in the pig's belly to cook. The hunter who returns with nothing must drink as many shots (*coups*) of wine or rum as the number of birds brought in by the most successful hunter. If bad luck, and not bad shooting, is the reason a hunter returns with no birds, he may choose the liquor he is compelled to drink. If he is a novice—that is, if this is his first barbecue or boucan— the penalty may be tempered. Hunters are recalled by firing consecutive shots into the air.

Last, the rules. The master of the barbecue carves the first platter—a large leaf—of pork, and his assistants carry it to the table. The older boucaniers carve next, then the novices. Once the first bite of pork is taken, no other food but pork and the birds cooked with it may be eaten. Except for a knife, metal instruments are forbidden: only fingers, brochettes, and knives may be used. Important—water may not be mixed with liquor! All liquor must be drunk full strength, punch being the only likely exception. Drinking is encouraged: "The law compels it, the sauce invites one to do so, and few err in this respect," wrote Father Labat. The master of the barbecue must fine anyone not eating, drinking, or working—or for any other reason his wisdom and experience compel! The fines, naturally, are shots of wine or rum.

# Appendix F
## *"Pieces-of-Eight! Pieces-of-Eight!"*

So screamed Long John Silver's parrot in Stevenson's *Treasure Island*, and the words were certainly more suited to the pirate and privateer of the Caribbean than to any other, for one result of piracy, privateering, and smuggling was the importation of Spanish silver directly into the French, English, and Dutch colonies. "One sees more Spanish money at Saint Domingue than that of France," wrote Father Labat, and accounts at Saint Domingue were tallied only in pieces-of-eight or *reales* (royals).[1] (The English, however, usually tallied in pounds, shillings, and pence, or £, s, and d). While Hollywood pirates have chests of gold and jewels, the real pirate had, more than anything else, Spanish silver: the piece-of-eight, short for "piece of eight reales," derived from the Spanish *peso de ocho reales*, commonly referred to simply as the *peso*, and from the weight of eight royals (the English equivalent was seventeen pennyweight).[2] The coin was also known among the English as the *Spanish dollar* (from *thaler*, originally a Bohemian silver coin, later used in reference to similar coins). Among the Spanish it was also known as the *real de a ocho*, *piastra*, *peso de plata*, and *peso de plata antigua*, and among the French variously as the *pièce de huit*, *piastre*, *piastre gourd*, *écu* or *écu espagnol*, and sometimes *reaux* (*reales*) *d'Espagne*.

Based on the *reale*, the piece-of-eight was the largest denomination of Spanish silver coin. Smaller coins of four, two, one, and a half reale were also minted, and were called by the English *half pieces*, *quarter pieces*, *rials*, and *half-reales*.[3] The piece-of-eight was worth 272 Spanish *maravedís*, while a single real was worth thirty-two.[4] (By 1686 the Spanish valued the piece-of-eight at ten reales.[5]) The coin was usually valued in the English colonies of the late seventeenth century at 4s.6d. (4 shillings, 6 pence), although in practice often at 5 or 6 shillings. Pieces-of-eight were "the standard of all the current coin" in the New World.[6] Most nations had similar silver coins, although usually not of the same value: the French écu, the Portuguese *cruzado*, the Dutch *gulden* or *ducatoon*, and the Danish *krone*, for example. Of these, the écu was "about the same value" as the piastre or pièce de huit, and the term

249

was often used to denominate the piece-of-eight. The coin outnumbered all others of silver by far.

About the size of a modern silver dollar, the seventeenth-century piece-of-eight has a unique look and feel, and none are identical. A small number of pieces-of-eight found in the New World were minted in Seville, but most were minted in Potosí (from 1575) and Mexico (from 1535). (The coins were also minted at Lima in 1568–88, and then from 1684, and at Santa Fe de Bogotá from 1620.) The English referred to these Spanish silver coins as "Seville, pillar and Mexico" dollars or pieces-of-eight, respectively.[7] Coin blanks were cut from silver bars hammered flat. Gemelli Careri, who visited the mint and royal office of the *Apartado* in Mexico, described the process: silver bars were assayed, then "put into the fire that they may be cut, and when cut, because the silver is harsh, they are wetted with water, and being put into the fire again are coin'd. . . . When cut according to their due weight, they return to the treasurer." The blanks were sent to the "whiteners," then "passing the officers who are to see it has the just weight of sixty seven rials to a mark," the coins were stamped, that is, placed between two dies and hit with a large hammer, leaving the often incomplete die marks on the coin.[8] In general, the coins produced in Mexico were of even poorer quality than those of Potosí and Lima. Because of its random shape and unmilled edges, the piece-of-eight was "liable to be clipped and debased," that is, to have silver clipped from the coin's edges to debase its actual value while retaining its face value and, when the clipped silver was added to other clippings, to even further enrich the thief.[9] Sometimes small plugs of silver were added to clipped pieces-of-eight to return them to the proper weight. Merchants preferred to tally the coins by weight, not by tale.

The Spanish dollar, both in its crude form as well as in its later form with milled edges, was the predominant colonial currency, and remained so up to the time of the American Revolution. Indeed, the unit of U.S. currency was derived from it. Some suggest that the dollar sign—$—derives from the pillar dollar, the two vertical strokes representing the two pillars of Hercules, and the S curve the waves beneath or the numeral 8. However, there are a dozen or more such theories on the derivation of the dollar sign, ranging from shorthand for shilling to abbreviations of peso or piece-of-eight. Shorthand for the piece-of-eight when keeping plunder books or tallying shares was often "pc. of 8/8" or "ps. 8/8," and it is easy to see how the dollar sign might have derived from this.[10] (One assumes a half-piece would be indicated by 4/8.) The resemblance of the S in the dollar sign to an 8 is strongly suggestive, and it is easy to see the numeral eight written with a slash through it to indicate a piece-of-eight, instead of using an 8 over another, and this being quickly transformed into the dollar sign.

A typical Spanish merchant's chest held two thousand pieces-of-eight, and one of the king's, three thousand.[11] Converting from Troy weights (seventeen pennyweight per coin, twenty-four grains per pennyweight, seven thousand grains per the modern avoirdupois pound), two thousand pieces-of-eight alone weighed approximately 117 pounds—heavy chests indeed!

A rich prize or otherwise successful cruise might earn a buccaneer a share of seven hundred pieces-of-eight (and weighing approximately forty-one pounds). Assuming an approximate equivalent value in 2007 of $50 to $55 per piece-of-eight (£26, EUR 40), he received the value of thirty-five thousand U.S. dollars in 2007, although such estimates often do not convey an accurate sense of value—the cost of living was much lower, and lifestyles in terms of material goods much simpler, in the buccaneer's period. In 1685, for example, forty shillings per month (roughly eight pieces-of-eight, or four hundred dollars in 2007) as a seaman aboard an armed galley (berthing and meals provided) was a decent wage.[12] At that rate of pay, seven hundred pieces-of-eight was more than a man might make in seven years.

And what could a pirate buy with this money? For five dollars he could buy a buccaneer gun or a parrot.[13] He could buy one hundred pounds of boucan for three dollars, although by the 1690s the price rose to six due to the overhunting of wild pigs.[14] At Jamaica he could buy a barrel of salted sea turtle for four to six pieces-of-eight (eighteen to twenty-five shillings).[15] In the Spanish colonies he could buy a dozen plantains for a half-reale, and in Havana he could buy a cardinal songbird for six to ten dollars.[16] He could buy cattle at four or five dollars a head, and a bull's hide was worth one dollar, as were two cowhides.[17] A good wild horse cost six to eight dollars on Saint Domingue (where they were exceptionally cheap), and twice that to break.[18] He could buy a canoe approximately thirty feet long, four feet wide, with five thwarts for fifteen dollars, plus a dollar apiece for two workers, and their food for fifteen days.[19] In Puerto Rico he could illicitly buy indigo at three reales per pound and annatto at four reales per pound, and sell them for twice this price at Jamaica.[20] The price of a black slave varied from $118 ready money to as little as fifty-eight dollars. Buccaneers and filibusters, as already noted, valued a slave at one hundred dollars (probably based on the 1662 asiento granted to Grillo and Lomelin, which valued slaves at this price), and Spaniards might pay buccaneers as much as two hundred for each captured slave.[21]

Unfortunately, we have little information on how much a pirate's entertainment in the taverns and stews of Petit Goave or Port Royal cost, particularly as these merchants of rum and pulchritude were known for raising their prices when pirates returned from successful cruises. Exquemelin's description of a drunken buccaneer or filibuster paying five hundred dollars to have a woman strip and dance naked for him, while it only may be the occasional practice, was not a good indication of the price of gratification ashore.[22] Or perhaps it was, after all—the rum surely burned as big a hole in this pirate's head as his money did in his purse, just as drink and dollars do with some sailors and adventurers even today.

# *Appendix G*
## *Places Plundered, 1674–1688*

*T*he following is almost certainly an incomplete list of the cities, towns, villages, and other places attacked by buccaneers and filibusters during the period under study, and also of English and French places attacked by the Spanish. *Sacked* indicates the capture of a place, *Attempted* indicates an attack that was repulsed, and *Threatened* indicates an attack intended or possible but called off just short of actual engagement, usually because surprise was lost. The lists below do not include raids on plantations and *estancias*, such as the filibuster raid on La Chua, Florida, and the Spanish raid on Laurens's plantation. Such descents were numerous, and many were not recorded.

## Buccaneer and Filibuster Attacks on Spanish Places

| PLACE | SACKED | ATTEMPTED | THREATENED |
|---|---|---|---|
| Acapulco, Mexico | ——— | ——— | 1685 |
| Alvarado, Mexico | 1676 (or 1677) | ——— | ——— |
| Apalache, Florida | 1677, 1682, 1684 | ——— | ——— |
| Arica, Chile | ——— | 1681 | 1680 |
| Campeche, Mexico | 1678, 1685 | ——— | ——— |
| Chepó, Darien | ——— | 1675 | ——— |
| Cotuí, Hispaniola | 1676 | ——— | ——— |
| Cumaná, Venezuela | 1681 | ——— | ——— |
| Gibraltar, Venezuela | 1678 | ——— | ——— |
| Granada, Nicaragua | 1686 | ——— | ——— |
| Guayaquil, Peru | 1684 | ——— | 1684 |
| Honduras, Port of | 1679 | ——— | ——— |
| Huasco, Chile | 1681 | ——— | ——— |
| Ilo, Peru | 1680, 1681 | ——— | ——— |
| La Guayra, Venezuela | 1680 | ——— | ——— |
| La Serena, Chile | 1680 | ——— | ——— |
| Leon, Nicaragua | 1685 | ——— | ——— |

| PLACE | SACKED | ATTEMPTED | THREATENED |
|---|---|---|---|
| Maracaibo, Venezuela | 1678 | ——— | ——— |
| Margarita, Venezuela | 1678 | ——— | ——— |
| Mérida, Mexico | ——— | 1685 | ——— |
| Mérida, Venezuela | ——— | 1678 | ——— |
| Paita, Peru | 1684 | ——— | 1681 |
| Portobello, Darien | 1680 | ——— | ——— |
| Pueblo Nuevo, Nicaragua | 1685 | 1680 | ——— |
| Puerto Principe, Cuba | 1679 | ——— | ——— |
| Realejo, Nicaragua | 1685 | ——— | 1684 |
| Río de la Hacha, Venezuela | 1681 | ——— | ——— |
| St. Augustine, Florida | 1683, 1686 | ——— | ——— |
| San Juan, Florida | 1683 | ——— | ——— |
| San Tomás, Venezuela | 1678 | ——— | ——— |
| Santa Maria, Darien | 1680, 1684 | ——— | ——— |
| Santa Maria, Florida | 1683 | ——— | ——— |
| Santa Marta, Venezuela | 1677, 1679 | ——— | ——— |
| Santiago de Cuba | ——— | 1678 | ——— |
| Segovia, Nicaragua | 1676 | ——— | 1688 |
| Tampico, Mexico | 1683, 1684 | ——— | ——— |
| Tihosuco, Mexico | 1686 | ——— | ——— |
| Trinidad (island of) | 1678 | ——— | ——— |
| Trujillo, Honduras | 1678 | ——— | ——— |
| Trujillo, Venezuela | 1678 | ——— | ——— |
| Valladolid, Mexico | ——— | ——— | 1686 |
| Veracruz, Mexico | 1683 | ——— | ——— |
| Xampolol, Mexico | ——— | 1685 | ——— |

To this list can probably be added Villa de Mosa, Mexico (attempted once and sacked twice, at least); Estapo, Mexico (attempted), and doubtless others.

## Spanish Attacks on English and French Places

| PLACE | SACKED | ATTEMPTED | THREATENED |
|---|---|---|---|
| Laguna de Terminos | 1680 | ——— | ——— |
| New Providence | 1684 | ——— | ——— |
| Petit Goave | 1687 | ——— | ——— |
| Samana, Hispaniola | 1676 | ——— | ——— |
| Tortola | 1686 | ——— | ——— |

# Appendix H
## New World Exports and Plunder

**Quoted From "A List of Commodities Brought From the Spanish West-Indies Into Europe," From Linaje's *Spanish Rule of Trade*:**

"*P*earls, Emeralds and Amethists; Virgin Silver; Ditto in Pigs; Ditto in Pieces of Eight; Virgin Gold; Ditto in Doblones [doubloons]; Cochinilla of several sorts [cochineal]; Grana Silvestre or wild [wild cochineal]; Ditto of Campeche; Indigo; Annatto [also achiote, otta, roucou: a red dye]; Logwood; Brasilette [Brasilwood, a red dyewood]; Nicaragua Wood [a red dyewood]; Fustick [a yellow dyewood]; Lignum Vitae [a dense wood]; Sugars; Ginger; Cacao; Bainillas [vanilla]; Cotton; Red Wooll; Tobacco in Roll; Ditto in Snuff; Hides raw; Ditto Tann'd; Ambergreese gray [from the sperm whale, a waxy substance found ashore or upon the sea, used in perfumery, gray ambergris was older, black was fresh]; Ditto black; Bezoar [ovoid calculus found in the digestive organs of various animals, especially ruminants, used for medicine and magic]; Balsam of Peru [from the *Myroxylon balsamum*]; Ditto of Tolu [from the *Myroxylon toluifera*]; Cortex Peru, or Jesuits Bark [cinchona bark, used to treat malaria]; Jallap; Mechoacan; Sarsaparilla; Sassafras; Tamarinds [a fruit]; Cassia [a bark related to cinnamon]; [Tortoiseshell]."

**Jamaican Exports, Quoted From Anonymous, *The Present State of Jamaica*:**

"Cacao; Sugar; Pimento [Allspice]; Cotton; Hides; Ginger; Tobacco; Tortoise Shell; Indigo; Fustick; Brazilletto [Brasilwood, a red dyewood]; Lignum Vitae; Granadilla [a fruit]; Ebony; Various Gums; Achiote."

**Other Jamaican Exports via Imports or Plunder, From Miscellaneous Sources:**

Logwood, Sarsaparilla, China [China root].

255

## Quoted From "Return of Imports From the American Colonies to London," October 1–November 1, 1681, *CSP 1681–1685*, no. 279:

"White Sugar [refined muscovado]; Brown Sugar [muscovado]; Ginger; Molasses; Aloes; Casticorum [probably *castoreum*, from the beaver, for medicine and perfume]; Indigo; Annatto; Tobacco; Cow Hides; Cat Skins; Buff Hides [possibly buffalo hides, or buff leather, a soft tanned leather used in military uniforms, "buff coats," for example]; Bearskins; Vizer Skins [possibly beaver skins]; Tortoise Shell; Elephants' Teeth [ivory via slavers from Africa]; Old Shruff [old brass or copper]; Cacao; Logwood; Brazelette [Brasilwood, a red dyewood]; Pimento; Fustic; Nicaragua Wood; Lignum Vitae; Hand Baskets; Bast Hats [hats made of various vegetable fiber such as palmetto]; Aqua Vitae [probably Rum]; Lime Juice; Cotton Wool."

### Various South Sea Plunder, 1681–1685, Listed in Various Journals

Pieces-of-eight; Gold dust; Pearls and jewels; Silver vessels; Church plate with silk hangings; Gilded ruby eagle with emeralds for eyes; Slaves; Spanish pilot books; Spanish letters and official documents; Annatto, or *otta*; Cochineal; Silvester (wild cochineal); Indigo; Chocolate; Brandy (in jars); Wine (in jars); Tobacco; Bags of flour; Grain (wheat, barley); Bread; "Jerke porke"; Hogs; Fowl and poultry; Salt beef; Mutton; Sweetmeats; "Marmalett" (marmalade, in boxes); Fruit; Sugar; "Cocoa-nut" (cacao) in "packs"; Cheeses; "Indian corn"; "Montego" (*manteca*, lard); Oil (in jars); Salt; Salt-fish; "*Quito*-cloth" (woolen serge and broadcloth from Quito, probably from the wool of the llama and its kin); Raw silks; Indian cloth; "Osnabrigs" (coarse linen cloth); Thread stockings; Linen; "Goat-skins drest"; Leather; Soap; Pitch; Rigging; Timber; Earthenware; Iron.

### A List of Plunder From *la Trompeuse*, Commanded by Jean Hamlin, Off-loaded at St. Thomas in 1683, Quoted From *Captain Carlisle's Adventures*, From Ayers:

"A very large Chest of Gold-Dust; 150 Piggs of Silver; 200 Baggs of Coined Money, besides Plate; Jewels; Elephants-Teeth; Other valuable Goods and Commodities."

### Colonial Imports

We cannot forget the goods exported to the New World from Flanders, Holland, England, France, Hamburg, Italy, Portugal, and Old Spain, via the ships of the colonial powers—everything from cloth to ironware to East Indian spices, and from wine to pins to sailcloth. Slaves were also valuable plunder, and various vessels were valuable as pirate vessels, storeships, prizes to be sold, and even for their ironwork alone, although many were burned or set adrift. At New England and Acadia, dried cod was a common cargo. Naval Stores-tar, pitch, cordage, timber, and masts, not to mention gunpowder and arms-were also valuable.

# Appendix I
## Weights, Measures, and Containers

### General Spanish Measures

*arroba*: twenty-five Spanish pounds (*libras*) dry measure, or three-quarters of a *quintal*; approximately three gallons in liquid measure
*azumbre*: four *quartillos*, approximately a half gallon
*barril* (barrel): six *barrils* equal one *pipa*, approximately half a ton
*carga*: two *fanegas*
*cuartilla*: three-quarters of a *fanega*
*fanega*: approximately one and a half bushels (four pecks or eight gallons) in the British imperial system
*legua*: the Spanish league, equals five thousand *varas*, approximately 2.6 miles
*libra*: the Spanish pound
*palmo de largo*: "large palm," or span, equals one-quarter of a *vara*; approximately eight and a quarter inches
*pie*: the Spanish foot of twelve *pulgadas*, approximately eleven inches
*pipa* (pipe): two *pipas* equal one ton
*pulgada*: the Spanish inch (thumb), approximately twenty-three centimeters
*quartillo*: one-quarter of an *azumbre*
*quintal*: one hundred *libras*; one hundred weight (approximately 101 pounds avoirdupois); four *arrobas*
*toesa*: slightly more than six feet
*tonelada* (ton): equals two *pipas*
*vara*: the Spanish yard of three *pies*, approximately thirty-three inches

### Spanish Measures From Linaje's *Spanish Rule of Trade* and *Norte de la Contratacion*

*arrove* (*arroba*): in liquid, thirty-two pounds
*barrel* (*barril*): fifteen barrels of one hundred weight (*barriles quintaleños*) equal one ton

*butt* (*vota*): five butts equal three tons

*chest* (*caxa*): a chest nine spans (*palmo de largo*) by four spans by three
      spans equals two-thirds of a ton. A chest seven spans by two and a half
      spans by two and a half spans equals one half ton. A chest six spans by
      two spans by two spans equals one quarter ton. Four chests five and a
      half spans by two and a half spans by two and a half spans equal one
      quarter ton.

*cloth*: "Bales of two Cloaths each, six to a Tun, of *French* Canvas six to a Tun"

*hogshead* (*quarto*): four hogsheads equal one ton, except from Santo Domingo
      where they were twice the size

*iron*: "Iron in Sheets 22 Quintals, or hundred weight and a half, to pay as a
      Tun"

*oil*: forty jars of oil equal one ton, one jar equals one-half *arrove* jar

*olives*: forty small barrels of olives equal one ton

*paper*: "3 large Bales of Paper of 60 Reams each" equal one ton

*pipe* (*pipa*): equals twenty-seven *arroves* (*arrobas*) or one half ton

*pitch*: sixteen quintals of pitch equal one ton

*span* (*palmo de largo*): four to the yard, approximately eight and a quarter
      inches

*wine*: forty-six jars of one and a quarter *arrove* equal one ton

## From "An Act for Regulating the Assize of Cask . . ." by the Government of the Colony of Massachusetts in New England, 1687

*butts*: one hundred and twenty-six gallons

*puncheons*: eighty-four gallons

*hogsheads*: sixty-three gallons

*tierces*: forty-two gallons

*barrels*: thirty-one and a half gallons

Listed also in the article were half-barrels, third-barrels, and *firkins* (a
*half-kilderkin*, eight to nine gallons). Casks were made of "sound well-
seasoned timber and free of sap." Coopers set their "distinct brand mark" on
their casks, and persons were appointed from time to time to "gage" (measure) casks to ensure they are properly proportioned.

## General Notes

Indigo, cochineal, and annatto dyes were usually packed in chests; tobacco in
barrels (hogsheads in Virginia); sugar in hogsheads or chests; and chocolate
in bags of approximately fifty pounds. Indigo was also noted packed in casks

and packs, tobacco in packs, and chocolate in *seróns* (hide-wrapped packages) of approximately one hundred pounds and also in barrels. Lime juice and butter were typically packed in firkins and kilderkins or, generally, kegs. Cotton was transported in bags, and grain in sacks, at least along the coast. Among the Spanish, wine, brandy, and oil were stored in jars of seven or eight gallons, and a bark might carry fifteen hundred or two thousand jars stowed together. Mercury, required for silver production, was carefully transported according to Linaje: fifty pounds (half a quintal) of the element were wrapped with a sheepskin and bound with hemp cord, which was fitted into a cask "nailed down." Three of the casks were put in a chest, which was then nailed shut, wrapped with hemp rope, wrapped with "course Mats," and bound again with hemp rope. On each chest was a linen cloth painted with the Spanish arms. Some chests contained only a quintal, and these were bound to Tierra Firma; those containing a quintal and a half were bound for New Spain. In New England, tar was to be shipped only in barrels of thirty gallons, or half-barrels (twenty gallons) or third-barrels (ten gallons). Allspice was often shipped in hogsheads or other barrels, and tortoiseshell in barrels or parcels. Cloth was mentioned in packs, parcels, and chests. Shot was usually shipped in bags or "rundlets" (small casks), and coin in chests or bags or both. In general, English goods were shipped variously in (or as) casks, cases, chests, boxes, bales, bags, bundles, parcels, packs, sacks, and trunks. Merchants of all nations had their own unique mark affixed to each shipping container, often a form of initials.

CREDITS: BREE LITTLE

## Examples of Merchants' Mark

# Appendix J
## A Brief Glossary of Sea Terms

**Battle Language**: to *make the ship ready for engaging* was to prepare the ship for battle. *Closed quarters*, *close quarters*, and *a close fight* referred to the barricading of a vessel in order to defend against a boarding action. In battle, the vessel with the *weather gage* had her adversary to leeward, while the vessel with the *lee gage* had her adversary to windward (see *Directions at Sea* below). To *strike* was to surrender, literally to strike (lower) topsails or colors, or both, as a sign of submission. *Strike amain!* was the usual demand from an enemy to surrender.

**Direction Aboard Ship:** the *bow* was the forward part of a vessel, the *stern* the rear, or *after*, part. *Starboard* was the right side, *larboard* the left when facing forward, although *port* was used instead of larboard when *conning* (giving orders to the helmsman). *Amidships* was the area at or near the center of the vessel. *Fore* meant the forward part of the vessel, or in that direction, and *aft* meant the rear part, or in that direction. *Abaft* meant behind, and *afore* in front of. One went *forward, aft, aloft* (into the masts and rigging), or *below*. To go *astern* was to go *aft*. *Fore and aft* indicated the entire vessel, as did *bow to stern* and *stem to stern*. The *maindeck* or the *gun deck* was the uppermost deck that ran the full length of the vessel. The *forecastle* (pronounced *foc'sl*) was the raised deck at the bow of the vessel (or the area there) and the space beneath. The *quarterdeck* was the first raised deck aft of the mainmast, and the *poop* was the deck above it. The *steerage* was the space beneath the quarterdeck, and the *roundhouse* the space beneath the poop. The *great cabin* was the captain's cabin at the stern, usually beneath the quarterdeck and aft of the steerage. Some large ships had a cabin that extended a few feet above the quarterdeck in front of the roundhouse, called the *carriage*. The *waist* was the open area between the steerage and the forecastle. The *hold* was the main storage area below. The *cook-room* was the location of the *fire hearth*; in later centuries it came to be called the *galley*. The *hawse* was the location at the bow where the *hawseholes* were, through which the anchor cables entered the vessel.

**Direction at Sea**: *windward* was the direction the wind blew from, *leeward* (pronounced *loo'ard*) the direction it blew to. When the wind *veered*, it changed direction. The *lee* was the leeward area adjacent to a vessel. *Astern* was behind the ship; *ahead* was directly forward; *abeam* was to the side; *on the weather quarter* or *on the lee quarter* was the direction forty-five degrees aft, starboard, or larboard; and *on the weather bow* or *on the lee bow* was the direction forty-five degrees forward, starboard, or larboard. *Within board* meant within the rails of the vessel (*aboard* the vessel, in other words), *overboard* was outside the vessel (gone from the vessel into the water, in other words), and *board and board* was used when one vessel was *alongside* another, touching it. To *bear in* or *stand in* was to sail toward something, and to *bear off* or *stand off* was to sail away from it. Something *in the offing* was in the distance toward the open sea. *To stand to the forefoot of a vessel* was to sail in a direction intended to cross its bow. To *tack* was to change direction—from one tack to the other—when sailing *close to the wind*. In other words, if the wind were on the starboard bow, to tack was to turn through the eye of the wind until the wind was on the larboard bow. In general, *tacking* was the means of sailing in the direction of the wind via a zigzag course.

**Fireworks**: a term for *grenades, firepots*, and *stinkpots*. Grenades were made of cast-iron spheres, clay pots, or glass bottles, and were filled with gunpowder. Bottles, especially *case bottles*, were sometimes wrapped or filled with scrap metal, and clay pots sometimes had musket balls embedded in them. Firepots were filled with combustibles, and stinkpots created a noxious smoke. Firepots, stinkpots, and grenades made from clay pots or bottles all had slow matches attached in order to ignite the gunpowder or combustibles when they struck the deck and broke. A *powder chest* was a small chest filled with a powder charge and musket balls or scrap metal, nailed to the deck, and fired with a fuse.

**Great Guns or Cannon**: at sea, cannon were referred to as *great guns* or simply as *guns*. They were mounted on wooden *carriages*, whose wheels were called *trucks*. They were fired with *slow match* (slow-burning cord) wrapped on a *linstock*. A gun was restrained by a *breeching* or *breech rope*, and was *run in* or *run out* by *gun tackles*. A *broadside* was the firing of all the great guns on either side of the vessel. *Chase guns* fired forward or astern: *bow chase* were those in the bow that pointed forward, and *stern chase* were those in the stern and pointed aft. Cannon fired a variety of projectiles, including *round shot* (cannonballs), *chain shot*, *bar shot*, and *canister* and *partridge* (cases or bags of musket balls or scrap metal). The term *grapeshot* appears to be an eighteenth-century term.

**Hull, Fittings, and Machinery**: *burthen* or *burden* was the carrying capacity in tons of a vessel, although the number in itself was not entirely accurate as to the actual capacity of the vessel. *Channels* (from *chainwale*), also called *chains*, were narrow platforms outboard on a vessel, which spread the *shrouds* (the main rigging supporting the lower masts). A *gunwale* (pronounced *gun'l*) was the upper rail that ran fore and aft—in other words, the upper edge of the hull. A *windlass* was a horizontal timber (a winch, in other words) used in small ships and vessels to raise the anchors. A *capstan* was a vertical windlass used to raise the anchors in most ships; *capstan bars* were used to turn the capstan. *Scuppers* were drains along the deck. A *hatch* was a large entry through the deck, a *scuttle* a small one, and *coamings* were the raised timbers around them. *Lights* were windows. Small ships and vessels were steered directly by helmsmen at the *tiller*, while larger ships were steered by a helmsman at the *whipstaff*, a vertical pole that moved the tiller. The *ship's wheel* was not yet invented. The *bittacle* (binnacle) housed the ship's *compass* and a candle to see it by at night.

**Masts**: Aboard a ship, the masts were the *foremast, mainmast*, and *mizzenmast. Topmasts* (*fore-topmast* and so on) were smaller masts *stepped* on the lower, main masts, and above them on some vessels were *topgallant masts* (often pronounced *t'gallant*), although in general the terms mainmast, foremast, and mizzenmast referred to the entire mast—lower masts, topmasts, and topgallant masts. A *pole mast* was a mast with no topmast, even if it carried a topsail. A *made mast* was a lower mast made from more than a single tree. When a mast cracked, it was *sprung*. At the bow was the *bowsprit*, an angled *spar* that often carried a *spritsail* and *sprit topsail. Yards* were tapered timbers to which sails were *bent* (attached). In battle, the fore and main yards were usually *slung* with chain to prevent their halyards being shot through and the yards falling to the deck. *Tops* were round platforms set at the juncture of the lower masts and topmasts: *maintop, foretop, mizzentop*. They were used for posting lookouts and for posting musketeers and grenadiers in battle.

*Rigging*: strictly speaking, there were only thirteen "ropes" aboard a seventeenth-century vessel. The rest of the *rigging* was referred to by names such as *halyards, braces, lifts, clews,* and so forth. *Shrouds* and *stays* supported the masts, and *ratlines* were made of light *line* secured horizontally across the shrouds, so that sailors could go aloft. *Cordage* and *rigging* were the general terms used for a ship's "ropes."

*Sails*: the large lower sails on the fore and mainmasts were called the *foresail* and *mainsail,* or more generally, the *courses.* The *mizzen sail* on a ship was a *lateen*—triangular—sail. Above them were the *topsails,* and above them the *topgallants. Staysails* were fore and aft sails set between the masts, and *studding sails* (pronounced *stuns'ls*) were, in the late seventeenth century, sails set in light winds outboard of the main courses and topsails, and perhaps outboard of the fore courses and topsails as well. A *bonnet* was a sail extension laced as necessary to the courses or lateen mizzen (strictly speaking, the term *course* was used for a main or foresail without a bonnet). *Spritsails* were sails set on the bowsprit.

*Small Arms*: muskets, pistols, and other handheld firearms were called *small arms,* although sometimes the term was extended to edged weapons (pikes, boarding axes, and swords) as well. Muskets and pistols were loaded with *ball* (musket or pistol balls) and often with *shot* (smaller balls similar to buckshot). Common *locks* (ignition mechanisms) included *flintlocks* and *miquelet locks* (each used a flint to create a spark to ignite the powder), and *matchlocks,* which used a length of *slow match* to ignite the charge.

*Swivel Guns*: Small cannon—*guns*—mounted on *yokes* on the rails or in *stanchions* fitted at the *rails,* were called *swivels, swivel guns,* and *patereroes.* They were either cast-iron or *brass* (bronze) muzzle loaders that loaded and fired as did their *great gun* brethren, or they were cast brass or forged (wrought) iron breechloaders with removable chambers that were loaded with a charge of gunpowder (the projectile was inserted at the breech into the barrel). The cast muzzle loaders were stronger guns but were also more expensive to make. The breechloaders, sometimes also called *chambers,* often fired a smaller charge but, if of forged iron, were less expensive to make (anchor smiths or blacksmiths could forge them). With the usual two chambers per gun and a crew of two, a breechloader could be loaded and fired more quickly (three shots per minute). However, they were also more dangerous to fire because hot gases vented backward from the breech where the chamber seated in the barrel.

**Terms Relating to Vessel Types**: a *ship* was a three-masted vessel, and the term commonly referred to a vessel *square-rigged* on the fore and mainmasts, with a *lateen mizzen sail* and a square topsail above it on the mizzen. A vessel rigged with lateen sails was *fore and aft rigged.* A *boat* was a small craft used for utility purposes and was typically small enough to be hoisted aboard a ship, although large *longboats* and *launches* were often towed instead. *A ship was never (nor is today) referred to as a* boat *under any circumstances.*

# *Notes*

## Chapter 1

1. Dampier, *Voyages and Discoveries*, 156.
2. Dampier, *New Voyage*, 137.
3. Calendar of State Papers (*CSP*) *1681–1685*, no. 695. To understand how geography affected piracy on the Spanish Main, see Galvin, *Patterns of Pillage*, an excellent study on the subject.
4. *CSP 1681–1685*, no. 1,065. The French referred to the Spanish Main as *Terre-Firme*, *la coste de Terre-Firme*, the *Côte d'Espagne*, or sometimes *la coste d'Espagne*. The Spanish often referred to it as *Tierra-Firma*. During this period *the Main* was also a term for the open sea itself.
5. Michel le Bris suggests 1676 as the year Exquemelin departs. See Exquemelin, *Flibustiers*, 19. Others suggest 1672.
6. *CSP 1681–1685*, no. 16; Dampier, *Voyages and Discoveries*, 156; Uring, *Voyages and Travels*, 167.
7. Dampier, *Voyages and Discoveries*, 163.
8. *CSP 1681–1685*, no. 102.
9. Anonymous, *Present State*, 16.
10. Dampier, *Voyages and Discoveries*, 159.
11. Uring, *Voyages and Travels*, 241.
12. Atkins, *Voyage to Guinea*, 227.
13. Uring, *Voyages and Travels*, 240–43; Dampier, *Voyages and Discoveries*, 156, 159, 163, 180–83; Atkins, *Voyage to Guinea*, 226–28. In general, see Joseph, "John Coxon," and Joseph, "British Loggers."
14. Uring, *Voyages and Travels*, 241.
15. Dampier, *Voyages and Discoveries*, 163.
16. Joseph, "John Coxon," 74–76.
17. *CSP 1681–1685*, no. 668.
18. Uring, *Voyages and Travels*, 169; Dampier, *Voyages and Discoveries*, 163.

19. Uring, *Voyages and Travels*, 165; Labat, *Voyages aux isles*, 250–51 (author's translation).
20. Little, *Sea Rover's Practice*, 23–40.
21. [Durand], *Frenchman in Virginia*, 94–95.
22. "Le sieur de Pouancey à Monseigneur le marquis de Seigneley," September 25, 1682, French National Archives, Colonies, C9 A rec. 1, extract. Reproduced in *Les Archives de la Flibuste*, http://www.geocities.com/trebutor/archives/D1682/D8209pouancey.html.
23. Ward, *Trip to Jamaica*, 13.
24. Ibid., 9, 16.
25. Gemelli Careri, *Voyage Round the World*, 513.
26. Erauso, *Lieutenant Nun*, 38.
27. Barlow, *Barlow's Journal*, 2:342–43. See also Defoe, *Colonel Jack*, 172, and Defoe, *Moll Flanders*, 86.
28. Exquemelin, *Buccaneers of America* (1684), 45, 45n1.
29. Rogers, *Jouranl*, 228–29.
30. Uring, *Voyages and Travels*, 12–13, 242.
31. Linaje, *Spanish Rule of Trade*, 107–16, 311.
32. Burkholder and Johnson, *Colonial Latin America*, 111–16.
33. Wood, "Captain Wood's Voyage," 67.
34. [Cox], *Voyages and Adventures*, 85; Beeston, "Relation," 170.
35. Rogers, *Cruising Voyage*, 203.
36. Ibid., 204; Exquemelin, *Buccaneers of America* (1684), 25; *CSP 1681–1685*, no. 1,163.
37. Phillips, *Journal of a Voyage*, 214.
38. Dampier, *New Voyage*, 341.
39. *CSP 1681–1685*, no. 1,163, 1,938; Westergaard, *Danish West Indies*, 122; Burnside, *Spirits of the Passage*, 57; Barbot, *Description of the Coasts*, 571; de Lussan, *Journal of a Voyage*, 75, 151; Clayton, "Maritime Trade," 163; Leonard, *Baroque Times*, 47.
40. *CSP 1681–1685*, no. 275.
41. Gemelli Careri, *Voyage Round the World*, 496.
42. Dampier, *Voyages and Discoveries*, 163.
43. Ibid; *CSP 1685–1688*, no. 967.
44. Dampier, *Voyages and Discoveries*, 163.
45. Pitman, *Relation of the Great Sufferings*, 469.
46. Atkins, *Voyage to Guinea*, 226.
47. *CSP 1685–1688*, no. 193.
48. Ibid., no. 67.
49. *CSP 1681–1685*, no. 2,067.

## Chapter 2

1. Dampier, *Voyages and Discoveries*, 140–41.
2. [Aulnoy], *Ingenious Letters of the Lady*, 756.
3. *Merriam-Webster's Collegiate Dictionary*, 11th ed., s.vv. "piragua," "pirogue."
4. For more detail on canoes and periagers, see Little, *Sea Rover's Practice*, 49–52.
5. Funnell, *Voyage Round the World*, 33.
6. Little, *Sea Rover's Practice*, 52, 54–55; Dampier, *New Voyage*, 29; Labat, *Voyages aux isles*, vol. 1:248–50.
7. Daniel, *Histoire de la Milice*, 720–21; Dassie, *L'Architecture Navale*, 9; Guillet, *Arts de l'homme*, 40–41; d'Estrées, "Mémoire," 203n1, 208, in Villette, *Mémoires*; Bruseth and Turner, *Watery Grave*, 67–69; Aubin, *Dictionnaire*, s.vv. "barque," "barque-longue," and "barque en fagot." In the French Navy of the period, a *barque-longue* was also a category of small ship used for coastal transport or lightering duties and was sometimes referred to as a *petite frégate*. La Salle's *La Belle* was not the first *barque-longue* (of the small frigate type) of its name to be lost in the New World—one was lost at anchor at Petit Goave in 1683 during a storm. Also, a suggestion was made in 1680 to ship one of these vessels in pieces (i.e., *en fagot*) to the isles. See d'Estrées, Bruseth, and Aubin.
8. Anderson, "Brigantine," 109–16; Baker, *Colonial Vessels*, 128, 139; Baker, *Sloops*, 72–73; *CSP 1681–1685*, no. 1,126; Dampier, *Voyages and Discoveries*, 141; Daniel, *Histoire de la Milice*, 720–21; Dassie, *L'Architecture Navale*, 9–10; Guillet, *Arts de l'homme*, 40–41, 69, 274, 348; Labat, *Voyages aux isles*, vol. 1:248–51; Little, *Sea Rover's Practice*, 41–56, 228–38; Linaje, *Norte de la Contratacion*, lib. II, 168–69; Linaje, *Rule of Trade*, 271–72; Nance, "Brigantines," 22–24; Moore, "Round-Sterned Ships," 293–97; Nance, "Ketches," 363. Dampier described his ketch as having a foremast, although he was probably simply referring to the forward mast. The snow was rare in the Caribbean until the 1690s. Yachts were most often seen at New York, the Dutch colonies, and St. Thomas.
9. Linaje, *Rule of Trade*, 271–72; Linaje, *Norte de la Contratacion*, lib. II, 168–69.
10. Daniel, *Histoire de la Milice*, 720–21; Dassie, *L'Architecture Navale*, 9–10; Emke, "*Anna Maria*," 6–24; Guillet, *Arts de l'homme*, vol. 3:158–59, 166, 173, 260; Little, *Sea Rover's Practice*, 41–56, 228–38. *Armé en flute* was a term used in the French Navy of the period to indicate a store ship or hospital ship, no matter its hull type.
11. *CSP 1685–1688*, no. 1,449iii.

12. Ringrose,"Captains Sharp," 236; de Lussan, *Journal of a Voyage*, 43.

13. *CSP 1681-1685*, nos. 963, 1,934iv, 1,938; Caruana, *Sea Ordnance*, 113; Exquemelin, *Flibustiers*, 183–84.

14. Ward, *Wooden World*, 13.

15. Dampier, *Voyages and Discoveries*, 282.

16. Cooke, *Voyage to the South Sea*, 31; Temple, *Papers of Thomas Bowery*, 182.

17. Wycherley, *Plain Dealer*, 50 (act 3, sc. 1).

18. Gemelli Careri, *Voyage Round the World*, 459.

19. Dampier, *New Voyage*, 363.

20. Dièreville, *Relation of the Voyage*, 33, 51; Gemelli Careri, *Voyage Round the World*, 472.

21. Teonge, *Diary*, 190.

22. Rogers, *Journal*, 145; Teonge, *Diary*, 44.

23. Everard, *Relation*, 276.

24. Gemelli Careri, *Voyage Round the World*, 458; Sharp,"Captain Sharp's Journal," 10, 15; Shelvocke, *Voyage Around the World*, 303; Ringrose, "Buccaneers of America" (1684), 330; Linaje, *Rule of Trade*, 231.

25. May, *An Account of* Terra Nova, 345.

26. Barbot, *Description of the Coasts*, 575.

27. May, *An Account of* Terra Nova, 349–350; Gemelli Careri, *Voyage Round the World*, 459.

28. Pitman, *Relation of the Great Sufferings*, 456; Rogers, *Journal*, 162; Yonge, *Journal*, 86; Gemelli Careri, *Voyage Round the World*, 459; Fryer, *New Account*, vol. 3:185; *CSP 1681-1684*, no. 1,949vi; Linaje, *Rule of Trade*, 169, 197, 233.

29. May, *An Account of* Terra Nova, 349–350.

30. Phillips, *Journal of a Voyage*, 233.

31. Barbot,"Voyage to *New Calabar*," 462.

32. Navarette, *Travels and Controversies*, 2:356; Teonge, *Diary*, 233.

33. May, *An Account of* Terra Nova, 347; Yonge, *Journal*, 91.

34. May, *An Account of* Terra Nova, 347.

35. Labat, *Voyages aux isles*, 1:21; Ligon, *True and Exact History*, 5.

36. Dampier, *Voyages and Discoveries*, 212.

37. de Lussan, *Journal of a Voyage*, 98, 108.

38. May, *An Account of* Terra Nova, 345.

39. In general see Mountaine, *Seaman's Vade-Mecum*, and Little, *Sea Rover's Practice*.

40. Leyland,"Fighting Merchant," 275.

41. Everard, *Relation*, 259.

42. Dampier, *Voyages and Discoveries*, 141–42.

# Chapter 3

1. *CSP 1681-1685*, no. 1,938.
2. Labat, *Voyages aux isles*, 2:241.
3. Dampier, *Voyages and Discoveries*, 148-49.
4. *CSP 1681-1685*, no. 1,163.
5. *CSP 1675-1676*, no. 520; *CSP 1677-1680*, no. 1,624; *CSP 1681-1688*, no. 1,198; Pitman, *Relation of the Great Sufferings*, 474-76.
6. For more on the profit motive of "wealth by force of arms," see Little, *Sea Rover's Practice*, 23-28.
7. Gemelli Careri, *Voyage Round the World*, 479; Gemelli Careri, *Viaje*, 8; Navarrete, *Travels and Controversies*, vol. 1:36, 39.
8. Gemelli Careri, *Voyage Round the World*, 479, 496, 526.
9. Beeston, "Relation," 170.
10. Navarrete, *Travels and Controversies*, vol. 2:405.
11. Ibid., vol. 2:399-400, 403.
12. Joutel, *Last Voyage*, 189.
13. Ibid., 190.
14. Rogers, *Cruising Voyage*, 203-4.
15. Leonard, *Baroque Times*, 159.
16. Gemelli Careri, *Voyage Round the World*, 538.
17. Navarette, *Travels and Controversies*, vol. 1:34, 38, 39; vol. 2:403-6; [Povey?], "Buccaneers on the Isthmus," 114; Dampier, *New Voyage*, 101; Joutel, *Last Voyage*, 189, 194; Guzman, "Relation," 147; Gemelli Careri, *Voyage Round the World*, 479; Dampier, *Voyages and Discoveries*, 158.
18. Beeston, "Relation," 170.
19. Joutel, *Last Voyage*, 194.
20. Gemelli Careri, *Voyage Round the World*, 481.
21. Dampier, *New Voyage*, 128, 131-32; Duhalde and de Rochefort, "Mémoires," in Margry, *Relations*, 220; Juárez, *Régimen Jurídico*, 75-76, 368-70; Linaje, *Rule of Trade*, 191.
22. Dampier, *New Voyage*, 128, 131-32; Burkholder and Johnson, *Colonial Latin America*, 75.
23. Dampier, *New Voyage*, 128, 131-32.
24. Ibid.; Juárez, *Régimen Jurídico*, 75-76, 368-70; al-Mûsili, *An Arab's Journey*, 89-90; Gemelli Careri, *Voyage Round the World*, 539. In general, see Linaje, *Rule of Trade*, or Linaje, *Norte de la Contratacion*.
25. Labat, *Voyages aux isles*, vol. 1:225; Gemelli Careri, *Voyage Round the World*, 539; Duhalde and de Rochefort, "Mémoires," in Margry, *Relations*, 219-21.
26. See, for example, *CSP 1681-1685*, no. 1,563.
27. Linaje, *Rule of Trade*, 206.

28. *CSP 1685-1688*, nos. 1,406, 1,733.

29. [Aulnoy], *Letters*, 756.

30. Ringrose, "Buccaneers of America," 322.

31. Willughby, *Relation*, 597.

32. [Aulnoy], *Letters*, 735.

33. Beeston, "Relation," 165; Gage, *Travels*, 73.

34. [Aulnoy], *Letters*, 734, 746; Gemelli Careri, *Voyage Round the World*, 496, 500; Joutel, *Last Voyage*, 194; Labat, *Voyage aux isles*, vol. 2:262; Shelvocke, *Voyage Around the World*, 112; Vargas, *By Force of Arms*, 144; Anonymous, *Voyage*, 239.

35. [Aulnoy], *Letters*, 745, 746; de Toledo, *Two Hearts*, 57-59; Willughby, *Relation*, 598.

36. Joutel, *Last Voyage*, 189-90.

37. Gemelli Careri, *Voyage Round the World*, 496.

38. Linaje, *Rule of Trade*, 155.

39. Gemelli Careri, *Voyage Round the World*, 495, 496.

40. Joutel, *Last Voyage*, 189.

41. Willughby, *Relation*, 595. See also Gage, *Travels*, 151-59.

42. Gage, *Travels*, 153.

43. [Aulnoy], *Letters*, 744.

44. Leonard, *Baroque Times*, 159-60. Mescal and tequila (a regional mescal) are distilled from *pulque*.

45. Bakewell, *Silver*, 24.

46. al-Mûsili, *An Arab's Journey*, 34.

47. [Aulnoy], *Letters*, 758; Labat, *Voyages aux isles*, vol. 2:271-72.

48. Leonard, *Baroque Times*, 157-71.

49. Navarette, *Travels and Controversies*, vol. 2:357.

50. Willughby, *Relation*, 598; Anonymous, *Voyage*, 245; Fuentes, *Buried Mirror*, 144-47.

51. Burkholder and Johnson, *Colonial Latin America*, 94; [Aulnoy], *Letters*, 760.

52. [Aulnoy], *Letters*, 754.

53. Vargas, *Remote Beyond Compare*, 130-31.

54. Villete, *Mémoires*, 54.

55. Vargas, *Remote Beyond Compare*, 87.

56. Willughby, *Relation*, 597; La Hontan, *Voyage*, 928.

57. Willughby, *Relation*, 597, 598.

58. See, for example, [Aulnoy], *Letters*, 756.

59. Willughby, *Relation*, 598.

60. Gage, *Travels*, 141.

61. Labat, *Voyages aux isles*, vol. 2:264; [Cleirac], *Us, et coutumes de la mer*, 87.

62. [Aulnoy], *Letters*, 742, 758.

63. Gemelli Careri, *Voyage Round the World*, 496; Joutel, *Last Voyage*, 189.
64. Linaje, *Rule of Trade*, 155.
65. [Aulnoy], *Letters*, 756.
66. Behn, *Rover*, 191 (act 2, sc. 1).
67. Bartolomé Arzáns de Orsúa y Vela, *Historia de la Villa Imperial de Potosí*, quoted in Bakewell, *Silver*, 25.
68. *CSP 1681–1685*, nos. 1,065, 1,163, 1,249.
69. Gemelli Careri, *Voyage Round the World*, 480.
70. Navarette, *Travels and Controversies*, vol. 2:399–400, 403.
71. Whistler, "Extracts," 155–57; Anonymous, *Present State*, 31.
72. *CSP 1681–1685*, no. 1,198.
73. Marley, *Sack of Veracruz*, 18; Crouse, *French Pioneers*, 82; Camus, *L'Île de la Tor-tue*, 33.
74. Chapin, *Privateer Ships*, 246n2; Exquemelin, *Flibustiers*, 165–67 (author's translations); Moreno, *Corsarios*, 39–40, 137–38; Montero, "Acerca de Piratas," 16; Lepers, *Tragique histoire*, 201–2; "M. De Chasteaumorant au Ministre de la Marine," June 23, 1699, in Margry, *Découvertes*, vol. 4:103; Du Casse, "Lettre de M. Ducasse," 1692, in Margry, *Relations*, 301; "Demande de pardon du capitaine Laurens de Graff," January 25, 1685, Archives nationales: CAOM COL-F3 164, f. 401, reproduced in *Les Archives de la Flibuste*, http://www.geocities.com/trebutor/ADF2005/1685/16850125grace.html; "Le sieur de Pouancey à Monseigneur le marquis de Seigneley," September 25, 1682, extract, Archives nationales, Colonies, C9 A rec. 1, reproduced in *Les Archives de la Flibuste*, http://www.geocities.com/trebutor/archives/D1682/D8209pouancey.html. Lepers suggests Breda as de Graff's birthplace. See also chapter 7, note 47.
75. Chapin, *Privateer Ships*, 246n2; Exquemelin, *Flibustiers*, 165–67 (author's translations); Moreno, *Corsarios*, 39–40, 137–38; Montero, "Acerca de Piratas," 16; Lepers, *Tragique histoire*, 201–2; "M. De Chasteaumorant au Ministre de la Marine," June 23, 1699, in Margry, *Découvertes*, vol. 4:103; "Demande de pardon du capitaine Laurens de Graff," January 25, 1685, Archives nationales: CAOM COL-F3 164, f. 401, reproduced in *Les Archives de la Flibuste*, http://www.geocities.com/trebutor/ADF2005/1685/16850125grace.html; "Le sieur de Pouancey à Monseigneur le marquis de Seigneley," September 25, 1682, extract, Archives nationales, Colonies, C9 A rec. 1, reproduced in *Les Archives de la Flibuste*, http://www.geocities.com/trebutor/archives/D1682/D8209pouancey.html.

# Chapter 4

1. Dampier, *Voyages and Discoveries*, 193.
2. Ibid., 47.

3. Camus, "*L'Île de la Tortue*," 27–36.

4. Exquemelin, *Flibustiers*, 66; Exquemelin, *Buccaneers of America* (1684), 45; Labat, *Memoirs*, 176–77; Uring, *Voyages and Travels*, 143; Rogers, *Cruising Voyage*, 199; [Cox], *Adventures by Sea*, 22; [Povey?], "Buccaneers on the Isthmus," 97; Gage, *Travels*, 223, 334; Gemelli Careri, *Voyage Round the World*, 468; *Cassell's French Dictionary*, s.vv. "boucan," "boucaner"; *Merriam-Webster's Collegiate Dictionary*, 11th ed., and *Oxford English Dictionary*, 2nd ed., s.vv. "buccaneer," "jerky," "bacon."

5. Exquemelin, *Buccaneers of America* (1678), 44–45; Exquemelin, *Flibustiers*, 66–67; Labat, *Voyages aux isles*, vol. 2:205–7, 233, 256–57.

6. Exquemelin, *Buccaneers of America* (1678), 48; Labat, *Nouveau voyage*, vol. 5:204–5.

7. Exquemelin, *Flibustiers*, 33, 67; Exquemelin, *Buccaneers of America* (1678), 62; Labat, *Voyages aux isles*, vol. 2:256–57; Labat, *Memoirs*, 175; Lepers, *Tragique histoire*, 50.

8. Lepers, *Tragique histoire*, 49, 106–7, 115–16; Labat, *Voyages aux isles*, vol. 2:255; Exquemelin, *Flibustiers*, 70, 84 (author's translation); Exquemelin, *Buccaneers of America* (1678), 46, 48, 53–55, 245.

9. Exquemelin, *Flibustiers*, 67; [Cleirac], *Us, et coutumes*, 87.

10. Exquemelin, *Flibustiers*, 68–69; Labat, *Nouveau voyage*, vol. 5:195.

11. Dampier, *Voyages and Discoveries*, 194.

12. Exquemelin, *Flibustiers*, 68–69.

13. Ibid., 71.

14. Ibid., 68–69; Labat, *Nouveau voyage*, vol. 5:190; Dampier, *Voyages and Discoveries*, 186.

15. Exquemelin, *Buccaneers of America* (1678), 41, 49; Exquemelin, *Flibustiers*, 71; Labat, *Voyages aux isles*, vol. 2:69–72, 233, 255–57; Labat, *Memoirs*, 176–77; Gemilli Careri, *Voyage Round the World*, 535.

16. Exquemelin, *Buccaneers of America* (1678), 48–51.

17. "Déposition de José de Mora, habitant d'Alvarado," June 16, 1651, Mexican archives, translated by and reproduced in *Les Archives de la Flibuste*, http://www.geocities.com/trebutor/archives/D1650/D5106alvarado.html.

18. Exquemelin, *Buccaneers of America* (1678), 48, 62, 115; Exquemelin, *Flibustiers*, 67; Labat, *Voyages aux isles*, vol. 1:290–91; Boudriot, "*Fusil Boucanier*," 24–30; Little, *Sea Rover's Practice*, 57–66; Wells, *Small Arms*, 144–50; Saint-Méry, *Loix*, vol. 1:385, 389. On arrival in the islands and showing their passports, merchants were required to produce their muskets for inspection. Merchants were to be fined one hundred *livres* if the muskets were of poor quality.

19. Anonymous, *Carthagene*, 14; Exquemelin, *Buccaneers of America* (1678), 48, 62; Exquemelin, *Flibustiers*, 67; Labat, *Voyages aux isles*, vol. 1:290–

291; Lepers, *Tragique histoire*, 49; Little, *Sea Rover's Practice*, 57–66. At seventy-five yards all muskets shot a pattern significantly larger than a silver dollar; even perfect aim and conditions cannot guarantee a hit on a target this small.

20. Labat, *Voyages aux isles*, vol. 1:290–91; Exquemelin, *Buccaneers of America* (1678), 115.

21. Exquemelin, *Buccaneers of America* (1678), 59–60, 109–10; Exquemelin, *Flibustiers*, 74; Rogers, *Journal*, 228–29.

22. de Lussan, *Flibustiers*, 51; Margry, *Découvertes*, vol. 2:488; Minet, "Journal," 89; *Le Dictionnaire de l'Académie Françoise*, 1st ed., 1694, s.vv. "chassemarée," "galet," "passe par tout"; Guillet, *Arts de l'homme*, vol. 3:70, s.v. "brise."

23. *CSP 1681–1685*, no. 1,216i.

24. Lepers, *Tragique histoire*, 52 (author's translation). See also Exquemelin, *Flibustiers*, 95–96, 106, 116, 147–51, 303–15; Exquemelin, *Buccaneers of America* (1678), 64, 66.

25. Lepers, *Tragique histoire*, 90–91, 212; Exquemelin, *Flibustiers*, 53, 92; *G. H. C. Bulletin* 12, January 1990, 96, 97, and *G. H. C. Bulletin* 78, January 1996, 1527, *Généalogie et Histoire de la Caraïbe*, accessible at www.ghcariabe.org. In French, the boucanier's threat to his fiancée is a pun: *manquer* means both to miss (as in miss a target), as well as to be unfaithful. He suggests to her that if she misses (is unfaithful to) him, his musket will not miss her.

26. Vargas, *By Force of Arms*, 144.

27. [Povey?], "Buccaneers on the Isthmus," 108.

28. Exquemelin, *Flibustiers*, 75; Navarrete, *Travels and Controversies*, vol. 2: 399–400; Lepers, *Tragique histoire*, 57–63.

29. Lepers, *Tragique histoire*, 57–63; Saint-Méry, *Description*, vol. 2:89.

30. Exquemelin, *Buccaneers of America* (1678), 62; [Cox], *Adventures*, 36, 40, 56. Some researchers have suggested that cartridges were made up only immediately prior to use in order to prevent tropical humidity from spoiling the powder, but period documents dispute this, as do the author's tests with corned black powder exposed directly for several weeks to conditions of high heat, humidity, and dampness. Research into and re-creation of period gunpowders at the Middelaldercentret (Medieval Center), Nykøbing Falster, Denmark, suggest similar results. Jens Christiansen, personal communication to the author, May 13, 2007.

31. Margry, *Découvertes*, vol. 2: 499–500; Camus, "*L'Île de la Tortue*," 57.

32. Exquemelin, *Flibustiers*, 66.

33. Dampier, *Voyages and Discoveries*, 192; Exquemelin, *Flibustiers*, 74–75.

34. Exquemelin, *Flibustiers*, 74–75; Whistler, "Extracts," 156.

35. Whistler, "Extracts," 156.

36. Exquemelin, *Histoire*, vol. 2:449; Whistler, "Extracts," 156.
37. Ibid.; Dampier, *New Voyage*, 87; Du Casse, "Lettre de M. Ducasse," 1692, in Margry, Relations, 295.
38. Girard, *Traité*, 101–2, and plates 78–80.
39. Whistler, "Extracts," 156.
40. Exquemelin, *Flibustiers*, 55, 74, 76–77; Exquemelin, *Buccaneers of America* (1684), 202; Exquemelin, *Buccaneers of America* (1678); Labat, *Voyages aux isles*, vol. 2:213. In general, see Butel, *Les Caraïbes*.
41. Whistler, "Extracts," 156.
42. Ringrose, "Buccaneers of America," 322; Beeston, "Relation," 170; Lepers, *Tragique histoire*, 152; Guzman, "Relation," 152–53.
43. [Povey?], "Buccaneers on the Isthmus," 102.
44. Some have suggested that *flibustier* derived from *flibot* (flyboat), a light vessel used by sea rovers of the early seventeenth century. See Saint-Méry, *Description*, xviii, and Anonymous, "Horrors," 349 and note. The *Oxford English Dictionary* derives *flibustier* from the Dutch *vryjbuiter*. See OED, 2nd ed., s.vv. "filibuster," "freebooter."
45. Exquemelin, *Buccaneers of America* (1678), 27, 57.
46. In general see Lunsford, *Piracy*; Snelders, *Devil's Anarchy*; and Vrijman, *Zeer Aenmerkelijke*.
47. Labat, *Voyages aux isles*, vol. 1:23–24.
48. de Lussan, *Flibustiers*, 84.
49. "Memoire de l'Île de la Tortue," in Camus, 119; "Mémoire, envoyé par le sieur Bellinzani, sur les boucaniers. . . ," May 1677, Archives nationales, CAOM COL-C9B 1, reprinted in *Les Archives de la Flibuste*, http://www.geocities.com/trebutor/ADF2005/1672/16770504pouancey.html; *CSP 1681–1685*, no. 668.
50. *CSP 1681–1685*, no. 668.
51. Camus, *L'Île de la Tortue*, 27–36.
52. See, for example, the sampling of Spanish interrogations of pirates in Moreno, *Corsarios*, 148–50. See also CSP 1677–1680, nos. 2, 1,360, 1,425.
53. Ibid.
54. Dampier, *New Voyage*, 100; Exquemelin, *Flibustiers*, 55.
55. Whistler, "Extracts," 155–61. The ingestion of urine actually increases de-hydration, but perhaps the sense of liquid, of thirst-quenching, was sufficient psychologically to get these soldiers to their feet.
56. Dampier, *New Voyage*, 155.
57. [Cox], *Adventures*, 70.
58. Anonymous, *Ordonnance*, 188–89.
59. Dampier, *New Voyage*, 40; Senior, *Nation of Pirates*, 30–32.
60. Lepers, *Tragique histoire*, 51.
61. Crouse, *French Struggle*, 132.

62. Exquemelin, *Flibustiers*, 322; de Lussan, *Voyage into the South Seas*, 135–36; Dampier, *New Voyage*, 11.

63. Exquemelin, *Flibustiers*, 91.

64. "M. de Pouancey [au comte d'Estrées]," April 1, 1677, Archives nationales, Colonies, C9 A rec. 1, reprinted in *Les Archives de la Flibuste*, http://members.tripod.com/diable_volant/archives/D1670/D7704pouancey.html (author's translation).

65. Exquemelin, *Buccaneers of America* (1678), 67.

66. Anonymous, *Carthagene*, 17.

67. Dampier, *New Voyage*, 120.

68. Navarrete, *Travels and Controversies*, vol. 2:403, and note 3.

69. Exquemelin, *Buccaneers of America* (1678), 40–41; Labat, *Nouveau voyage*, vol. 5:192–94.

70. Camus, *L'Île de la Tortue*, 57, 119; Crouse, *French Struggle*, 134; Exquemelin, *Buccaneers of America* (1678), 45.

71. Exquemelin, *Flibustiers*, 89, 92.

72. Paraphrased from "Le sieur de Pouancey à Monseigneur le marquis de Seigneley," September 25, 1682, extract, Archives nationales, Colonies, C9 A rec. 1, reproduced in *Les Archives de la Flibuste*, http://www.geocities.com/trebutor/archives/D1682/D8209pouancey.html.

73. Camus, *L'Île de la Tortue*, 83, 85.

## Chapter 5

1. Anonymous, *Carthagene*, 9; Dampier, *Voyages and Discoveries*, 132; Barbot, *Description of the Coasts*, 574.

2. Forbin, *Mémoires*, 49.

3. Joutel, *Last Voyage*, 9.

4. Ibid., 9–10.

5. Anonymous, *Carthagene*, 14–15.

6. Moreno, *Corsarios*, 148.

7. Kricher, *Neotropical*, 266–67.

8. Labat, *Memoirs*, 78–79; al-Mûsili, *An Arab's Journey*, 92.

9. Dampier, *Voyages and Discoveries*, 212.

10. Coxere, *Adventures*, 34; Lyde, *True and Exact*, 503; Barrato, "Diary," 195.

11. Dampier, *Voyages and Discoveries*, 138.

12. Hutchinson, *Treatise*, 297.

13. [Povey?], "Buccaneers on the Isthmus," 88; Fryer, *East India*, vol. 1:55.

14. Exquemelin, *Flibustiers*, 89; Dampier, *New Voyage*, 88–89.

15. Labat, *Voyages aux isles*, vol. 2:419; Little, *Sea Rover's Practice*, 87–88.

16. Joutel, *Last Voyage*, 110, 117; Dièreville, *Relation of the Voyage*, 169–71,

296–297; Barroto, *Diary*, 180; Anonymous, *Voyage*, 238; Wafer, *Isthmus*, 22; Dampier, *New Voyage*, 344.

17. Wycherley, *Plain Dealer*, 28 (act 2, sc. 1).

18. Senior, *Pirates*, 37; Exquemelin, *Flibustiers*, 176 (author's translation).

19. Forbin, *Mémoires*, 48.

20. Ibid.

21. Anonymous, *Carthagene*, 13–14.

22. Coxere, *Adventures*, 40.

23. Dampier referred to Petit Goave as "Pettit Guavos" and "Petit Guavres."

24. "Mémoire, envoyé par le sieur Bellinzani, sur les boucaniers . . . ," May 1677, Archives nationales, CAOM COL-C9B 1, reprinted in *Les Archives de la Flibuste*, http://www.geocities.com/trebutor/ADF2005/1672/16770504pouancey.html.

25. Minet, "Journal," 88. See also Labat, *Memoirs*, 88.

26. Labat, *Voyages aux isles*, vol. 2:233; Phillips, *Journal*, 215; Dampier, *New Voyage*, 205; Exquemelin, *Buccaneers of America* (1684), 44–45; Saint-Méry, *Description*, vol. 2:540.

27. *CSP 1681–1685*, no. 668; Moitt, *Women and Slavery*, 25; Chapin, *Privateer Ships*, 214, 274; Crouse, *French Struggle*, 133–34.

28. Anonymous, "Horrors of San Domingue," 360. Crouse, *French Struggle*, 133, suggested that only the original fifty were ever sent.

29. *CSP 1685–1688*, no. 1,356, 1,382; Gemelli Careri, *Voyage Round the World*, 540; Phillips, *Journal*, 179.

30. Du Casse, "Lettre de M. Ducasse," 1692, in Margry, *Relations*, 295. Labat, *Nouveau voyage*, 191; Labat, *Voyages aux isles*, 245; Labat, *Memoirs*, 165.

31. Dampier, *New Voyage*, 40; "Brevet de naturalité pour le nommé Laurens de Graff et sa femme," August 15, 1685, Archives nationales: CAOM COL-B 11, ff. 193–194, reprinted in *Les Archives de la Flibuste*, http://www.geocities.com/trebutor/ADF2005/1685/16850805naturalite.html.

32. Crouse, *French Struggle*, 141.

33. Saint-Méry, *Description*, vol. 2:538; Saint-Remy, *Mémoires*, 279; Little, *Sea Rover's Practice*, 252.

34. Lepers, *Tragique histoire*, 115–16; Saint-Méry, *Description*, vol. 1:298; "M. de Pouancey [au comte d'Estrées]," April 1, 1677, Archives nationales, Colonies, C9 A rec. 1, reprinted in *Les Archives de la Flibuste*, http://members.tripod.com/diable_volant/archives/D1670/D7704pouancey.html.

35. Margry, *Découvertes*, vol. 4:498–500 (author's translation).

36. Joutel, *Last Voyage*, 7; Camus, *L'I le de la tortue*; 85–86.

37. Dampier, *New Voyage*, 47; Saint-Méry, *Description*, vol. 2:538.

38. Gasser, "Mystérieuses," 225. Estimates ranged from one thousand in 1677 to three thousand in the mid-1680s.

39. Dampier, *New Voyage*, 136.
40. Cowley, *Cowley's Voyage*, 2; [Povey?], "Buccaneers on the Isthmus," 132.
41. Exquemelin, *Flibustiers*, 107.
42. *CSP 1685-1688*, nos. 1,161, 1,449.
43. *CSP 1685-1688*, no. 1,555.
44. Zahedieh, "Trade, Plunder," 216; *CSP 1677-1680*, no. 375; May, *An Account of* Terra Nova, 345.
45. Rogers, *Journal*, 225-27; Anonymous, *Present State*, 11-12; Barlow, *Journal*, 321; Pawson, *Port Royal*, 52, 53, 111.
46. Ward, *Trip to Jamaica*, 13; Whistler, "Extracts," 146; Rogers, *Journal*, 228-29.
47. Rogers, *Journal*, 226-29; Ward, *Trip to Jamaica*, 16; *CSP 1685-1688*, no. 1,382; Pawson, *Port Royal*, 160-61, 232.
48. Exquemelin, *Flibustiers*, 178-79.
49. Rogers, *Journal*, 226; Barlow, *Journal*, vol. 1:313-14, 328, 345; May, *An Account of* Terra Nova, 345; Anonymous, *Present State*, 16; *CSP 1681-1685*, no. 963; Pawson, *Port Royal*, 129, 159-60, 223-31.
50. *CSP 1681-1685*, no. 1,759.
51. Westergaard, *Danish West Indies*, 46, 48-49, 53-55, 56, 285; *CSP 1681-1685*, nos. 1,471-1,474, 1,535i, 1,597, 1,947i, 1,759, 1,909.
52. [Povey?], "Buccaneers on the Isthmus," 132; Westergaard, *Danish West Indies*, 121-22.
53. Labat, *Memoirs*, 200-4.
54. *CSP 1681-1685*, no. 1,474, 1,168, 1,537; Westergaard, *Danish West Indies*, 41.
55. Ibid.
56. *CSP 1681-1685*, nos. 1,509, 1,540, 1,590i; Pitman, "Relation," 464.
57. Ibid.
58. Pitman, *Relation*, 464-65; *CSP 1685-1688*, no. 1,718.
59. Hubbard, *Swords, Ships & Sugar*, 55-56, 79, 85, 86; Barlow, *Journal*, vol. 2:330.
60. *CSP 1685-1688*, no. 1,356.
61. Newe, "Letters," 185.
62. *CSP 1681-1685*, nos. 1,299, 1,563; *CSP 1685-1688*, nos. 639, 1,161, 1,449iv, 1,555; Dampier, *New Voyage*, 55; Gasser, "Mystérieuses," 225.
63. Ward, *Trip to Holland*, 7, 8.
64. de Lussan, *Journal of a Voyage*, 47-48.
65. Lunsford, *Piracy*, 146; Dampier, *New Voyage*, 40.
66. *CSP 1681-1685*, nos. 2,008, 2,042.
67. *CSP 1681-1685*, no. 1,249.
68. *CSP 1681-1685*, no. 1,854; Pitman, "Relation," 474.

69. [Povey?], "Buccaneers on the Isthmus," 102–103; Ringrose, "Buccaneers of America," 331.

70. The attack on Alvarado may have occurred in early 1677.

# Chapter 6

1. Exquemelin, *Flibustiers*, 133–34, 159–61; Linaje, *Rule of Trade*, 207–9; *CSP 1677–1680*, no. 53; Villette, *Mémoires*, 255; Gage, *Travels*, 193–94; Dampier, *New Voyage*, 160; Duhalde and Rochefort, "Mémoires," 220. A *hourque* (in French also *hourcre*, *houcre*, and *ourcre*) was also a Dutch vessel with a round hull like a flute's, and one or two masts. Vessel types varied by region, period, nationality, and even organization or group using the vessel. The same term may have referred to two different vessel types depending on region and nationality, even in the same period. The etymology or relationship to similar terms, however, is often obvious or likely.

2. Exquemelin, *Buccaneers of America* (1684), 112; Exquemelin, *Flibustiers*, 140 (author's translation).

3. Smith, *Seaman's Grammar*, 49–50.

4. *CSP 1677–1680*, nos. 53, 203, 203i; Exquemelin, *Flibustiers*, 133–34, 158.

5. Dampier, relying on what he heard, suggested "silvester" was made from seeds.

6. *CSP 1681–1685*, no. 167; Zadediah, "Frugal, Prudential," 207.

7. Anonymous, *Present State*, 2; Zadediah, "Frugal, Prudential," 210.

8. al-Mûsili, *An Arab's Journey*, 49.

9. Villette, *Mémoires*, 54.

10. Uring, *Voyages and Travels*, 12–13.

11. Ligon, *Barbados*, 85–96; Rochefort, du Tertre, and de Poincy, *Caribby-Islands*, 194–96; Anonymous, *Present State*, 10; Atkins, *Voyage*, 216; Uring, *Voyages and Travels*, 143.

12. Uring, *Voyages and Travels*, 229–30.

13. Middleton, *Tobacco Coast*, 109–13.

14. Dampier, *New Voyage*, 52.

15. Exquemelin, *Buccaneers of America* (1684), 91.

16. Mather, *Angel of Bethesda*, 302–3, 307, 308.

17. Dampier, *New Voyage*, 159; Rochefort, du Tertre, and de Poincy, *Caribby-Islands*, 197–98.

18. Kricher, *Neotropical*, 187–88; Dampier, *New Voyage*, 51–52; Gage, *Travels*, 153.

19. al-Mûsili, *An Arab's Journey*, 44, 59–61; Burkholder and Johnson, *Colonial Latin America*, 127.

20. Daniel, *Histoire*, 720–21; Guillet, *Arts de l'homme*, vol. 158–59.

21. In general, see Little, *Sea Rover's Practice*.

22. Little, *Sea Rover's Practice*, 153–61; Labat, *Memoirs*, 25–28; Labat, *Voyages aux isles*, vol. 1:99; Duguay-Trouin, *Mémoires*, 21–22. Labat described filibusters firing pistols—*coups de pistolet*—into powder chests to render them largely inert, but cutting the fuses (if exposed) with cutlasses, or *coups de sabre*, seems safer and more effective. The hot gases alone from a discharging pistol might detonate the powder chest. The author has seen similar devices detonated, and their effect is devastating within ten feet. However, the use of a musket loaded with ball and shot at a greater range might be effective—and safer.

23. Exquemelin, *Buccaneers of America* (1699), 84–85; Exquemelin, *Flibustiers*, 139; Exquemelin, *Histoire*, vol. 1:275–76; Camus, *L'Île de la Tortue*, 77; *Dictionnaire de l'Académie Française*, 1st ed., 1694, s.v. "saucisson."

24. Exquemelin, *Flibustiers*, 159–61; *CSP 1681–1685*, nos. 963, 1,163; Gasser, "Mystérieuses," 212–15.

25. *CSP 1685–1688*, nos. 1,449iv, 1,449, 1,705.

26. Villette, *Mémoires*, 255.

27. *CSP 1677–1680*, no. 53.

## Chapter 7

1. *CSP 1677–1680*, nos. 375, 383, 867; Chapin, *Privateer Ships*, 217–18.

2. *CSP 1681–1685*, no. 1,563.

3. *CSP 1677–1680*, nos. 375, 383, 867; Chapin, *Buccaneers*, 217–18.

4. Anonymous, *Present State*, 70–71.

5. Ibid., 71.

6. Evelyn, *Diary*, 486 (entry of September 16, 1685).

7. Atkins, *Voyage*, 208.

8. *CSP 1681–1685*, no. 1,475.

9. Behn, *Oroonoko*, ix, 8.

10. Thomas, *Slave Trade*, 192–95, 201–2, 213–18, 224.

11. *CSP 1681–1685*, no. 712.

12. Zadediah, "Merchants," 590.

13. Labat, *Memoirs*, 59–60.

14. Beeston, "Relation," 167; Zadediah, "Frugal, Prudential," 152.

15. Uring, *Voyages and Travels*, 90–105; Tattersfield, *Forgotten Trade*, 69–80, 123–40; Labat, *Memoirs*, 60; Phillips, *Journal*, 206, 218, and in general; Barbot, "Voyage to *New Calabar*," 465; Dampier, *New Voyage*, 341.

16. Dickenson, *Journal*, 2.

17. Ringrose, "Captains Sharp," 270, 275; Ringrose, "Buccaneers of America," 435.

18. Gemelli Careri, *Voyage Round the World*, 537.

19. Zadediah, "Trade, Plunder," 210.

20. Labat, *Memoirs*, 126.

21. Saint-Méry, *Loix*, vol. 1:414–24.
22. Labat, *Memoirs*, 167.
23. Saint-Méry, *Loix*, vol. 1:203.
24. Labat, *Memoirs*, 127.
25. Saint-Méry, *Loix*, vol. 1:203.
26. Ibid., vol. 1:248.
27. Ibid., vol. 1:414–24.
28. *CSP 1681–1685*, no. 1,805.
29. *CSP 1681–1685*, no. 1,475.
30. Brindenbaugh and Brindenbaugh, *No Peace*, 363; Buisseret, *Historic Jamaica*, 56.
31. Genovese, *Rebellion*, 35, 64; Brindenbaugh and Brindenbaugh, *No Peace*, 361–62.
32. Barlow, *Journal*, vol. 2:314.
33. Lepers, *Tragique histoire*, 124–25; Saint-Méry, *Description*, vol. 1:694.
34. Genovese, *Rebellion*, 38–39.
35. Labat, *Memoirs*, 127.
36. Exquemelin, *Buccaneers of America* (1684), 234.
37. See, for example, Kupperman, *Providence Island*, 338–39.
38. de Lussan, *Freebooters*, 460.
39. Ringrose, "Buccaneers of America," 435–36; *CSP 1681–1685*, no. 872.
40. *CSP 1685–1688*, no. 1,313.
41. Barlow, *Journal*, vol. 2:314.
42. Ringrose, "Captains Sharp," 275, 302, 311; [Cox], *Adventures*, 79; Dampier, *New Voyage*, 114; Exquemelin, *Buccaneers of America* (1678), 179, 180; Moreno, *Corsarios*, 148.
43. Ringrose, "Captains Sharp," 311.
44. Labat, *Memoirs*, 221–22.
45. [Dick], "Brief Account," 282.
46. Chapin, *Privateer Ships*, 201, 201n3.
47. *CSP 1675–1676*, no. 1,178. Captain Francis may have been the Spaniard Don Francisco. Some researchers state that Captain Laurens was a mulatto escaped slave, apparently based partly on the resemblance of de Graff to *grifo* or *griffe*, words variously indicating in this period the offspring of or descent from an African and a Native American (*mulatto* was the period term for the offspring of a black and a white, and often for those of any mixed African heritage as well), and partly on the existence of a Spanish mulatto pirate named Lorenzo Jácome (Weddle, *Spanish Sea*, 399; Moreno, *Corsarios*, 38–39). While intriguing, the argument is also highly speculative and unsupported by numerous documentary sources. The author has seen no published accounts that cite primary sources in support of the thesis that he was a mulatto or an escaped slave, and has seen no

description of Laurens as a mulatto prior to a few nineteenth-century Mexican histories that identify him as the mulatto Lorenzo Jácome. Moreno (*Corsarios*, 38–39) identifies Lorenzo Jácome as a *tabas-queño* who attacked Zinzantum in 1652, and notes that both Jácome and an eighteenth-century individual (both called Lorencillo) have been confused with Laurens by a few historians. None of the French, English, and Spanish records and accounts of the period the author has reviewed, including various official correspondence associated with Laurens's consideration of English citizenship and of his French naturalization, nor eye-witness accounts describe Laurens as a mulatto or former slave. In 1682, for example, Governor Pouançay, who was personally acquainted with Laurens, described him simply as a Dutchman from Doort (Dordrecht) in the Netherlands. Likewise, Governor Du Casse, who also knew Laurens, described him in a letter in 1692 as a "Dutch foreigner." Governor Lynch of Jamaica described him as a "Dutch pirate." Laurens's naturalization papers describe him as a Dutchman from Dordrecht. Exquemelin, who returned to Saint Domingue as part of the French expedition against Cartagena in 1697 (and possibly returned in earlier years) and may have met Laurens, described Laurens during his lifetime (1699; the author has not examined earlier editions) as a blond Dutchman, although this description in itself is certainly not an absolute indicator of ethnicity. Indeed, Laurens's consistent quarter and mercy toward his Spanish enemies are not what one would expect of a man who had been worked as their slave. Captain Diego, the escaped slave from Havana, would murder the native Spaniards among his prisoners, for example. *Graff* (modern spelling *graaf*) is a common Dutch word meaning *earl*, from which one of de Graff's Spanish nicknames, *el conde* (the count), surely derived (Moreno, *Corsarios*, 39–40). Some suggest that Laurens's status as an escaped slave was omitted from accounts, and his description altered in them, in order to avoid inciting slave rebellions. However, this argument, among other weaknesses, fails to account for such omissions in correspondence and other records not intended for publication.

48. Gage, *Travels*, 314–17, 333.
49. Jameson, *Privateering*, 10n4; Chapin, *Privateer Ships*, 273. According to some historians, there were three seventeenth-century mulatto pirates known as Diego.
50. *CSP 1677–1680*, no. 383; Chapin, *Privateer Ships*, 217–18.

# Chapter 8

1. Dampier, *New Voyage*, 131.
2. Forbin, *Mémoires*, 47.

3. Ringrose, "Buccaneers of America," 330.
4. *CSP 1681-1685*, no. 668.
5. Ibid., no. 769.
6. Zadediah, "Trade, Plunder," 218.
7. *CSP 1681-1685*, no. 1,949.
8. Zadediah, "Merchants," 582.
9. *CSP 1681-1685*, no. 668.
10. Zadediah, "Merchants," 581.
11. *CSP 1681-1685*, no. 769.
12. Ibid., no. 668; Dampier, *New Voyage*, 41; Zadediah, "Merchants," 593.
13. Zadediah, "Merchants," 579-80; Fortune, *Merchants*, 46-47, 64.
14. Zadediah, "Merchants," 574; *CSP 1685-1688*, no. 1,311.
15. Labat, *Memoirs*, 170-73; Labat, *Voyages aux isles*, vol. 2:251-57.
16. Ibid.
17. Dampier, *New Voyage*, 212.
18. Labat, *Memoirs*, 168-69, 74-75; Labat, *Voyages aux isles*, vol. 2:251-67; Labat, *Nouveau voyage*, vol. 5:224-25.
19. Dampier, *Voyages and Discoveries*, 206; Labat, *Nouveau voyage*, vol. 5:224.
20. Labat, *Nouveau voyage*, vol. 5:224-25.
21. Labat, *Memoirs*, 168-69, 174-75; Labat, *Voyages aux isles*, vol. 2:251-67.
22. Uring, *Voyages and Travels*, 113-14.
23. Ibid.
24. Dampier, *New Voyage*, 39; Uring, *Voyages and Travels*, 114.
25. *CSP 1681-1685*, no. 668.
26. Zadediah, "Trade, Plunder," 218.
27. Dampier, *New Voyage*, 52.
28. [M.W.], *Mosqueto*, 286; *CSP 1685-1688*, no. 1,281.
29. Labat, *Memoirs*, 179-99; Labat, *Voyages aux isles*, vol. 2:251-67.
30. *CSP 1677-1680*, no. 1,497.
31. *CSP 1681-1685*, no. 1,938.
32. Zadediah, "Merchants," 585-86.
33. *CSP 1681-1685*, no. 2,042.

# Chapter 9

1. "Le commissaire Jolinet au ministre Colbert [extrait]," December 19, 1678, Archives nationales, Colonies, C8 A rec. 1, fol. 130-131, reproduced in *Les Archives de la Flibuste*, http://us.geocities.com/trebutor/archives/D1670/D7808lemoign.html; "L'intendant Patoulet au ministre Colbert [extrait]," November 2, 1679, Archives nationales, Colonies, C8 A rec. 1, fol. 222-229, reproduced in *Les Archives de la Flibuste*, http://us.geocities.com/trebutor/archives/D1670/D7808lemoign.html.

2. Means, *Spanish Main*, 174–86.
3. *CSP 1681–1685*, nos. 1,845, 1,851; Gasser, "Mystérieuses," 222–24.
4. *CSP 1681–1685*, nos. 1,563, 2,042; Gosse, *Who's Who*, 136–37, 159, 324; Dow, *Pirates*, 27–32. See also *CSP 1685–1688*, nos. 207, 210, 1,405, 1,449, 1,449i, 1,555.
5. Ward, *A Trip to New England*, 5, 7.
6. Means, *Spanish Main*, 173.
7. *CSP 1677–1680*, no. 1,188.
8. *CSP 1681–1683*, no. 1,299.
9. *CSP 1681–1685*, xix.
10. *CSP 1681–1685*, nos. 1,845, 1,851.
11. *CSP 1677–1680*, no. 258; *CSP 1681–1685*, no. 559.
12. Mather, *Wonders*, 14, 67.
13. *CSP 1681–1685*, no. 559.
14. *CSP 1681–1685*, no. 1,589.
15. Ward, *A Trip to New England*, 6.
16. *CSP 1681–1685*, no. 98i.
17. Dow and Edmonds, *Pirates*, 25–27.
18. *Public Records of the Colony of Connecticut (PRCC)*, vol. 3:54.
19. Phillips, *Salem*, 280–83. See also *CSP 1675–1676*, no. 543, 849, 1,067.
20. Ringrose, "Buccaneers of America," 398.
21. *CSP 1681–1685*, nos. 552, 668, 668i. In general, see Webb, *Governors-General*.
22. Little, *Sea Rover's Practice*, 130–31; *Oxford English Dictionary*, 2nd ed., s.v. "amain." From the French *amener*, to lower, and perhaps also phonologically in the sense of "to the main," that is, toward the sea.
23. Jameson, *Privateering and Piracy*, 76–81; Chapin, *Privateer Ships*, 28–30; Apestegui, *Pirates*, 211, 219–20; Bourne, *Red King's Rebellion*, 112; Schultz and Tougias, *King Philip's War*, 42–43; Dow and Edmunds, *Pirates*, 44–53; *PRCC*, vol. 3:318; *CSP 1675–1676*, nos. 821, 1,071; *CSP 1677–1680*, no. 1,083.
24. Jameson, *Privateering and Piracy*, 76–81; Chapin, *Privateer Ships*, 28–30; Apestegui, *Pirates*, 211, 219–20; Bourne, *Red King's Rebellion*, 112; Schultz and Tougias, *King Philip's War*, 42–43; Dow and Edmunds, *Pirates*, 44–53.

## Chapter 10

1. Ringrose, "Buccaneers of America," 398, 407, and in general.
2. de Lussan, *Journal of a Voyage*, 89.
3. Labat, *Memoirs*, 36.
4. Ringrose, "Buccaneers of America," 360.

5. Exquemelin, *Flibustiers*, 94 (author's translation); de Lussan, *Journal of a Voyage*, 127; Labat, *Memoirs*, 221–23.
6. Labat, *Memoirs*, 36, 222.
7. Ibid, 36.
8. Exquemelin, *Flibustiers*, 93.
9. Ward, *Trip to Holland*, 6, 8.
10. Labat, *Memoirs*, 224.
11. Ibid., 59; al-Mûsili, *An Arab's Journey*, 49; Wendell, *Cotton Mather*, 52; Norton, *Devil's Snare*, 18–24.
12. Marley, *Pirates and Engineers*, 51.
13. Saint-Méry, *Loix*, vol. 1:414–24.
14. Cervantes, *Devil*, 35, 37, and in general.
15. Labat, *Memoirs*, 107.
16. See, for example, Gage, *Travels*, 278–85; and Anonymous, *Voyage*, 245.
17. Gage, *Travels*, 237.
18. Labat, *Voyages aux isles*, vol. 2:44.
19. Olmos and Paravisini-Gebert, *Creole Religions*, 1–16.
20. Labat, *Voyages aux isles*, vol. 2:44.
21. See, for example, Ward, *London Spy*, 258–65.
22. Robbins, *Encyclopedia of Witchcraft*, 211, 317–19, 456–57.
23. Coxere, *Adventures*, 44–45.
24. See, for example, C. W., *Dæmon of Burton*, 1–5; and Mather, *Wonders*, 89–90.
25. Pepys, *The Shorter Pepys*, 655–56 (entry of August 21, 1666).
26. Ibid., 850–51 (entry of November 29, 1667).
27. Defoe, *Further Adventures*, 189.
28. Fryer, *New Account of East India*, 34.
29. Joutel, *Last Voyage*, 5–6; Gemelli Careri, *Voyage Round the World*, 471.
30. Dièreville, *Relation of the Voyage*, 57.
31. Cowley, *Cowley's Voyage*, 6–7.
32. Ward, *A Trip to New England*, 4.
33. Ibid.
34. Dièreville, *Relation of the Voyage*, 204.

## Chapter 11

1. Dampier, *New Voyage*, 227.
2. Earle, *Wreck of the Almiranta*, 93; Swanson, *Documentation*, 75.
3. Barlow, *Journal*, vol. 2:421.
4. Fryer, *New Account of East India*, vol. 3:30–31.
5. Atkins, *Voyage*, 225.
6. Barlow, *Journal*, vol. 2:333, 315.

7. Ibid., vol. 2:336.

8. [Cox], *Adventures*, 33.

9. Cooke, *Voyage*, vol. 2:29; May, *An Account of* Terra Nova, 350.

10. Norwood, *Voyage to Virginia*, 82.

11. May, *An Account of* Terra Nova, 349; Norwood, *Voyage to Virginia*, 83, 86.

12. Dampier, *New Voyage*, 195.

13. Gasser, "Mystérieuses," 220.

14. Barbot, *Description of the Coasts*, 575–76.

15. Dampier, *Voyages and Discoveries*, 264–65.

16. Barbot, *Description of the Coasts*, 577–78.

17. Ibid.

18. *New World of English Words*, 2nd ed., 1662, s.v. "Tornado"; Dampier, *Voyages and Discoveries*, 280–83.

19. Forbin, *Mémoires*, 47–48.

20. Dampier, *New Voyage*, 304–5.

21. Dampier, *Voyages and Discoveries*, 266–67; May, *An Account of* Terra Nova, 346. Bonnets were in use at least as late as 1689.

22. Dampier, *Voyages and Discoveries*, 266–67.

23. [Cox], *Adventures*, 97.

24. Ibid., 267; Shelvocke, *Voyage Around the World*, 240.

25. Dièreville, *Relation of the Voyage*, 203–4.

26. Barlow, *Journal*, vol. 2:349.

27. Fryer, *New Account*, vol. 1:72.

28. [Povey?], "Buccaneers at Portobello," 85.

29. Everard, "A Relation of Three Years," 270.

30. May, *An Account of* Terra Nova, 345–54.

31. Thacher, "Letter," 62.

32. Forbin, *Mémoires*, 48.

33. Dampier, *New Voyage*, 43–44. For studies in the archaeology of piracy, see Skowronek, *X Marks the Spot*.

34. Swanson, *Documentation*, 22–26.

35. *CSP 1681–1688*, no. 769.

36. Swanson, *Documentation*, 26, 80.

37. "L'intendant Patoulet au ministre Colbert [extrait]," November 2, 1679, Archives nationales, Colonies, C8 A rec. 1, fol. 222–229, reprinted in *Les Archives de la Flibuste*, http://us.geocities.com/trebutor/archives/D1670/D7808lemoign.html.

38. *CSP 1681–1685*, no. 1,590i.

39. *CSP 1681–1685*, no. 552.

40. Swanson, *Documentation*, 80–84.

41. *CSP 1681–1685*, no. 600.

42. Ibid.; Earle, *Wreck of the Almiranta*, 126–27.
43. *CSP 1681–1685*, no. 668i.
44. Phillips, *Journal*, 228.
45. Labat, *Memoirs*, 112–14. Based on the author's experience as a Navy SEAL, these stories, with the possible exception of the attack on the shark (which may be somewhat exaggerated), are all credible.
46. Fryer, *New Account*, vol. 3:177–78.
47. [Walker?], *Voyages and Cruises*, 152.
48. Teonge, *Diary*, 214.
49. Dampier, *New Voyage*, 177; de Lussan, *Journal of a Voyage*, 99–100.
50. [Walker?], *Voyages and Cruises*, 71–72.
51. Dampier, *New Voyage*, 273.
52. Smith, *Seaman's Grammar*, 47.
53. Teonge, *Diary*, 214.
54. Ibid., 65.
55. Joutel, *Last Voyage*, 21.
56. Teonge, *Diary*, 32. Perhaps the victim was hypothermic, with slow, shallow respirations, and the process helped rewarm him.
57. Earle, *Wreck of the Almiranta*, 112–14; Lane, *Pillaging*, 161–63; Peterson, "Reach for the World," 729; *CSP 1681–1685*, no. 600; *U.S. Navy Diving Manual*, 1–3.
58. Author's experience free diving as a Navy SEAL in a dive tower and in open water to sixty feet, as well as free swimming in descents to submarine escape trunks.
59. Earle, *Wreck of the Almiranta*, 111–12.
60. Author's experience free diving as a Navy SEAL in dive towers, open water, and from submarine escape trunks.
61. See Peterson, "Reach for the World," 729.
62. Author's experience as a diver, skin diver, and Navy SEAL.
63. Lane, *Pillaging*, 161–63; Earle, *Wreck of the Almiranta*, 112–14.
64. Earle, *Wreck of the Almiranta*, 112.
65. See Kohshi, "Neurological Diving Accidents."
66. Author's experience as a Navy SEAL.
67. Kohshi, "Neurological Diving Accidents," 57–59. The possibility of decompression sickness brought on by repeated breath-hold dives was first brought to the author's attention by Basic Underwater Demolition/SEAL Dive Phase instructors in 1982, and later by SEAL Diving Supervisor Course instructors.
68. Earle, *Wreck of the Almiranta*, 183, 184.
69. Dampier, *New Voyage*, 107.
70. Exquemelin, *Buccaneers of America* (1684), 113.
71. Phillips, *Journal*, 213; Everard, "A Relation of Three Years," 280–81.

72. Barlow, *Journal*, vol. 2:321–32.
73. Shelvocke, *Voyage Around the World*, 239; Linaje, *Rule of Trade*, 183.
74. [Cox], *Adventures*, 43.
75. Ringrose, "Buccaneers of America," 388. According to Ringrose, the bladder was a horsehide.
76. Dampier, *New Voyage*, 134–35.
77. Labat, *Memoirs*, 205–6.
78. *CSP 1681–1685*, no. 2,067.
79. Ibid., no. 2,067i. This was the wreck of the *Nuestra Señora de Concepción*, whose enormous treasure Phips recovered, and the aforementioned private map referred to it.

## Chapter 12

1. Ringrose, "Buccaneers of America," 297–98.
2. Dampier, *New Voyage*, 15.
3. *CSP 1681–1685*, no. 1,949iii.
4. A few of the more useful period references on sea turtles include Dampier, *New Voyage*, 76–81; Dampier, *New Holland*, 85; Rogers, *Cruising Voyage*, 261–63, 276–77; Cooke, *Voyage to the South Sea*, vol. 1:311–12; Funnell, *Voyage Round the World*, 72–74; Pitman, "Relation," 456–58; Uring, *Voyages and Travels*, 166; Rogers, *Journal*, 162, 230; Yonge, *Journal*, 86; Ashe, *Carolina*, 152–54; Gage, *Travels*, 334; Fryer, *New Account*, 185–86; Rochefort, du Tertre, and de Poincy, *Caribby-Islands*, 133–38 (or the French edition); Ligon, *True and Exact History*, 4, 36–37; and all editions of Exquemelin.
5. Rochefort, du Tertre, and de Poincy, *Caribby-Islands*, 135.
6. Dampier, *New Voyage*, 49, 76–81; Wafer, *Isthmus*, 115; Rogers, *Cruising Voyage*, 276; M.W., *Mosqueto*, 298; Cooke, *Voyage*, vol. 1:311–12; Spotila, *Sea Turtles*, 16.
7. Barlow, *Journal*, vol. 2:315.
8. *CSP 1681–1685*, no. 236; Exquemelin, *Buccaneers of America* (1684), 62.
9. Dampier, *New Voyage*, 79.
10. Ibid.; Funnell, *Voyage Round the World*, 72–74.
11. Yonge, *Journal*, 86.
12. Dampier, *New Voyage*, 79.
13. Fryer, *New Account*, 185–86; Rogers, *Cruising Voyage*, 261.
14. Ligon, *True and Exact History*, 36; Spotila, *Sea Turtles*, 41–42.
15. Pitman, "Relation," 458.
16. Yonge, *Journal*, 86.
17. Dampier, *New Voyage*, 34–35.
18. Cooke, *Voyage*, vol. 1:311–12.

19. Ibid., 79; Rochefort, du Tertre, and de Poincy, *Caribby-Islands*, 135.
20. Cooke, *Voyage*, vol. 1:311-12; Pitman, "Relation," 456.
21. Dampier, *New Voyage*, 76-77; Ashe, *Carolina*, 153.
22. *CSP 1681-1685*, no. 1,949v.
23. Rochefort, du Tertre, and de Poincy, *Caribby-Islands*, 135; Ashe, *Carolina*, 153.
24. Ashe, *Carolina*, 153; Yonge, *Journal*, 86.
25. *CSP 1681-1685*, nos. 963, 1,949iii, 1,949iv.
26. Ibid., no. 1,938.
27. Rogers, *Journal*, 162, 230.
28. Ashe, *Carolina*, 153.
29. Yonge, *Journal*, 86.
30. Labat, *Memoirs*, 241; Rochefort, du Tertre, and de Poincy, *Caribby-Islands*, 135.
30. Dampier, *New Holland*, 85; Gage, *Travels*, 223, 334.
32. Exquemelin, *Buccaneers of America* (1678), 60.
33. Dampier, *New Voyage*, 33-35.
34. Exquemelin, *Buccaneers of America*, 177.
35. Atkins, *Voyage*, 43.
36. Dampier, *New Voyage*, 33-35; Atkins, *Voyage*, 43.
37. Ashe, *Carolina*, 154.
38. Ibid.
39. Reeves, *Marine Mammals*, 485.
40. Dampier, *New Voyage*, 33-35.
41. Reeves, *Marine Mammals*, 482-85.
42. Dampier, *New Voyage*, 32.
43. Ibid., 69; Dampier, *Voyages and Discoveries*, 146.
44. Dampier, *New Voyage*, 32; Reeves, *Marine Mammals*, 69.
45. Dampier, *New Voyage*, 70.
46. Wafer, *Isthmus*, 129-30.
47. *CSP 1675-1676*, no. 971; *CSP 1685-1688*, no. 1,718.

## Chapter 13

1. [Povey?], "Buccaneers at Portobello," 84; [Dick], "Account," 257-58. In general, buccaneers and filibusters did not have to post a bond or other security for good behavior when receiving a commission. See *CSP 1685-1688*, no. 558.
2. [Povey?], "Buccaneers at Portobello," 84-92; [Dick], "Account," 257-59; Wafer, *Isthmus*, 39, 42.
3. Ibid.
4. Ibid.

5. Gage, *Travels*, 212–13; Anonymous, *Voyage*, 244.
6. Fryer, *New Account*, vol. 1:55.
7. Joutel, *Last Voyage*, 46.
8. Radisson, *Explorations*, 20.
9. Ibid., 21.
10. See, for example, Atkins, *Voyage*, 210–14.
11. de Lussan, *Journal of a Voyage*, 145–46.
12. Labat, *Memoirs*, 102–3.
13. See, for example, Lafitau, *Moeurs*.
14. Behn, *Oroonoko*, 3.
15. Gage, *Travels*, 91.
16. See, for example, Malone, *Skulking Way*; and Labat, *Memoirs*, 112.
17. Davis, *Expedition*, 160.
18. Labat, *Memoirs*, 112.
19. Pitman, *Relation of the Great Sufferings*, 459; Jens Christiansen of the Middelaldercentret, Denmark, personal communication with the author, May 13, 2007, relating the results of a shooting exercise between muskets and bows.
20. Labat, *Memoirs*, 111; Jens Christiansen and Peter Vemming Hansen of the Middelaldercentret, Denmark, personal communication with the author, May 13, 2007, relating the results of extensive research into and testing of fire arrows.
21. *CSP 1681–1685*, no. 204.
22. Little, *Sea Rover's Practice*, 57–66; Malone, *Skulking Way*, 21–22; Vargas, *By Force of Arms*, 144; Anonymous, *Voyage*, 239. In the author's tests, musket balls routinely passed through two-inch boards, brush piles, and dense undergrowth, but arrows fired from a bow failed to in all cases. Both arms were shot from twenty yards. The bow had a sixty-five-pound draw, and arrows were tipped with broad steel hunting points.
23. Exquemelin, *Flibustiers*, 148–49.
24. Malone, *Skulking Way*, 22.
25. Labat, *Memoirs*, 110–12.
26. [Povey?], "Buccaneers on the Isthmus," 97; Davis, *Expedition*, 160; Exquemelin, *Flibustiers*, 313; Dampier, *New Voyage*, 184. See also Wells, *Small Arms*, 33–35, and Janclot, "Relation," 78.
27. Exquemelin, *Buccaneers of America* (1684), 187.
28. Ayers, "Chagre," 130.
29. Dampier, *Voyages and Discoveries*, 131.
30. *CSP 1681–1685*, nos. 204, 1,126; Labat, *Memoirs*, 73–75. Similar attacks and reprisals occurred in 1675. See *CSP 1675–1676*, no. 748.
31. Whistler, "Extracts," 148.
32. In general see Beck, *American Indian*.

33. In general see Crane, *Southern Frontier*; Gallay, *Indian Slave Trade*; Steele, *Warpaths*.
34. Steele, *Warpaths*, 57.
35. Dampier, *Voyages and Discoveries*, 213–14.
36. Ibid., 163.
37. Exquemelin, *Buccaneers of America* (1684), 233.
38. Uring, *Voyages and Travels*, 143.
39. Exquemelin, *Buccaneers of America* (1678), 182, 185.
40. [Cox], *Adventures*, 4.
41. Kupperman, *Providence Island*, 97–99.
42. Dampier, *New Voyage*, 15–16. In general see M.W., *Mosqueto*.
43. Dampier, *New Voyage*, 35, 129–31.
44. Davis, *Expedition*, 156–57.
45. Dampier, *New Voyage*, 20.
46. Ibid., 181; Ringrose, "Captains Sharp," 204.
47. Ringrose, "Captains Sharp," 275.
48. Exquemelin, *Flibustiers*, 304–15.

## Chapter 14

1. [Povey?], "Buccaneers on the Isthmus," 106; Ringrose, *Buccaneer's Atlas*, 262.
2. Ringrose, "Buccaneers of America," 445.
3. Smith, *Grammar*, 38.
4. Ward, *London Spy*, 244, 268–69.
5. Ward, *Trip to Jamaica*, 10.
6. Ibid., 9.
7. Smith, *Grammar*, 27.
8. Johnson, *General History*, 202.
9. Ward, *Wooden World*, 98.
10. *CSP 1681–1685*, no. 98i.
11. *Oxford English Dictionary*, 2nd ed., and *Merriam-Webster's Collegiate Dictionary*, 11th ed., s.v. "fuck." The *OED* suggests the word's roots are indeterminate. *Merriam-Webster* suggests Dutch and Swedish links, *fokken* and *fókka*, respectively.
12. Ward, *Wooden World*, 74.
13. Ibid., 75; the author's experience in the U.S. Navy.
14. Ward, *Wooden World*, 77.
15. *CSP 1681–1685*, nos. 1,294, 1,348, 1,502.
16. English Statutes of the Realm, Act of Parliament, "An Act to Prevent and Reform Profane Cursing and Swearing," 21 Jac. I. c. 20.
17. Rogers, *Journal*, 229; Ward, *Jamaica*, 16; Atkins, *Voyage*, 208.

18. Navarette, *Travels and Controversies*, vol. 2:345, 357.
19. Gay, *Polly*, 563 (act 2, sc. 4).
20. Most persons in hazardous professions today, the combat arms of the military, and of the U.S. Navy especially, are plainspoken. Navy SEALs, both officer and enlisted, are particularly so, given their operational environment and naval tradition. For the argument that such language derives instead from the working class and class warfare, see Rediker, *Between the Devil*, 167–69.
21. Shakespeare, *Romeo and Juliet* (Cambridge), act 1, sc. 5; Shakespeare, *The Tempest* (Cambridge), act 1 sc. 1.
22. Sturmy, "Mariner's Magazine," 83.
23. Barbot, *Description of the Coasts*, 575–76. To *shiver* is to shatter, to break into small pieces.
24. [Povey?], "Buccaneers on the Isthmus," 93, 119; Joutel, *Last Voyage*, 141.
25. [Povey?], "Buccaneers on the Isthmus," 120.
26. [Povey?], "Buccaneers on the Isthmus," 119; Exquemelin, *Flibustiers*, 106–7; [Cox], *Adventures*, 80; Ringrose, "Captains Sharp," 194; Ringrose, "Buccaneers of America," 315; Dick, "Account," 276; Wafer, *Isthmus*, 105–11, and in general.

# Chapter 15

1. Sharp, *Journal*, 2.
2. [Povey?], "Buccaneers on the Isthmus," 95.
3. Ringrose, "Buccaneers of America," 300. The device of a hand and sword was used on the Ostend battle ensign.
4. Gerhard, *Pirates*, 144.
5. See for example *CSP 1681–1685*, no. 2,067.
6. de Lussan, *Journal of a Voyage*, 155.
7. Dick, "Brief Account," 265; Ringrose, "Buccaneers of America," 321–25; Sharp, *Journal*, 12–13; [Cox], *Adventures*, 13–14; [Povey?], "Buccaneers on the Isthmus," 99–100.
8. Ibid.
9. Ibid.
10. Ibid.
11. [Cox], *Adventures*, 24.
12. Ringrose, "Buccaneers of America," 358.
13. Sharp, *Journal*, 39.
14. Ringrose, "Buccaneers of America," 358, 366.
15. [Cox], *Adventures*, 24.
16. Dick, "Brief Account," 270.
17. Ringrose, *Buccaneer's Atlas*, 158.

18. Ringrose, "Buccaneers of America," 358–60.
19. de Lussan, *Freebooters*, 425.
20. [Povey?], "Buccaneers on the Isthmus," 124.
21. Ibid.; *CSP 1681–1685*, no. 872.
22. de Lussan, *Journal of a Voyage*, 84, 86, 221.
23. See for example de Lussan, *Journal of a Voyage*, 118–19. In her excellent translation of de Lussan's work, Marguerite Eyer Wilbur mistakenly translated *fusil* as *pistol*. A fusil is a flintlock musket.
24. Dampier, *New Voyage*, 135–36.

## Chapter 16

1. [Povey?], "Buccaneers on the Isthmus," 100.
2. Ibid.
3. [Dick], "Account," 266–67; [Cox], *Adventures*, 14–15; Sharp, *Journal*, 14; [Povey?], "Buccaneers on the Isthmus," 114.
4. Sharp, *Journal*, 14.
5. Ringrose, "Buccaneers of America," 326.
6. Evelyn, *Diary*, 364 (entry of March 24, 1671).
7. Coxere, *Adventures by Sea*, 42; Lyde, *True and Exact*, 503, 505.
8. Dampier, *New Holland*, 125; Cooke, *Voyage*, vol. 2:93; Fryer, *New Account*, vol. 1:58.
9. Doublet, *Mémoires*, 179.
10. See for example Jameson, *Privateering and Piracy*, 456–61.
11. Phillips, *Journal*, 215.
12. See for example Northcote, *Extracts*.
13. Dampier, *Voyages and Discoveries*, 188.
14. Dampier, *New Holland*, 85–86.
15. M. W., *Mosqueto*, 292.
16. Dampier, *New Voyage*, 48; Funnell, *Voyage Round the World*, 72.
17. Funnell, *Voyage Round the World*, 60; Dampier, *New Voyage*, 203.
18. Dampier, *New Voyage*, 173–74.
19. Ibid., 194.
20. Ringrose, "Buccaneers of America," 379.
21. Ibid., 11; Ringrose, "Buccaneers of America," 381.
22. [Cox], *Adventures*, 46; Ringrose, "Buccaneers of America," 299.
23. Dampier, *New Voyage*, 82, 210.
24. Funnell, *Voyage Round the World*, 226.
25. Dampier, *New Holland*, 123.
26. Linaje, *Rule of Trade*, 206.
27. Pitman, *Relation of the Great Sufferings*, 474, 475.
28. de Lussan, *Journal of a Voyage*, 199.

29. Exquemelin, *Flibustiers*, 92; Exquemelin, *Buccaneers of America* (1678), 58; Anonymous, *Carthagene*, 17.
30. See, for example, la Hontan, *Voyage*, 925.
31. Dampier, *New Voyage*, 155.
32. [Povey?], "Buccaneers at Portobello," 88.
33. Dampier, *New Voyage*, 240.

## Chapter 17

1. Exquemelin, *Buccaneers of America* (1684), 74.
2. Doublet, *Mémoires*, 179.
3. Beckles, *White Servitude*, 83.
4. Dampier, *New Holland*, 86; Moitt, *Women and Slavery*, 99-100.
5. Gage, *Travels*, 199.
6. Moitt, *Women and Slavery*, 99.
7. Dunn, *Sugar and Slaves*, 252-56.
8. Gage, *Travels*, 68-70. See also Ligon, *Barbados*, 12-13, 15-17, and Yonge, *Journal*, 87-88, for similar but less prudish descriptions.
9. Fryer, *New Account*, vol. 1:33; Anonymous, *Carthagene*, 13-14.
10. Dampier, *New Voyage*, 365-66.
11. Cowley, *Cowley's Voyage*, 6.
12. Sharp, *Journal*, 52; Ringrose, "Captains Sharp," 279.
13. Laurens, Van Horn, Dampier, Look, Swan, Beare, and Spurre were married men, for example, and at least the first two had families.
14. Hrodej, "La flibuste," 299-300.
15. [Povey?], "Buccaneers on the Isthmus," 120-21; [Cox], *Adventures*, 80. Cox, Dick, and Ringrose did not mention Marquess's infatuation.
16. de Lussan, *Journal of a Voyage*, 217-19.
17. [Aulnoy], *Ingenious Letters*, 743, 745, 748, 754, 758, 759.
18. Fuentes, *Buried Mirror*, 210.
19. Behn, *Rover*, 196 (act 2, sc. 2).
20. Fraser, *Weaker Vessel*, 51.
21. Wycherley, *Country Wife*, 6 (act 1, sc. 1), and note 4.
22. Stone, *Family*, 334.
23. Bloch, *Account*, xiii.
24. Ringrose, "Captains Sharp," 253-54.
25. Ibid.; Ringrose, "Buccaneers of America," 398; Sharp, *Journal*, 46; *CSP 1677-1680*, no. 869. For an extremely speculative view, see Burg, *Sodomy and the Pirate Tradition*. Regarding the paper with names on it, Burg (148) states that it was discovered on Captain Cook, but Ringrose and Sharp were clear that it was found on his servant. Had Captain Cook been discovered with the list of names, none would ever have served under him again.

26. Stone, *Family*, 265–67.
27. Fraser, *Weaker Vessel*, 59.
28. Stone, *Family*, 265–67, 325.
29. Dampier, *New Voyage*, 144; *Merriam-Webster's Collegiate Dictionary*, 11th ed., s.v. "avocado"; Phillips, *Journal of a Voyage*, 221.
30. For example, Wycherley's *Plain Dealer* and *Country Wife*.
31. Dampier, *New Voyage*, 173.

## Chapter 18

1. Uring, *Voyages and Travels*, 148.
2. Dampier, *Voyages and Discoveries*, 209–10.
3. Joutel, *Last Voyage*, 189–91; Gemelli Careri, *Voyage Round the World*, 526–27, 539.
4. de Lussan, *Journal of a Voyage*, 195–96.
5. de Lussan, *Freebooters*, 452–53.
6. Guzman, "Relation," 154.
7. de Lussan, *Freebooters*, 395.
8. de Lussan, *Journal of a Voyage*, 67.
9. Guzman, "Relation," 152.
10. Dampier, *New Voyage*, 169.
11. Guzman, "Relation," 152–53.
12. de Lussan, *Freebooters*, 439; Moreno, *Corsarios*, 40.
13. Beeston, "Relation," 170.
14. Moreno, *Corsarios*, 133.
15. Le sieur de Grammont, "Relation de la prise de Gouaire par Granmont," Archives nationales, Colonies, F# 164, fol. 332, reprinted in *Les Archives de la Flibuste*, http://www.geocities.com/trebutor/archives/D1680/D8008laguayra.html.
16. Moreno, *Corsarios*, 133.
17. Linaje, *Rule of Trade*, 233, 300.
18. Apestegui, *Pirates*, 178.
19. Daniel, *Histoire*, vol. 2:594.
20. This is confirmed not only by period texts, but also by a demonstration provided in October 2005 by a Jamestown reenactor who could load and fire on average in thirteen to sixteen seconds, using a paper cartridge instead of a charger on his bandolier, and simulating the loading of a ball, which, per period practices, was held in his mouth until needed.
21. Daniel, *Histoire*, vol. 2:594; *CSP 1685–1688*, no. 805i.
22. Moreno, *Corsarios*, 133.
23. Whistler, "Extracts," 160–61.
24. *CSP* 1675–1676, no. 525; *CSP* 1677–1680, nos. 403, 1,109, 1,141; *CSP* 1681–1685, nos. 486, 1,919.

25. [Cox], *Adventures*, 41; *CSP 1681-1685*, no. 1,126.

26. Daniel, *Histoire*, vol. 2:594.

27. Little, *Sea Rover's Practice*, 63; Wells, *Small Arms*, 152-53, 155-156; *CSP 1681-1685*, no. 1,126; Labat, *Voyages aux isles*, vol. 2:97.

28. Joutel, *Last Voyage*, 123-24.

29. Pitman, "Relation," 452.

30. de Lussan, *Voyage to the South Sea*, 163, 164-65.

31. *CSP 1681-1688*, no. 1,857.

32. *CSP 1677-1680*, no. 347.

33. Dampier, *Voyages and Discoveries*, 212.

34. Rogers, *Cruising Voyage*, 167 quoting Dampier.

35. Le sieur de Grammont, "Relation de la prise de Gouaire par Granmont," Archives nationales, Colonies, F# 164, fol. 332, reprinted in *Les Archives de la Flibuste*, http://www.geocities.com/trebutor/archives/D1680/D8008laguayra.html.

36. [Cox], *Adventures*, 16, 56. Based on test firings by the author, a load of one musket ball and seven 00 buckshot produced a pattern averaging nine inches in diameter at ten yards and eighteen inches at twenty yards. However, the patterns varied greatly—some were roughly circular, some tall and narrow, some wide and flat.

37. Ayers, "Chagre," 136.

38. Exquemelin, *Buccaneers of America* (1678), 162.

39. Uring, *Voyages and Travels*, 149.

40. de Lussan, *Freebooters*, 399, 452.

41. Exquemelin, *Flibustiers*, 332.

42. "Relation anonyme d'un voyage de Granmont," February 11, 1679, Archives nationales, Colonies, F3 164, fol. 325, reprinted in *Les Archives de la Flibuste*, http://www.geocities.com/trebutor/ADF2005/1672/16790211maracaibo.html.

43. Le sieur de Grammont, "Relation de la prise de Gouaire par Granmont," Archives nationales, Colonies, F# 164, fol. 332, reprinted in *Les Archives de la Flibuste*, http://www.geocities.com/trebutor/archives/D1680/D8008laguayra.html.

44. Dampier, *Voyages and Discoveries*, 158.

45. Exquemelin, *Flibustiers*, 325-31; Apestegui, *Pirates*, 192-93; Moreno, *Corsarios*, 331-66.

46. Dampier, *New Voyage*, 113.

47. de Lussan, *Journal of a Voyage*, 203-10; in general Bernal Ruiz, *Toma del Puerto*.

48. Cooke, *Voyage*, vol. 1:290-92; [Cox], *Voyages*, 54-60, 70; Dagnino, *Correjimiento*, 136-38; Dampier, *New Voyage*, 175-76; [Dick], "Account," 274-75; Little, *Sea Rover's Practice*, 214-17; [Povey?], "Buccaneers on

the Isthmus," 114–15; Ringrose, *Atlas*, 18–19, 214, 216; Ringrose, "Buccaneers of America" (1684), 404–9; Ringrose, "Captains Sharp," 259–62, 265–66, 279; Sharp, "Journal," 47–48; Wafer, *Isthmus*, 121.

49. Ibid.
50. Dampier, *New Voyage*, 52.
51. Dampier, *Voyages and Discoveries*, 210–11.
52. Exquemelin, *Flibustiers*, 162; Ayers, *Van Horn*, 117.
53. Uring, *Voyages and Travels*, 148–49; Marley, *Veracruz*, 28.
54. Ayers, *Van Horn*, 117.
55. Uring, *Voyages and Travels*, 148–49.
56. For period accounts see Exquemelin, *Flibustiers*, and Ayers, *Van Horn*. For modern accounts see Moreno, *Corsarios*, and Marley, *Veracruz*. For filibuster activities in 1683–85, see Gasser's "Mystérieuses."
57. Marley, *Veracruz*, 38–39.
58. Ayers, *Van Horn*, 118; *CSP 1681–1685*, no. 1,163.
59. Moreno, *Corsarios*, 423.
60. Ibid., 225.
61. Ayers, *Van Horn*, 115–20; Exquemelin, *Flibustiers*, 159–64; Moreno, *Corsarios*, 165–54, and in general; Marley, *Veracruz*; "Relation du voyage des flibustiers aux Andoures et Nove Espagne," November 16, 1683, Archives nationales, CHAN MAR-B4 9, fol. 389, reprinted in *Les Archives de la Flibuste*, http://www.geocities.com/trebutor/ADF2005/1680/16831116veracruz.html.
62. Ringrose, "Buccaneers of America," 361.
63. See, for example, [Cox], *Adventures*, 54; and in general Ringrose, "Buccaneers of America."
64. de Lussan, *Journal of a Voyage*, 402.
65. Exquemelin, *Buccaneers of America* (1684), 140, and in general.
66. *CSP 1681–1685*, no. 1,313.
67. See, for example, Robbins, *Encyclopedia of Witchcraft*, 501.

## Chapter 19

1. Exquemelin, *Flibustiers*, 164.
2. Ibid.
3. *CSP 1681–1685*, nos. 963, 1,163.
4. Marley, *Veracruz*, 57–58.
5. Exquemelin, *Flibustiers*, 173.
6. *CSP 1681–1685*, no. 1,163.
7. Ayers, *Van Horn*, 119; al-Mûsili, *An Arab's Journey*, 84.
8. "Relation du voyage de flibustiers aux Andoures et Nove Espagne," November 16, 1683, Archives nationales, CHAN MAR-B4 9, fol. 389, re-

printed in *Les Archives de la Flibuste*, http://www.geocities.com/trebutor/ADF2005/1680/16831116veracruz.html.

9. Exquemelin, *Flibustiers*, 173.
10. See, for example, McBane, *Expert*, and Drake, *Amiable Renegade*.
11. Exquemelin, *Flibustiers*, 164; Ringrose, "Buccaneers of America," 435.
12. Ringrose, "Buccaneers of America," 435.
13. al-Mûsili, *An Arab's Journey*, 84.
14. Snelders, *Anarchy*, 118-20, 152. See also Vrijman, *Reyning*.
15. Sharp, *Journal*, 3; [Povey?], "Buccaneers on the Isthmus," 129.
16. Exquemelin, *Flibustiers*, 331.
17. Forbin, *Mémoires*, 31-32, 40.
18. Phillips, *Journal*, 207, 236.
19. [Aulnoy], *Ingenious Letters*, 756; Kiernan, *Duel*, 61.
20. See Kelly, *Damn'd Thing*.
21. Spierenburg, "Knife Fighting," 108-9; McBane, *Expert*, 74.
22. Ward, *London Spy*, 241; Ward, *Wooden World*, 92.
23. Rogers, *Journal*, 208. See also Labat, *Voyages aux isles*, 2:264.
24. Wycherley, *Plain Dealer*, 5 (act 1, sc. 1).
25. Rogers, *Journal*, 228-29.
26. de Lussan, *Flibustiers*, 89.
27. Rogers, *Journal*, 228-29.
28. Wycherley, *Plain Dealer*, 50 (act 3, sc. 1).
29. See also Kiernan, *Duel*, 55.
30. Drake, *Amiable Renegade*, 331.
31. Exquemelin, *Flibustiers*, 331; McBane, *Expert*, 26-27, 35.
32. Silver, *Paradoxes of Defense*, 2.
33. For example, see Liancour, *Maitre d'armes*; Hope, *New Method*; McBane, *Expert*; and Wylde, *English Master*.
34. Blackwell, *Fencing Master*, 52; Hope, *New Method*, 119-20, 166; L'Abbat, *Art of Fencing*, 1-2.
35. [Aulnoy], *Ingenious Letters*, 735; *CSP 1677-1680*, no. 520.
36. Ibid., 740.
37. *New World of English Words*, 2nd ed., edited by E. Phillips (London: E. Tyler for Nath. Brooke, 1662), s.v. "Husares." However, some etymologies suggest the word has its origins in the Serbian and Croatian word for pirate. See for example *Merriam-Webster*, 11th ed., s.v. "hussar."
38. Hope, *New Method*, 166.
39. McBane, *Expert*, 60.
40. Szabó, *Fencing*, 235; Lukovich, *Fencing*, 106, 160; Du Casse, "Lettre de M. Ducasse," 1692, in Margry, *Relations*, 301.
41. See, for example, Quevedo, *Swindler*, 105-8.
42. Martin, *Islands*, 130. See also Liancour, *Maitre d'armes*; Hope, *New Method*; McBane, *Expert*; Page, *Broad Sword*; and Wylde, *English Master*.

43. Evelyn, *Diary*, 556.
44. Castle, *Schools*, 202.
45. Ligon, *True and Exact Account*, 52.
46. Gage, *Travels*, 73.
47. CSP 1675-1676, nos. 543, 849; Duguay-Trouin, *Mémoires*, x; [Walker?], *Voyages*, 158-59.
48. Exquemelin, *Flibustiers*, 107.
49. The two broad approaches to fencing (technician and warrior) described by Czajkowski in *Understanding Fencing* (165-79) to a fair degree can be used to compare the differences between duel and battle.
50. Liancour, *Maître d'armes*, 24; Hope, *New Method*, 158.
51. This rule remains in effect in modern foil and saber fencing, although the associated rule as to what constitutes an attack has been debased.
52. Drake, *Amiable Renegade*, 327.
53. "Never hesitate!" warned Dr. Francis Zold in 1977, saber in hand. It is a lesson that sticks with the author to this day.
54. Silver, *Paradoxes*, 3.
55. Hope, *New Method*, 161; Wycherley, *Plain Dealer*, 85 (act 5, sc. 1).
56. McBane, *Expert*, 57.
57. Ayers, *Van Horn*, 119.
58. Exquemelin, *Flibustiers*, 173-76. Accounts vary as to how soon Van Horn died.
59. Ibid.
60. Ibid.
61. al-Mûsili, *An Arab's Journey*, 84.
62. Exquemelin, *Flibustiers*, 173-76.

## Chapter 20

1. Horne, *Account*, 3; Macaulay, *History*, vol. 1:531-619; Whiles, *Sedgemoor*.
2. Pitman, *Relation of the Great Sufferings*, 433-43.
3. Le Fevre, "Loss," 76.
4. [Povey?], "Buccaneers on the Isthmus," 104.
5. Ibid.
6. Rogers, *Cruising Voyage*, 167.
7. [Cox], *Adventures*, 82; CSP 1681-1685, no. 963; Dampier, *New Voyage*, 44-45, 246, 270; de Lussan, *Journal of a Voyage*, 96-97; [Povey?], "Buccaneers at Portobello," 90; [Povey?], "Buccaneers on the Isthmus," 103-4; Rogers, *Cruising Voyage*, 159-62.
8. Mountaine, *Vade-Mecum*, 139-42.
9. CSP 1685-1688, no. 961; Saint-Méry, *Partie Espagnole*, vol. 1:172.

10. Barlow, *Journal*, vol. 1:27–28.
11. Pitman, *Relation of the Great Sufferings*, 431–76; Barlow, *Journal*, vol. 2:342–43; Beckles, *White Servitude*, 5–6, 49–52.
12. Rogers, *Cruising Voyage*, 94.
13. Exquemelin, *Flibustiers*, 93.
14. *CSP 1685–1688*, no. 1,010.

## Chapter 21

1. Chapin, *Privateer Ships*, 254–55; Moreno, *Corsarios*, 403–9; Torres Ramirez, *Armada*, 125–27.
2. Torres Ramirez, *Armada*, 125–27; Moreno, *Corsarios*, 286–87, 299–303; Gasser, "Mystérieuses," 219; Marley, *Veracruz*, 67.
3. Gasser, "Mystérieuses," 229, 240–41; Moreno, *Corsarios*, 374–75; Torres Ramirez, *Armada*, 126–27, 133.
4. Pitman, *Relation of the Great Sufferings*, 468–76.
5. *CSP 1681–1685*, nos. 1,163, 1,198, 1,563, 1,630, 1,866, 1,949v.
6. *CSP 1681–1685*, no. 1,163.
7. Weddle, *Wilderness Manhunt*, 41–45, 48–49, 100–1; Barroto, *Diary*, 181.
8. Pitman, *Relation of the Great Sufferings*, 468–76. John Whicker is probably Sabatini's inspiration for Dr. Whacker in *Captain Blood*.
9. Ibid.
10. "Jugement du Conseil de Guerre, contre des Forbans qui avoient fait une descente au Petit Goave," August 11, 1687, in Saint-Méry, *Loix*, vol. 1:458; *CSP 1685–1688*, no. 1,406; Saint-Méry, *Description Topographique*, vol. 2:538; "Audition des Espagnols qui ont mis à terre au Petit Gouave...," August 11, 1687, Archives nationales, Colonies, C9A rec. 1, reproduced in *Les Archives de la Flibuste*, http://www.geocities.com/trebutor/archives/D1686/D8708audition.html, accessed November 30, 2006; Moreno, *Corsarios*, 407; Apestegui, *Pirates*, 217.
11. Ibid.
12. Labat, *Memoirs*, 49–50.
13. Exquemelin, *Flibustiers*, 166–68; Gasser, "Mystérieuses," 240–42; Moreno, *Corsarios*, 375–89; Torres Ramirez, *Armada*, 133–35.
14. Ibid.

## Chapter 22

1. Exquemelin, *Flibustiers*, 165–66; Vaissière, *Origines de la colonisation*, 46–47, note 5; CSP 1689–1692, no. 980.
2. Apestegui, *Pirates*, 196; Chapin, *Privateer Ships*, 246n2, 258, 262n1; Crouse,

*French Struggle*, 212; *CSP 1681-1685*, nos. 1,461, 1,649, 1,718; *CSP 1689-1692*, no. 980; "Demande de pardon du capitaine Laurens de Graff," January 25, 1685, Archives Nationales, CAOM COL-F3 164, fol. 401, reproduced in *Les Archives de la Flibuste*, http://www.geocities.com/trebutor/ADF2005/1685/16850125grace.html;"Brevet de naturalité pour le nommé Laurens de Graff et sa femme,"August 5, 1685, Archives nationales: CAOM COL-B 11, ff. 193-94, reproduced in *Les Archives de la Flibuste*, http://www.geocities.com/trebutor/ADF2005/1685/16850805naturalite.html; Lepers, *Tragique histoire*, 219.

3. Sabatini, *Captain Blood*, 138, 219-22.

4. In general see Lloyd,"Bartholomew Sharp"; Ringrose, *Buccaneer's Atlas*, 30-32; *CSP 1681-1685* and *CSP 1685-1688*; and the journals of [Cox], Dampier (*New Voyage*), Dick, [Povey?], Ringrose, and Sharp.The record of Sharp's commission is provided in Tanner, *Descriptive Catalog*, 404.

5. *CSP 1681-1685*, nos. 1,223, 1,313, 1,376, 1,642, 1,759, 1,839, 1,962, 2,042.

6. Ibid.

7. [Povey?],"Buccaneers on the Isthmus," 100.

8. Ibid., 102.

9. [Cox], *Adventures*, 59.

10. *CSP 1685-1688*, no. 1,877; *CSP 1693-1696*, no. 207.

11. Dampier, *New Voyage*, 84, 300.

12. de Lussan, *Journal of a Voyage*, 166, 213.

13. *CSP 1685-1688*, no. 1,127; Johnson, *History*, 505; M.W., *Mosqueto*, 289.

14. Barroto,"Diary," 181, 182, 195.

15. Moreno, *Corsarios*, 148-49, 374.

16. Gasser,"Mystérieuses," 247-50.

17. M.W., *Mosqueto Indian*, 289.

18. Apestegui, *Pirates*, 211.

19. Lunsford, *Piracy and Privateering*, 146, 202-3; *CSP 1693-1696*, nos. 1,201iii, 1,236.

20. Chapin, *Privateer Ships*, 64-69.

21. Gosse, *Pirate's Who's Who*, 136-37.

22. French, *Historical Collections*, 34; G.H.C.Bulletin 78, January 1996, 1527, *Généalogie et Histoire de la Caraïbe*, accessible at www.ghcariabe.org; Vaissière, *Origenes de la colonisation*, 46-47, note 5.

23. Exquemelin, *Flibustiers*, 25.

24. Shomette, *Pirates*, 76-92; Wafer,"Secret Report," 133-51.

25. *CSP 1681-1685*, no. 1163; *CSP 1677-1680*, no. 1646.

26. Exquemelin, *Flibustiers*, 166-67 (author's translation).

27. [Povey?],"Buccaneers at Portobello," 91.

## Appendix F

1. Labat, *Nouveau voyage*, vol. 5:190; Labat, *Voyages aux isles*, vol. 2:233.
2. McCusker, *Money and Exchange*, 246; Linaje, *Rule of Trade*, 150.
3. *PRCC*, vol. 3:416; Labat, *Nouveau voyage*, vol. 5:190; Gemelli Careri, *Voyage Round the World*, 510.
4. Earle, *Wreck of the Almiranta*, 13.
5. McCusker, *Money and Exchange*, 99.
6. *CSP 1681–1685*, nos. 1,875, 1,876; *PRCC*, vol. 3:416.
7. *PRCC*, vol. 3:416.
8. Gemelli-Careri, *Voyage Round the World*, 510; Marx, *Shipwrecks*, 115–16; Budde-Jones, *Coins*, 3.
9. *CSP 1681–1685*, no. 1,875.
10. [Cox], *Adventures*, 80; Jameson, *Privateering*, 400.
11. Gemelli Careri, *Voyage Round the World*, 537.
12. *CSP 1681–1685*, no. 2,067. In general, see McCusker, *How Much*, and McCusker, *Money and Exchange*. Thirty shillings was the typical wage of a naval seaman. See *CSP 1677–1680*, no. 988.
13. May, *An Account of* Terra Nova, 349–50.
14. Labat, *Voyages aux isles*, vol. 2: 233.
15. Ashe, *Carolina*, 153.
16. Dampier, *New Voyage*, 216; Gemelli Careri, *Voyage Round the World*, 539.
17. Labat, *Memoirs*, 167.
18. Ibid.
19. Labat, *Voyages aux isles*, vol. 1:343–44.
20. Dampier, *New Voyage*, 160.
21. Ringrose, "Buccaneers of America," 330.
22. Exquemelin, *Buccaneers of America*, 75.

# Bibliography

## Period Sources

al-Mûsili, Elias. *An Arab's Journey to Colonial Spanish America: The Travels of Elias al-Mûsili in the Seventeenth Century.* Translated and edited by Caesar E. Farah. Syracuse, NY: Syracuse University Press, 2003.

Anonymous. *An Abridgment of the English Military Discipline.* London: John Bill, 1685.

Anonymous. *Ordonnance de la marine du mois d'Août 1681.* Paris: Charles Osmont, 1714.

Anonymous. *The Present State of Jamaica.* London: Fr. Clark for Tho. Malthus, 1683.

Anonymous. *Relation de ce qui s'est fait à la Prise de Carthagene, située aux Indes Espagnoles par l'escadre commandée par M. de Pointis.* Bruxelles: Jean Fricx, 1698.

Anonymous. *Voyage to the Mississippi Through the Gulf of Mexico.* Translated by Ann Linda Bell. Annotated by Robert S. Weddle. In Weddle, *La Salle,* 225–58.

Ashe, Thomas. *Carolina, or a Description of the Present State of That Country, by Thomas Ashe, 1682.* In Salley, *Narratives of Early Carolina,* 138–59.

Atkins, John. *A Voyage to Guinea, Brazil, and the West Indies.* 1735. Facsimile reprint, London: Frank Cass, 1970.

Aubin, Nicolas. *Dictionnaire de marine.* 3rd ed. Haag, Netherlands: Adrien Moetjens, 1742.

[Aulnoy, Marie Catherine le Jumelle de Barneville, baronne d']. *The Ingenious Letters of the Lady's—Travels into Spain.* 1691. Reprinted in Harris, *Navigantium,* vol. 2, 733–62.

Ayers, Philip (P. A.), ed. *Captain Van Horn with His Buccanieres Surprizing of la Veracruz.* 1684. In Ayers, *Voyages and Adventures,* 115–20.

———, ed. "Of the Taking the Castle of Chagre." In Ayers, *Voyages and Adventures,* 130–31.

————, ed. *The True Relation of Admiral Henry Morgan's Expedition Against the Spaniards in the West-Indies, in the Year 1670*. 1684. In Ayers, *Voyages and Adventures*, 132–44.

————, ed. *The Voyages and Adventures of Capt. Barth. Sharp and Others, in the South Sea*. London: P. A., Esq. [Philip Ayers], 1684.

Baker, Thomas. *Piracy and Diplomacy in Seventeenth-Century North Africa: The Journal of Thomas Baker, English Consul in Tripoli, 1677–1685*. Edited by C. R. Pennell. London: Associated University Presses, 1989.

Barbot, James. "An Abstract of a Voyage to *New Calabar* River, or *Rio Real*, in the Year 1699." In Churchill and Churchill, *Collection of Voyages*, vol. 5, 455–66.

Barbot, John. *A Description of the Coasts of North and South-Guinea*. In Churchill and Churchill, *Collection of Voyages*, vol. 5, 1–588.

Barlow, Edward. *Barlow's Journal*. 2 vols. Edited by Basil Lubbock. London: Hurst & Blackett, Ltd., 1934.

Barroto, Enríquez. "The Enríquez Barroto Diary." Translated and annotated by Robert S. Weddle. In Weddle, *La Salle*, 149–205.

Beeston, William. "The Relation of Colonel Beeston, His Voyage to Carthagena, for Adjusting the Peace Made in Spain, for the West-Indies, &c." 1684. In Ayers, *Voyages and Adventures*, 160–72.

Behn, Aphra. *Oroonoko or, The Royal Slave*. 1688. Reprint, New York: W. W. Norton, 1973.

————. *The Rover*. 1677. Reprint edited by Scott McMillin. In *Restoration and Eighteenth-Century Comedy*. 2nd ed. New York: W. W. Norton, 1997.

Blackwell, Henry. *The English Fencing-Master*. London: J. Downing, 1702.

Bloch, Julius M., et al., eds. *An Account of Her Majesty's Revenue in the Province of New York, 1701–09: The Customs Records of Early Colonial New York*. Ridgewood, NJ: The Gregg Press, 1966.

Boteler, Nathaniel. *Boteler's Dialogues*. 1685. Reprint edited by W. G. Perrin. London: Navy Records Society, 1929.

C. W., ed. *The Daemon of Burton. Or a True Relation of Strange Witchcraft*. London: C. W., 1671.

*Calendar of State Papers (CSP), Colonial Series, America and West Indies*, 1574–1738. 44 vols. W. Noel Sainsbury, Edited by J. W. Fortescue et al. London: 1860–1969.

Capo Ferro, Ridolfo. *Italian Rapier Combat: Capo Ferro's "Gran Simulacro."* 1610. Reprint edited by Jared Kirby. London: Greenhill Books, 2004.

Churchill, Awnsham, and John Churchill, eds. *A Collection of Voyages and Travels*. 6 vols. London: John Walthoe et al., 1732.

[Cleirac, Estienne]. *Us, et coutumes de la mer*. Bordeaux, France: Guillaume Millanges, 1647.

Cooke, Edward. *A Voyage to the South Sea and Round the World in the Years 1707 to 1711*. 1712. 2 vols. Facsimile reprint, New York: Da Capo Press, 1969.

Cowley, Abraham. *Cowley's Voyage Round the Globe*. In Hacke, *Original Voyages*, 1–45.

[Cox, John]. *The Adventures of Capt. Barth. Sharp and Others, in the South Sea*. In Ayers, *Voyages and Adventures*, 1–114.

Coxere, Edward. *Adventures by Sea of Edward Coxere*. Edited by E. H. W. Meyerstein. London: Oxford University, 1946.

Dampier, William. *A New Voyage Round the World*. 1697. Reprint, New York: Dover, 1968.

———. *A Voyage to New Holland*. 1729. Reprint, Gloucester, England: Alan Sutton, 1981.

———. *Voyages and Discoveries*. 1729. Reprint, London: Argonaut Press, 1931.

Daniel, R. P. [and Gabriel Daniel]. *Histoire de la Milice Françoise et des Changements qui s'y sont faits depuis l'établissement de la Monarchie dans les Gaules jusqu'à la fin du Règne de Louis le Grand*. 2 vols. Paris: Jean-Baptiste Coignard, 1721.

Dassie, F. *L'Architecture Navale*. 2nd ed. Paris: Laurent D'Houry, 1695.

Davis, Nathaniel. *The Expedition of a Body of Englishmen to the Gold Mines of Spanish America, in 1702*. 1704. In Wafer, *Wafer's Description*, 152–65.

Defoe, Daniel. *Colonel Jack*. 1722. Reprint, London: Hamish Hamil-ton, 1947.

———. *The Further Adventures of Robinson Crusoe*. 1719. Reprinted in *The Best Known Works of Daniel Defoe*. Garden City, NY: Nelson Double-day, n.d.

———. *Moll Flanders*. 1722. Reprint, Oxford: Oxford University Press, 1981.

de Lussan, Raveneau. *Journal of a Voyage into the South Seas in 1684 and the Following Years with the Filibusters*. 1689. Reprint translated and edited by Marguerite Eyer Wilbur. Cleveland: Arthur C. Clark Company, 1930.

———. *Journal of a Voyage Made by the Freebooters into the South Sea, 1684, and in the Following Years*. 1699. In Exquemelin, *Buccaneers of America*, 314–464.

———. *Les flibustiers de la mer du sud*. 1695. Reprint edited by Patrick Villiers. Paris: Éditions France-Empire, 1992.

[Dick, William]. "A Brief Account of Captain Sharp." In Exquemelin, *Buccaneers of America*, 257–83.

Dickinson, Jonathan. *Jonathan Dickinson's Journal*. 1699. Reprint edited by Evangeline Walker Andrews and Charles McLean Andrews. Stuart: Valen-tine Books, 1975.

Dièreville, Sieur de. *Relation of the Voyage to Port Royal in Acadia or New France*. 1708. Reprint edited by John Clarence Webster and translated by Mrs. Clarence Webster. Toronto: Champlain Society, 1933.

Doublet, Jean. *Mémoires, 1655–1728*. In *Le Honfleurais aux Sept Naufrages*, edited by Noël le Coutour. Paris: L'Harmattan, 1996.

Drake, Peter. *Amiable Renegade: The Memoirs of Captain Peter Drake, 1671–1753.* 1755. Reprint edited by Sidney Burrell. Stanford, CA: Stanford University Press, 1960.

Duguay-Trouin, René. *Mémoires de Duguay-Trouin, Lieutenant général des Armées Navales.* 1741. Reprint edited by Philippe Clouet. Paris: Éditions France-Empire, 1991.

[Durand]. *A Frenchman in Virginia: Being the Memoirs of a Huguenot Refugee in 1686.* 1687. Reprint edited and translated by Fairfax Harrison. Richmond, VA: privately printed, 1923.

Erauso, Catalina de. *Lieutenant Nun: Memoir of a Basque Transvestite in the New World.* 1829. Reprint translated by Michele Stepto and Gabriel Stepto. Boston: Beacon Press, 1996.

Evelyn, John. *The Diary of John Evelyn, Esq., F.R.S., from 1641 to 1705–6, with Memoir.* London: W. W. Gibbings, 1890.

Everard, Robert. "A Relation of Three Years Suffering of Robert Everard, Upon the Coast of Assada Near Madagascar, in a Voyage to India, in the Year 1686." In Churchill and Churchill, *Collection of Voyages,* vol. 6, 259–82.

Exquemelin, A. O. *The Buccaneers of America.* 1678. 2nd ed. Reprint translated from Dutch by Alexis Brown. London: Folio Society, 1969.

———. *Les flibustiers du nouveau monde.* 1699, with additional passages from the 1688 edition. Reprint edited by Michel le Bris. Paris: Éditions Phébus, 1996.

———. *Histoire des aventuriers flibustiers qui se sont signalez dans les Indes.* 2 vols. Paris: Jacques Le Febvre, 1699.

———[Joseph Esquemeling]. *The History of the Buccaneers of America.* 1699. Reprint, Boston: Sanborn, Carter, and Bazin, 1856.

———[John Esquemeling]. *The Buccaneers of America.* 1684. Reprint, New York: Dorset Press, 1987.

———. *Piratas de la America, y luz à la defensa de las costas de Indias Occidentales.* Translated from Dutch by Alonso de Buena-Maison. Colonia Agrippina: Lorenza Struickman, 1681.

Forbin, comte de [Claude de Forbin-Gardanne]. *Mémoires du Comte de Forbin.* 1729. Reprint, Paris: Mercure de France, 1993.

French, B. F., ed. *Historical Collections of Louisiana and Florida, Including Translations of Original Manuscripts Relating to Their Discovery and Settlement: Historical Memoirs and Narratives, 1527–1702.* New York: Albert Mason, 1875.

Fryer, John. *A New Account of East India and Persia, Being Nine Years' Travels, 1672–1681.* 1698, 1909–1915. 3 vols. Reprint edited by William Crooke. Millwood, NY: Krause Reprint, 1967.

Funnell, William. *A Voyage Round the World.* 1707. Facsimile reprint, New York: Da Capo Press, 1969.

Gage,Thomas. *Thomas Gage's Travels in the New World*. 1648. Reprint edited by J. Eric S. Thompson. Norman: University of Oklahoma Press, 1969.

Gay, John. *Polly: An Opera*. 1729. Reprinted in *The Poetical Works of John Gay*. London: Oxford University, 1926.

———. *Travels Through Europe*. 1700. Reprinted in Churchill and Churchill, *Collection of Voyages*, vol. VI, 43–142.

———. *Viaje a la Nueva España*. 1700. Reprint, Mexico City: Universidad Nacional Autónoma de México, 1976.

Gemelli Careri, Giovanni Francesco [John Francis Gemelli Careri]. *A Voyage Round the World*. 1700. Reprinted in Churchill and Churchill, *Collection of Voyages*, vol. IV, 1–572.

Girard, P.J. F. *Traité des Armes*. Paris: Pierre de Hondt, 1740.

Godfrey, John. *A Treatise Upon the Useful Science of Defence, Connecting the Small and Back-Sword, and Shewing the Affinity Between Them*. London: T. Gardner, 1747.

Guillet, Georges. *Les arts de l'homme d'epée, ou le dictionnaire du gentilhomme*. Paris: Gervais Clouzier, 1678.

Guzman, Juan Perez de. "Don Juan Perez de Guzman, His Relation of the Late Action of the English in the West-Indies." In Ayers, *Voyages and Adventures*, 145–59.

Hacke, William. *A Collection of Original Voyages*. 1699. Facsimile reprint edited by Glyndwr Williams. New York: Scholars' Facsimiles & Reprints, 1993.

Harris, John, ed. *Navigantium atque Itinerantium Bibliotheca: or, a Compleat Collection of Voyages and Travels*. London: Bennet et al., 1705.

Hennepin, Lewis. 1705. *An Account of Mr. La Salle's undertaking to discover the River Missisipi, by Way of the Gulph of Mexico*. In Harris, *Navigantium*, vol. 2, 911–15.

"Historical Journal; or, Narrative of the Expeditions Made by Order of His Majesty Louis XIV, King of France to Colonize Louisiana, Under the Command of M. Pierre le Moyne d'Iberville, Governor General." [1698?] In French, *Historical Collections*, 29–121.

Hope, William. *New Method of Fencing*. 1707. Reprinted in Rector, *Highland Swordsmanship*, 87–193.

Horne, Robert, et al. *An Account of What Passed at the Execution of the Late Duke of Monmouth*. London: Robert Horne et al., 1685.

Hutchinson, William. *A Treatise on Naval Architecture*. 1794. Reprint, Annapolis, MD: Naval Institute Press, 1969.

Ingram, Bruce, ed. *Three Sea Journals of Stuart Times*. London: Constable & Co. Ltd., 1936.

Jameson, John F., ed. *Privateering and Piracy in the Colonial Period: Illustrative Documents*. New York: Macmillan Company, 1923.

Janclot. "Relation de l'officer Janclot." 1690. In Ernest Myrand, *Sir William*

*Phips devant Quebec: histoire d'un siege.* Quebec: L. J. Demers & Frère, 1893, 74–79.

Jeaffreson, Christopher. A Young Squire of the Seventeenth Century: From the Papers (A.D. 1676–1686) of Christopher Jeaffreson, of Dullingham House, Cambridgeshire. Edited by John Cordy Jeaffreson. 2 vols. London: Hurst and Blackett, 1878.

Johnson, Charles [Daniel Defoe?]. *A General History of the Robberies and Murders of the Most Notorious Pirates.* 1726. Reprint, New York: Dodd, Mead & Company, 1926.

Joutel, Henri. *The Last Voyage Perform'd by La Salle.* 1714. Facsimile reprint, Ann Arbor, MI: University Microfilms, 1966.

Labat, Jean Baptiste. *The Memoirs of Père Labat, 1693–1705.* Edited and abridged by John Eaden. London: Frank Cass, 1970.

————. *Nouveau voyage aux isles d'Amérique.* 6 vols. Paris: Guillaume Cavelier, 1722.

————. *Voyages aux isles de l'Amérique.* 1722. Reprint edited by A. t'Serstevens. 2 vols. Paris: Èditions Duchartre, 1931.

L'Abbat [Labat]. *The Art of Fencing: Or the Use of the Smallsword.* 1696. Reprint edited and translated by Andrew Mahon. Dublin: James Hoey, 1734.

Lafitau, Joseph François. *Moeurs des sauvages Ameriquains, comparées aux moeurs des premiers temps.* Paris: Saugrain et al., 1724.

Lahontan [Louis Armand de Lom d'Arce, baron de la Hontan]. *A Voyage to North America.* 1703. Reprinted in Harris, *Navigantium*, vol. II, 915.

Lepers, Jean-Baptiste [P. le Pers]. *La tragique histoire des flibustiers: Histoire de Saint-Domingue et de l'Ile de la Tortue, repaires des flibustiers, écrite vers 1715 par le Rév. P. Lepers.* Edited by Pierre-Bernard Berthelot. Paris: Éditons G. Crès, n.d.

Liancour, André Wernesson de [le Sieur de Liancour]. *Le maitre d'armes ou l'exercice de l'épée seule.* Amsterdam: Daniel de la Feuille, 1692.

Ligon, Richard. *A True and Exact History of the Island of Barbados.* 1673. Facsimile reprint, London: Frank Cass, 1998.

Linaje, José de Veita [Ioseph de Veitia Linage]. *Norte de la Contratacion de las Indias Occidentales.* Seville: Juan Francisco de Blas, 1672.

————. *The Spanish Rule of Trade to the West-Indies.* 1702. Translated and edited by John Stevens. Facsimile reprint, New York: AMS Press, 1977.

Lyde, Robert. *A True and Exact Account of the Retaking of a Ship, Called The Friend's Adventure, of Topsham, from the French.* 1693. Reprinted in Edward, Arber, and Thomas Seccombe, eds., *An English Garner: Stuart Tracts, 1603–1693*, vol. 8, 477–514. New York: E. P. Dutton, n.d.

M. W. *The Mosqueto Indian and His Golden River: Being a Familiar Description of the Mosqueto Kingdom in America.* 1699. In Churchill and Churchill, *Collection of Voyages*, vol. 6, 284–98.

Margry, Pierre. *Découvertes et établissements de Français dans l'ouest et dans le sud de l'Amerique Septentrionale (1614–1754), mémoires et documents originaux.* 4 vols. Paris: D. Jouaust, 1880.

———. *Relations et mémoires inédits pour servir à l'histoire de la France dans pays d'outre-mer.* Paris: Challamel Aimé, *1867.*

Marsden, R. G., ed. *Documents Relating to Law and Custom of the Sea.* 2 vols. N.p.: Navy Records Society, 1916.

Martin, Martin. *A Description of the Western Islands of Scotland.* 1703. Reprint, Edinburgh: Birlinn Limited, 1999.

Mather, Cotton. *The Angel of Bethesda: An Essay Upon the Common Maladies of Mankind.* Edited by Gordon W. Jones. Barre, MA: American Antiquarian Society, 1972.

———. *The Wonders of the Invisible World.* 1692. Reprint, New York: Dorset Press, 1991.

May, Charles. *An Account of the Wonderful Preservation of the Ship* Terra Nova *of London.* 1694. In Churchill and Churchill, *Collection of Voyages,* vol. 6, 345–54.

McBane, Donald. *Expert Sword-Man's Companion.* 1728. Reprinted in Rector, *Highland Swordsmanship,* 21–85.

Miller, James. "A Short Treatise of the Gladiatory Art of Defence." Folio, 1738.

Minet. "Journal of Our Voyage to the Gulf of Mexico." Translated by Ann Linda Bell, annotated by Robert S. Weddle. In Weddle, *La Salle,* 83–126.

Molière [Jean-Baptiste Poquelin]. *Le bourgeois gentilhomme.* 1670. Reprint, Sorbonne: Librairie Larousse, 1970.

Montauban, Sieur de. *A Relation of a Voyage Made by the Sieur De Montauban.* In Exquemelin, *History of the Buccaneers,* 464–84.

Mountaine, William. *The Seaman's Vade-Mecum and Defensive War by Sea.* 1756. Reprint, London: Conway Maritime Press, 1971.

"Narrative of the Expedition of M. Cavalier de la Salle to Explore the (Mississippi) Colbert River." [1682?] In French, *Historical Collections,* 17–27.

Navarrete, Domingo Fernández de. *The Travels and Controversies of Friar Domingo Navarrete, 1618–86.* 2 vols. Edited by J. S. Cummins. Cambridge: Cambridge University Press, 1962.

Newe, Thomas. "Letters of Thomas Newe, 1686." In Salley, *Narratives of Early Carolina,* 179–87.

Northcote, William. *Extracts From the Marine Practice of Physic and Surgery.* Philadelphia: R. Bell, 1776.

Norwood, Henry. *Voyage to Virginia.* 1732. In Wharton, *Trough of the Sea,* 65–119.

Page, Thomas. *The Use of the Broad Sword.* Norwich, England: M. Chase, 1746.

Pepys, Samuel. *The Shorter Pepys.* Selected and edited by Robert Latham from *The Diary of Samuel Pepys, a New and Complete Transcription,* edited by Robert Latham and William Matthews. Berkeley: University of California Press, 1985.

Petter, Nicolaes. *Klare Onderrichtinge der Voortreffelijcke Worstel-Konst.* Amsterdam: Johannes Janssonius Van Waesberge, 1674.

Phillips, Thomas. *A Journal of a Voyage From England to Africa, and so Forward to Barbados, in the Years 1693 and 1694.* In Churchill and Churchill, *Collection of Voyages*, vol. 6.

Pitman, Henry. *A Relation of the Great Sufferings and Strange Adventures of Henry Pitman.* 1689. Reprinted in Edward, Arber, and Thomas Seccombe, eds., *An English Garner: Stuart Tracts, 1603-1693*, vol. 8, 431-76. New York: E. P. Dutton, n.d.

[Povey, Edward?]. "The Buccaneers on the Isthmus and in the South Sea, 1680-1682." In Jameson, *Privateering and Piracy*, 92-135.

————. "The Buccaneers at Portobello, 1680." In Jameson, *Privateering and Piracy* (PRCC), 84-92.

*The Public Records of the Colony of Connecticut.* 15 vols. Hartford, CT: Brown & Parsons, 1850-90.

Quevedo, Francisco de. *The Swindler (El Buscún).* 1626. Reprint translated by Michael Alpert. In Quevedo and Alpert, *Lazarillo de Tormes and the Swindler*, 61-197.

Quevedo, Francisco de, and Michael Alpert. *Lazarillo de Tormes and the Swindler: Two Spanish Picaresque Novels*, rev. ed. London: Penguin Books, 2003.

Rector, Mark, ed. *Highland Swordsmanship: Techniques of the Scottish Masters.* Union City, CA: Chivalry Bookshelf, 2001.

Ringrose, Basil. *A Buccaneer's Atlas: Basil Ringrose's South Sea Waggoner.* Edited by Derek Howse and Norman J. W. Thrower. Berkeley: University of California Press, 1992.

————. "The Buccaneers of America: The Second Volume." In Exquemelin, *The Buccaneers of America* (1684), 285-475.

————. "Captains Sharp, Coxon, Sawkins, and Others . . ." In Exquemelin, *The History of the Buccaneers of America*, 180-313.

Roch, Jeremy. *The Journals of Jeremy Roch.* In Ingram, *Three Sea Journals of Stuart Times*, 25-139.

Rochefort, César de, Jean-Baptiste du Tertre, and Louis de Poincy. *Histoire naturelle et morale des îles Antilles de l'Amérique avec un vocabulaire caraïbe.* 2 vols. Rotterdam: A. Leers, 1658.

————. *The History of the Caribby-Islands, viz. Barbados, St Christophers, St Vincents, Martinico, Dominico, Barbouthos, Monserrat, Mevis, Antego, &c. in all XXVIII.* Translated by John Davies. London: Thomas Dring and John Starkey, 1666.

Rogers, Francis. *The Journal of Francis Rogers.* In Ingram, *Three Sea Journals of Stuart Times*, 141-230.

Rogers, Woodes. *A Cruising Voyage Round the World.* 1712. Facsimile reprint, New York: Da Capo Press, 1969.

Saint-Méry, M. L. E. Moreau de. *Loix et constitutions des colonies Françaises de l'Amérique sous le vent*. 2 vols. Paris: privately printed, n.d.

Saint-Remy, Pierre Surirey de. *Mémoires d'Artillerie*. Paris: Jean Anisson, 1697.

Salley, Alexander S., Jr., ed. *Narratives of Early Carolina, 1650-1708, Original Narratives of Early American History*. New York: Charles Scribner's Sons, 1911.

Seller, John. *The Sea Gunner*. 1691. Facsimile reprint, Rotherfield, England: Jean Boudriot Publications, 1994.

Sharp, Bartholomew. "Captain Sharp's Journal of His Expedition." In Hacke, *Original Voyages*, 1-55.

Shelvocke, George. *A Voyage Around the World*. 1726. Facsimile reprint, New York: Da Capo Press, 1971.

Silver, George. *Paradoxes of Defence*. 1599. Facsimile reprint, New York: Da Capo Press, 1968.

Smith, John. *The Seaman's Grammar and Dictionary*. London: Randal Taylor, 1691.

Sturmy, Samuel. "The Mariner's Magazine—1669." Excerpted in C. E. Kenney, *The Quadrant and the Quill*. London: Metchim and Son, Ltd., 1947.

Sue, Eugène. *Histoire de la Marine Française*. 2nd ed. 4 vols. Paris: Depot de la Librarie, 1845.

Tanner, J. R., ed. *A Descriptive Catalogue of the Naval Manuscripts in the Pepysian Library at Magdalene College, Cambridge*. Vol. 1. [London]: Navy Records Society, 1903.

Temple, Richard Carnac, ed. *The Papers of Thomas Bowery, 1669-1713*. London: Hakluyt Society, 1927.

Teonge, Henry. *The Diary of Henry Teonge, 1675-1679*. 1825. Reprint edited by G. E. Manwaring. New York: Harper and Brothers, 1927.

Thacher, Anthony. "Some Part of a Letter . . ." 1635. In Wharton, *Trough of the Sea*.

Thevenot, Melchisedech [M. Thevenot]. *L'Art de nager, demontré par figures*. Paris: Thomas Moette, 1696.

Uring, Nathaniel. *The Voyages and Travels of Captain Nathaniel Uring*. 1726. Reprint, London: Cassell, 1928.

Vargas, Diego de. *By Force of Arms: The Journals of Don Diego de Vargas, 1691-1693*. Edited by John L. Kessel and Rick Hendricks. Albuquerque: University of New Mexico, 1992.

———. *Remote Beyond Compare: Letters of Don Diego de Vargas to His Family From New Spain and New Mexico, 1675-1706*. Edited by John L. Kessell. Albuquerque: University of New Mexico Press, 1989.

Villehuet, Jaques Bourdé de. *Le Manoeuvrier, ou essai sur la théorie et la pratique de mouvements du navire et des évolutions navales*. Paris: H. L. Guerin and L. F. Delatour, 1765.

Villette, Marquis de [Philippe le Valois Villete]. *Mémoires du marquis de Villette*. Paris: Jules Renouard, 1844.

Wafer, Lionel. *A New Voyage and Description of the Isthmus of America.* 1699. Reprint edited by L. E. Elliott Joyce. Oxford: Hakluyt Society, 1934.

————. "Wafer's 'Secret Report' of 1698." In Wafer, *Wafer's Description*, 133–51.

[Walker, George?] *The Voyages and Cruises of Commodore Walker.* 1760. Reprint, London: Cassell and Company, 1928.

Ward, Edward [Ned Ward]. *Five Travel Scripts Commonly Attributed to Edward Ward.* Facsimile reprints. New York: Columbia University Press, 1933.

————. *The London Spy: The Vanities and Vices of the Town Exposed to View.* 1703. Reprint edited by Arthur L. Hayward. London: Cassell and Company, 1927.

————. *A Trip to Holland.* 1699. Facsimile reprint in Ward, *Five Travel Scripts.*

————. *A Trip to Jamaica.* 1700. Facsimile reprint in Ward, *Five Travel Scripts.*

————. *A Trip to New England.* 1699. Facsimile reprint in Ward, *Five Travel Scripts.*

————. *The Wooden World.* 1707. Reprint, [London?]: Society for Nautical Research, 1929.

Weddle, Robert S., ed. *La Salle, the Mississippi, and the Gulf: Three Primary Documents.* College Station: Texas A&M University Press, 1987.

Wharton, Donald P., ed. *In the Trough of the Sea.* Westport: Greenwood Press, 1979.

Whistler, Henry. "Extracts From Henry Whistler's Journal of the West India Expedition." In Firth, C. H., ed. *The Narrative of General Venables.* New York: Longmans, Green, and Co., 1900.

Willughby, Francis. *A Relation of a Voyage Made Through a Great Part of Spain.* In Harris, *Navigantium*, vol. 2, 592–98.

Wood, John. "Captain Wood's Voyage Through the Streights of Magellan, &c." In Hacke, *Original Voyages*, 56–100.

Wycherley, William. *The Country Wife.* 1675. Reprinted in Scott McMillin, ed. *Restoration and Eighteenth-Century Comedy.* 2nd ed. New York: W. W. Norton, 1997.

————. *The Plain Dealer.* 1677. Facsimile reprint, Yorkshire: The Scholar Press, 1971.

Wylde, Zachary. *English Master of Defence Or, The Gentleman's Al-a-mode Accomplish....* Tork, England: John White, 1711.

Yonge, James. *The Journal of James Yonge (1647–1721).* Edited by F. N. L. Poynter. London: Longmans, 1963.

## Modern Sources

Anderson, R. C. *Seventeenth Century Rigging.* London: Percival Marshall, 1955.

———— . "Some Additions to the Brigantine Problem." *Mariner's Mirror* 8, no. 2 (1922): 109–16.

Apestegui, Cruz. *Pirates of the Caribbean.* Translated by Richard Lewis Rees. Edison, NJ: Chartwell Books, 2002.

Arana, Luis Rafael. "Don Manuel de Cendoya and Castillo de San Marcos, 1669-1673." *El Escribiano* 36 (1999): 29-36.

———. "Pirates March on St. Augustine, 1683." *El Escribiano* 36 (1999): 64-72.

Baker, William A. *Colonial Vessels: Some Seventeenth-Century Sailing Craft.* Barre, MA: Barre Publishing Company, 1962.

———. *Sloops and Shallops.* 1966. Reprint, Columbia: University of South Carolina Press, n.d.

Bakewell, Peter. *Silver and Entrepreneurship in Seventeenth-Century Potosí: The Life and Times of Antonio López de Quiroga.* Dallas: Southern Methodist University, 1988.

Beck, Horace P. *The American Indian as a Sea-Fighter in Colonial Times.* Mystic, CT: Marine Historical Association, Inc., 1959.

Beckles, Hilary McD. *White Servitude and Black Slavery in Barbados, 1627-1715.* Knoxville: University of Tennessee, 1989.

Bernal Ruiz, María del Pilar. *La Toma del Puerto de Guayaquil en 1687.* Sevilla, Spain: Escuela de Estudios Hispano-Americanos de Sevilla, 1979.

Besson, Maurice. *The Scourge of the Indies.* Translated by Everard Thornton. London: George Rutledge, 1929.

Billacois, François. *The Duel: Its Rise and Fall in Early Modern France.* 1986. Reprint edited and translated by Trista Selous. New Haven, CT: Yale University Press, 1990.

Boudriot, Jean. "Le Fusil Boucanier Français." *Gazette des Armes* 40 (July-August 1976): 24-30.

Bourne, Russell. *The Red King's Rebellion: Racial Politics in New England, 1675-1678.* New York: Oxford University, 1990.

Boyd, Mark F. "The Fortifications at San Marcos de Apalache." *Florida Historical Quarterly* 15, no. 1 (1936): 3-34.

Bradley, Peter T. "The Ships of the Armada of the Viceroyalty of Peru in the Seventeenth Century." *Mariner's Mirror* 79, no. 4 (1993): 393-402.

———. "Some Considerations on Defence at Sea in the Viceroyalty of Peru During the Seventeenth Century." *Revista de Historia de America* 79 (1975): 77-97.

Brindenbaugh, Carl, and Roberta Brindenbaugh. *No Peace Beyond the Line: The English in the Caribbean, 1624-1690.* New York: Oxford University Press, 1972.

Briost, Pascal, Hervé Drévillon, and Pierre Serna. *Croiser le fer.* Seyssel, France: Champ Vallon, 2002.

Bruseth, James E., and Toni S. Turner. *From a Watery Grave: The Discovery and Excavation of La Salle's Shipwreck, La Belle.* College Station: Texas A&M University Press, 2005.

Budde-Jones, Kathryn. *Coins of the Lost Galleons.* 3rd ed. Winter Park, FL: Printing-Action Graphics, 2004.

Buisseret, David. *Historic Jamaica From the Air*. Photography by Jack
    Tyndale-Biscoe, cartography by Tom Willcockson. Kingston; Jamaica: Ian
    Rundle, 1996.
Burg, B. R. *Sodomy and the Pirate Tradition: English Sea Rovers in the
    Seventeenth-Century Caribbean*. New York: New York University, 1984.
Burkholder, Mark A., and Lyman L. Johnson. *Colonial Latin America*. New
    York: Oxford University, 1990.
Burney, James. *History of the Buccaneers of America*. 1816. Reprint, New
    York: W. W. Norton, 1950.
Burnside, Madeleine. *Spirits of the Passage: The Transatlantic Slave Trade in
    the Seventeenth Century*. New York: Simon and Schuster, 1997.
Bushnell, Amy Turner. "How to Fight a Pirate: Provincials, Royalists, and the
    Defense of Minor Ports During the Age of Buccaneers." *Gulf Coast His-
    torical Review* 5 (1990): 18–35.
Butel, Paul. *Les Caraïbes au temps des flibustiers*. Paris: Aubier Montaigne,
    1982.
Camus, Michel Christian. *L'Île de la Tortue au coeur de la flibuste caraïbe*.
    Paris: Éditions l'Harmattan, 1997.
Caruana, Adrian B. *The History of English Sea Ordnance, 1523–1875:
    Volume I, The Age of Evolution, 1523–1715*. Rotherford, England:
    Jean Boudriot Publications, 1994.
Castle, Egerton. *Schools and Masters of Fence*. 1885. Facsimile reprint, York,
    PA: George Shumway, 1969.
Cervantes, Fernando. *The Devil in the New World: The Impact of Diabolism
    in New Spain*. New Haven, CT: Yale University Press, 1994.
Chapelle, Howard I. *The Search for Speed Under Sail*. New York: W. W. Norton,
    1967.
Chapin, H. M. *Privateer Ships and Sailors: The First Century of American
    Colonial Privateering, 1625–1725*. Toulon: Imprimerie G. Mouton, 1926.
Chartrand, René. *The Spanish Main, 1492–1800*. Illustrated by Donato
    Spedaliere. Oxford, England: Osprey Publishing, 2006.
Chatelain, Verne E. *The Defenses of Spanish Florida, 1565 to 1763*. Washing-
    ton, DC: Carnegie Institute of Washington, 1941.
Clayton, Lawrence A. "The Maritime Trade of Peru." *Mariner's Mirror* 72, no. 2
    (1986): 159–77.
———. "Ships and Empire: The Case of Spain." *Mariner's Mirror* 62, no. 3
    (1976): 235–48.
Clifford, Barry. *The Lost Fleet: The Discovery of a Sunken Armada From the
    Golden Age of Piracy*. New York: Harper Collins, 2002.
Corbett, Julian. "Galleys and Runners." *Mariner's Mirror* 7, no. 2 (1921):
    133–35.
Crane, Vernor W. *The Southern Frontier, 1670–1732*. Ann Arbor: University of
    Michigan, 1956.

————. *French Pioneers in the West Indies, 1624-1664.* 1940. Reprint, New York: Octagon Books, 1977.

Crouse, Nellis M. *The French Struggle for the West Indies, 1665-1715.* New York: Columbia University Press, 1943.

Czajkowski, Zbigniew. *Understanding Fencing: The Unity of Theory and Practice.* New York: SKA Swordplay Books, 2005.

Dagnino, Vicente. *El Correjimiento de Arica: 1535-1784.* Arica, Chile: La Epoca, 1909.

Dobrenko, Alexander, and Ann Palmer. "The Model of *La Légère* in the Central Naval Museum, St. Petersburg: Master Shipbuilder Blaise Pangalo in Peter the Great's Shipyards." *Mariner's Mirror* 86, no. 1 (2000): 37-49.

Dow, George Francis, and John Henry Edmonds. *The Pirates of the New England Coast, 1630-1730.* 1923. Reprint, New York: Argosy-Antiquarian, 1968.

Druett, Joan. *Rough Medicine: Surgeons at Sea in the Age of Sail.* New York: Routledge, 2000.

Dunn, Richard S. *Sugar and Slaves: The Rise of the Planter Class in the English West Indies, 1624-1713.* Chapel Hill: University of North Carolina, 1972.

Dunn, William Edward. "The Spanish Search for La Salle's Colony on the Bay of Espíritu Santo, 1685-1689." *Southwestern Historical Quarterly* 19, no. 4 (April 1916): 324-69.

Earle, Peter. *The Wreck of the Almiranta.* London: Macmillan London Limited, 1979.

Emke, C. A. "*Anna Maria*: A Late Seventeenth Century Fluyt." *Model Shipwright*, no. 126 (June 2006): 6-24.

Engen, David K. "The Appearance of the Eighteenth Century Ship, Part One." *Nautical Research Journal* 37, no. 3 (1992): 161-68.

Fortune, Stephen Alexander. *Merchants and Jews: The Struggle for West Indian Commerce, 1650-1750.* Gainesville: University of Florida Press, 1984.

Franklin, John. *Navy Board Ship Models, 1650-1750.* Annapolis: Naval Institute Press, 1989.

Fraser, Antonia. *The Weaker Vessel.* New York: Knopf, 1984.

Fuentes, Carlos. *The Buried Mirror: Reflections on Spain and the New World.* New York: Houghton Mifflin, 1992.

Gallay, Alan. *The Indian Slave Trade: The Rise of the English Empire in the American South, 1670-1717.* New Haven, CT: Yale University Press, 2002.

Galvin, Peter R. *Patterns of Pillage: A Geography of Caribbean-Based Piracy in Spanish America, 1536-1718.* New York: Peter Lang, 2000.

Gasser, Jacques. "Les mystérieuses disparitions de Grammont." In Le Bris, *L'Aventure de la flibuste*, 211-50.

Genovese, Eugene D. *From Rebellion to Revolution: Afro-American Slave*

*Revolts in the Making of the Modern World*. Baton Rouge: Louisiana State University, 1979.

Gerhard, Peter. *Pirates of the Pacific, 1575-1742*. 1960. Reprint, Lincoln: University of Nebraska Press, 1990.

Gilkerson, William. *Boarders Away I: With Steel-Edged Weapons and Polearms*. Lincoln, RI: Andrew Mowbray, Inc., 1993.

———. *Boarders Away II: Firearms of the Age of Fighting Sail*. Lincoln, RI: Andrew Mowbray, Inc., 1993.

Gosse, Philip. *The Pirate's Who's Who*. 1924. Reprint, Glorietta, NM: Rio Grande Press, 1988.

Haring, C. H. *The Buccaneers in the West Indies in the 17th Century*. 1910. Reprint, Hamden, CT: Archon Books, 1966.

———. *Trade and Navigation Between Spain and the Indies*. Cambridge: Harvard University Press, 1918.

Hrodej, Philippe. "La flibuste domingoise à la fin du XVIIe siècle: une composante économique indispensable." In Le Bris, *L'Aventure de la flibuste*, 289-312.

Hubbard, Vincent K. *Swords, Ships & Sugar: History of Nevis*. Corvallis, OR: Premiere Editions International, 2002.

Hughson, Shirley Carter. *The Carolina Pirates and Colonial Commerce, 1670-1740*. 1894. Reprint, Spartanburg, SC: The Reprint Company, 1992.

Joseph, Gilbert M. "British Loggers and Spanish Governors: The Logwood Trade and Its Settlements in the Yucatan Peninsula." *Caribbean Studies* 14, no. 2 (1974): 7-36.

———. "John Coxon and the Role of Buccaneering in the Settlement of the Yucatán Colonial Frontier." *Terrae Incognitae* 12 (1980): 65-84.

Juárez, José Antonio Caballero. *El Régimen Jurídico de las Armadas de la Carrera de Indias: Siglos XVI y XVII*. México City: Universidad Nacional Autónoma de México, 1997.

Kelly, James. *That Damn'd Thing Called Honour: Duelling in Ireland, 1570-1860*. Cork, Ireland: Cork University Press, 1995.

Kiernan, V. G. *The Duel in European History: Honor and the Reign of Aristocracy*. Oxford: Oxford University Press, 1989.

Kinkor, Kenneth J. "Black Men Under the Black Flag." In Pennell, *Bandits at Sea*, 195-210.

Knaut, Andrew L. *The Pueblo Revolt of 1680*. Norman: University of Oklahoma, 1995.

Kohshi, Kiyotaka, et al. "Neurological Diving Accidents in Japanese Breath-Hold Divers: A Preliminary Report." *Journal of Occupational Health* 43, no. 1 (January 2001): 56-60.

Kricher, John. *A Neotropical Companion: An Introduction to the Animals, Plants, and Ecosystems of the New World Tropics*. 2nd ed. Illustrated by William E. Davis, Jr. Princeton: Princeton University Press, 1997.

Kupperman, Karen Ordahl. *Providence Island, 1630-1641: The Other Puritan Colony.* Cambridge: Cambridge University Press, 1995.

Lane, Kris E. *Pillaging the Empire: Piracy in the Americas, 1500-1750.* Armonk, NY: M. E. Sharpe, 1998.

Lavery, Brian. *The Arming and Fitting of English Ships of War, 1600-1815.* Annapolis: Naval Institute Press, 1987.

Le Bris, Michel, ed. *L'Aventure de la flibuste.* Paris: Éditions Hoëbeke, 2002.

Le Fevre, Peter. "The Loss of the *Date Tree* While Careening at Cadiz in 1679." *Mariner's Mirror* 68, no. 1 (1982): 75-76.

Leonard, Irving A. *Baroque Times in Old Mexico.* Ann Arbor: University of Michigan Press, 1959.

Leyland, John. "An Old Fighting Merchant Seaman." *Mariner's Mirror* 1, no. 4 (1911): 271-75.

Little, Benerson. *The Sea Rover's Practice: Pirate Tactics and Techniques, 1630-1730.* Washington, DC: Potomac Books, 2005.

Lloyd, Christopher. "Bartholomew Sharp, Buccaneer." *Mariner's Mirror* 42, no. 4 (1956): 291-301.

Lukovich, István. *Fencing.* 1975. Reprint translated by István Butykay and John Harvie. Budapest: Corvina, 1986.

Lunsford, Virginia W. *Piracy and Privateering in the Golden Age Netherlands.* New York: Palgrave MacMillan, 2005.

Macaulay, Thomas Babington. *The History of England From the Accession of James II.* 4 vols. New York: Harper & Brothers, Publishers, 1849-1856.

Malone, Patrick M. *The Skulking Way of War.* Baltimore: Johns Hopkins University Press, 1991.

Marley, David F. *Pirates and Engineers.* Windsor, Ontario: Netherlandic Press, 1992.

————. *Sack of Veracruz.* Windsor, Ontario: Netherlandic Press, 1993.

Marx, Robert F. *Shipwrecks in the Americas.* 1971. Rev. ed. New York: Dover Publications, 1987.

McCusker, John J. *How Much Is That in Real Money? A Historical Price Index for Use as a Deflator of Money Values in the Economy of the United States.* Worcester, MA: American Antiquarian Society, 1992.

————. *Money and Exchange in Europe and America, 1600-1775: A Handbook.* Chapel Hill: University of North Carolina Press, 1978.

Means, Philip Ainsworth. *The Spanish Main.* New York: Charles Scribners Sons, 1935.

Merrien, Jean. *La vie des marins au grand siècle.* Rennes, France: Terre de Brume Éditions, 1995.

Middleton, Arthur Pierce. *Tobacco Coast: A Maritime History of Chesapeake Bay in the Colonial Era.* 1953. Reprint, Baltimore: Johns Hopkins University Press, 1984.

Moitt, Bernard. *Women and Slavery in the French Antilles, 1535-1848.* Indianapolis: Indiana University Press, 2001.

Montero, Pablo. "Acerca de Piratas y de Imperios." *Diario de Campo*, no. 31 (2005): 14–23.

Moore, Alan, and R. Morton Nance. "Round-Sterned Ships: No. II The Hooker." *Mariner's Mirror* 1, no. 4 (1911): 293–97.

Moreno, Juan Juarez. *Corsarios y Piratas en Veracruz y Campeche*. Sevilla, Spain: Escuela de Estudios Hispano-Americanos de Sevilla, 1972.

Nance, R. Morton. "Brigantines." *Mariner's Mirror* 7, no. 1 (1921): 22–24.

———. "Ketches." *Mariner's Mirror* 2, no. 4 (1912): 362–70.

Newton, A. P. *The European Nations in the West Indies, 1493–1688*. 1933. Reprint, New York: Barnes and Noble, 1967.

Norton, Mary Beth. *In the Devil's Snare: The Salem Witchcraft Crisis of 1692*. New York: Alfred A. Knopf, 2002.

Olmos, Margarite Fernández, and Lizabeth Paravisini-Gebert. *Creole Religions of the Caribbean: An Introduction From Vodou and Santería to Obeah and Espiritismo*. New York: New York University Press, 2003.

Parry, J. H. *The Spanish Seaborne Empire*. London: Hutchinson & Co., 1966.

Pawson, Michael, and David Buisseret. "A Pirate at Port Royal in 1679." *Mariner's Mirror* 57, no. 3 (1971): 303–5.

———. *Port Royal, Jamaica*. 1974. 2nd ed. Kingston: University of the West Indies Press, 2000.

Pennell, C. R., ed. *Bandits at Sea: A Pirate Reader*. New York: New York University Press, 2001.

Peterson, Harold L. *Arms and Armor in Colonial America, 1526–1783*. New York: Bramhall House, 1956.

Peterson, Mendel. "Reach for the World." *National Geographic* 152, no. 6 (1977): 724–67.

Phillips, James Duncan. *Salem in the Seventeenth Century*. Boston: Houghton Mifflin, 1933.

Reeves, Randall R., et al. *National Audubon Society Guide to Marine Mammals of the World*. Illustrated by Pieter A. Folkens. New York: Knopf, 2002.

Robbins, Rossell Hope. *The Encyclopedia of Witchcraft and Demonology*. New York: Crown Publishers, 1959.

Sabatini, Rafael. *Captain Blood: His Odyssey*. New York: Grosset and Dunlap, 1922.

Saint-Méry, M. L. E. Moreau de. *Description topographique, physique, civile, politique et historique de la partie Françiase de l'isle Saint-Domingue*. 2 vols. Philadelphia: privately printed, 1797.

———. *Description topographique et politique de la partie Espagnole de l'isle Saint-Domingue*. 2 vols. Philadelphia: privately published, 1796.

Schama, Simon. *The Embarrassment of Riches: An Interpretation of Dutch Culture in the Golden Age*. New York: Knopf, 1987.

Schultz, Eric B., and Michael J. Tougias. *King Philip's War: The History and*

*Legacy of America's Forgotten Conflict.* Woodstock, VT: Countryman Press, 1999.

Segovia Salas, Rodolfo. *Las fortificationes de Cartagena de Indias.* Bogotá: Carlos Valencia Editores, 1982.

Senior, Clive. *A Nation of Pirates: English Piracy in Its Heyday.* New York: Crane, Russak & Company, 1976.

Shomette, Donald. *Pirates on the Chesapeake.* Centreville, MD: Tidewater Publishers, 1985.

Skowronek, Russell K., and Charles R. Ewen, eds. *X Marks the Spot: The Archaeology of Piracy.* Gainesville, FL: University Press of Florida, 2006.

Snelders, Stephen. *The Devil's Anarchy.* Brooklyn: Autonomedia, 2005.

Spierenburg, Pieter. "Knife Fighting and Popular Codes of Honor in Early Modern Amsterdam." In *Men and Violence: Gender, Honor, and Rituals in Modern Europe and America.* Edited by Pieter Spierenburg. [Columbus?]: Ohio State University, 1998.

Spotila, James R. *Sea Turtles: A Complete Guide to Their Biology, Behavior, and Conservation.* Baltimore: Johns Hopkins University Press, 2004.

Steele, Ian K. *Warpaths: Invasions of North America.* Oxford: Oxford University, 1994.

Stone, Lawrence. *The Family, Sex and Marriage in England, 1500-1800.* 1977. Abridged ed. New York: Harper Torchbooks, 1979.

Swanson, Gail. *Documentation of the Indians of the Florida Keys and Miami, 1513-1765.* Haverford, PA: Infinity Publishing, 2003.

Szabó, László. *Fencing and the Master.* 1977. Reprint translated by Gyula Gulyás, John Harvey, and Stephen E. Vamos. Staten Island: SKA Swordplay Books, 1997.

Tattersfield, Nigel. *The Forgotten Trade.* London: Jonathan Cape, 1991.

Thomas, Hugh. *The Slave Trade: The Story of the Atlantic Slave Trade, 1440-1870.* New York: Simon and Schuster, 1997.

Torres Ramirez, Bibiano. *La Armada de Barlovento.* Sevilla, Spain: Escuela de Estudios Hispano-Americanos de Sevilla, 1981.

*U.S. Navy Diving Manual,* Revision 5. Washington, DC: Naval Sea Systems Command, 2005.

Vaissière, Pierre de. *Les origines de la colonisation et la formation de la société française á Saint-Domingue.* Paris: Bureaux de la Revue, 1906.

Vrijman, L. C. *Dr. David van der Sterre: Zeer Aenmerkelijke Reysen Gedaan Door Jan Erasmus Reyning.* Amsterdam: P. N. Van Kampen, 1937.

Waddell, Peter J. A. "The 1996 Excavation of a Ship From Sir William Phips' Fleet, 1690." In *Underwater Archaeology Conference Proceedings From the Society for Historical Archaeology Conference, 1997,* edited by Denise C. Leakey. Washington, DC: Society for Historical Archaeology, 1997.

Webb, Stephen Saunders. *The Governors-General: The English Army and the*

*Definition of the Empire, 1569-1681*. 1979. Reprint, Chapel Hill: University of North Carolina Press, 1987.

Weddle, Robert S. *Spanish Sea: The Gulf of Mexico in North American Discovery, 1500-1685*. College Station: Texas A&M University, 1985.

———. *Wilderness Manhunt: The Spanish Search for La Salle*. 1973. Reprint, College Station: Texas A&M University, 1999.

———. *The Wreck of the Belle, the Ruin of La Salle*. College Station: Texas A&M University, 2001.

Weiss, John. "The Horrors of San Domingo, Chapter IV." *Atlantic Monthly* 10, no. 59 (1862): 347-58.

Wells, Noel. *Small Arms of the Spanish Treasure Fleets*. Dallas: Rock Bottom Publications, 2006.

Wendell, Barrett. *Cotton Mather*. 1891. Reprint, New York: Barnes and Noble, 1992.

Wenhold, Lucy L. "The First Fort of San Marcos de Apalache." *Florida Historical Quarterly* 34, no. 4 (1956): 302-15.

Westergaard, Waldemar. *The Danish West Indies Under Company Rule (1671-1754)*. New York: Macmillan, 1917.

Whiles, John. *Sedgemoor 1685*. 1975. 2nd ed. Chippenham, England: Picton Publishing, 1985.

Williams, Glyndwr. *The Great South Sea: English Voyages and Encounters, 1570-1750*. New Haven, CT: Yale University Press, 1997.

Wright, J. Leitch, Jr. "Andrew Ranson: Seventeenth Century Pirate?" *Florida Historical Quarterly* 39 (1960-1961): 135-44.

Zadediah, Nuala. "'A Frugal, Prudential and Hopeful Trade': Privateering in Jamaica, 1655-89." *Journal of Imperial and Commonwealth History* 18 (1990): 145-68.

———. "The Merchants of Port Royal, Jamaica, and the Spanish Contraband Trade, 1655-1692." *William and Mary Quarterly*, 3rd ser., 43 (1986): 570-93.

———. "Trade, Plunder, and Economic Development in Early English Jamaica, 1655-89." *Economic History Review*, 2nd ser., 39, no. 2 (1986): 205-22.

4, 44, 55, 68, 71, 91, 155, 178, 181; death of, 220; as lieutenant-governor, 36, 105; as pirate hunter, 157; rules of engagement, 84; swearing, 148; 157
Morgan's Line (Port Royal), 64
Morris, Captain (buccaneer), 104-5
Mosely, Samuel (soldier and buccaneer), 104-5
Moseley's Privateers, 105
Mosquito Coast, 71, 89, 130, 134
mulattos: dress of, 30; as men-at-arms, 22, 34-35; part of New World culture, 8, 9, 10, 40; at Petit Goave, 60-62; as pirate captains, 91; as slaves, 90; social status, 33-34
mule trains, 25
murder: common crime, 35, 164; among filibusters, 108; of La Salle, 213; during piratical act, 128, 156; of prisoners, 22, 180, 189-90
Murphy, John. *See* Morfa, Juan
muscovado sugar, 77
music, 185, 191, 215
musket shot (distance), 63
*mustee. See* mestizos
mutiny, 164, 213
Myngs, Christopher (naval commander), 182

Native Americans: in general, 1, 9, 10, 22, 27-28, 31, 34-35, 40, 67, 72, 76, 90, 105, 121-23, 136-43, 149, 170; and pirates, 129, 131, 133, 134, 135-36, 141-42, 203; as seen by Europeans, 137-38; as slaves, 90, 109, 140-42; Abenaki, 10; Apalache, 10; Aztec, 10; Carib, 10, 14, 69, 72, 106, 109-110, 121-23, 139-40, 158; Cherokee, 139; Creek, 139, 143; Cuna (Darien), 10, 134, 138; Guale, 139; Gulf Coast, 123, 209; Huron, 10; Inca, 10; Iroquois, 10; language, 40; Lucayas, 121; Maya, 10; Moskito, 10, 89, 129, 131, 133, 134, 141-42, 161, 203, 218; Narragansett, 10; Powhatan, 139, 140; Timucuan, 10; Wampanoag, 10, 105, 140; Westos, 10, 139, 140; Yamassee, 10, 186
Native American warfare, 138-40
navigation, 115-16
Navigation Acts, 70, 95
Navy SEALs, 125
Needham, Captain (naval commander), 213
Netherlands: characterized, 108; Exquemelin destination, 3; logwood shipped to, 6; rasp houses, 8-9; slave trade, 94; trade with Spain, 95; war with France, 37, 83.

*See also* European immigrants
Nevil, Captain (buccaneer), 239
Nevis, 67, 69-70, 72, 98, 158
New England, 6, 70, 98, 99-106, 109, 132
Newgate, 8
New Hampshire, 101, 103
New Holland, 104
New Jersey, 101
New Mexico, 32, 142
New Providence, 72, 121, 134, 164, 185, 213; described, 68-69; attacked, 206
New Spain: population composition, 23-25; regional characteristics, 25, 32
New Wrack. See ships, by name: *Nuestra Señora de Concepción*
New York, 37, 101, 132
Nicaragua, 72
nicknames. *See* false names, pseudonyms, nicknames
Nicolás, Jorge (Spanish pirate), 209
Nieuw Amsterdam, 37. *See also* New York
*nom de guerre. See* false names, pseudonyms, nicknames
no prey no pay (no purchase no prey), 14, 54, 223

Obeah, 110
*obedesco pero non cumplo*, 27, 94
Ogeron, Bertrand d' (governor of Saint Domingue), 36, 45, 50, 62, 72
oil, rendered from fat, 43
Old Christians, 33
Old Wrack. See ships, by name: *Nuestra Señora de las Maravillas*
Onan, Pasqual (Spanish pirate), 35, 141-42, 210-11, 218, 240
One Bush Key, 202
Orange, Pierre l' (filibuster), 218, 240
oranges, orange trees, 57
Organos Bank, 185
Orinoco River, 143, 186
*Oroonoko* (Aphra Behn), 85
osnabrig cloth, 4, 256
Ostend, 158
Ostend privateers, 28
Oviedo, Gaspar de (Spanish commander), 182
Ovinet, le Grand (filibuster), 53
Ovinet, Pierre (filibuster), 53

Padrejan (rebel slave), 88-89, 127
Paine, Peter (merchant captain), 164
Paine, Thomas (buccaneer), 101, 105, 121, 142, 164, 185, 218, 240

Palitinate, 220
Panama: forces dispatched from, 136, 154–55; sack of, 3, 36, 71, 91, 155, 177; smuggling at, 94, 97; treasure fleet rendezvous, 25, 27;
Panama, Bishop of, 71
Panama, Governor of, 71–72
*para y pinto*, 31
Parris, Samuel (Puritan minister), 109
parrots, 17–18, 58, 86, 251
partisan warfare, 34
patache, 15, 25, 27, 80
patereroes. *See* swivel guns
pavilions (tents), 4
Peace of Casco, 105
Peche, Thomas (pirate), 152
Pedneau, Captain (filibuster), 186, 240
Pennon, Captain (filibuster), 164, 240
Pennsylvania, 101
Penn, William (founder of Pennsylvania), 101
Pepys, Samuel (diarist), 111, 170, 246
Peralta, Francisco de (Spanish commander), 154–55, 159, 221
periager. *See* vessel types: piragua
Perico Island, 25, 127, 186
Persia, 138
Peru, 10, 23, 24, 25, 34, 86
Peterson, Captain (buccaneer), 240
Petit, Captain (filibuster), 186, 240
Petit Fond, 48
Petit Goave, 1, 3, 135, 142, 166, 185; described, 57–64; great storm at, 120; La Salle visit, 186; sacked, 210–11, 213. *See also* Saint Domingue
Philippine Islands, 206, 218
Phips, William (governor of Massachusetts), 121, 126
Picard, Captain (filibuster), 164, 219, 240
*pícaros*, 21
Pie de Palo (Wooden Leg). *See* Jol, Cornelis
pieces-of-eight, 66, 249–52, 255–56
Pierre le Picard (Pierre Santot, filibuster), 45, 56, 240
pigs (swine), 18, 39–43, 55, 247–48
pimento. *See* allspice
pink. *See* vessel types: pink
piracy, 4, 12, 64, 67, 72; justification for, 22, 39
pirate flag. *See* colors
pirates: Anglo-American (eighteenth century), 2, 12, 59, 217, 220; Asian, 58; bases of operation, 57–71; black, 53, 58, 59, 90–91; character of (especially buccaneers and filibusters), 7, 11, 21–22, 53–56, 71–72, 81, 90–91, 113–14, 152, 161, 163, 164, 165–70; customs of, 53–55, 113–14, 167; deaths of, 72, 81, 92, 152, 155, 180, 208, 218; disagreements among, 157, 159–60; literacy of, 149–50; mestizo, 22, 58; mulatto, 22, 58; Native American, 58, 59; organization of, 231–34; as plain-dealers, 148–49, 294n20; racial composition of, 22, 58; recreation ashore, 59–61; social composition of, 53, 58, 64; Spanish, 3, 14, 21–23, 28, 35, 36, 63, 68–69, 97, 98, 206–13; virtues of, 12, 220–21. *See also* buccaneers; filibusters
Pitman, Henry (transported rebel), 69, 70, 131, 175, 209; literary work, 244–45; marooned, 201–2, 204, 206, 213
*Plain Dealer, The* (William Wycherley), 59, 192
plantation economy, 76
plantations, 9, 61–62, 66, 67, 76–78, 86–89; owned by pirates, 45, 219; owned by priests, 76
planters, 43, 52, 55, 76–77
plate fleets. *See* treasure fleets
plunder, pirate: at sea, 36, 75, 90, 157, 164; ashore, 90, 128, 164, 183, 222; lists of, 255–61. *See also* pieces-of-eight
poetry contests, 31
Pointis, baron de (privateer), 219, 246
*Polly* (John Gay), 148
Port Bayaha (Saint Domingue), 41
Port-de-Paix (Saint Domingue), 63, 88
Portes Arson, sieur de (supercargo), 96, 98
Port Margot (Saint Domingue), 41, 88
Port Morant (Jamaica), 128, 135
Portobello, 25, 27, 93, 97, 130, 163; attacked, 135–36, 142, 143
Port Royal (Carolina), 206
Port Royal (Jamaica), 3, 62, 63, 119, 127, 167; described, 64–67; importance of, 53, 63; reliance on turtle, 130–32; trade, 77. *See also* Jamaica
Port Scrivan. *See* Puerto del Escribano
Portugal, 15
Potosí (Chile), 25, 31, 34, 78
Pouançay, Jacques Nepveu, sieur de (governor of Saint Domingue), 7, 55, 56, 72, 89, 185, 284–85n47
poverty, 33
Povey, Edward (buccaneer author), 145, 151, 159, 219, 222, 244
powder chests, 19
Price, Major (planter), 205

prickly pear cactus, 67, 76
pride and bravado, Spanish, 28, 33–34, 156, 171
priests' tobacco, 77
prisoners, treatment of by pirates, 108, 155, 156, 180, 183–84, 189–90, 209–210, 220
privateering: as piracy, 3–4; distinguished from piracy, 11; legitimate, 4, 35, 36, 165
privateering commissions. *See* commissions, privateering
privateers, legitimate: 4, 5, 28, 79, 92, 99; *See* also buccaneers; filibusters; pirates
prostitution, 59, 61, 66, 103, 165, 252
Providence Company, 91
Providence Island, 89, 100, 141
provisioning: while careening, 203; at Jamaica, 64, 164; live animals aboard, 17–18; pirate diet, 161–62; with pork, beef, and horse, 39–43, 55; in port, 55; with sea turtle, 129–34, 186
pseudonyms. *See* false names, pseudonyms, nicknames
Puerto Cavallos (Honduras), 25, 73–74, 81
Puerto de Garrote (Darien), 97
Puerto del Escribano, 135
Puerto Franco. *See* Charlestown (Carolina)
Puerto Nova (Darien), 97
Puerta Pee. *See* Puerto del Escribano
Puerto Principe, 127
Puerto Rico, 27, 39, 98, 164. *See also* San Juan
*pulque. See* beverages: *pulque*
punishment: among Europeans, 137, 201; among Native Amerians, 137; among pirates, 117, 137, 205, 227; of indentured servants, 133, 204; Naval, 169; of pirate prisoners, 155, 156; of pirates by authorities, 104–5, 208, 211, 218; of slaves, 87–88, 133. *See also* prisoners, treatment of by pirates
Punta Brava. *See* Cape San Blas
Punta de Maisí (Cuba), 210
Puritans, 68, 99–106, 141, 147, 170; influence on piracy, 103
purity of blood, 33

*quarteroon de Negroes,* 9
Quintano (Spanish admiral), 92

race relations, 33–34
racial ethnicities, 9
racial stereotypes, 32, 33, 60–61
racism, 8, 33, 84–85, 90–91. *See also* slavery
Rackam, Calico Jack, 12, 59
raids, 48, 63

rake (dissolute gentleman). *See* Wilmot, John
rake (slant of mast), 14
ranches, 24
Rancho-Reys (Venezuela), 97
Randolph, Edward (king's agent for Massachusetts), 102
rape, 166, 184
rasp houses, 8
rats, 18, 116
Read, Captain (buccaneer), 157, 213, 219, 240
Realejo (Nicaragua), 173
rebellion, social and political, 8, 10–11
recuas. *See* mule trains
Red Sea, 100, 101
regional stereotypes, 25, 32
registry ships, 27, 73
religion: in general, 22, 23, 67, 69, 84–85, 107–110, 143, 156; among Native Americans, 31, 109–110, 143; among pirates, 57, 61, 103, 107–8; among Puritans, 100–103, 106; among slaves, 84–85, 110; among Spaniards, 31, 34, 208
religious persecution, 8, 9
*renegados,* 35, 62
*repartimiento,* 27–28
revenge, 34. *See also* dueling
Reyning, Jan Erasmus (Dutch filibuster): with Binkes, 72, 92; death, 219; dueling, 191; epitomizing the freebooter, 216; indentured, 52; under L'Ollonois, 56; under many flags, 35, 70, 104, 109
Rhoades, John (pirate), 104
Rhode Island, 70, 101
Riet, Willem (Dutch freebooter), 240
Ringrose, Basil (buccaneer surgeon and author), 149, 151–52, 155, 156, 167; death, 219; literary work, 244–45
Río de la Hacha, 25, 97, 158
Río de la Plata, 134
Río Dulce (Honduras), 73, 80
Rio Grande Basin. *See* New Mexico
Rivera, Manoel Pardal (Spanish pirate), 104–5
Roatan Island, 74
Roberts, Bartholomew (pirate), 12, 59, 220
Robert, William (buccaneer), 240
Rock the Brazilian (filibuster), 45, 55, 64, 149, 191, 196
Roderigo, Peter (pirate), 104–5
Rodrigo, Don (Spanish officer), 172
Rodriguez, Manuel (Spanish pirate), 35, 71, 240
Rogers, Francis (supercargo), 192
Rogers, Thomas (buccaneer), 36

Rogers, Woodes (privateer), 23, 219
romance, 60, 167-68. *See also* sex
*Romeo and Juliet*, 149
Romney Marsh (England), 217
Rose, Jean (filibuster), 135, 143, 186, 240
Rosiers, Vincent de (boucanier), 42
*roucou*. See achiote
*Rover, The* (Aphra Behn), 34, 168
Royal Africa Company, 83
rum. *See* beverages: rum
rum production, 77
running, 163
Russel, James (deputy governor of Nevis),
      69-70

Saba, 105
Sabatini, Rafael (novelist), xiii, 202, 216
Sacrificios Island, 189, 198, 202
saëtia. *See* vessel types: settee
sails: 14, 20, 118, 146
Saint Domingue (Haiti), 3, 16; described, 40,
      43, 47, 57-64; population growth, 50,
      52, 61, 62, 63, 87; slavery at, 87-89
Salem, 121
Salinas, 1-2, 12
salt, 1, 43
salt barks, 2, 3
salt rakers, 94
Salt Tortuga, 39, 70, 204
Saltatudos Island. *See* Salt Tortuga
Samana (Santo Domingo), 41, 63, 72, 203
Samballos Islands. *See* San Blas Islands
Samson, Captain (filibuster), 96, 98
San Andrés. *See* Henrietta Island
San Antonio (St. Anthony), 31
San Blas Islands, 130, 141
Sandy Key (Port Royal), 64
*sangliers*. *See* pigs, wild
San Juan (Florida), 185
San Juan (Puerto Rico), 24, 71, 206
San Marcos de Apalache (Florida), 92, 142-
      43, 163, 206, 209
Santa Catalina. *See* Providence Island
Santa Helena, 167
Santa Maria (Darien), 143, 186
Santa Maria (Florida), 185
Santa Marta (Colombia), 25, 71, 92, 128, 142
Santa Marta, Bishop of, 71
Santiago (rebel slave), 89
Santiago de Cuba, 71, 97, 98, 164, 209-210
Santiago de los Caballeros (Santo Do-
      mingo), 23
Santo Domingo, 23, 27, 34, 46, 71, 89, 97,
      142, 164

San Tomás (Venezuela), 105
Santot, Pierre. *See* Pierre le Picard
Sanz, Gaspar (composer), 185
Sapodilla Cays, 74
sarsaparilla, 66, 75, 98, 255
*Savanne Brulée* (Saint Domingue), 41, 48
Sawkins, Richard (buccaneer), 6, 50, 71, 103,
      128; death, 50, 218; at Perico, 154-55;
      vessels, 240; wounded, 139
scarlet letter, 102-3
*Scarlet Letter, The*, 103
Scottish Company of Darien, 219
Scottow, Captain (militia officer), 105
sea dogs, Elizabethan, 2
sea hibiscus. *See* Maho tree
sea hounds. *See* seals and sea lions
seals and sea lions, 133-34
Searles, John (buccaneer), 140, 202
*Sea Rover's Practice, The* xiii
sea shanties. *See* shanties
sea swine. *See* seals and sea lions
sea terms, 263-67
sea turtles: described, 129-30; fished, 130-
      32; consumed by logwood cutters, 4;
      medicinal use, 161; provisions at sea,
      18, 161-62, 186, 203; tortoise shell, 66,
      128; turtle sloops, 7, 94, 98
Sedgemoor, Battle of, 201, 205
Segovia (Nicaragua), 72
Senegal (Africa), 106
Sénégal companies, 85
Serles Key, 202
settee. *See* vessel types: settee
sex, 7, 29, 32, 46, 141, 160; on the Main, 59-
      61, 165-70; Puritan attitude toward,
      102-3
sex (vessels as female), 16, 32
sexually transmitted disease, 160, 161, 165
Shakespeare, 149
shanties, 147
sharks, 18, 120, 123, 126
Sharp, Bartholomew (buccaneer): at Arica,
      181-82; biography, 216-17; firing on
      Hendricks, 191; at Honduras, 128;
      journal, 246; logwood cutting, 6; under
      Morgan, 56; multilingual, 149; at
      Portobello, 135; at Segovia, 72; in South
      Sea, 89, 143, 151, 158, 167, 191; tried
      for piracy, 163, 216-17; vessels, 240
shipbuilding, 16, 103
ships. *See* vessel types
ships, by name:
      *Aletta*, 163
      *Aventurière*, 96-97

*Batchelor's Delight*, 186, 237
*Belle*, 206
*Betty* sloop, 239
*Bonetta*, 216–17
    *Bristol* man-of-war, 123
*Buen Jesus de las Almas*, 36, 75, 236
*Cadiz Merchant*, 244
*Cacafuego* (*Shitfire*), 236
*Cascarille*, 238, 240
*Chasseur*, 237, 240
    *Chester* man-of-war, 80
*Concordia*, 207, 241
*Cygnet of London*, 240–41, 244
    *Dartmouth* man-of-war, 206
    *Dauphin* (l'Orange's), 240
*Dauphin* (merchantman), 63
*Dauphine*, 241
*Diligent* (*Fortune*), 208, 236
*Drake* man-of-war, 203, 216, 218
*Edward and Thomas*, 104
*Elisabeth*, 186
*Falcon* man-of-war, 203
*Flying Post-Horse*, 104
*Fortune*, 81
*Fortune's Adventure*, 68, 236
*Francesa* (*Françoise, Dauphine*), 100, 164, 220, 238, 241
*Francis* man-of-war, 68, 218
*Gaillard* man-of-war, 81
*Gallant*, 239
*Gideon*, 67
*Golden Fleece*, 205, 235
*Grand Gustaphus*, 213
*Great Dolphin*, 128
*Guagone* (*Quagone*), 236
*Guannaboe*, 116, 243
*Hannibal*, 62, 191
*Hunter* man-of-war, 128, 143
*Irondelle*, 239
*Leon*, 237
*Loire*, 80
*Louise*, 241
*Loyal Merchant*, 243
*Margarita*, 207, 240
*Mayflower*, 237
*Nicholas*, 237
*Nouvelle Trompeuse*, 100, 218
*Nuestra Señora de Burgos* man-of-war, 207–8, 211–12
*Nuestra Señora de Candelaria*, 117, 163, 186
*Nuestra Señora de Concepción* man-of-war, 207–8, 211–12
*Nuestra Señora de Concepción*

(*Almiranta*) wreck, 121, 125, 210, 213, 290n79
*Nuestra Señora de Consolación*, 80–81
*Nuestra Señora de la Atocha* wreck, 105
*Nuestra Señora de la Paz* (*La Mutine*), 100, 235
*Nuestra Señora de las Maravillas* wreck, 68, 72, 92, 105, 115, 120–21, 128, 142, 163, 164, 185, 186
*Nuestra Señora del Honhón* (*Leon Coronado*) man-of-war, 212, 237
*Nuestra Señora de Rega* (*Reglita*) patache, 80–81, 185, 208, 209, 212, 236, 241
*Padre Ramos*, 241
*Pearl*, 240
*Penobscot* Shallop, 104
*Phillip* Shallop, 104
*Plantanera*, 186
*Postillon*, 241
*Presbyter* (*Isabella*), 208, 239
*Profète Daniel* (*Samuel*), 207, 236
*Profond*, 80
*Prosperous*, 238
*Rainbow of London*, 245
*Resolution* (*Baldivia Josiah*), 238, 240
*Revenge*, 185–86, 237
*Rose of Algeree*, 121, 186
*Ruby* man-of-war, 186
*Ruzé*, 240
*Saint Françoise* (*Saint Joseph*), 238
*Saint-Jean* (L'Ollonois's), 80
*Saint Jean*, 91
*Saint Nicolas* (*Mary and Martha, Hardy*), 80, 117, 221, 238, 241
*Salisbury* Ketch, 104
*San Francisco* (*Neptune*), 100, 186, 238
*Santissima Trinidad* (*Trinity*), 155, 156, 158, 159, 163, 181–82, 202, 218, 237, 240
*Santo Rosario*, 157
*Schitié*, 236
*Sevillana*, 212
*Soldada* (*James*), 70, 236
*Sorcière*, 105
*Stad Rotterdam*, 186
*St. David*, 237
*Subtille*, 240
*Success* man-of-war, 128
*Summer Island*, 236
*Sun*, 83
*Terra Nova*, 64, 119

*Tiger*, 240
*Tigre*, 235, 238, 239
*Toison d'Or*, 99, 239
*Trompeuse* (Dumesnil's), 237
*Trompeuse* (Guernsey's), 238
*Trompeuse* (Hamlin's), 67, 68, 164, 238
*Virgin de Populo y San Antonio de Padua*, 239
*Virgin Queen*, 75
*White Lamb*, 239
shipwrecks: in general, 115-27; d'Estrées, 105, 120; Grammont's, 179; Henry Morgan's 36; pirate, 206; slave ships, 89, 106; treasure ships, 68, 72, 92, 105
silver, 75, 78-79, 81
Silver, George (swordsman author), 193, 198
slavery: in general, 49, 76, 81, 83-92, 96, 133, 161, 166; Moorish and Islamic slaves, 106, 109; Native American slaves, 90, 109, 140-42, 204, 208; pirates and, 90, 163, 183; price of, 251-52; rationalization of, 84-85; slave rebellions, 36, 88-90, 163, 205; slave trade, 3, 9, 28, 60-62, 63, 69, 70, 83-86, 91-92, 94-96, 106, 127, 163, 164; smuggling of slaves, 94, 97, 158. *See also* Africans; maroons; militia: Spanish
sloops. *See* vessel types, sloop
sloop trade, 3, 7, 93-98
smallpox, 9
Smith, John (soldier of fortune), 74, 146
smuggling, 25, 93-98, 251. *See also* sloop trade; slavery: smuggling of slaves
snow. *See* vessel types: snow
social change, 9-11
social mobility, 8, 62, 64
social prejudices (other than racism), 8, 32, 33, 64, 65-66
Sotomayor, Lorenzo (Spanish gentleman), 181
South Carolina. *See* Carolina
South Cays (Cuba), 132, 133
South Sea expeditions, 67, 90, 127, 128, 141-42, 143; battles during, 151-58, 180-82, 186
Spain, 27, 31-32, 37, 93, 95
Spanish Hispaniola. *See* Santo Domingo
Spanish Main: in general, 1-12; defined, 2-3; popular image of, 23; seventeenth century image of, 13-14
Spanish missions, 143
speech, pirate. *See* language: of pirates
Springer, Captain (buccaneer), 143
Springer's Key, 135, 203

spirits. *See* kidnappers
Spurre, George (buccaneer), 164, 183, 218, 240, 297n13
Stapleton, William (governor of Leeward Islands), 67, 70
St. Augustine, 103, 140, 202, 218
St. Catherine Island, 143
St. Christopher, 98, 123
St. Croix, 72
steep tub, 17
St. Eustace, 105
Stevenson, Robert Louis, 147, 249
St. Kitts. *See* St. Christopher
St. Malo (France), 96
St. Marks River. *See* Toscache River
St. Martin, 72
storms. *See* weather at sea
Straits of Magellan, 158
striking the bell, 233
St. Thomas, 36, 70, 105, 142, 145, 163, 202; described, 67-69; population, 67, 142, 164
St. Tomás de Castilla, 73
Stuart, Mary (Queen of England), 220
St. Vincent, 72, 139
sugar production, 77, 261
sugar droghers, 77
superstition, 31, 110-114; in general, 110-112; among seamen and pirates, 111-14
Surinam, 2, 36, 86, 133, 139
Swan, Charles (buccaneer), 157, 180, 186, 206, 213, 218; death, 218; married, 297n13; vessels, 240-41;
swashbuckling, 8, 67
swearing, 6, 31, 66, 113, 147-48, 189. *See also* language
Sweden, 127
Sweet Virginia tobacco, 77
swimming, 121-24, 289n45
swords, 46, 64, 98, 140, 180, 189-98. *See also* dueling; fencing
synagogues. *See* churches and synagogues
syncretism, 110

*tabaco de sacerdotes*. *See* priests' tobacco
Tabary, Captain (Carib warrior), 140
Taino (language), 40
Tampico (Mexico), 185, 186, 207-8, 209
Tarare Mountain (Saint Domingue)
tartan (tartana, tarteen). *See* vessel types, tartan
Tartary, 138
*tasajos*, 40

tattoos, 59
taverns, 66, 103, 252
Taylor, John (Jamaica planter), 126
*Tempest, The*, 149
tempests. *See* weather at sea
Thacher, Anthony (shipwreck victim), 119-20
theater, 31
Thevenot, Melchisedech (author), 123
Thomas, Captain (pirate), 158
Thrower, Norman (scholar), 145
thunderstorms. *See* weather at sea
Tihosuco (Mexico), 206
Tindall's Point (Virginia), 164
Tituba (slave), 109
Tobago, 92
tobacco: health issues, 77; production, 43, 52, 61, 75, 77, 255, 261; use, 59, 77, 180
topsail vessels, 16
Tocard, Jean (filibuster), 241
tortoises (land turtles), 130
Tortue, La. *See* Tortuga
Tortuga (Saint Domingue), 39-40, 56, 63, 64, 91
Tortuga (near Margarita). *See* Salt Tortuga
Tortugas. *See* Dry Tortugas
torture, 22, 109, 184, 209
Toscache River, 142
Towers (pirate), 241
Townley, Francis (buccaneer), 121, 142, 157, 180, 218, 241
trade: Dutch attitude toward, 71, 101; fairs, 27; goods, 86, 96; Puritan practices of, 100-101; Spanish, 93-94; with pirates, 94. *See also* exports, New World; imports, New World
trade versus piracy, 64, 66-67
trading by stealth. *See* sloop trade
*traiter à la pique. See* sloop trade
treasure, 17, 121, 249-52. *See also* wrecking; treasure fleets
treasure chests, 17, 251
treasure fleets, 24, 25-27, 62, 73, 93, 127, 171, 172. *See also* wrecking
treasure maps, 128
Treaty of Nymwegen, 106
Treaty of Westminster, 105
trials for piracy, 163, 208, 211, 216-17, 219, 244
Trinidad, 92, 105, 143, 186
Trinidad (Cuba), 27
Tripoli, 123
Trist (Mexico), 4, 13. *See also* logwood cutting

Tristian, Captain (filibuster), 158, 185, 207, 218, 237, 241
Trujillo (Honduras), 25, 73-74, 105
Tupi (language), 40
Tuxpan (Mexico), 209

Underwater Demolition Teams (UDTs), 125
urca. *See* vessel types; Honduras ship
Uring, Nathaniel (mariner), 6, 7, 9, 76, 97, 171
utopia, pirate, 22, 91

*vacadas*, 24
Valens, Ritchie (pop musician), 185
Vandelmof (commander of La Cinquantaine), 46-48
Van der Sterre, David (biographer), 191
Van Horn, Nicolas (Dutch filibuster), character of, 199; death, 198-99, 215, 218; duel with Laurens, 189-90, 198; at Honduras, 80-81, 207; jewelry, 158; as slaver, 163, 164; marriage, 297n13; at Veracruz, 182-84, 189-90, 198-99, 202
vanilla, 30
Vargas, Diego de (governor of New Mexico), 31-32, 114
Vaughn, Lord (governor of Jamaica), 36, 99
Veale, Captain (pirate), 100
Venables, General (conqueror of Jamaica), 34
vendetta, 192. *See also* assassination
Venecia, 209
Venta Cruz (Venta de Cruzes), 25, 93
Vent-en-Panne (filibuster), 45
Vent-Cruz: in general, 23, 24, 27, 33, 70, 71; attacked, 68, 171-72, 174, 182-84, 189-90, 198-99; described 171-72;
Verina tobacco, 77
Verpré (filibuster), 241
vessel types: 14-19, 235-41; bark, 1, 4, 14, 98; barcalonga, 14-15, 35, 68; barque, 14, 81, 119, 154-55; barque longue, 14-15, 271n7; Bermuda sloop, 14, 16, 96-97; brigantin, 15; brigantine, 15, 75; canoe, 14, 25, 93, 129, 133, 135, 139, 154-55; corvette, 15, 80; flute, 15, 25, 72, 73-75, 79-81; flyboat, 15; fragatta, 15, 27; frigate, 15, 16, 27; galleon, 15, 25-27; galley, 16, 35, 63, 98; ketch, 13, 15, 19-20, 186; launch, 14; longboat, 14; piragua, 14, 16, 25, 35, 63, 68, 93, 98, 135, 139, 140; pink, 15, 116; settee, 15; ship, 15, and throughout; sloop, 14, 64, 77, 94, 209-210; snow, 271n8; tartan, 15; urca, 15, 25, 72, 73-75, 79-81, 282n1; yacht, 271n8

Vigneron, Captain (filibuster), 186, 241
Vigot, Guillaume (filibuster), 241
Villette, marquis de (French officer), 76, 243-44
Virgin Mary, 32
Virginia, 9, 70, 72, 139, 164, 185
Vizcayans. *See* Biscayers
Vlissingen (Flushing), 158
*vryjbuiter*, 52

Wafer, Lionel (buccaneer surgeon and author), 134, 149, 151-52, 158, 219, 244-46
Wakulla River. *See* Guacara River
Wallis, Daniel (buccaneer), 123
Ward, Ned (satirist Edward Ward), 8, 16, 65, 100, 102, 146-47
watches at sea, 233
Water Key, 202, 237
Watling Island, 202
Watling, John (buccaneer), 56, 143, 181-82, 202, 218, 241
wealth: pursuit of, 22, 54-55, 71, 76, 91; pirate wealth, 45, 62, 219
weather at sea, 19, 114, 115-20
weights and measures, 259-61
West Africans, 10. *See also* Africans; slave trade
Western Design, 103
whaling, 134
Wheeler, Captain (militia officer), 105
Whicker, John (transported rebel), 209-210
whirlwinds. *See* weather at sea
Whistler, Henry (English soldier), 50, 65
Will (Moskito striker), 204
Willems, Jan. *See* Yanky, Captain
William of Orange, King (England), 220
Williams, John (pirate), 104-5
Wilmot, John, Earl of Rochester (rake and poet), 147
Windward Islands, 69, 91
witch hunt, 102, 121
witches and witchcraft, 102, 110-111, 121
Willemstad, 70
wolding: as torture, 184; of a vessel's hull, 119

women: disguised as men, 8, 62, 167, 169; of Jamaica, 66; mistreatment of, 183; multiracial in New World, 8, 9; Native American, 141; of New Spain, 29-30, 33-34; passengers at sea, 116, 119; Puritan, 102-3; role underrepresented, 46; of Saint Domingue, 45-46, 60-61, 62; sex and romance, 165-70; slaves, 90. *See also* marriage among boucaniers and pirates; sex
wood cutters. *See* logwood cutting
Woodward, John (surgeon, slaver), 140
Woolery, Thomas (pirate), 100, 185, 206, 213
wrecking (treasure salvage): buried treasure, 128; techniques of, 120-21, 124-27; treasure wrecks, 7, 68, 72, 92, 105, 163, 164, 185

Wright, William (buccaneer): adopted son, 36, 141; attacks on Spanish, 72, 142, 158; under Morgan, 56; received at Petit Goave, 62; vessels, 241; at Virginia, 70, 164, 186
Wycherley, William (playwright), 59, 192

yacht. *See* vessel types
Yanky, Captain (Dutch filibuster Jan Willems): offer of amnesty, 185, 213; attacks on Spanish, 158, 186, 205; logwood cutting 6; at Carolina, 70; death, 218; dispute with Wright, 228; with Evertson, 70, 157; Hamlin's crew joins, 217; attack on hulk, 81, known by nickname, 45; vessels, 100, 241
Yellows, Captain (Dutch filibuster Helles de Lecat), 6, 109
Yonge, James (sea surgeon), 130, 132
Young, George (buccaneer), 121, 185, 241
Youring, Edward (seaman), 104
Ýskenderun (Turkey), 103

*zambos*, 9, 10
*zaramullos*, 21

*zee-roovers*, defined, 70

# About the Author

**Benerson Little** is a former Navy SEAL officer, military analyst, and intelligence analyst, among other trades. He is also the author of *The Sea Rover's Practice: Pirate Tactics and Techniques, 1630–1730*. His daughters, writing, and teaching fencing occupy most of his time.